OVID RENEWED

OVID RENEWED

Ovidian influences on literature and art
from the Middle Ages to the twentieth century

edited by
CHARLES MARTINDALE
University of Sussex

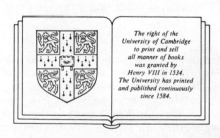

The right of the
University of Cambridge
to print and sell
all manner of books
was granted by
Henry VIII in 1534.
The University has printed
and published continuously
since 1584.

CAMBRIDGE UNIVERSITY PRESS

Cambridge
New York   Port Chester
Melbourne   Sydney

Published by the Press Syndicate of the University of Cambridge
The Pitt Building, Trumpington Street, Cambridge CB2 1RP
32 East 57th Street, New York, NY 10022, USA
10 Stamford Road, Oakleigh, Melbourne 3166, Australia

First published 1988
Reprinted 1989

Printed in Great Britain by the University Press, Cambridge

British Library cataloguing in publication data
Ovid renewed: Ovidian influences on
literature and art from the Middle Ages to
the twentieth century.
1. Ovid – Influence – English literature
2. English literature – History and
criticism
I. Martindale, Charles
820.9   PR138

Library of Congress cataloguing in publication data
Ovid renewed.
Bibliography.
Includes index.
1. English literature – Roman influences.
2. Ovid, 43 B.C.–17 or 18 A.D. – Influences.
3. Metamorphoses in literature. 4. Mythology, Classical,
in literature. 5. Metamorphoses in art. 6. Mythology,
Classical, in art. I. Martindale, Charles.
PR127.O95   1988   820'.9   87-11703

ISBN 0 521 30771 6

The sources of the extracts printed in this book are as follows:
Excerpts from 'The Waste Land' and the notes to accompany 'The Waste Land' from *Collected Poems 1909–1962* by T. S. Eliot, copyright 1936 by Harcourt Brace Jovanovich, Inc.; copyright 1963, 1964 by T. S. Eliot; from *The Waste Land: a Facsimile and Transcript* by T. S. Eliot, copyright © 1971 by Valerie Eliot; from *Selected Essays* by T. S. Eliot, copyright 1950 by Harcourt Brace Jovanovich, Inc.; renewed 1978 by Esme Valerie Eliot; from 'The Death of Narcissus' from *Poems Written in Early Youth* by T. S. Eliot, © 1967 by Valerie Eliot; from *The Dial* New York LXXI 4 (October 1921) 452–5 by T. S. Eliot.
An extract from Johann Wolfgang Von Goethe: *Faust Part One*, translated by Philip Wayne (Penguin Classics, 1949) copyright © the Estate of Philip Wayne, 1949; and an extract from Johann Wolfgang Von Goethe: *Faust Part Two*, translated by Philip Wayne (Penguin Classics, 1959) copyright © the Estate of Philip Wayne 1959.

In memoriam
L. P. WILKINSON (1907–1985)
scholar, man of letters,
anima naturaliter Ovidiana

en ego, cum caream patria vobisque domoque,
    raptaque sint, adimi quae potuere mihi,
ingenio tamen ipse meo comitorque fruorque:
    Caesar in hoc potuit iuris habere nihil.
quilibet hanc saevo vitam mihi finiat ense,
    me tamen extincto fama superstes erit,
dumque suis victrix omnem de montibus orbem
    prospiciet domitum Martia Roma, legar.

Although I am without fatherland and you and home,
and although everything which could be taken from me
has been snatched away, yet I find company and pleasure
in my own *ingenium* – Caesar could have no jurisdiction
over that. Let anyone who wants end this life of mine
with a cruel sword; yet though I shall be dead, my fame
will live, and as long as warlike Rome looks out victorious
from its hills at the whole world which it has conquered,
I shall be read.   *Tristia* 3.7.45–52

CONTENTS

CONTENTS

PLATES

9   Luca Giordano (1634–1705), *Perseus and the companions of Phineus* (National Gallery, London). Oil on canvas, 285 × 366 cm, *c.* 1680. Reproduced by courtesy of the Trustees, The National Gallery, London.

10a   Jean-Léon Gérôme (1824–1904), *Pygmalion and Galatea* (Metropolitan Museum of Art, New York. Gift of Louis C. Raegner, 1927 (27.200)). Oil on canvas, 88.9 × 68.6 cm, 1890.

10b   Gian Lorenzo Bernini (1598–1680), *Apollo and Daphne* (Galleria Borghese, Rome). Marble, 243 cm high, finished by September 1625. Photo: Alinari.

11a   Antonio Allegri, called Correggio (*c.* 1490–1534), *Jupiter and Io* (detail) (Kunsthistorisches Museum, Vienna). Oil on canvas, 163 × 74 cm, *c.* 1533.

11b   Antoine Watteau (1684–1721), *The Judgement of Paris* (Musée du Louvre, Paris). Oil on wood, 47 × 30 cm, probably 1718. Photo: Réunion des Musées Nationaux.

12   Roman *Europa and the Bull* (Villa, Lullingstone, Kent). Mosaic, *c.* AD 330. Reproduced by courtesy of the Royal Commission on the Historical Monuments of England.

13   Titian, *Rape of Europa* (Isabella Stewart Gardner Museum, Boston). Oil on canvas, 185 × 205 cm, 1559–62.

14   François Boucher (1703–70), *Jupiter and Europa* (Wallace Collection, London). Oil on canvas, 234 × 277 cm, 1734. Reproduced by permission of the Trustees of the Wallace Collection.

15   François Boucher, *Jupiter and Europa* (Musée du Louvre, Paris). Oil on canvas, 160.5 × 193.5 cm, 1747. Photo: Réunion des Musées Nationaux.

16   Paolo Caliari, called Veronese (1528(?)–88), *Jupiter and Europa* (Palazzo Ducale, Venice). Oil on canvas, 240 × 303 cm, 1573. Photo: Alinari.

NOTES ON CONTRIBUTORS

COLIN BURROW is writing a D. Phil. thesis on *The English Humanist Epic, 1580–1614* at New College Oxford, and has been elected to a Research Fellowship at Gonville and Caius College, Cambridge.

HELEN COOPER is a fellow of University College, Oxford, and the author of *Pastoral: Mediaeval into Renaissance* (Ipswich and Totowa NJ 1977) and *The Structure of the Canterbury Tales* (London 1983).

CHRISTOPHER GROCOCK wrote his thesis on Gilo of Paris' *Historia Vie Hierosolimitane* at Bedford College, London, and is editing the work for the Oxford Medieval Latin Texts series. He has also edited the *Ruodlieb* (Warminster and Chicago 1985).

BRUCE HARBERT, formerly lecturer at Merton College, Oxford, is Roman Catholic chaplain at the University of Sussex; he is the author of articles on medieval literature and theology, and editor of *A Thirteenth-Century Anthology of Rhetorical Poems* (Toronto 1975).

DAVID HOPKINS, lecturer in English at Bristol University, is the author of *John Dryden* (Cambridge 1986), and has a special interest in Dryden's translations from the Latin.

LAURENCE LERNER, poet and critic, Professor of English, formerly at Sussex University, now at Vanderbilt, is the author of numerous books including *Love and Marriage* (London 1979) and *The Literary Imagination* (Brighton 1982).

NIGEL LLEWELLYN is lecturer in the History and Theory of Art at Sussex University; he contributed to *Virgil and his Influence*, has a special interest in eighteenth-century art and historiography, and is writing a book on English Renaissance funeral monuments.

CHARLES MARTINDALE, lecturer in Classical and Medieval Studies at Sussex University, shortly to move to Bristol University, is the editor of *Virgil and his Influence* (Bristol 1984) and author of *John Milton and the Transformation of Ancient Epic* (London and Sydney 1986).

STEPHEN MEDCALF, Reader in English at Sussex University, has published on Virgil, Golding and *The Later Middle Ages* (London 1981), and is writing a study of the poetry of T. S. Eliot.

JANE MILLER wrote her thesis (under the name Jane Keen) at the University of Southampton entitled *The Perseus and Pygmalion Legends in later Nineteenth-Century Literature and Art, with special reference to the Influence of Ovid's Metamorphoses* (1983).

A. D. NUTTALL, formerly Professor of English at Sussex University, is now a fellow of New College, Oxford; his writings on Shakespeare include *The Winter's Tale* (London 1966), *Two Concepts of Allegory* (London 1967) and *A New Mimesis* (London and New York 1983).

NIALL RUDD is Professor of Latin and Dean of Arts at Bristol University; his writings on Latin literature include *Lines of Enquiry* (Cambridge 1976) and *Themes in Roman Satire* (London 1986).

RACHEL TRICKETT is Principal of St Hugh's College, Oxford; her publications include *The Honest Muse: A Study in Augustan Verse* (Oxford 1967), and she has contributed to *Augustan Studies: Essays in honour of Irvin Ehrenpreis* (Newark, University of Delaware 1986).

NORMAN VANCE is lecturer in English at Sussex University; he has written widely on nineteenth-century literature, and is author of *The Sinews of the Spirit* (Cambridge 1985).

PREFACE

Ovid would have thought Britain little better than Tomis, to which Augustus maliciously confined him for the last years of his life. But he would perhaps be pleased that the *ultimi Britanni* have come to share in that *cultus* to which he had so unswervingly committed himself and to which he made no small contribution. His culture, handed down by tradition, may now be drawing to its close. The disappearance of classics from most of our schools and its shrinkage in universities is a ruination, and it is still too soon to say what will eventually survive the wreck. But if nothing else, the crisis has brought classicists to speak more openly of the importance of their subject for understanding the world in which we live, so many aspects of which – its languages, its political structures and discourses, its thought, its art, its law – are grounded in the civilisations of Greece and Rome. So as classics has declined, the study of the classical tradition has actually burgeoned.

This book was designed as a successor to the present editor's *Virgil and his Influence: Bimillennial Studies*. It had its immediate origin in the Faculty Latin Reading Group of the University of Sussex and the enthusiastic discussions of its members: Bruce Harbert, Larry Lerner, Michelle Martindale, Keith McCulloch, Stephen Medcalf, Tony Nuttall, Norman Vance. It is still too soon to write a complete account of Ovid's influence (at times almost coterminous with the history of education), but these essays provide material for such an account. Contributors were asked to provide something critical and comparative, not merely descriptive, but otherwise no attempt was made to enforce uniformity; differences of opinion and approach will be evident. The focus is primarily on English literature, but within the wider European cultural context.

The book was not initially planned as a memorial volume for L. P. Wilkinson, but as it took shape so many of the contributions appeared to continue and elaborate his interests that it seemed appropriate to dedicate the collection to his memory, which his widow has kindly given us permission to do. L. P. Wilkinson wrote what is still the best general introduction to Ovid in English; he made a substantial contribution to the study of *Nachleben*; he always saw classics as part of the European cultural tradition. His humane approach, together with the very ease and grace of his writing, perhaps led him to be underestimated within the austere and often limited world of classical scholarship. Like Ovid he wore his learning lightly, but there can be no doubt about the enduring value of his books on Latin poetry (all published by CUP): *Horace and his Lyric Poetry* (1945), *Ovid Recalled* (1955, later abridged as *Ovid Surveyed*), *Golden Latin Artistry* (1963), arguably his masterpiece, and *The Georgics of Virgil* (1969). And, like Ovid's, his books are read.

I am grateful to Professor E. J. Kenney, another distinguished Cambridge Ovidian, who gave help and advice in the early stages of the project (he is in no way to be held responsible for the results), and to the staff of Cambridge University Press for their assistance throughout.

Unless otherwise stated the texts of Ovid cited are as follows: OCT for the amatory poems and *Tristia*, Palmer for *Heroides*, Teubner for *Metamorphoses* (Anderson) and *Fasti*.

C.A.M.

Shoreham-by-Sea
December 1986

I

INTRODUCTION

Charles Martindale

I

Si monumentum requiris, circumspice. Ovid is everywhere. His importance for European literature is immense. Medievalists call a whole epoch the *aetas Ovidiana* (what this means in practice is shown in Christopher Grocock's essay on Gilo of Paris). A list of the major English poets alone on whom he has been a key influence is impressive: Chaucer, Gower (in some ways the leading Ovidian of the Middle Ages, as Bruce Harbert shows), Spenser, Marlowe, Shakespeare, Donne, Milton, Pope. On the arts, both fine and decorative, his influence has been at least as great. Ovidian stories have provided the material for innumerable musical compositions – the first opera, Peri's *Dafne* (c. 1597), had an Ovidian subject. He has influenced the history of gardening from the Renaissance onwards: the interplay of nature and art, the exotic world of the antique gods conjured up in grotto, grove and statue, the shifts and transformations which bedazzle the visitor's eyes, including automata worked by hydraulic systems to create metamorphic effects – all these and more are the gift of Ovid to the garden.[1] He can turn up in the most unexpected places: one may find a story from the *Metamorphoses* decorating a medieval cathedral;[2] a bizarre pottery group of Cephalus and Procris was issued in the 1790s in grimy Burslem by the Staffordshire firm of Lakin and Poole.[3] In short, from the twelfth century onwards Ovid has had a more wide-ranging impact on the art and culture of the West than any other classical poet. Only the critics have stood aloof.

This is a book about Ovid's influence, but it is also a book about Ovid himself. 'The greatest commentator on Virgil is Dante, the greatest commentator on Ovid – Shakespeare'; so writes J. K. Newman.[4] That artists are the best interpreters of other artists is a slogan containing truth and falsity in about equal measure. Critics have their own job to do, and artists, for all their intuitive insights, are often both idiosyncratic and egocentric when responding to the work of others. Yet in the case of Ovid the claim has a larger measure of truth than usual. There is a striking contrast between the rich and varied response of artists, and the comparative poverty of the critical tradition, which has often done little more than reiterate the complaints made in antiquity by the school-

1

masterly Quintilian and the Senecas, father and son. David Hopkins shows how this dichotomy existed within the same man in the case of Dryden, who criticised Ovid along familiar lines in his prose, while responding to him with instinctive sensitivity in his translations.

There are many reasons for studying the afterlife of a great writer;[5] here it is enough to say that tradition is a two-way process and closely bound up with hermeneutics, as T. S. Eliot observed in 'Tradition and the Individual Talent':

> what happens when a new work of art is created is something that happens simultaneously to all the works of art which preceded it. The existing monuments form an ideal order among themselves, which is modified by the introduction of the new (the really new) work of art among them. The existing order is complete before the new work arrives; for order to persist after the supervention of novelty, the *whole* existing order must be, if ever so slightly, altered; and so the relations, proportions, values of each work of art toward the whole are re-adjusted; and this is conformity between the old and the new. Whoever has approved this idea of order, of the form of European, of English literature will not find it preposterous that the past should be altered by the present as much as the present is directed by the past.[6]

Since the notion that the present affects the past may seem unduly mystical and anti-historical, it is worth trying to show briefly what Eliot's formulation might mean. For example a development of a distinct genre of science fiction has allowed the critic to identify what we might call the science fiction impulse in the literature of the past, as in Lucian, *Gulliver's Travels* and the *Divine Comedy*. Again it was Sainte-Beuve in the nineteenth century who first popularised the notion of Virgil as the poet of the tears of things, because the Romantic movement in poetry had made it easier to identify such qualities in Virgil. Texts – all texts to an extent and great texts in particular – are complex and multi-faceted; no reading, even a true reading, can be more than partial. No reader or age can notice all that is potentially present, and any reader will be more inclined to notice what chimes with present preoccupations, whether his own or those of his society. When an important new work is produced, it may thus alter not perhaps an earlier work, strictly speaking, but the elements in that work we are able to see. Furthermore sometimes later artistic responses to a work of art are quite straightforwardly the best way of approaching it. The study of the tradition can help us to relativise ourselves, see the works of the past with fresh eyes, escape our own parochialism; it is important to avoid the teleological assumption that only the responses of one's own age have any validity. Certainly the tradition can often teach us to understand Ovid better. Pythagoras' speech in *Metamorphoses* 15, which provides a philosophical *ratio* for a poem about flux, is generally not taken seriously today; it is regarded either as parody (by the more sympathetic) or as sheer opportunism to give some semblance of unity to the poem.[7] Of course the speech is not philosophy of a technical kind like Lucretius' *De Rerum Natura*, but it is philosophical poetry, as earlier ages had no difficulty in understanding. Dryden, who excelled in such writing, thought it 'the masterpiece of the whole *Metamorphoses*'.[8]

Introduction

Shakespeare, obsessed throughout his work by time and change, echoes lines from it in several sonnets, for example at the beginning of 60 (cf. *Met.* 15.181–3, with Golding's translation):

> Like as the waves make towards the pebbled shore,
> So do our minutes hasten to their end.

Spenser pays tribute to the philosophical poet in Ovid in the Mutabilitie Cantos and elsewhere in the *Faerie Queene*, as Colin Burrow shows.

Those who think that Ovidian wit is inconsistent with seriousness might reflect on the kaleidoscopic tones in the Elizabethan epyllia inspired by Ovid, discussed by Laurence Lerner. Those who believe that metamorphosis is no more than a structural device in the *Metamorphoses* might contemplate Bernini's *Apollo and Daphne* in which the youthful sculptor, with impressive virtuosity, shows the flesh of Daphne at the very moment of transformation (Pl. 10b).[9] A moralising epigram was added at the suggestion of the future Pope Urban VIII while the work was in progress:

> quisquis amans sequitur fugitivae gaudia formae
> fronde manus implet baccas seu carpit amaras.
>
> (Whatever lover pursues the joys of fleeting beauty
> fills his hands with leaves or plucks bitter fruit.)

Bernini conveys the brio of Ovid's story with its numerous witty touches (for example as Ovid's Apollo pursues Daphne he offers to run slower if she will do the same, and also incongruously delivers a kind of hymn to his own powers, *Met.* 1.510ff); in particular Bernini cleverly takes the Apollo Belvedere – that most revered of ancient statues – and metamorphoses him into a sprinter. But Ovid's story is not only ebullient, there are disturbing undercurrents in the nymph's fear of rape and above all in the strangeness of her transformation to which Bernini also does justice. The contrasted textures of the sculpture convey the paradoxes of Ovid's description of the metamorphosis – heavy torpor seizing the running limbs, soft flesh ringed with bark, hair growing into leaves, swift feet sticking in clinging roots (548ff):

> vix prece finita torpor gravis occupat artus:
> mollia cinguntur tenui praecordia libro,
> in frondem crines, in ramos bracchia crescunt;
> pes modo tam velox pigris radicibus haeret,
> ora cacumen habet: remanet nitor unus in illa.
>
> Scarce had she finished, when her feet she found
> Benumbed with cold and fastened to the ground;
> A filmy rind about her body grows,
> Her hair to leaves, her arms extend to boughs.
> The nymph is all into a laurel gone,
> The smoothness of her skin remains alone.   (Dryden)

3

There is an intense, tactile, almost surreal concentration on the details of metamorphosis, particularly marked in the treatment of fingers and toes, the latter becoming, horribly, claw-like at the tips as they put down roots. Daphne's face seems to express fear and horror, which could be as much in response to her metamorphosis as to the imminent approach of the lustful god (for a different view see p. 160). In general the sculpture embodies a characteristic baroque paradox, on the one hand sweeping theatrical movement creating an impression of careless ease, on the other a technical perfection in the surfaces and a mastery of precise detail, not in the least impressionistic. The paradox is perfect for the combination of movement and stasis as the fleeing Daphne becomes 'root-bound', as Milton puts it in *Comus* (661). The witty, the erotic and the grotesque are miraculously fused as in the original, in an image at once polished and fluid, sprightly and troubling.

It seems likely that metamorphosis also has a profound if obscure psychological significance.[10] A particularly striking instance in literature which concerns the story of Apollo and Daphne occurs in a lyric by Petrarch (*Canzoniere* 23), in which the poet imagines himself transformed into a laurel, image at once of his beloved Laura and of poetry. The story of Daphne seems to have caught the imagination of artists of all kinds, perhaps because it could readily be taken as a 'metaphor for the pursuit of perfection'.[11] The best-known reference in English poetry occurs in Marvell's 'The Garden' (27–32):

> The gods that mortal beauty chase
> Still in a tree did end their race.
> Apollo hunted Daphne so,
> Only that she might laurel grow.
> And Pan did after Syrinx speed
> Not as a nymph, but for a reed.

There is a typical Ovidian ambivalence at work here, depending on whether we are dealing with intention or result. If Apollo is chasing Daphne for the purpose of stimulating new plant life, we have a clever paradox, mischievous in tone; however, if the god's lust for female flesh finds as its object only vegetation, there is a more melancholy undertow to the wit – and 'mortal beauty' certainly obliquely suggests the sort of moralisation inscribed on the Bernini statue.

Those to whom the violence in the *Metamorphoses* is merely a trivial gratification of a Roman taste for cruelty might have their view modified by contemplation of Titian's disturbing late masterpiece *The Flaying of Marsyas*.[12] Part of what is troubling in some Ovidian episodes is the combination of cruelty with a certain wit and detachment and the unruffled stylishness with which acts of violence are described; in consequence the reader is left uncertain of how to react. For example in Ovid's version itself of the story of Marsyas, the satyr, while being flayed by Apollo for his presumption in challenging him to a musical contest, is made to say, with pointed ingenuity, *quid me mihi detrahis?* (*Met.* 6.385 why do you tear me from myself?), while Ovid cleverly observes of his flayed body *nec quicquam nisi vulnus erat* (388 he was nothing but wound). The cleverness coexists with authentic pathos, horror and the mysterious sense of release in the transformation of the tears of the onlookers into the Marsyas, the clearest river in Phrygia (*Phrygiae liquidissimus amnis* 400), perhaps also reflecting the earlier exposure to vision of the victim's uncovered inwards (*perlucentes* 391). Titian's painting presents problems which if not identical are in some respects analogous. The sense of detachment emanating from all the characters (there is no pain in Marsyas' face and no writhing or contortion), the strange serenity of the painting with its muted but sensuous colour and its creamy surface so at odds with the violence of the subject, the thoughtful industry with which, like artists and without seeming brutality, the flayers perform their terrible work, all intensify the troubling horror of the image; while we see no raw nerves, the bucket gleams upon our attention with a sickening significance, and a small dog laps up blood. There is a telling combination of the impressionistic with precise detail like the sharp outline of the skin peeled away from Marsyas' body. As in Ovid, the artist's virtuosity seems to have outrun his human sympathy; some have thought the result so disgusting that they have questioned Titian's authorship. Yet, though it may have a kind of decadence, the image is not easily dismissed as merely trivial or callous, and it has the capacity to haunt the imagination. Titian's mythological paintings after Ovid (whose *Metamorphoses* he read in translation) are not in general exactly based on Ovid's words like Bernini's statue, rather, as Nigel Llewellyn shows, they are poetic evocations of the spirit of the original, towards which Titian seems to have had a special responsiveness (see Pls. 4, 8, 13).

2

The variousness of the response to Ovid (illustrated for particular stories in the essays by Niall Rudd and Jane Miller) mirrors the variety of Ovid's own writings. Ovid is sometimes thought of as monotonous, and partly because he wrote more voluminously than other Latin poets he occasionally repeated himself, particularly in the *Heroides* and the exile poems. But at the same time he is a protean artist, whereas images of him are frequently only two-dimensional. Recent criticism regularly emphasises the wit and humour (valued anew and no longer seen as proof of essential triviality) at the expense of other equally important qualities. For example the exuberance and rhetorical facility of his style is rightly stressed, but it is less often remarked that he can write with a simplicity which few Latin poets dare to venture. An instance is the bitter directness of his address to his friends in *Ex Ponto* 3.7, or these moving lines from *Tristia* 3.8 (8–10):[13]

> [ut] aspicerem patriae dulce repente solum,
> desertaeque domus vultus, memoresque sodales,
> caraque praecipue coniugis ora meae.

5

...that I might see the sweet soil of my fatherland on a sudden and the look of my deserted home and my friends who remember me and especially the dear face of my wife...

It has been observed that Ovid's Lucretia (*Fasti* 2.723ff) is presented *less* rhetorically than Livy's (let alone Shakespeare's).[14]

Along with the cleverness the writing regularly displays poetic imagination of a high order, as two of Ovid's nineteenth-century admirers rightly insisted. 'Of all the ancient Romans, Ovid had the finest imagination' wrote W. S. Landor,[15] while James Henry, the engagingly verbose commentator on Virgil, unexpectedly declared for Ovid in some comments on *Met.* 15.603-4, *qualia succinctis, ubi trux insibilat eurus, | murmura pinetis fiunt* (such a murmur as comes from girt-up pine-woods when the fierce east wind whistles through them):

Whoever has been in a pine wood will require no further comment on *succincta*, in its literal application to the female dress. A pine wood is indeed a wood of bare legs. Let no one say that Ovid is not a poet, or subscribe to Dryden's most unjust opinion of him. He was a more natural, more genial, more cordial, more imaginative, more playful poet not only than Dryden, but than our author, or any other Latin poet.[16]

Such strokes of imagination are to be found throughout Ovid's work. At the beginning of *Tristia* 4.3 Ovid asks the two Bears which never set to turn their shining faces towards Rome and his *domina* to see whether she is mindful of him or no; as R. G. M. Nisbet has observed, this fantasy about the stars is hard to match, and the picture beautifully emphasises the poet's loneliness as the vast night is contrasted with the lover's bed (23ff).[17] In *Remedia Amoris* 169ff Ovid shows he can draw as memorable vignettes as Horace in praise of the countryside, an unaccustomed theme:

> temporibus certis desectas alligat herbas
> et tonsam raro pectine verrit humum. (191–2)

At set times the countryman binds the cut grasses, and sweeps the shaven ground with wide-toothed comb.

It is characteristic of Ovid to see the resemblances between a mown field and a man's head of hair (*pecten*, a comb, is here used for *furca*). Ovid's imagination is frequently of a plastic or visual kind, which helps to account for his influence on painters and sculptors; a particularly fine example is the rainbow simile in the story of Arachne (*Met.* 6.63ff), used to illustrate an artistic effect in a tapestry. Sometimes indeed a picture in Ovid may have been inspired by a work of art, for example Cupid bending his bow in *Amores* 1.1.21ff.

Likewise Ovid's mythological world is not only amusing, but rich in romance:[18] the delicate picture of Ariadne gradually awakening on her lonely island in *Heroides* 10, Leander gazing sadly across the deep towards Hero's tower, seeing or thinking that he sees (a Virgilian echo) her wakeful light (*Her.* 18.29ff), the moon glimmering on the water as he swims across to her (59–60;

77ff) – Ovid is full of such touches. The poets of the Renaissance can point us towards this underemphasised aspect of his art. Here, for example, is Spenser (*FQ* III vi 45):

> And all about grew every sort of flowre,
> To which sad lovers were transformd of yore;
> Fresh *Hyacinthus*, *Phoebus* paramoure,
> And dearest loue,
> Foolish *Narcisse*, that likes the watry shore,
> Sad *Amaranthus*, made a flowre but late,
> Sad *Amaranthus*, in whose purple gore
> Me seemes I see *Amintas* wretched fate,
> To whom sweet Poets verse hath given endlesse date.

In this passage we have the pathos of the Ovidian transformations – 'sad', 'fresh', 'foolish' – rueful memories of distant untimely fatalities (with a presumably deliberate catch in the voice in the half-line 4, a Virgilian cadence which first appeared in the 1609 edition). The phrase about Narcissus 'that likes the watry shore' deftly conflates person and flower in true Ovidian fashion. With carefully controlled rhetoric the stanza then builds to its powerful climax as it moves into the present to lament a recently dead poet–lover, probably Sidney; there is an affective emotional repetition and a fine poise between resigned grief and the grandeur of the characteristically Ovidian claim for the power of poetry. The whole is suffused with a kind of sweet melancholy frequently found in such Ovidian imitations. Shakespeare can strike a not dissimilar note:

> In such a night
> Did Thisbe fearfully o'ertrip the dew,
> And saw the lion's shadow ere himself
> And ran dismayed away.
> In such a night
> Stood Dido with a willow in her hand
> Upon the wild sea banks, and waft her love
> To come again to Carthage.
> In such a night
> Medea gathered the enchanted herbs
> That did renew old Aeson.

In *The Merchant of Venice* V i, in alternating speeches, the lovers Lorenzo and Jessica relate the moonlit night in which they find themselves to episodes from four great love stories (Troilus and Cressida, Pyramus and Thisbe, Dido and Aeneas, Medea and Jason, the first from Chaucer, the remaining three Ovidian, though all also handled by Chaucer) before the mood evaporates into mild teasing. Since all four are in fact stories of tragic love, a modern critic might feel that Shakespeare is being wry or ironic at the expense of his complacent lovers (the following banter reminds us of the deception of Shylock), but the timbre of the verse lends little support to such a reading; the romantic sweetness has been isolated from stories which turn out tragic or squalid or sinister. The lines on Dido (which seem to derive from *Heroides* 10, Ariadne to Theseus, as

7

well as 7, Dido to Aeneas) in particular are exquisitely modulated, with several romantic details, the willow branch of the forsaken lover, the wild sea bank, the word 'waft' suggesting gentle melancholy and yearning. Milton too sees the world of classical myth with a soft Ovidian focus:

> Not that fair field
> Of Enna, where Proserpine gathering flowers
> Herself a fairer flower by gloomy Dis
> Was gathered... (*PL* 4.268–72)

I have argued elsewhere that Milton used the *Metamorphoses* as a gateway to faery lands forlorn,[19] and the Proserpina passage inspired by Ovid later haunted a long line of Romantic poets, including Keats, Shelley, Tennyson and Swinburne.

The romantic is not the only unfamiliar Ovid. Another is the poet of marriage. The slick cynic of the *Ars Amatoria* who enraged Augustus and mocked at Roman *gravitas* is an engaging figure, and it was not surprising that he should strike a chord in the 1960s as an apostle of sexual liberation. (W. R. Johnson revealingly talked in 1970 of Ovid's opposition to Augustus' 'anti-sex laws'.)[20] But Ovid's interest in human love and sexuality goes deeper than this, and shows him, in more respects than one, a child of his time. Augustus' attempts to promote marriage were not without their ironies: the original legislation had been brought forward by unmarried, childless consuls and lauded by the bachelor Horace, whilst the greatest poet of the new age devoted his energies to the portrayal of a tragic love-affair outside marriage. It was the disgraceful Ovid who was truly concerned with *socialis amor*, to use his own phrase (*Tr.* 5.14.28; *Pont.* 3.1.73). Perhaps not since Homer had a major poet written with more sympathetic interest about married love; one thinks for example of Ceyx and Alcyone, Cephalus and Procris, and Baucis and Philemon, or Ovid's own relationship with his third wife as conveyed in the exile poetry. In the fine *Tristia* 4.3 Ovid, in R. G. M. Nisbet's words, 'professes an Augustan idea of marriage, even if the celestial pattern is marred by the imperfections of earth'.[21] Allied to this is a feeling for children.[22] Such an interest had been characteristic of Hellenistic poetry, and was sympathetically taken up by a number of Latin writers. A tender verse in a wedding hymn by Catullus (61.209–13) looks forward to the birth of a child, the *parvulus Torquatus* who inspired the most intimate moment in the *Aeneid* (4.328–9) when Dido appeals to Aeneas by the child they might have had. But Ovid goes into further detail: *Heroides* 11 explores the feelings of the young mother Canace for her baby son, while in *Heroides* 8.89ff we see the effects on the child Hermione of her abandonment by her mother, Helen.

This familial Ovid is perhaps part of a more generally paradoxical figure, Ovid the moralist. The Middle Ages notoriously moralised Ovid, everywhere seeking the hidden senses, searching for what the Elizabethan poet Thomas

Howell called 'Ovid's meaning strange / That wisdom hideth with some pleasant change,'[23] and the habit continued into the Renaissance and beyond, to fall eventual victim to the historicism of the Enlightenment. Certainly the majority of such readings seem to us reductive or arbitrary, but to see Ovid as unvaryingly amoral or trivial is a yet worse misreading. Ovid is no moraliser but his sympathetic interest in so many aspects of the human predicament has its own moral dimension. His belief in *cultus*, including the rejection of contemporary cant about the past, is a principled one, however debonair its expression; he prefers the present not because it is luxurious but because it is civilised (*Ars* 3.113–28). In *Ex Ponto* 2.9.47–8 he tells King Cotys that study of *ingenuae artes* softens character and prevents cruelty. One cannot imagine him recreating at length the harsh heroic world of traditional martial epic; he would surely have agreed with Dryden's comments on 'those ungodly man-killers whom we poets, when we flatter them, call heroes; a race of men who can never enjoy quiet in themselves, till they have taken it from all the world'.[24]

The variousness of Ovid's poetry is also to be found within individual poems, where Ovid is seldom to be tied down to a single attitude or tone, embarrassing his critics with his shifts from grave to gay. Many of the Ovidian works discussed in this volume are similarly kaleidoscopic. Music will afford some further instances. Few would think of Handel, composer of heroic operas and solemn oratorios, as a natural Ovidian, but so it proved; three of his most honeyed works are settings of texts which derive from Ovid, and they display that constellation of qualities which we have learned to see as Ovidian.[25] The cantata *Apollo e Dafne* belongs to Handel's early Hanover years. There is beguiling lyricism as in Dafne's opening aria with oboe and pizzicato strings, where she complacently expresses her preference for peace and calm over love (the libretto throughout alludes to the moral tradition though it is not obsessed by it). There is wit, particularly in the depiction of the pursuit, where the violin representing Dafne races at twice the speed of Apollo's plodding but insistent bassoon. There is a melancholy undertow in Apollo's seduction aria *Come rosa in su la spina* and thoughtful pathos in the final lament, where the word-play *pianta/pianto* is an Ovidian feature (*cara pianta co' miei pianti/il tuo verde irrigherò* – dear plant, with my plaints I shall water your green). The masque *Acis and Galatea* (*c.* 1718), written for performance at Cannons to an excellent libretto by Gay, with some help from Pope and others, offers an analogous range of tones but greater musical complexity. Again there is the romantic sweetness and languor with its underlying pastoral melancholy, most hauntingly in the stylised eroticism of Acis' air 'Love in her eyes sits playing'. Polyphemus is a fully drawn Ovidian character; the picture of the fearsome monster attempting to play love songs has an Ovidian quality of comedy, grotesqueness and pathos combined. 'Bring me a hundred reeds of decent growth / To make a pipe for my capacious mouth', he sings in a recitative – the music takes the last word to a comically low pitch, and then in the famous air 'O ruddier than the cherry' a high recorder (flageolet) wittily accompanies the bass voice in a jaunty and somewhat rustic-sounding melody for the perfect musical equivalent of Ovid's amusing cascade of comparisons (*Met.* 13.789ff). But the giant is also genuinely threatening, as the grand fugal chorus 'Wretched lovers' has already powerfully warned us, and Acis' death and Galatea's lament introduce a more straightforward plangency. This complex of emotions is delicately resolved by the metamorphosis and by the more tranquil sadness of Galatea's sublime air 'Heart, the seat of soft delight' with its accompanying chorus, as the violence is transmuted into something perpetually fresh and life-giving and Acis becomes a fountain and stream. Warbling treble recorders deftly suggest the flowing waters, and there is a moving and typically Ovidian equivocation about whether Acis – 'murm'ring still his gentle love' – is river or river god. The last of these Ovidian works is the secular oratorio *Semele*, first performed in 1744 and composed in Handel's maturest manner to another fine libretto, this time by Congreve, based on Ovid's story of Semele with some details from the Sleep episode in *Metamorphoses* 11 and the seduction of Zeus in *Iliad* 14. When the sleepy Somnus is suddenly aroused at Juno's insistent reminder that 'Pasithea shall be thine', the humour of the music is broad indeed. Wit and near-tragedy are tellingly juxtaposed when Jupiter tries to avoid immolating Semele ('My softest lightning yet I'll try, / And mildest melting bolt apply'). To the features we have seen in the earlier works Handel now adds a much richer female characterisation, with the jealous Juno and above all Semele herself, vain, silly, sexy, irresistible, to create the full Ovidian range of qualities. In *Semele* European music achieved its most complete Ovidian masterpiece.

3

Whatever, then, happened to Ovid? He has continued to influence writers in modern times, as Stephen Medcalf shows,[26] but, despite the pioneering work of L. P. Wilkinson, he has scarcely been restored to his rightful position as one of the central figures in the European tradition. Within the world of classical scholarship, books and articles are written about him, but with results that are in general less impressive than in the case of other great Latin poets. There are still no commentaries in English on substantial portions of his output. Some reasons for this comparative twentieth-century neglect may be suggested. First there are institutional factors. Classical scholarship tends to conservatism and Victorian attitudes to Ovid, investigated here by Norman Vance, continued to prevail in classical studies where equivalent attitudes had long been jettisoned elsewhere. Ovid is still today not a standard school author in quite the way that Virgil is, and it is possible to read classics in some universities without seriously studying his works, even the *Metamorphoses*. Secondly the genius of Ovid in his masterpiece the *Metamorphoses* is a genius for sheer narration; however refashioned the tale, the tale is the thing, and some people in the twentieth century have expressed hostility to such mere story-telling, like E. M. Forster in 1927: 'Yes – oh dear yes – the novel tells a story. That is the fundamental aspect without which it could not exist. That is the highest factor common to all novels, and I wish that it was not so, that it could be something different – melody, or perception of the truth, not this low atavistic form.'[27] Allied to this suspicion of story is what a recent Reith lecturer called 'the rage for interpretation', which leads to readings which are reductive, thin, over-intellectual, and in the case of Ovid distract us from the all-important surface quite as much as the excesses of the *Ovide moralisé*. Again literary critics – and in the twentieth century it is these who largely create the prevailing climate of literary opinion and taste – naturally prefer works which they can write about well. Accordingly they tend to put a high value on those authors who respond to the techniques which are fashionable and to ignore or be dismissive of authors who are more recalcitrant. This may help to explain, for example, the continued modern reputation of Donne, a difficult poet who, in contrast with, say, Herrick, makes it easy for the critic to show his paces. Virgil suits many modern literary-critical techniques and accordingly remains secure in his traditional – and justifiable – position. Ovid has in general responded badly, worse, not only than his poetic equals, but than his inferiors, for example Propertius or Juvenal, and in consequence his work is easily undervalued. It is a curious fact that probably as many university students today encounter Catullus' 'Peleus and Thetis' as the *Metamorphoses*. There is, I would submit, some cultural provincialism here.

Interpretations of the story of Salmacis and Hermaphroditus (*Met.* 4.285ff) will serve to illustrate typical approaches of contemporary criticism which may be thought less than wholly fruitful. In this tale the androgynous Hermaphroditus, child of Venus and Mercury, comes to the pool of Salmacis, a nymph who rejects hunting for more enervate pleasures.[28] She instantly desires the handsome youth and propositions him, but he rejects her advances and she pretends to leave. She watches while he strips and bathes naked in her pool, and then unable to contain herself longer leaps into the water. She clings to him but he continues to repel her, and both make a prayer and have it granted, she that they may never be separated – their two bodies are at once fused to form the first hermaphrodite – he that whoever in future enters the water will be made effeminate; hence the Asian pool acquired its properties. What have the critics done with this story, which held so strong an appeal for the poets of the Renaissance? First it is treated as a parody, and in particular as a parody of part of the *Odyssey*.[29] It has often been argued that parody lies at or near the centre of twentieth-century Anglo-Saxon literary culture, which takes as one of its foundation texts James Joyce's parodic novel *Ulysses*. If Ovid can be shown to be a parodist, perhaps he too can be made to appeal to twentieth-century sensibilities. So the *Metamorphoses* becomes a kind of burlesque epic or anti-epic, or even specifically an anti-*Aeneid*. In the story of Hermaphroditus the

eagle and snake simile (361ff) describing Salmacis' 'attack' on Hermaphroditus
in the water has been taken as epic parody, and the initial encounter between
the pair as parodying that between Nausicaa and Odysseus in *Odyssey* 6. It
seems clear that Ovid did have Homer at the back of his mind, because
Odysseus' adroitly diplomatic speech to Nausicaa (149ff) seems to have helped
to shape Salmacis' propositioning one (320ff), and because the polypus simile
(366–7) used of Salmacis' clinging embraces derives from one in *Odyssey* 5
(432–5). There may be a humorous implied contrast, for those who pick up the
allusion, between the suavity of Odysseus and the rampant nymphomania of
Salmacis. But I doubt whether there is consistent parody of the *Odyssey*, not
least because this part of Homer's poem is itself not straightforwardly epic or
heroic in manner at all, but witty and irreverent, if in a more delicate way than
Ovid. For example when Odysseus holding a bush in front of his genitals is
compared to a ravening lion (6.130ff), the unusual application of a typical Iliadic
wild beast simile is a delightful stroke of wit. Ovid may even have recalled the
Odyssean passage precisely *because* its atmosphere is so elegantly sub-heroic.
In general, to treat the *Metamorphoses* essentially as parody is to flatten it.
Certainly it contains parody, this poem of constant changes, as it contains so
much else, but Ovid cannot be tied down to one set of static attitudes, even if
lascivia is never very far away. As with Dr Johnson's friend who tried to be a
philosopher, so with Ovid cheerfulness was always breaking in. When he tells
the story of Pyramus and Thisbe, the tone is pathetic, until the outpouring
blood of the dying Pyramus is compared to water spurting out of a drainpipe
(*Met.* 4.121ff). But this unexpected moment of grotesque wit, while it may
undercut, does not destroy the pathos of the tale as a whole, which is certainly
not merely a parody of a tragic love story.

If parody is not the all-opening key, neither is symbolism, another shibboleth
of modern criticism. Virgil's *Aeneid* responds well to treatment as symbolic
narrative, so the same treatment is tried with Ovid.[30] A few successful efforts
have been made with Ovid's landscapes, but even here one can have doubts.
The pool of Narcissus certainly suggests the boy's isolation and virginity, so
perhaps Salmacis' pool symbolises the sexual inexperience of Hermaphroditus,
particularly as after the sexual encounter its pure waters are stained: *incesto*
(*incerto*: Anderson) *medicamine tinxit* (388). An obvious objection is that the
pool belongs to Salmacis, the very embodiment of languid sensuality. Accordingly it is noted that water is also life-giving and associated with fertility.
Perhaps so, but we may become suspicious of a pool which can so readily
symbolise both virginity and lust; better simply to say that it adds much to the
atmosphere and tension of the tale.

Pure narrative is difficult to write about, and its triumphs difficult to account
for. This point is well made in an essay by C. S. Lewis 'On Stories', which
includes the useful observation that a story is not just a sequence of events but
the flavour generated by its principal ingredients; one of the most important

things about a story concerning giants is the sense of giantness[31] (here it is the 'aura' of the sultry nymph and her pool). However some particular aspects of the story's appeal can be suggested. The account of how Salmacis' pool got its qualities offers the satisfactions of the Just-So story, which Kipling was not alone in appreciating. Ovid produces much delicate magic from the dual nature of Salmacis, part pool, part nymph of the pool, culminating in her watery embraces of Hermaphroditus (360: *circumfunditur*). The story contains one perfect narrative moment, when a hidden Salmacis watches the naked boy swimming in her pool. There is a special quality of sensuality about such unseen watching, perfectly caught by Milton in *Paradise Lost* 9.421ff when, unobserved, Satan watches Eve moving among the flowers. Bartholomäus Spranger chose to illustrate the scene from Ovid in a painting now in Vienna, a superbly evocative image of voyeurism,[32] while Shakespeare transfers it to the story of Venus and Adonis (*The Taming of the Shrew*, Induction ii.47ff):

> Dost thou love pictures? We will fetch thee straight
> Adonis painted by a running brook,
> And Cytherea all in sedges hid,
> Which seem to move and wanton with her breath
> Even as the waving sedges play wi' th' wind.

Ovid, after Homer the most accomplished story-teller among the ancient poets, is full of such moments: to give one further example, Hypermestra, awake on her wedding night hearing her sisters murdering their husbands in adjacent rooms, unwilling herself to take part (*Her.* 14.33ff). Finally, Ovid achieves a beautifully subdued sensuality of tone. *Mollitia* would be an appropriate Latin term for it, and *mollis* with its cognates is in fact a key word in the story.[33] An undercurrent of erotic suggestion runs throughout, as with the picture of Salmacis gathering flowers (315), suggesting the loss of virginity (though it is not she who is to be plucked). The sultry atmosphere is intensified by the similes. The first group (331–3) describes the traditional roses-and-cream complexion of the blushing loved one, while even more evocatively the nymph's eyes shine like sunlight reflected from a mirror (347–9), and the white body of Hermaphroditus in the translucent water is like ivory or lilies seen through glass (354–5), an image with a long subsequent history:

> in liquidis translucet aquis, ut eburnea siquis
> signa tegat claro vel candida lilia vitro.

> Like iv'ry then his snowy body was,
> Or a white lily in a crystal glass.
>
> (Beaumont, *Salmacis and Hermaphroditus*, 863–4)

Oddly such Ovidian sensuality does not become decadent. By contrast in an analogous Virgilian passage (*Aen.* 12.64ff), almost certainly in Ovid's mind, the lushly over-ripe sensuality is pushed over into excess by the word *violaverit*:

accepit vocem lacrimis Lavinia matris
flagrantis perfusa genas, cui plurimus ignem
subiecit rubor et calefacta per ora cucurrit;
Indum sanguineo veluti violaverit ostro
si quis ebur, aut mixta rubent ubi lilia multa
alba rosa: talis virgo dabat ore colores.

Lavinia heard her mother's words, her burning cheeks bathed in tears, and a deep
blush revealed its fires and suffused her hot face, as it is when one corrupts Indian
ivory with blood-red dye, or when many white lilies blush when mixed with roses;
such were the colours the maiden showed in her cheeks.

By contrast Ovid does not leave a sickly taste in the mouth.

4

Outside strictly classical circles Ovid has in recent years been receiving more
sympathetic treatment, and some of the reasons for this merit attention.
Modern critical theory stresses the extent to which art creates rather than
reflects reality, and in some quarters this has been accompanied by a definite
preference for texts like *Tristram Shandy* which proclaim their own artificiality
and fictionality, which breach traditional canons of what constitutes smooth
and consistent realism. Likewise many theorists argue for the reflexivity of
texts, regarding poetry as being in essence about poetry. One can see that such
attitudes would be likely to lead to a revaluation of Ovid. It is interesting that
two of Ovid's admirers earlier in this century (after the Victorian period in
which as one of them said 'Ovid died, for at least the third time..., and was
buried deep under mountains of disparaging argument to make a throne for
Virgil')[34] stressed the extent to which his poetry constituted an autonomous
sphere. Gilbert Murray in his Henry Sidgwick Lecture of 1920, 'Poetry and
Mimesis', claimed in a spirited defence of Ovid that, while he ranks supreme
among 'creators of mimic worlds', 'his criticism of life' is that 'passed by a
child, playing alone and peopling the summer evening with delightful shapes,
upon the stupid nurse who drags it off to bed'; Ovid is 'a man who seems
hardly to have lived at all except in the world of his imagination'.[35] T. F.
Higham, in his seminal essay of 1934, talks of Ovid as 'living in a world of
poetry with standards of its own'.[36]

This approach to Ovid certainly yields insights. The extreme literariness of
his work, aspects of which offended Romantic taste, can be seen again as a
virtue, as it was to Shakespeare and the Elizabethans. This literariness can be
prettily illustrated from *Tristia* 1, a book of poems which more clearly than
almost anything else in ancient literature has a definite autobiographical basis,
yet paradoxically has equally an overwhelmingly literary flavour.[37] It is thus
significant that the autonomy of poetry, which in Ovid's case allows his art to
survive the disaster of his life, is one of the main themes of the exile poetry. In
Tristia 1 the gaiety and wit which result from this literariness differentiate these

14

poems from the more insistent plaintiveness of later work. In poem 2 Ovid is an epic hero rescued by the gods from a *poetica tempestas*; in poem 5 he develops an elaborate *synkrisis* of himself and Odysseus, though his labours are real and no *fabula* (80). In poem 6 his wife is like one of his own heroines (33) and his description of his final night in Rome in poem 3 is intensely literary and elegiac, he and his wife behaving like, say, Ceyx and Alcyone, while there are also constant echoes of Aeneas' departure for exile in *Aeneid* 2. In poem 1 he treats his own fate as a metamorphosis (119–20), in 7 the *Metamorphoses* is an image of himself (his attempt to burn the poem is another literary gesture given the story of Virgil's wish to have the *Aeneid* destroyed), while in 11 his *ingenium* persists despite the danger of his journey to Pontus. Throughout the Emperor is treated as a typical Ovidian god in his arbitrary sway. Life has been subsumed into art.

Equally significant is Ovid's explicit preoccupation with the role and nature of art. In *Amores* 3.12 and *Ex Ponto* 4.8 he praises the transforming power of the imagination. It is poets who create the world of myth, even in a sense, the poet audaciously affirms, the gods themselves (*Pont.* 4.8.55–6):

> di quoque carminibus, si fas est dicere, fiunt,
> tantaque maiestas ore canentis eget.

> (the gods too, if it is permitted to say so, are made by poetry, and their great majesty needs the poet's mouth.)

The *Metamorphoses* may be much more than a poem about writing poetry, but art and artists are certainly central to it. Indeed this may help to explain Ovid's choice of subject, for, as one critic puts it, 'what is poetry but a metamorphosing power, turning fantasy to shapes and giving what is mortal a kind of immortality?'[38] A number of stories directly concern artistic creation: the Pierides, Arachne, Marsyas, Orpheus, Pygmalion. Others could easily be seen in this light, including Midas who 'carries out a travesty of artistic transformation'[39] and Icarus who has been taken as a type of the aspiring artist. It has been argued that many of these stories indicate that Ovid stressed the frailty of the artist and his tragic destiny, but the proud epilogue which proclaims the transcendence of poetry in a world of change shows that Ovid's overall view was far from such a narrowly pessimistic one:

> And now the work is ended which Jove's rage
> Nor fire nor sword shall raze nor eating age.
> Come when it will my death's uncertain hour,
> Which of this body only hath a power,
> Yet shall my better part transcend the sky,
> And my immortal name shall never die.
> For, wheresoere the Roman eagles spread
> Their conquering wings, I shall of all be read,
> And, if we poets true presages give,
> I in my fame eternally shall live.   (Sandys)

The *Metamorphoses* also seem implicitly to raise questions about the nature of narrative. For example we find series of tales within tales creating a 'Chinese box' effect[40] which dissolves the normal stable authority of story-telling. Again there are ecphrases which are, as has been observed, 'mirrors of the poem itself'.[41] Thus Arachne's tapestry shows, reflexively, scenes of transformation beginning with the story of the rape of Europa which Ovid has already told at length (*Met.* 6.103ff); Arachne subsequently experiences treatment of the sort she has been depicting. The painting which most fully reflects this aspect of Ovid's narrative world is Velasquez' *The Spinners*, part of the profundity of which seems to reside, as in the better-known *Las Meninas*, in its ability to prompt in the viewer questions about the nature of perception.[42] The painting, which is marked by a tremendous technical virtuosity, is hard to decipher. The foreground scene is generally supposed to represent the tapestry workshop in Madrid, but some have argued that the young spinner with her back to us is Arachne, while the old lady with the oddly youthful leg is the disguised Minerva. In the background a group of elegantly dressed ladies is looking at a tapestry; figures which we can identify as Minerva and Arachne in the centre of this in-set may be part of the tapestry (where otherwise one can make out the outlines of Titian's version of the rape of Europa), but appear to be standing in front of it on a different plane. The allusion to Titian's painting (Pl. 13), which was in the Spanish royal collection at this date, is a witty touch worthy of Ovid himself. The whole painting is an image at once lucid and puzzling, which prompts questions about art and narrative and the nature of reality, and finds a painterly equivalent for Ovid's subordination of story to story.

Ovid's fluently witty style obviously plays a central role in the creation of this literariness. The stylishness of the writing is obtruded, not concealed, so that Richard Lanham in his discussion of the rhetorical character of the *Metamorphoses* can call the style the central principle in the poem and 'an act of pure display'.[43] There is an amusing story told about Ovid by Seneca the Elder which if not true is at least *ben trovato* (*Contr.* 2.2.12). Friends of Ovid asked to select for removal three lines in his work and Ovid agreed on condition that he could keep three – predictably the same lines were chosen on both sides; the two that survive in Seneca's apparently lacunose text are *Amores* 2.11.10 *et gelidum Borean egelidumque Notum* and *Ars* 2.24 *semibovemque virum semivirumque bovem.* Such rhetorical playfulness is apt to offend the serious-minded. It is not that Ovid's style is any more mannered and artificial than Virgil's – rather less so in fact – but that Ovid's stylishness proclaims itself more stridently irrespective of what is being said, while the excellences of the style are less closely connected with the other excellences, less obviously functional, than they are in Virgil. For example the ostentatious rhetorical patterning of *Heroides* 3.5–6 *si mihi pauca queri de te dominoque viroque / fas est, de domino pauca viroque querar* is delighted in for its own sake (for an instance where it may have point in suggesting the mutuality of love see *Her.* 13.2 and 166).

This characteristic dance of language has wide consequences for tone and manner. It helps to create a sense of detachment, and enables Ovid to evade the kind of high seriousness which Matthew Arnold thought a prerequisite of the greatest literature. We are reminded that we are dealing with a sceptical, sophisticated mind playing in the world of myth, which is seen not as a mirror of reality, as it was in the main by the Greek tragedians, but as the creation of a fictive world. The *Metamorphoses* is nothing so crude as an anti-*Aeneid*, but it is possible to see that the *Aeneid* with its constellation of qualities – its consistent *gravitas*, its presentation of a stable world order centred on eternal Rome, its implicit view that war and politics constitute the greatest subject, its static pathos – is deconstructed in the *Metamorphoses*. The shifts of tone in Ovid disconcert critics for whom Virgil constitutes an unalterable norm. Even the sympathetic Wilkinson apparently finds only 'sheer comedy' in the story of Callisto (*Met.* 2.409ff),[44] where in fact Ovid moves from frivolity with more than a hint of nastiness to a disturbing combination of surreal horror, pathos and grotesque humour in the metamorphosis of girl into bear. Formally too Ovid deconstructs the unified Aristotelian form of epic to provide an alternative model for narrative poets, a model later praised by Cinthio, the theorist of romance; Ovid flamboyantly emphasises the randomness of structure by ignoring book divisions in the case of a number of stories (e.g. Phaethon) in a way which could easily have been avoided and by the sheer effrontery of some of his transitions, censured by the classicising Quintilian (4.1.77).

This post-structuralist image of Ovid, if we may so term it, is a helpful one, enabling us to make sense of features of Ovid's writing which many working within different critical traditions have attacked or tried to explain away. But it like others is two-dimensional; in insisting on the purely autonomous nature of Ovid's world, it limits the poet's appeal and the human relevance of his work.[45] Once again the tradition as a whole can rescue us from such one-sidedness, for Ovid has long been valued for his acuteness as a psychologist, as a successor to Euripides, as a poet interested in many facets of human behaviour and what the eighteenth century called 'the passions', in particular the whole range of emotions associated with love. Ovid is perhaps best described as a psychologist rather than as a delineator of character and personality of the sort which we encounter in Homer or Shakespeare or Jane Austen. (To demonstrate the difference one can compare Sophocles, rightly admired in antiquity for his supreme command of *ethos*, with Euripides; Philoctetes is a more delicately drawn and interesting individual than Pentheus, but Euripides uses the latter as a vehicle for some remarkable psychological insights about repression and sexuality.) Ovid's concern is with the behavioural patterns and psychological drives which constitute the ground of human nature.

The importance attached to this side of Ovid's achievement is perhaps best illustrated by the long-continued interest in a collection that is undervalued today, the *Heroides*, those 'soliloquies of the irresolute mind' as R. G. M. Nisbet terms them,[46] in which we see, in Dryden's words, 'the various movements of a soul combating betwixt two different passions'.[47] Rachel Trickett explores the attractions of this collection for Augustan writers, an attraction which culminates in the one undoubted masterpiece of the genre in English, Pope's weird *Eloisa to Abelard*. It has been observed that these free-floating explorations of consciousness and intense subjectivity raise interesting philosophical questions about the nature of the real.[48] They likewise illustrate Ovid's sympathy (snide though it sometimes is) for women, another feature of the Ovidian tradition shared, as Helen Cooper reminds us, by Chaucer, who was described by Gavin Douglas as 'evir (God wait) all womanis frend' (Prologue to *Aeneid* 1.449). In *Heroides* 19.9ff Hero contrasts the varied interests of men with her lot as a woman forced to concentrate on love alone by lack of alternative activities: *superest praeter amare nihil* (16).[49] She thus anticipates by eighteen centuries the sentiments of Julia's much admired letter in *Don Juan*, Canto 1.194: 'Man's love is of man's life a thing apart, / 'Tis woman's whole existence'. In *Heroides* 3 Ovid points the way to the Middle Ages by making the love interest central to the story of Troy (as happens later in Tiepolo's fine fresco in the Villa Valmarana, in Vicenza).

In Ovid's handling of myth there is thus often a tension between the ancientness of the story and the up-to-date treatment, in particular the psychology. At its worst, as in *Heroides* 4, this results in a debasement of the myth through a pert modernisation which saps it of its vitality.[50] Here Ovid flamboyantly chooses the trivial, as when Phaedra claims that chastity was old-fashioned even when Saturn was king (130–1); this is the silly side of Ovid, which held an appeal for Juvenal. Altogether more agreeable, though still frivolous, is the treatment of the affair between Paris and Helen in *Heroides* 16 and 17 where the lovers are transported into the cynical world of the *Amores* and *Ars Amatoria*. For example we have the triangular banquet scene (16.213ff) or the amusing way in which Helen reveals that she has fallen for the handsome stranger even as she denies it (17.75ff) – *La Belle Hélène* indeed. This is the ancient equivalent of Shaw's *Caesar and Cleopatra*, minor art but with its own appeal. But at its best, as in most of the *Metamorphoses*, the world of Ovidian myth is a wonderful amalgam of old and new, of the glamorously remote and the familiarly human, as Ovid with a uniquely sympathetic detachment unfolds, in a world of wonders, all the wonders of the human heart.

5

A. D. Nuttall observes that 'the Latin poet who ran constantly in Shakespeare's thoughts was not Virgil but Ovid'. Many of the Ovids we have met in this

18

Introduction

introduction – the psychologist, the narrator, the creator of a world of glamour
and romance, the rhetorician who revelled in the possibilities of style – must
have appealed to him. So we may end with Shakespeare and with one of the
most wondrous tributes ever paid by one great poet to another:

> Ye elves of hills, brooks, standing lakes, and groves
> And ye that on the sands with printless foot
> Do chase the ebbing Neptune and do fly him
> When he comes back, you demi-puppets that
> By moonshine do the green sour ringlets make
> Whereof the ewe not bites, and you whose pastime
> Is to make midnight mushrooms, that rejoice
> To hear the solemn curfew, by whose aid –
> Weak masters though ye be – I have bedimm'd
> The noontide sun, call'd forth the mutinous winds
> And 'twixt the green sea and the azur'd vault
> Set roaring war; to the dread rattling thunder
> Have I given fire and rifted Jove's stout oak
> With his own bolt, the strong-bas'd promontory
> Have I made shake and by the spurs pluck'd up
> The pine and cedar; graves at my command
> Have wak'd their sleepers, op'd and let 'em forth
> By my so potent Art. But this rough magic
> I here abjure, and when I have requir'd
> Some heavenly music, which even now I do,
> To work mine end upon their senses that
> This airy charm is for, I'll break my staff,
> Bury it certain fathoms in the earth,
> And deeper than did ever plummet sound
> I'll drown my book.   *(The Tempest* V i 33–57)

This speech of Prospero which starts by closely imitating Medea's invocation
in *Metamorphoses* 7.197ff, with some help from Golding's translation of it, is
as electrifying as anything in English poetry. The invocation does not reach the
expected climax in a prayer or demand – this is relegated to a series of subordinate clauses and turns out to be merely a request for background music –
but leads instead to a resignation of magical powers (the details of the invocation being dismissed, with some irony presumably, as 'rough magic').
Prospero switches from energy, enthusiasm and increasing exultation in his
powers – powers reflected in the power of language – to a wistful weariness;
the syntax (the invocation never coming to a proper conclusion) is oddly
unsettling, even dizzying. If not Shakespeare's farewell to the stage, at any rate
the passage has a valedictory quality, and Prospero's Art is not only that of the
magician, but also, as the play's language strongly suggests, of the poet and
playwright.

Before that Art is abjured, it is celebrated in a passage of breathtaking
virtuosity. The verse line is elastic whilst under an extraordinary control, and
gives an impression that it is only just within the parameters of blank verse in

rhythm and sound (the unusual frequency of enjambements, elisions and especially feminine endings should be noted). In line 33 the monosyllabic words run helter-skelter, skipping from the fifth syllable, against the grain of the metre, the plurals making the line a mouthful of sound; a lighter, more regular line follows, befitting the lovely detail of elvish lightness – 'with printless foot'. In line 35 the extra syllable 'him' (as with 'magic' in 50) creates a slight rhythmic hiccup, while there is a beautiful sense of elves running out and back by the shore, at once playful children and disturbing powers. The beginning of line 38, in addition to the monosyllables, has the powerful compression of 'not bites' (for 'does not bite'), whereby the English is given something of the solid presence of Latin (translators from Latin often complain about the mass of little auxiliary words in English). The light lithe patter of language which dominates in the lines about the elves now modulates, via the romantic 'solemn curfew' – the sort of touch which haunted Milton in his early poetry – to a grandeur which, after onomatopoeia for the thunder, ends in abruptly stifled near-rant. Look, the passage seems to be saying; look at what can be done by a supreme master. And then, with a change of register and a hard-won simplicity, Prospero says farewell to his magic, and Shakespeare to his Ovid. In the words of Muriel Bradbrook:

Prospero's farewell to his art is not only Shakespeare's most important debt to Ovid, and one of the few direct and unmistakable quotations in all his work: it is also a measure of his debt to the whole Ovidian tradition of his youth, as the masque of Juno and Ceres which precedes it is the most perfect statement of what others had tried to put into the Ovidian Romance. Here, in these richly habited masquers and their pastoral attendants, the sunburnt sicklemen and the Nayades of windring brookes, transferred by a final metamorphosis to the celebration of chastity, the Gods and mortals of the antique world appear in all their purfled splendour, all their harvest ripeness, before their final dissolution into air.[51]

2

DAEDALUS AND ICARUS
(i) FROM ROME TO THE END OF THE MIDDLE AGES

Niall Rudd

IN A VOLUME DEVOTED TO OVID and his influence it is fair to give pride of
place to his versions of the story as found in the *Ars Amatoria* and the
Metamorphoses. In fact they deserve that position anyway, not only because
they possess certain qualities which will shortly be acknowledged, but also
because they represent the first full literary treatment that has survived from
antiquity. The earlier, Greek, chapter in the history of the myth is unfortunately
lost; and I will not try to recover it, even in outline, by using the titles of plays,
the remarks of scholiasts, and the accounts of later writers like Diodorus,
Apollodorus and Pausanias.[1] Instead I propose a swift tour, starting from
Augustan Rome, calling briefly at various places of interest, and covering in all
a span of 2,000 years. Such tours, of course, are never satisfactory. But they can
and should give a general impression of the area; and when a particular place
seems attractive one can always note it and return to explore it later.

Like Virgil's Daedalus, we call first at Cumae, where we look at the temple
doors (*Aen.* 6.14ff). One door shows the killing of Androgeos and below that,
it seems, the selection of the Athenian victims. On the other door (*contra* in
l.23) we also expect two scenes. One is taken up with the bull, the counterfeit
cow, and the minotaur; the second (*hic* in l.27) with the maze and probably
Theseus finding his way out with the thread supplied by Daedalus.[2] What,
then, of Icarus? Whether the scene of his fall was never started or never
completed, it could hardly have been accommodated within any symmetrical
plan. I mention the point merely to indicate that Virgil was not always
interested in exact correspondences. I am not even sure how far the temple
doors may be said to provide an entry to Book 6 in the way that the gates of
Sleep provide an exit. More important is the fact that they allow the epic to
extend backwards into the legendary past as the parade of heroes points
forwards to the historical future. As for any larger theme, although scholars
like Jackson Knight and Poeschl would disagree, I cannot find any single idea
connecting the scenes as a whole with anything that happens later in the book.
But one can discern a thread connecting Androgeos with Marcellus, Lausus and
Pallas. That series, in turn, forms part of the larger theme of father and son
which runs through the epic. It is here that Daedalus, grieving over Icarus, finds

21

his place. There was no occasion to develop the story, but Virgil did refer to it in a characteristically sympathetic way.

The note of censure was sounded in Latin for the first time by Horace. In *Odes* 1.3, a good but untypically reactionary poem, he rebukes Daedalus for invading the air: *expertus vacuum Daedalus aera / pennis non homini datis* (34–5). The other three elements were violated by the first mariner, by Prometheus (who stole fire), and by Hercules (who penetrated beneath the earth). It may seem odd that man could violate his own element, but the proper place for human-beings was the *surface* of the earth. Delving into it for precious metals was a sign of greed and discontent;[3] breaking into the underworld was a more extreme kind of hybristic invasion.

Icarus makes his appearance in a very different context. In *Odes* 2.20 we are told that Horace will be *Daedaleo notior Icaro* as his fame flies across the world. The poem has certain incongruities. It reads like a parting declaration, though the writer is not going to leave just yet; it describes a metaphorical transformation in grotesquely literal terms – *iam iam residunt cruribus asperae / pelles*; and in general it represents an uneasy mixture of boasting and self-mockery. Icarus contributes to the ambiguity, being winged and famous but also fallen and dead. Yet, whatever we think of the ode, the flying boy was destined to have a long history as a symbol of poetic aspiration. In *Odes* 4.2 that symbol is used ironically. While Pindar soars as naturally as a swan, any overambitious poet who tries to make his way aloft with wax-fastened wings (i.e. with artificial aids) will give his name to a glassy sea. Giving one's name to a sea is not, of course, meant as a consolation (as with Palinurus and his *terra* in *Aen.* 6.381). It is more like the soldier's sardonic idea of getting one's name on a monument.

Another of the myth's possibilities is hinted at by Ovid in *Ars Amatoria*, Book 2. I say 'hinted at' because the point is not firmly established; in fact Ovid has been less clever than usual. In ll.17–20 he notes how difficult it is to make Amor, the winged boy, stay. He then continues:

> hospitis effugio praestruxerat omnia Minos;
> audacem pinnis repperit ille viam.

> Minos had blocked the foreigner's escape;
> He found a way by wings – a daring feat.

We realise that *ille* is not Amor. It ought, one feels, to be the other winged boy, Icarus. But the *hospes* must be Daedalus, and that is confirmed by *repperit...viam*. At the end of the story Icarus' wings float on the sea (95) and he is buried by his father. Ovid then adds a couplet to link the story with his general theme of elusive Amor:

> non potuit Minos hominis compescere pinnas,
> ipse deum volucrem detinuisse paro.　　　　　　　　(97–8)

> Minos could not detain a human's wings,
> Yet I intend to hold a winged god.

Daedalus and Icarus (i)

Here the *pinnae* are not the floating wings mentioned four lines previously. The *homo* who owns them is Daedalus; for Ovid is referring back to Minos' failure to detain his prisoner. So the connection of Amor with Icarus, so frequently exploited in the later tradition, is not established here.

After his fruitless request to Minos, Daedalus observes that there is no escape by land or sea, but the air remains. He has not mentioned the fourth element, fire. But that will play a crucial part in the action, a part foreshadowed when in constructing the wings Daedalus uses fire to melt the wax – *ceris...igne solutis* (47). The coming catastrophe is again glanced at when Daedalus warns Icarus about the sun – *impatiens cera caloris erit* (60). Finally, the worst happens – *cera deo propiore liquescit* (85). In his later version in *Metamorphoses* 8 Ovid employs less obvious signals. In the construction of the wings the wax is not melted by fire; instead we have the delightful yet ominous picture of the young Icarus softening the yellow wax with his thumb, like a child at primary school messing around with plasticene. The Latin is *pollice ceram / mollibat* (198–9), which foreshadows *vicinia solis / mollit...ceras* (225–6). He also tries to catch the feathers as they wave in the wind. We are told that by his play Icarus was interfering with his father's miraculous work. Every father has had that experience, whether his miraculous work is bashing a typewriter or papering the kitchen wall. In the *Ars*, Daedalus and Icarus take off from a hill-top (71–2). Unlike some writers,[4] Ovid does not show them as imprisoned. More important, he deliberately minimises the element of hybris by making Daedalus beg Jupiter's pardon: he has no wish to approach the gods' abode; he is driven to fly by his urge for freedom (38–40).

In the *Metamorphoses* more emphasis is laid on Daedalus' craftsmanship; it is, after all, his innovation that brings about the quasi-metamorphosis from man to bird. A shepherd and a ploughman now share the fisherman's astonishment at the flying pair; and again we are given an amazing aerial view of the Aegean islands. There are one or two slight changes in emotional focus. The *Ars* conveys a more vivid sense of Icarus' panic; we experience that horrifying moment when he looks down:

> territus a summo despexit in aequora caelo;
>   nox oculis pavido venit oborta metu.   (87–8)

> From heaven's height
> Appalled he gazed upon the deep below,
> And in his panic darkness veiled his eyes.

We hear his actual cry as he falls: *pater o pater, auferor* (91). The later passage gives a sharper account of Icarus' exhilaration:

> puer audaci coepit gaudere volatu
> deseruitque ducem caelique cupidine tactus
> altius egit iter   (223–5)

> The lad exulted in his daring flight;
> He left his guide, and eager for the sky
> Climbed higher.

23

The *Metamorphoses* presents a more poignant view of Daedalus. Tears run down the old man's cheeks, and his hands tremble – rhetorical/pathetic touches which have the effect of making him more like a grandfather. Again, Daedalus' reaction to the tragedy is more sensitively observed. In an agony of remorse he curses his skill – *devovitque suas artes* (234). In neither work is there any mention of the boy's disobedience. Moreover, since Ovid's Icarus is a child, portentous judgements about his arrogance are out of place. The *Ars* speaks of his 'incautious years' (83), and it is true that Icarus' disaster comes from his youthful impetuosity: *si jeunesse savait*. But the rest of that saying is equally apposite: *si vieillesse pouvait*. For the other side of Icarus' imprudence is his energy, his excitement, and his eagerness to rise higher – feelings which Daedalus, with his caution and wisdom, has long forgotten.

As well as dramatising the generation-gap (which was not invented in the 1960s), Ovid presents scientific inventiveness in all its ambivalence. Unlike so many of his successors, he does not indulge in simplistic condemnation; after all, without technology we would still be savages. Nor does he encourage the equally naive assumption that human progress is assured by the proliferation of ingenious gadgets. What *can* be inferred from his story is that revolutionary discoveries occasionally do take place, but that they entail costs which, if foreseen, might have been thought unacceptable; also that when disasters occur they come not always from greed and evil intent but sometimes just from thoughtless enthusiasm. This sophistication of judgement, mediated through a vivid and economical narrative, makes Ovid's version classical in every sense.

A word now about the aeronauts' route. Taking off from Crete for Attica, they fly north between Naxos and Paros to Delos. So far so good. But then, instead of turning north-west, they turn *east* and eventually find Calymna to starboard and Samos to port. As a way of getting to Attica this is an absurdity. True, Icarus had to fall into the Icarian sea, but that leaves the geographical puzzle unsolved. Now, as Stephanus of Byzantium tells us (under Ἰκαρία). Icaria was an Attic deme of the Aegeid tribe; it was located about 5 km from Marathon;[5] and scholars have long believed that Icarus was its eponymous hero. One of these scholars, Carl Robert, considered the possibility that Icarus' fall had originally taken place when Daedalus was escaping from Attica.[6] But more attractive than this, I think, is Peter Green's suggestion that Icarus originally fell into the sea off Attica on the last stage of his flight from Crete.[7] If that is so, how did the story become transferred to the other end of the Aegean? Perhaps when Ionians from Attica colonised the island in the tenth or eleventh century BC they named it Icaria after the old-country's deme, and as a result the legend of Icarus suffered geographical dislocation. That, you may say, is a rather precarious hypothesis, but it does try to make sense of the story. I should be interested to hear of anything better.

Ovid used the myth once more, in a touching passage prompted by his misery as an exile. Just as he thinks of Actaeon when speaking of his error (*Tr.* 2.105–6), so he thinks of Daedalus when longing for home. Dreams of self-generated flight are idle; but Augustus can give feathers; if he grants a return, the poet will instantly take wing (*Tr.* 3.8.5–16). Alas, it never happened.[8]

We leave aside two choric passages of Seneca, where the myth is used in a pleasant but conventional way to recommend the middle course as opposed to perilous glory.[9] The wisdom of such advice is well illustrated by the case of Silius Italicus, who tried to embroider his account with a couple of original touches, and came to grief as a result. In *Punica* 12.95, according to Virrius of Capua, when Daedalus took to the air the gods were terrified by the strange new bird; and later, when Daedalus beat his breast in grief, the flapping of his wings propelled him on his course (99–101). Unfortunately there is not the slightest evidence that Silius meant to be funny. Juvenal's case was different. By the second century AD the theme was as well worn as that of Hylas, and so when Juvenal wanted to satirise safe but vacuous mythological subjects he included 'the youngster's splash-down into the sea and the flying joiner' – *et mare percussum puero fabrumque volantem* (1.54). Equally familiar is Juvenal's description of the versatile and compliant Greek:

> Teacher of grammar and speaking, geometer, painter, masseur,
> prophet and tight-rope-walker, doctor, wizard – your hungry
> Greekling can manage the lot; he'll climb to the sky if you ask him.[10]

Then, as often, Juvenal sights another peak of wit farther up:

> In fact it wasn't a Moor, nor yet a Sarmatian or Thracian
> who sprouted wings, but a man born in the centre of Athens.   (3.76–80)

So, through the sarcasm of a Roman satirist, the great inventor who flew to freedom is reduced to the status of a typical Greek know-all.

From Juvenal's flying joiner we pass easily to celestial lore of another kind. In the piece *On Astrology* attributed to Lucian we are told that Daedalus was an adept in this art.[11] He taught Pasiphae about the constellation Taurus, and as a result she became enamoured of the doctrine – an elegant rationalisation. He also taught Icarus, but the latter, because of his youthful rashness, sought after intractable things; he was raised by his mind into the sky; then, abandoning reason, he fell from truth into a sea of perplexities. We meet the same idea again in Eustathius' note on the Icarian sea (*Iliad* 2.145). Here Icarus is equated with all the clever astrologers of the present time 'who wing their way upward…to discover truth and then falling down are drowned in a sea of falsehood'.[12] That was written in twelfth-century Constantinople; the author may well have been thinking of Lucian. The idea occurs again in Alciati's emblem-book at the time of the Renaissance, when Lucian's influence was widely felt.[13]

A number of other passages in Lucian illustrate the story's endless adaptability. There is a financial application – the rich sometimes fly too close to the sun and then fall like Icarus (*The Dream*, 23); and a social application – when the lowly are suddenly elevated by fortune they tend to fall like Icarus (*Essays in Portraiture*, 21). But the most interesting passage comes in *The Ship*, where Timolaos wants Hermes to give him a ring which will enable him to fly. He will then travel over the world, seeing the marvels of India, locating the source of the Nile, ascertaining how much of the earth is inhabited, and whether people in the southern hemisphere live upside down. A companion predicts that the traveller will have a nasty shock when he suffers the fate of Icarus. In this remarkable passage the Icarian figure of Timolaos is associated with the ranging intellect in a way that foreshadows the aspirations of Faust.

Clearly the idea of flight appealed to Lucian, perhaps because it offered new vantage-points for observing human absurdity. In another piece, entitled *Icaromenippus*, the cynic Menippus, despairing of learning the truth from philosophers, decides to fly to heaven. Taking a hint from Daedalus, he makes himself a pair of wings, using eagle- and vulture-feathers, and making sure not to fasten them with wax. Then, after a series of test-flights, he takes off. He witnesses several entertaining revelations on Olympus; then his wings are confiscated and Hermes leads him back to earth by the ear.

So far we have considered only literary treatments. But Lucian also refers to a dance on the subject (*The Dance*, 49). One wonders what form it took. Actual elevation seems unlikely; for a hoist or a trapeze would have put this dance quite out of line with the others mentioned. So presumably the performance was some kind of ballet. One thinks initially of people flapping and scurrying around as though in a rather hectic production of *Swan Lake*. But such frivolity is misconceived. To go no further back than our own century, a ballet score *Icare* was written by Igor Markevich in 1932. A ballet of the same name was devised by Serge Lifar and performed in Paris in 1935. The choice of theme may have been deliberate; for Lifar was keen to emancipate dance from the trammels of music. And in fact the score of *Icare* consisted simply of Lifar's rhythms, orchestrated by George Szyfer, conductor of the Paris opera. The most memorable feature was Lifar's own performance as Icarus, a feat which seemed to defy gravity. Photos show him dressed in a short belted tunic with gauzy wings on his arms.[14] The ballet was revived at Monte Carlo in 1938 and again in Paris in 1962, when Picasso painted the scenery and the curtain.[15]

Lucian's dance, then, was a ballet; but something more sensational seems to lie behind a remark of Suetonius. Describing a show attended by Nero, he says that Greek boys performed a number of ballets on mythological themes. One of the acts went wrong when Icarus at his first attempt fell close to the emperor's couch and spattered him with blood (*Nero* 12.2). Had some contraption failed to work, or was this Icarus an early 'tower-jumper'? In any case it seems to have been an accident, not a punishment; for the other dancers in the show were awarded certificates of citizenship.

Daedalus and Icarus (i)

Punishment, however, clearly supplied the context of Martial's epigram (*De Spectaculis* 8):

> Daedale, Lucano cum sic lacereris ab urso,
> quam cuperes pinnas nunc habuisse tuas!

> Torn, Daedalus, by a bear upon the sand,
> How gladly would you have your wings to hand![16]

Daedalus, presumably, was the unfortunate slave's name; perhaps he had earned it by his manual dexterity. One writer has suggested that the victim was equipped with wings and urged to fly over the lumbering bear – a suitably sick idea. Unfortunately it is ruled out by the pentameter.

As a last example from antiquity, we will take an affectionate exchange of letters in fourth-century Bordeaux between Ausonius and his son Paulinus. The young man had written of himself and his father:

> audax Icario qui fecit nomina ponto
> et qui Chalcidicas moderate enavit ad arces

> One in his rashness named the Icarian blue;
> The other prudently to Cumae flew

– an elegant conceit with one Horatian and one Virgilian allusion. Ausonius was delighted at being regarded as a wise model, but he refused to accept that his son was rash; the names had been wrongly chosen: *nam tu summa sic expetis ut non decidas; senectus mea satis habet si consistat* (*Epist.* 23) – 'You make for the heights without falling, while I in my old age am glad enough to stay on the ground.'

By the end of antiquity summaries of the story had appeared in various collections, like those of Apollodorus and Hyginus. Here is the account given in the anonymous *Narrationes*:[17]

Daedalus...cum propter commissa Minoem, a quo clausus tenebatur, profugere vellet, pennas sibi et filio Icaro aptavit, quibus ut volucres profugerent regis imperium. quorum Icarus, quia praeceptis parentis obtemperare nequiverat, in insulam maris decidit...

On account of what he had done, Daedalus was keen to escape from Minos who was holding him prisoner. He therefore fitted wings to himself and his son Icarus so that they might escape like birds from the king's authority. Icarus, however, because he failed to obey his father's instructions, fell onto an island of the sea...

As a digest, that serves well enough, but in the centuries that followed more ambitious Ovidian commentators sought to add a deeper significance by means of allegorical interpretations. The practice, of course, was already well established. One thinks of Heraclitus and the Stoic Cornutus in the first century, the neoplatonists Porphyry and Sallust in the third and fourth centuries, and Fulgentius in the sixth.[18] Following this thread into the Middle Ages, we pause

27

for a moment at Theodulf of Orleans in the Carolingian period. In one of his poems he speaks of Virgil and the chatty Ovid (*Naso loquax*):

> in quorum dictis quamquam sint frivola multa
>   plurima sub falso tegmine vera latent.
> falsa poetarum stylus affert, vera sophorum;
>   falsa horum in verum vertere saepe solent.
>   (Migne, *PL* 105, 331–2)

Though much frivolity attends their words,
Truths oft lie hid behind a cozening screen.
The bard pens lies, the sage reality.
(He turns the poet's fiction into truth.)

The last line reminds us that more than one attitude to allegory was possible. Heraclitus had argued that, since so great a poet as Homer could not have been guilty of impiety, he must have been using allegory when he described the gods' misconduct.[19] That, as far as we can tell, was straightforward naivety. When Theodulf says that philosophers change the poets' falsehoods into truth, he is not being naive – or not at least in the same way; for he is claiming that philosophers confer a deeper meaning on the literal, and sometimes disreputable, sense intended by the poets. Others again, no doubt, enjoyed pagan literature in its own terms, but when discussing it in public clothed it in allegorical garments for the sake of decency. Many of Ovid's stories, however, did not have to be saved by edifying interpretations since they were clearly moral already. Thus in the thirteenth century John of Garland, in his *Integumenta Ovidii*,[20] could sum up the message of Philemon and Baucis quite fairly in a single couplet:

> Baucidis ostendit timidique Phylemonis alma
>   Religio superos quod timeas et ames   (335–6)

Baucis' and shy Philemon's piety
Proclaims that one should fear and love the gods.

John of Garland did not mention Daedalus and Icarus, but in *Le Roman de la Rose* we are told that, as Daedalus made wings for Icarus, men make wings for Wealth so that she may fly and they themselves may gain glory and esteem.[21] A more elaborate treatment of the myth, including theological and moral allegory, is found in the *Ovide moralisé*, a fourteenth-century poem of some 70,000 verses. God is the artificer of the world. His son, after his incarnation and death, rose on wings to the sky, thus showing the way to others:

> Et quel voie doivent tenir
> Cil qui vuelent aus sieulz venir?
> Par deus eles doivent voler
> Cil qui là s'en vuelent aler.
> L'amour de Dieu, c'est l'ele destre;
> L'amour dou proisme est la senestre   (8. 1819–24)[22]

And what, then, is the path that should be taken
By those who would attain unto the heavens?
Two wings there are, by which all those must fly
Who hope to mount unto that region;
The right wing mirrors forth the love of God,
The left the love we owe our fellow men. (Cf. note 18)

Then comes a moral warning: those who fly too low are those who direct their affections evilly; those who fly too high in their mad arrogance will be sent hurtling to destruction, and their grave will be in hell: *en enfer ert sa sepulture* (1867). Later in the same century the story was used rather less sternly by Chaucer's friend John Gower. In Book 4 of his *Confessio Amantis* he says

And whan tei weren bothe alofte,
This Icharus began to monte,
And of the conseil non accompte
He sette which his fader tawhte   (1060–63)

Like Phaethon, Icarus is cited as an example of heedlessness (*Negligentia*); one flew too low, the other too high.

As well as asserting the moral value of pagan myths – *gentiles poetas mythicos esse theologos* (*Genealogy*, Tabula, Book 15) – Boccaccio summarises and rationalises the tale of Daedalus and Icarus as a story (*ibid*. ll.26). He claims that in writing his compendium he has risen to the skies *quasi sumptis Dedali pennis* (*ibid*. 15, *prohemium*), thus employing the myth as a conventional metaphor. In addition to all this he refers to Varro's three levels of under-standing religious material – the popular, the poetic, and the philosophical (*ibid*. 15.8). Most classicists, I think, would find that variety of approach quite surprising. The medieval response was not invariably confined to didacticism and allegory.

To pick up another medieval thread (which runs this time through love lyric) we must go back 200 years to the world of the troubadours. Of the few references which I have noticed the most interesting comes in the poem by Rigaut de Barbesieux beginning *Altressi con l'orifanz* ('Just like the banner'):

Ben sai qu' amors es tan granz
que leu mi pot perdonar
s'ieu failli per sobramar
ni reingnei com Dedalus [or Ycarus or lo Magus]
que dis qu'el era Iesus
e vole volar al cel outracuidanz[23]

So great (I know it) is love's power,
I hope for absolution
For failing through devotion;
I seemed like Daedalus of yore
Who claimed that he was Christ and tried
To fly to heaven in his pride.

One notices the variants in line 4. Whoever wrote *Dedalus* or *Ycarus*, whether the poet himself or a scribe, had clearly no conception of chronology. Like Jesus, they both belonged to the past; so what else mattered? We are even left wondering whether the same kind of belief operated in each case. As for *lo Magus*, the magician, that was Simon Magus, an amalgam of history and fiction, to whom I shall return presently. Daedalus too is doubtless regarded as a magician. (That reputation was accorded to everyone who possessed extraordinary ability.) In this poem, he, or Icarus, is compared with the lover. But the comparison is not taken too far. For the writer goes on to say that as *his* pride is nothing but love (*e mos orgoills non es res mas amors*) he does not deserve the fate of Icarus; rather he needs to be saved by his lady's grace. In the courtly love-poetry of Provence the high and unapproachable lady is offered service by the adoring poet. So spiritual is his devotion (at least in expression) that it easily merges into religious language. Hence the mention of Jesus is not wholly surprising.

While Petrarch (1304–74) speaks of Phaethon, the Phoenix, and other winged creatures like birds and butterflies, he does not actually name Icarus. But it is clear that when he wrote the following stanzas Icarus was very much in his mind:

> I pensava assai destro esser su l'ale
> (non per lor forza, ma di chi le spiega)
> per gir cantando a quel bel nodo eguale
> onde Morte m'assolve, Amor mi lega.
>
> Trovaimi a l'opra via più lento et frale
> d'un picciol ramo cui gran fascio piega,
> et dissi: 'A cader va chi troppo sale,
> né si fa ben per uom quel che 'l ciel nega.'[24]

> I thought me fleet enough upon the wing
> (Not through its power but his who gave it me)
> Full worthily of that fair knot to sing
> Which Love has tied and Death alone will free.
>
> For such a task I proved languid and slow,
> Like a small branch which a great burden plies;
> 'Who mounts too high,' I said, 'will fall below,
> Nor can a man achieve what Heaven denies.'

Here, as often, Petrarch is at once heir to the troubadours and ancestor of the poets of the Renaissance.

Half a century earlier, Dante had used the myth largely in a rhetorical way. In the *Inferno*, as he flies through the sky on the back of the monster Geryon, he looks around and sees nothing but air. What greater terror had ever been experienced? Not Phaethon's, not even that of Icarus:

> Nè quando Icaro misero le reni
> Senti spennar per la scaldata cera,
> Gridando il padre a lui 'Mala via tieni!'

Daedalus and Icarus (i)

> Che fu la mia, quando vidi ch' i' era
>   Nell' aere d'ogni parte, e vidi spenta
>   Ogni veduta, fuor che della fiera   (17.109–14)
> Nor was poor Icarus' fear, when he perceived
> His back unfeathered by the melted wax
> (His father shouted 'No! That's not the way!'),
> Greater than mine when I beheld myself
> Surrounded by the air on every hand
> And nothing visible except the beast.

Dante, then, used Ovid, not to convey a moral, or to express his love, but simply to describe what his terror was like. Chaucer has a somewhat similar purpose in Book 2 of *The House of Fame*, where he is carried aloft by the eagle of Jupiter. As the world falls away, the poet can no longer make out the details. No wonder, says the eagle, for no one has risen half as high as this, neither Alexander, nor Scipio,

> No eke the wrechche Didalus,
> Ne his childe, nyse Ykarus,
> That fleegh so highe, that the hete
> His wynges malte, and he fel wete
> In myd the see, and ther he dreynt,
> For whom was maked moch compleynt.   (411–16).

So Icarus is used to illustrate not fear, as in Dante, (for Chaucer's fear has already been allayed) but simply height. Whereas Dante's fear was *as great as* that of Icarus, Chaucer's height is *more than twice* that of Icarus. Such rhetorical expansion is familiar enough, but where did Chaucer find the idea of compleynt or lament? Mourning nymphs were shown on various Pompeian frescoes, but of course Chaucer knew nothing of that. Perhaps the idea came to him independently as he sought a rhyme for *dreynt*. At any rate the idea proved fruitful. Draper, for instance, made the lament of Icarus the theme of his highly romantic painting, which may be seen in the Tate Gallery. Just before the quotation one notices the name of Alexander. We all know him as a conqueror, and most of us have heard of the Alexander romance; but it comes as a surprise to learn that the great man was also an aviator. Yet so he was, and some works which represent him on his celestial journey are referred to in the Appendix.

Another man of unusual powers who inspired many stories was Simon Magus, mentioned in the quotation above by the troubadour Rigaut. According to Acts 8.9–24, Simon the Magician was converted by Philip in Samaria, but later angered Peter by his naive attempt to buy the ability to impart the Holy Spirit. In the course of time layers of fiction were added. Many stories placed him in Rome in the time of Nero, and the most famous described him as a blasphemous heretic who claimed he could outdo Jesus and fly up to heaven. Some say he took off in a chariot drawn by demons; but the writer of the

31

History of the Jewish War (now believed to be Ambrose rather than Hegesippus) reports that he used wings. As Simon flew overhead, St Peter directed a stream of powerful prayers at him, like spiritual anti-aircraft shells, which impeded his wings and brought him crashing to the ground. But notice how the wings are described: *remigiis alarum quas sumserat* (Hegesippus 3.2) – a clear echo of *remigium alarum*, the phrase used of Daedalus' wings in *Aeneid* 6.19.[25] Simon's fall is portrayed in a wide range of medieval monuments – e.g., Celtic crosses in Ireland, a Romanesque capital in Autun, Sicilian mosaics, Roman frescoes, and stained glass in Bourges, Chartres and Tours.[26] It is worth adding that according to one tradition he fell onto the temple of Romulus, an appropriate symbol of paganism.

Also like Daedalus was the Norseman Wayland, whose story is recounted in the Edda.[27] This cunning smith was imprisoned by a king, Nidud of N. Jutland, who severed his hamstrings to prevent his escape. But Wayland got his brother Egill to gather birds' feathers, from which he made a pair of wings and eventually soared to freedom. The story has several versions and numerous ramifications, but two features are noteworthy, one primitive and the other pointing forward. The first is the element of revenge: Wayland raped the king's daughter and murdered his two sons. The second feature emerges from the version in the Thidrek saga which tells us that Wayland got Egill to test the wings, instructing him to take off into the wind and to land with the wind behind him. So Egill took off, flew, and crashed painfully on landing. Wayland then said, 'I shall repair what is amiss.' Having done so, he climbed onto a roof with Egill's help. Then, as he launched himself into the air, he said 'I told you wrong when I instructed you to land down wind, because I didn't trust you to return the wings. Remember, all birds take off into the wind and land *the same way*.' After that brief lesson in aerodynamics Wayland flew off home.[28]

From there we pass to a Greek folk-tale from Zacynthus about a certain Captain Thirteen – 'ὁ καπιτάνος Δεκατρεῖς' – so called no doubt, because of his great physical powers. After being thrown into a pit by his enemies, the Captain found a dead bird lying there. Removing its wings, he fastened them to his arms with clay and then rose into the air. Unfortunately, however, he encountered a shower of rain which dissolved the clay, and he fell into the sea. Presumably the tale represents a rather crude conflation of Daedalus and Icarus, based on dim recollections of the original.[29]

In England the earliest aeronaut was King Bladud, the legendary founder of Bath and the father of King Lear. We are told that he travelled to Athens, where he learned much secret lore, including the art of Daedalus. On returning he decided to demonstrate his magical abilities by leaping from the top of Apollo's temple in London, which was then called Trinaventum or Troy-novant, that is, New Troy. Like Simon Magus, he crashed through the roof of the pagan temple, and according to Geoffrey of Monmouth (writing about 1147) he ended up *in multa frusta contritus* – 'smashed to pieces'. A variant version of the story acknowledges the parallel to Daedalus: *ad ultimum, ceu Daedalus, alis sibi factis, per aera volare praesumpsit, unde summo infortunio lapsus cecidit super templum Apollinis*...(In the end, like Daedalus, he made himself wings and had the temerity to fly through the air. He came to grief disastrously by falling onto the temple of Apollo.)[30]

Later, in the epilogue to the *Mirour for Magistrates* (1587 edn), Bladud was compared to Icarus:

> Who so that takes in hand the aire to scale
> As Bladud here did take him on to flie,
> Or Dedals sonne (as Poets tell the tale)
> Yong Icarus, that flew (they say) so hie;
> Or else as Simon Magus flew perdy.

Later still, in the seventeenth century, Bladud was ridiculed in a splendid passage by Percy Enderbie: 'He provides feathers, wax, glew, and all such utensils as his abused brains apprehended necessary to quillifie him into the nature of a fowl or rather a fool, and thus like Esops crow deckt with feathers not his own he appears more formidable and monstrous than the Griffons in the Mountains of Armenia.' (The Griffons, no doubt, were those that transported Alexander.) The above passage is then followed by 40 lines of Ovid's Latin, describing the fall of Icarus. And eventually comes the moral:

> Thus destitute of help he falls headlong,
> A just reward for his temerity.[31]

The classical '*exemplum*' was also acknowledged by William of Malmesbury in his account of the Benedictine monk Eilmer, who at the beginning of the eleventh century dared a deed of remarkable boldness.

He had...fastened wings to his hands and feet, so that, mistaking fable for truth, he might fly in the manner of Daedalus (*ut Daedali more volaret*). Collecting the breeze on the top of the tower of Malmesbury Abbey, he flew for over a furlong. But buffeted by the strong wind and currents of air, as well as by the awareness of his own rashness, he fell, broke his legs, and was lame thereafter. He himself used to say that the reason why he failed was that he forgot to put a tail on his backside: *ipse ferebat causam ruinae quod caudam in posteriore parte oblitus fuerit*.[32]

Eilmer's flight became famous in the Middle Ages and was still being reported in the seventeenth century. It is now commemorated in Malmesbury Abbey by a stained-glass window, erected in 1928. For centuries the town had a pub called 'The Flying Monk', of which there is a painting in the hotel behind the Abbey. Alas, the pub has now been demolished to make way for a supermarket. However, I am glad to say that there is an establishment near the Abbey called 'Elmer's Hair Stylists', with a drawing of two air-borne monks in the window.

For our next example we move east, to an incident which took place about 1161, when the Turkish Sultan was visiting the Greek Emperor in Constantinople. Inspired by the occasion, one of the Sultan's followers donned a wide white garment, climbed to the top of the hippodrome, and proclaimed he could fly. As he stood there hesitating, the crowd became impatient and began shouting 'πέτασον, πέτασον', 'Fly, fly!' But as an aeronaut he turned out to be more pitiable than Icarus – 'ἦν οὐρανοδρόμος 'Ικάρου ἐλεεινότερος', and he came tumbling down 'εἰς μωκίαν καὶ γέλωτα' – to the accompaniment of jeers and laughter. So says Nicetas Choniates, rather unsympathetically, in his history, which was written in 1206.[33] Clearly the tower-jumper's action, like that of Icarus, was regarded as foolish to the point of idiocy. Richard Knolles, who repeats the story in his *Generall Historie of the Turks* (1621), allows himself a little embroidery: 'The Turks attending upon the Sultan could not walk the streets underided; the artificers in their shops shaking their armes with their tooles in their hands, as did the Turk, and still crying out "Flie, Turk, flie!"' (p. 37). One can perhaps detect an element of relief in the cruel amusement – relief that one who had threatened to reveal himself as a superhuman genius had suddenly rejoined the mass of earth-bound humanity and had paid with his broken body for his pretensions to uniqueness and glory.

To close this medieval section I propose to cheat by bringing in a non-literary artist. In the opening chapter of his famous book *The Survival of the Pagan Gods* Jean Seznec speaks of the euhemeristic tradition whereby pagan gods, and even heroes like Prometheus and Hercules, were treated with the highest respect in the Middle Ages on account of their achievements as men on earth; they were even placed beside the great figures of Judaeo-Christian history like Moses. A striking instance of this practice is to be found on the lowest zone of bas-reliefs on the Campanile of Florence. There, shortly before 1350, Andrea Pisano, going on designs by Giotto, executed a series of carvings in marble, starting from the creation of man and moving on to the labours of Adam and Eve; further on we have Orpheus, the father of poetry. Other inventors and pioneers are also represented – the navigator, the painter, the sculptor, and so on. But what is really breath-taking in this parade of culture-heroes is the presence of Daedalus, the first aviator (see Pl. 2a). By including him Andrea revealed himself as a harbinger of the Renaissance in his thinking as well as in his style. Andrea's other great achievement was the pair of bronze doors which he had executed for the Baptistery in 1336.[34] Is it too fanciful to imagine that as he fashioned those miraculous panels (now on the south side of the building) Andrea remembered his Virgil and thought of himself as doing what Daedalus had done at Cumae? Such an idea would add an even deeper resonance to the figure on the Campanile relief.

By now a few general reflections suggest themselves. First, the myth is seen to have an extraordinary iridescence. Daedalus employs his inventiveness to surmount obstacles, asserting his control over nature in order to obtain freedom. But in doing so he raises the urgent question whether scientific enquiry and technological development should be given *carte blanche*. With pollution, over-population, and the threat of nuclear war the problem is now all too familiar; but of course it was foreseen many years ago. Two books claim mention here: *Daedalus, or Science and the Future*, by J. B. S. Haldane (1924) and *Icarus, or the Future of Science*, by Bertrand Russell (1926); but no doubt the reader can think of earlier examples. Like Daedalus, Icarus can be seen as representing the quest of the intellect, the urge to transcend human limitations, the yearning for divinity. But he is also the meddler whose foolishness amounts to blasphemy – Simon Magus as well as Christ. Again, while Icarus stands for youthful exuberance and the sense of adventure, the intoxication of new experience and sensation, and the soaring delights of art and love, he also represents not only excessive ambition (political, social, sexual, financial) but also the triumph of astrology, the occult, and other weak-minded nonsense. And allied to the lack of wisdom is a fatuous exhibitionism. The sky provides the most natural and available of all theatres. The spectators need only look up. Then there is the whole question of parent–child relationships. Everyone agrees that up to a certain point obedience is vitally important – 'don't try to cross the road or climb on that rock'. Most people also agree that at some stage self-assertion is necessary for growth. But how do we judge when that stage has come? And if self-assertion leads to disaster, whether through a rash business-venture, a hasty marriage, or even just a fast motor-bike, is the parent still responsible? All these issues are somehow present in the myth, and they do not exhaust it.

Again, as we review the period we have covered, we may wonder how a myth like this is perpetuated. We soon abandon the simple idea that the tradition works like a chain, with B drawing on A, and C on B. It seems rather to depend on a dual process of re-enactment and recognition. The two operations come together in the case of the boy who fell at Nero's games; for he was consciously acting the part. Similarly, a poet–lover may re-enact the myth in his imagination, recognising it for what it is, and using it as a framework, model, or point of reference for his own emotional situation. (Some more examples will be offered in Part ii.) In other instances, as with Captain Thirteen and Wayland the Smith, the myth is recast, modified, and even concealed; yet its essential shape can still be recognised by later observers.[35] Such recognition can be seen taking place in historical or quasi-historical narratives like Enderbie's account of Bladud, or William of Malmesbury's account of Eilmer, or Nicetas's account of the flying Turk. In all such cases the writer asserts that what has happened recalls or illustrates or recreates the original, archetypal, myth. In the case of such material there is no point in asking whether art imitates life or *vice versa*. For both life and art return to the myth, and draw meaning and sustenance from that.

Of course it was all a fiction. There was no bronze-age Greek who did what Daedalus or Icarus did. The story of their success and failure is not fact. But provided we know what we are doing, we still have a right to call it true.

35

3

DAEDALUS AND ICARUS
(ii) FROM THE RENAISSANCE TO THE
PRESENT DAY

Niall Rudd

IN THE FOURTEENTH CENTURY, allegorical interpretations of the *Metamorphoses* were still usually written in Latin. Some were rudimentary, like those of Giovanni del Virgilio. His method, say Wicksteed and Gardner, was 'to moralise the stories after the fashion of the crudest conceivable rationalism, and then to sum up the result in a few doggerel verses'. This unkind verdict is, alas, confirmed by an inspection of Giovanni's comments on Daedalus and Icarus: *quia navigio veloci ut aves abiere, ideo fictum est quod alis sibi factis fugerunt. Forte autem filius e puppi decidit* – 'Because they departed like birds in a swift ship the tale was invented that they escaped on wings which they had made for themselves. The son, however, happened to fall overboard.' He then adds a finger-wagging moral:

> credite dicenti, nati, tam sepe parenti
> ut medium pariter contineatis iter
>
> Obey your father's bidding, sons, I pray,
> and hold unswerving to the middle way.[1]

The suggestions of Pierre Bersuire (d. 1362) in his *Ovidius Moralizatus* were a good deal more sophisticated: *Istud applica historialiter contra illos qui cogitant labirintos...Vel dic moraliter quod Dedalus est peccator quem Minos i diabolus in labirinto negociorum et bonorum huius mundi includit...Expone si vis exemplariter allegando contra filios inobedientes et presumptuosos...Vel quod Dedalus architectus est Deus qui mundi machinam fabricavit, filius est quilibet Christianus...* 'Apply it historically against those who devise labyrinths...or say in moral terms that Daedalus is a sinner whom Minos, i.e. the devil, shut up in a maze of the concerns and blessings of this world...Set it forth if you wish as an example, applying the story to disobedient and presumptuous sons...Or say that Daedalus the architect is God, who made the structure of the world, his son is any Christian...'[2]

Latin works, old and new, were still being printed in the sixteenth and seventeenth centuries;[3] but gradually more and more studies began to be published in the vernacular. The author of the *Ovide moralisé* was followed eventually by Bonsogni, Bonsignore and Dolce in Italy, and by Boner, Lorch

37

and Spreng in Germany.[4] In Spain the version by Bustamante (after 1541) was reprinted sixteen times within a hundred years; there too allegories were supplied, notably by Perez Sigler (1580) and Sánchez de Viana (1589).[5]

In England (1567) Arthur Golding published his version of the *Metamorphoses*, written in lumbering fourteen-syllable iambic couplets, along with allegorical comments. This was the standard English translation during the greatest period of our literature, and it still holds a special place as 'Shakespeare's Ovid'. In Golding's view, Daedalus showed how all men love liberty and how necessity brings forth invention, while Icarus illustrated the importance of moderation and obedience.[6] All very sensible, and very traditional. But in the following century a new note is heard. In 1626 George Sandys finished his much neater translation in heroic couplets and dedicated it to King Charles. For the 1632 edition he added an allegorical commentary in prose. There, after praising the golden mean, he says 'Icarus falls in aspiring. Yet more commendable then those who creepe on the earth like contemptible wormes; such the *other* extreme, whereas *this* has something of magnanimity, and mounts like the bird of Jove to his kindred heaven.'[7] That comment is the more interesting because it did not originate with Sandys. In 1609, in his *De Sapientia Veterum*, Francis Bacon had already written: *defectus recte aestimantur excessibus praviores. Quandoquidem excessui nonnihil magnanimitatis subsit et cognationis cum caelo, ad instar volucris; defectus vero humi serpat instar reptilis* – 'Defects are rightly considered worse than excesses. An excess has an element of magnanimity and of kinship with heaven, like a bird; whereas a defect creeps on the earth like a snake.'[8] This shows that Sandys's sentiment was shared by the most adventurous mind of that robust and stirring age. Lowliness was ceasing to be a virtue, and the pride of the questing intellect was ceasing to be a sin. Sandys himself was not only a scholar but a man of affairs. After travelling extensively in the Near East, he sailed to Virginia in 1621 as treasurer of the Virginia Company. There on one occasion he took part in a reprisal against the red Indians for a massacre of settlers; yet such adventures still left him time to get on with his writing. Though we may have mixed feelings about colonial enterprises (now that our own period of expansion is over), it is pleasant to recall that the earliest piece of English verse written on the North American continent was a translation of Ovid.

The myth was also available as a political parable. An Irish poem (*c.* 1580) urges Richard MacOliverus MacShane to follow the *via media* in pursuit of the chieftainship. It tells of the King of Greece's three sons who are on an island with the Emperor of the World's daughter. She and the boat are stolen away by an interloper, whereupon the three brothers glue feathers to their arms and fly off in pursuit. One flies too high and falls like Icarus, the other flies too low and drowns, the eldest wins through. The girl, we are then told, is the chief's rod of office, the feathers are mercenaries, the glue is their pay, and so on. It is all a conscious adaptation of Ovid, as is clear from the fact that the eldest son is called Dédsholus which in Irish means 'He of the gleaming teeth'.[9]

We will now take a different approach to our myth, starting from the dualism of body and soul. The dichotomy is, of course, very ancient; but for our purpose we need not go further back than Plato. In *Timaeus* (35A) soul is said to be compounded of that which is transient and divisible and that which is eternal and *in*divisible. Though enclosed in an earthly body, the soul of a lover aspires to a knowledge of absolute beauty. In *Phaedrus* the lover feels wings growing on his soul and longs to fly upwards (249D). Finally (still by way of preparation), we may refer to two famous sections of the *Republic*, those of the divided line and the cave, where the good in the intelligible world is seen as analogous to the sun in the visible world (508B–C, 516A–B).

These ideas were taken over and developed by influential Christian thinkers in the fifteenth century. Marsilio Ficino (1433–99) commented on the three works just mentioned and also referred to them in his own treatises and epistles.[10] Within this framework of ideas it was easy for Daedalus and Icarus to make their appearance. Daedalus, in fact, had already done so. In the *De Libero Arbitrio* of Lorenzo Valla (*c.* 1440) the interlocutor Antonio Glarea says he is unable to restrain the impulse of his mind. 'Why,' he asks, 'should I foreswear wings if I could possibly obtain them by Daedalus' example (*Daedali exemplo*)? And indeed how much finer are the wings that *I* long for. With them I might fly, not from the prison of walls, but from the prison of errors; and arrive, not as he did, in the fatherland which breeds bodies, but in the one where souls are born.'[11]

There the myth is mentioned explicitly. At other times it is alluded to without the use of names. Pico della Mirandola studied in Florence with Ficino, who was 30 years his senior. In about 1486 he composed his *Oratio de Hominis Dignitate*, in which he longed for those Socratic frenzies sung by Plato in the *Phaedrus*, so that 'escaping quickly from there by the oarage of feet and wings' he might arrive by the swiftest course to the heavenly Jerusalem.[12] 'Oarage of...wings' (*alarum...remigio*) – that tell-tale phrase again shows that Daedalus is in the writer's mind.

The idea of a lover's soul winging its way to heaven occurs quite commonly in the poetry of the period. One thinks of the pieces by Lorenzo de' Medici beginning *Due ale ha la nostr' alma pur e bella* and *O Dio, o Somma Bene, or come fai?* and of Girolamo Beniveni's sonnet *La donna mia non è cosa mortale*.[13] (Lorenzo was a pupil of Ficino's, and Girolamo belonged to the same circle.) But the most apposite illustration of this common ground between philosophy and poetry comes nearly a century later, in Giordano Bruno's *De gli heroici furori* – 'Heroic Frenzies' (1585). In the third dialogue the poet Tansillo (1510–68) is represented as saying that every heroic love has divinity as its object, aspiring to divine beauty. Few can reach that goal, but 'the heroic soul is happier to fall or fail worthily in that high endeavour…rather than to succeed perfectly in lower, less noble, matters'.[14] The interlocutor agrees, whereupon Tansillo recites one of his own sonnets *Poi che spiegate ho l'ale al bel desio*.[15] Richard Garnett's translation begins:

> Now that my wings are spread to my desire,
> The more vast height withdraws the dwindling land,
> Wider to wind these pinions I expand,
> And earth disdain, and higher mount and higher;
> Nor of the fate of Icarus inquire,
> Or cautious droop, or sway to either hand;
> Dead I shall fall, full well I understand;
> But who lives gloriously as I expire?…[16]

For our next example we move back half a century to Sannazaro (1458–1530). In his famous sonnet Sannazaro does not project himself into Icarus' situation, as Tansillo does; he rather reflects on what Icarus did, and ponders on the reward which outweighed his failure:

> Icaro cadde qui: queste onde il sanno
> che in grembo accolser quelle audaci penne;
> qui finì il corso, e qui il gran caso avvenne
> che darà invidia agli altri che verranno.
>   Aventuroso e ben gradito affanno,
> poi che, morendo, eterna fama ottenne!
> Felice chi in tal fato a morte venne,
> c'un sì bel pregio ricompensi il danno!
>   Ben pò di sua ruina esser contento,
> se al ciel volando a guisa di colomba,
> per troppo ardir fu esanimato e spento;
>   et or del nome suo tutto rimbomba
> un mar sì spazïoso, uno elemento!
> Chi ebbe al mondo mai sì larga tomba?[17]

> Here Icarus fell; these waves beheld his fate,
> which drew the daring wings to their embrace;
> here the flight ended; here the event took place,
> which those unborn will yearn to emulate.
> Thrilling and welcome was his sorrow's weight,
> since dying he achieved immortal praise;
> happy that, since he died above disgrace,
> so fair a prize his loss should compensate.
> With such a fall well may he be content,
> if, soaring to the sky dove-like and brave,
> he with too fierce a flame was burnt and spent;
> his name now echoes loud in every wave,
> across the sea, throughout an element;
> who ever in the world gained such a grave?

What a magnificent poem it is! Even in a jaded cynical age it conveys something of the audacity, the defiance of human limitations, the sheer *joie de vivre*, which we associate with the Renaissance. At the same time it reminds us of the myth's elemental power, which we first learned of in Horace: spirit soars above earth into air, is consumed by fire, and drops into water to achieve lasting glory.

Naturally enough, both Sannazaro and Tansillo had a considerable influence on the Europe which had emerged from the Middle Ages. They were joined and reinforced by others, of whom some were primarily lyric poets and others, like Ariosto and Tasso, were better known for their work in other genres (Turner, 51–8). Spain was the country most affected. This was because, by 1503, Spain had taken control of Naples – a control which it retained, despite continual unrest, for 200 years. Sannazaro came from Naples, and it was in Naples in the 1530s that the Spanish poet Garcilaso de la Vega met Tansillo.[18]

In the lyrics of Spain's golden age (1550–1650) the myth of Icarus played a notable part. This phenomenon has been studied by J. H. Turner, who ranges, with generous quotations, from Garcilaso to José Delitala y Castelví. I mention just a few of the conceits employed by these poets: the writer fears that his attempts to praise his beloved will be as perilous as the venture of Icarus (an adaptation of Horace's *recusatio* in *Odes* 4.2 to an amatory context); the lover's tears are like the ocean into which Icarus fell; the poet burns alive in the fire of his lady's eyes; the wings of Icarus consist of a single quill – the poet's pen. In the same works Icarus is associated with symbols which we encountered earlier in Petrarch – Phaethon, the Phoenix, the eagle (which can gaze at the sun), and the butterfly (which is consumed by the object of its own desire).[19]

Turner remarks how, as courtly love and neoplatonism gave way to the Counter-Reformation, Icarus ceased to be admired and became, as he had been before, the object of ridicule and censure. As a generalisation no doubt that is true; but some qualifications are in order. The realist Cervantes (b. 1547) already questioned the wisdom of aiming too high; conversely, in the late seventeenth century Sor Juana Inés de la Cruz still expressed an Icarian yearning for transcendence.[20]

The first French sonnet on our theme was Ronsard's version (*Amours* 167) of a poem by Ariosto.[21] That by its nature was derivative, but Ronsard's characteristic self-reference appears in another Icarian piece, ending with the epitaph:

> Ronsard voulant aux astres s'eslever,
> fut foudroyé par une belle Astrée.[22]
>
> Eager to soar, among the stars to dwell,
> Ronsard was blasted by a fair Estelle.

Making a very different use of the myth, Ronsard chides a lady for her excessively spiritual concerns. Like Icarus, she is too airy: *aimer l'esprit, Madame, est aimer la sottise*.[23] The theme also recurs in several poems by Philippe Desportes, of which the most famous is the imitation of Sannazaro's

Icaro cadde qui. The piece, beginning *Icare est cheut ici le jeune audacieux*,[24] is rendered thus by Maurice Baring:

> Here fell the daring Icarus in his prime,
> He who was brave enough to scale the skies;
> And here, bereft of plume, his body lies,
> Leaving the valiant envious of that climb.
> O rare performance of a soul sublime,
> That with small loss such great advantage buys;
> Happy mishap fraught with so rich a prize,
> That bids the vanquished triumph over time.
> So new a path his youth did not dismay.
> His wings, but not his noble heart, said nay;
> He had the glorious sun for funeral fire;
> He died upon a high adventure bent;
> The sea his grave, his god the firmament.
> Great is the tomb, but greater the desire.[25]

Enfin Malherbe vint. The classical critic found much amiss with Desportes' work, including his use of myth; in one poem he had confused Icarus with Phaethon (a common enough mistake), and in another he had used the phrase *jeune Dédale* for Icarus, thus overlooking the contrast between father and son.[26] The rights and wrongs of such matters are not our concern; but it is interesting to note that here the myth supplied material for a major literary controversy.

Before leaving France we pause to glance at a satire which appeared in 1652, entitled *L'Icare sicilien, ou la cheute de Mazarin avec sa metamorphose*. The man in question was Jules Mazarin, a French statesman of Italian origin, who succeeded Richelieu.[27] The metamorphosis is an innovation. Instead of being drowned, the wretched man will be turned into – what?

> Ah pardon, Mazarin, pardon!
> Les Dieux te feront un chardon
> Pour être sous cette figure
> Des Asnes la noble pasture.

He will become a thistle and provide food for asses.

In English, there is space just to note the attractive anonymous lyric beginning 'Love winged my hopes and taught me how to fly'.[28] In this Icarian poem Daedalus has been replaced by Love – a natural enough substitution since Love is appropriately winged and Daedalus' instruction had been of a rather different kind. Even more to our purpose is one of Michael Drayton's *Amours* (1594), in which the roles of Daedalus and Icarus have been combined:

> My Hart imprisoned in a hopeless Ile,
> Peopled with Armies of pale jealous eyes,
> The shores beset with thousand secret spyes,
> Must passe by ayre, or else dye in exile.

Daedalus and Icarus (ii)

He framd him wings with feathers of his thought,
Which by theyr nature learn'd to mount the skye,
And with the same he practised to flye,
Till he himself thys Eagles art had taught.

Thus soring still, not looking once below,
So neere thyne eyes celestiall sunne aspyred,
That with the rayes his wafting pyneons fired.
Thus was the wanton cause of hys owne woe.
Downe fell he in thy Beauties Ocean drenched,
Yet there he burnes, in fire thats never quenched.[29]

In the first stanza the lover's environment is seen as a hostile Crete. By taking thought he contrives to liberate himself, soaring above his enemies. But in doing so he flies too close to the burning radiance of his beloved's eyes, and his wings catch fire (which shows how easily Icarus can be conflated with Phaethon). He falls into the ocean of his loved one's beauty, which like Milton's lake of fire burns perpetually. That, or something like it, is surely what the poem means. I do not know how much weight should be attached to the details of the opening lines. But if the 'hopeless Ile', with its 'spyes', is a political reference, the Cretan parallel becomes correspondingly important.

From sixteenth-century lyric to sixteenth-century lampoon. In 1504 a quack doctor, alchemist, and general con-man called John Damian, who had insinuated himself into the good graces of King James IV of Scotland, was made Abbot of Tungland near Galloway. On 27 September 1507, when the King had sent ambassadors to France, Damian declared he would be there before them. He climbed onto the top of Stirling Castle, donned a pair of feathered wings, and dropped straight onto a dunghill, fracturing his thigh in the process. John Leslie in his history of Scotland (1578) says *omnes risu emori, illum qui modo tanquam alter Icarus coelum alis petebat, terram nunc suis pedibus, contuso paene corpore, tanquam Simonem illum Magum, non potuisse premere* – 'They all died laughing, to think that a man who shortly before was winging his way to heaven like a second Icarus was now lying with his body almost shattered, like Simon Magus, unable to stand on the earth.' Damian blamed the mishap on his feathers, many of which had come from hens; unlike an eagle's, they were not suitable for soaring, but by a natural affinity (*vi quadam insita*) they had drawn him to a dunghill (*sterquilinium*).[30]

Now by his success with the King, Damian had apparently obstructed the preferment of the poet William Dunbar. In protest the latter wrote two trenchant invectives, one called 'The Birth of the Anti-Christ' (for which Damian was allegedly responsible) and the other called 'The Fenyeit Freir of Tungland' (*fenyeit* meaning 'bogus'). In the second piece the birds of the air wondered what the flying abbot might be:

Sum held he had bene Dedalus
Sum the Menatair marvelous
Sum Martis blaksmyth Vulcanus
    And Sum Saturnus kuke. (Cf. Ganymede?)

43

> And evir the cuschettis at him tuggit, (wood-pigeons)
> The rukis him rent, the ravynis him druggit,
> The hudit crawis his hair furth ruggit,
> The hevin he micht not bruke.

(That is, to prevent his enjoying possession of the sky.)[31] But the poor man's misfortunes did not stop there. Other birds moved into the attack, and a buzzard snatched off his testicles. In his extremity the victim then defecated and besmirched a hundred head of cattle peacefully grazing below. (Dunbar was not a man for half measures.) There is, needless to say, personal animus here. But there is more than that. In Dunbar's view Damian's welcome at court was an indictment of the King, and his attempted flight represented a blasphemous outrage against God's heaven.

The myth has also tragic possibilities, as the Greeks knew. It haunted Marlowe, who alluded to it in three of his plays in passages of splendidly extravagant rhetoric:

> Ile frame me wings of waxe, like Icarus,
> And ore his ships will soore unto the Sunne,
> That they may melt and I fall into his armes.

So Dido in *Dido, Queen of Carthage* (V i 243–5). For the Duke of Guise the propelling agent is power rather than sexual passion:

> What glory is there in a common good,
> That hanges for every peasant to atchive?
> That like I best that flyes beyond my reach.
> Set me to scale the high Peramides
> And thereon set the Diadem of Fraunce,
> Ile either rend it with my nayles to naught
> Or mount the top with my aspiring wings,
> Although my downfall be the deepest hell.
>
> (*The Massacre at Paris* 2.97–104)

There we have, not Icarus–Christ, but Icarus–Lucifer. One recalls Isaiah's verses beginning 'How art thou fallen from heaven, o Lucifer, son of the morning!' and ending 'Yet thou shalt be brought down to hell, to the sides of the pit' (14.12–15).

Hell, too, is the destination of Dr Faustus, another Icarus-figure, as the opening chorus makes plain. He excelled all in theology

> Til swolne with cunning of a self-conceit,
> His waxen wings did mount above his reach,
> And melting heavens conspired his overthrow. (20–2)

The punctuation of the last line is debated,[32] but it is the image of reaching that immediately concerns us. 'That like I best,' says the Duke of Guise, 'that flyes beyond my reach.' The Elizabethan critic Puttenham explained the figure of hyperbole as 'the over-reacher', and that was used by Harry Levin in the title of his interesting book on Marlowe.[33] Levin also used as frontispiece Alciati's emblem of the falling Icarus. The emblem (no. 104) is entitled *In Astrologos*, which recalls the passage of Lucian mentioned in Part (i).[34] Icarus and his supposed interest in astrology prefigures Faustus, who has fallen into 'cursed necromancy'.

> Nothing so sweete as Magicke is to him,
> Which he preferres before his chiefest blisse.

In a famous chorus of *Antigone* Sophocles wrote πολλὰ τὰ δεινὰ κοὐδὲν ἀνθρώπου δεινότερον πέλει (332–3), 'Many are the world's wonders, and nothing is more wonderful than man.' Ἄιδα μόνον φεῦξιν οὐκ ἐπάξεται (360–1), 'From death alone will he effect no escape.' Since magic has always attempted what cannot be achieved by natural means, it follows that death is magic's ultimate challenge. True, Faust has not been rendered immortal, but he has succeeded in deferring death for 24 years – no small span, especially in a time of plague. But now his time is up. When the play opens, he, like Oedipus, is already a doomed man; and he is presented to us as such: 'And this the man that in his study sits'. Is it true, then, that, as Santayana said, Faustus is a martyr to everything that the Renaissance prized – power, curious knowledge, enterprise, wealth, and beauty? Or is *Dr Faustus* fundamentally a morality play about pride and punishment? Perhaps in the end we do not have to decide. As Hegel might have said, *Dr Faustus* dramatises the struggle between two equally legitimate and equally vital claims – innovation and stability.[35] As in Marlowe's other two plays, the figure of Icarus illuminates the character in question. It also illuminates Marlowe himself, that brawling blasphemous genius whose flamboyant brilliance seemed to clamour for an early death, if only to avoid the humiliations and tedium of middle age.

It seems odd to talk of 'descending' to Shakespeare. Yet, in a sense, that is what we must do; for although the myth is evoked twice in *Henry VI*, Part 1, and once in *Henry VI*, Part 3, the treatment in each case is personal, and indeed familial. That in itself is unusual. The last instance we noted was in the letters of Ausonius and Paulinus. Again, the mythological references are by no means casual or decorative. In Part 1 Shakespeare leads up to them over two scenes in which Talbot tries to persuade his son, John, to make good his escape from the French. The lad persistently refuses to leave his father, thus establishing his courage and nobility – proving himself 'commendable'. Linguistically, too, the myth is prepared for. Early in Act IV Scene v Lord Talbot urges the boy to escape 'by sudden flight'. Young John answers 'Is my name Talbot? And am I your son? / And shall I fly?' (not 'flee'). There are ten more occurrences of 'fly' or 'flight', after which the son says:

> Then talk no more of flight, it is no boot;
> If son to Talbot, die at Talbot's foot.

The boy, then, has disobeyed, not by flying too high, but by refusing to 'fly' at all. The father accepts the alteration of the myth and alters it again on his own account, calling on his son to follow him by standing his ground:

> Then follow thou thy desperate sire of Crete,
> Thou Icarus, thy life to me is sweet.
> If thou wilt fight, fight by thy father's side,
> And commendable prov'd, let's die in pride.

At the opening of the next scene the wounded Talbot speaks of his son's death, saying that he charged

> Into the clustering battle of the French;
> And in that sea of blood my boy did drench
> His overmounting spirit; and there died
> My Icarus, my blossom, in his pride.

Not only the final rhyme, but the entire image provides continuity between the two scenes. And notice the final alteration whereby Icarus' pride, or arrogance, is transmuted into the pride of self-respect. There is another, equally interesting, scene in Part 3, when King Henry explicitly refers to himself as Daedalus. But space forbids discussion. Enough to note that Shakespeare, like Virgil, has reasserted the poignancy of the father–son relationship. I suspect, moreover, (though here I am open to correction) that in Shakespeare, for the first time, the scene of Icarus' daring is transferred from the sky to the battlefield. Our own century has achieved the opposite feat by transferring bellicosity to the sky, and making Icarus into a fighter-pilot.

In the late seventeenth century more research was being done on flight. Bishop John Wilkins and his friend Robert Hook reported on their investigations to the Royal Society in 1660. In 1680 Borelli's *De motu animantium* demonstrated that flight of the Daedalian kind was impossible – human musculature could not sustain it. Also, though his positive contentions had to be modified, Borelli showed that a bird's wing does not produce lift by striking down and backwards like an oar. So the old metaphor, which goes back at least as far as Aeschylus (*Ag.* 52), turned out to be misleading. Though there was less scientific progress in the eighteenth century, several fantastic novels were published – some comic and some romantic – which served to fuel public interest in flight.[36]

The most distinguished writers, however, remained sceptical. In the *Guardian* of 20 July 1713 Addison spoke of Bishop Wilkins's researches and went on to print a letter from a correspondent who signed himself 'Daedalus'. Part of it runs as follows:

I think fit to acquaint you that I have made a considerable progress in the art of flying. I flutter about my room two or three hours in a morning, and when my wings are on can go above a hundred yards at a hop, step, and jump. I can fly already as well as a turkey-cock, and improve every day.

'Daedalus' intends to patent the wings to forestall commercial competition, and to set up a monopoly in teaching persons of quality. The invention, moreover, will ease congestion on the roads and greatly facilitate trade. The editor replies in the persona of Mr Ironside, who is gravely concerned about the implications for sexual morality: 'You should have a couple of lovers make a midnight assignation upon the top of the monument, and see the cupola of St. Paul's covered with both sexes like the outside of a pigeon-house.' Again 'The poor husband could not dream what was doing over his head. If he were jealous, indeed, he might clip his wife's wings, but would this avail when there were flocks of whoremasters perpetually hovering over his house?' In view of all this frivolity one turns back to the Horatian epigraph prefixed to Addison's article: *udam / spernit humum fugiente penna* (*Carm.* 3.2.23–4) – 'spurns the damp ground with flying wing'. The Roman poet's subject was *Virtus*.

That is Addison in playful mood. It is worth pausing a moment to recall the developments which helped to produce that urbane, confident, teasing tone – the economic changes which were bringing increased prosperity; the emergence of a new middle class, eager to learn the manners appropriate to a gentleman; the appearance of editors who were willing to teach them, while also providing entertainment; the periodicals which gave some writers a chance to earn a living without truckling to the aristocracy. All these factors somehow contributed to Addison's style. And for his subject classical myth as ever offered a paradigm.

One notes that Addison did not attempt to *refute* Bishop Wilkins. Nothing so dogmatic was called for. He simply assumed, and expected his readers to assume, that all attempts to fly were ridiculous. Johnson took a slightly different line in *Rasselas*. While contemplating escape from the valley of happiness, Rasselas, Prince of Abyssinia, met a man who was convinced he could fly. In conversation the man pointed to some of the blessings which would accrue as a result of flight, including (as with Lucian) the discovery of the sources of the Nile; he was also level-headed enough to foresee the possibility of air raids. Some time later the man took off from a promontory and 'in an instant dropped into the lake. His wings, which were of no use to him in the air, sustained him in the water, and the Prince drew him to land, half dead with terror and vexation' (Section 6). There is less fantasy here than in Addison, and a good deal less facetiousness. The flyer is not depicted as farcical; and Johnson takes the point that there is no *a priori* argument against human flight. As Rousseau had remarked a few years earlier in *Le nouveau Dédale*, 'by what right do birds exclude us from their element when fish admit us to theirs?'[37] Nevertheless, by having an eye-witness record the man's failure, Johnson provided empirical proof of the theory's unsoundness – rather as he refuted Berkeley by kicking a stone.

When *Rasselas* was published (1759), Goethe was ten years old. As a boy, he saw a marionette performance based on Marlowe's *Dr Faustus*, and his imagination was kindled. Only two passages of Goethe can be mentioned here. The first is Faust's magnificent speech in *Faust*, Part 1, outside the city gate (1064ff), in particular the lines beginning

> O dass kein Flügel mich vom Boden hebt,
> Ihr nach und immer nach zu streben!

> I long to join his quest
> On tireless wings uplifted from the ground.
> Then should I see, in deathless evening-light,
> The world in cradled stillness at my feet,
> Each valley hushed, fire touching every height,
> While silver brooks in golden rivers meet.
> Then mountains could not check my god-like flight,
> With wild ravine or savage rocky ways;
> But lo, the sea, with warm and tranquil bays,
> Would hold its beauty to my wondering sight.

(Philip Wayne's Penguin translation)

An almost mystical contemplation of nature, reminding us of Wordsworth.[38]

The other passage, in Part 2, concerns the boy Euphorion, a strange figure who is the son of Faust and Helen of Troy. As such, he is meant to symbolise the modern blend of Romantic and Classical poetry; but in fact his Romantic genes are clearly dominant. In l.9607 his mother warns him not to attempt flight, and his father reminds him that he is really a creature of the earth. But all to no avail. He climbs to a mountain top; looking down he sees a battle taking place below. Determined to participate heroically, he hurls himself into the air:

> ein Flügelpaar
> Faltet sich los!

> And here are wings
> Spreading for flight.

His robes keep him up for a moment. Then, as the chorus shouts 'Ikarus! Ikarus!' (9901) he falls at his parents' feet. 'We fancy,' says the text, 'that we recognise in the dead a well-known figure.' Elsewhere Goethe tells us that the well-known figure is that of Byron; the war which Euphorion saw was the war of Greek independence.

The mature Goethe, then, perceived the appeal of Euphorion and what he stood for; but in Euphorion's fate, and finally in Faust's, Goethe may well have uttered a warning against 'uncontrolled Titanism, which had been associated with his own *Sturm und Drang*, had lived on in Byronism, and could only...have disastrous consequences'.[39]

One doubts whether an adequate essay on French Romanticism could be written around the theme of Icarus. (M. Z. Shroder's study interprets the myth very broadly.[40]) But it is certainly true that images of flight recur at numerous points in the movement. In 1821, concluding *Le poète dans les révolutions*, Victor Hugo wrote:

Daedalus and Icarus (ii)

L'alcyon, quand l'océan gronde,
Craint que les vents ne troublent l'onde
Où se berce son doux sommeil;
Mais pour l'aiglon, fils des orages,
Ce n'est qu' à travers les nuages
Qu'il prend son vol vers le soleil.

The halcyon, at the storm's alarm,
dreads that the wind will toss the calm
whereon his cradle lies.
The eaglet, child of the tempest loud,
knows he must battle through the cloud
as toward the sun he flies.

Forty years later, in very different mood, Baudelaire concluded one of his poems thus:

En vain j'ai voulu de l'espace
Trouver la fin et le milieu;
Sous je ne sais quel œil de feu
Je sens mon aile qui se casse;
Et brûlé par l'amour du beau
Je n'aurai pas l'honneur sublime
De donner mon nom à l'abime
Qui me servira de tombeau.

In vain my passion to survey
The limits of infinity;
I feel, beneath a fiery eye,
my wings falling away.
And I whom beauty's rays consume
shall never know the final bliss
of giving my name to that abyss
which will provide my tomb.

Thus Baudelaire sardonically rejects the comfort of a glorious death offered by Sannazaro and Desportes. In case we have any doubt about the speaker, the poem is entitled *Les plaintes d'un Icare*. To take another instance, in his *Notices romantiques* Gautier says in connection with de Vigny's *Chatterton*:

La jeunesse de ce temps-là était ivre d'art, de passion, et de poésie...Le sort d'Icare n'effrayait pas personne. Des ailes! des ailes! des ailes! s'écriait-on de toutes parts, dussions-nous tomber dans la mer!

Young people in those days were drunk with art, passion, and poetry...No one was deterred by Icarus' fate. 'Wings! Wings! Wings!' came the cry on every side, 'even if it means falling into the sea!'

One can hardly fail to recall that one of Gautier's own poems, *Ce que disent les hirondelles*, contained the line *Des ailes! des ailes! des ailes!*

In our own century four main areas can be distinguished in which the myth has had a significant function: the purely artistic, the communist, the fascist, and the psychological. As examples from the artistic, non-political, area one might choose Serge Lifar's ballet, which I spoke of in Part (i); or possibly Gide's

Thésée (1946); or perhaps the work of Michael Ayrton, who in his writing and painting and, above all, in his sculpture reverted to Daedalus and Icarus again and again.[41] Instead I shall say a little about James Joyce. There is no problem about establishing relevance. The epigraph to *A Portrait of the Artist as a Young Man* reads *et ignotas animum dimittit in artes* – the innovations of Daedalus as described in *Metamorphoses* 8.18; and the chief character is called Stephen Daedalus. This young man, who is a persona of Joyce himself, comes to find the Irish intellectual atmosphere restricting and oppressive. 'When the soul of a man is born in this country,' he says, 'there are nets flung at it to hold it back from flight. You talk to me of nationality, language, religion. I shall try to fly by those nets' (211).[42] Already, in a reverie he has seen 'a hawklike man flying sunwards above the sea' (184); and later, standing in the classical portico of the National Library on a spring evening,[43] he watches like an augur the flying birds and experiences a sense of fear – 'a fear of symbols and portents, of the hawklike man whose name he bore soaring out of his captivity on osierwoven wings, of Thoth, the god of writers, writing with a reed upon a tablet and bearing on his narrow ibis head the cusped moon' (229). The work closes with two entries: April 26th 'I go to…forge in the smithy of my soul the uncreated conscience of my race.' April 27th 'Old Father, old artificer, stand me now and ever in good stead.' As a metaphorical smith, the speaker identifies himself with the mythical Daedalus – 'I go to forge etc.' But what of the last entry? Does he still see himself as Daedalus? Perhaps as the reincarnation of Daedalus he is asking the original Daedalus for help. That is possible, though not strictly logical. It seems more likely that he has switched to Icarus.

For a closely related passage we turn to *Ulysses*, where Stephen reflects to himself 'Fabulous artificer, the hawklike man. You flew. Whereto? Newhaven –Dieppe, steerage passenger. Paris and back. Lapwing. Icarus. *Pater, ait.* Seabedabbled, fallen, weltering. Lapwing you are. Lapwing he.'[44] Here there plainly *is* a switch from Daedalus to Icarus. As a biographical fact, Joyce had received a telegram from his father, urging him to come home because his mother was dying. So the first bid for freedom had ended ingloriously. The etymology of lapwing is hlēap-wince, 'leap-waver'; in spring the bird gives an odd aerobatic display, climbing upwards and then plunging down, rolling and twisting, apparently out of control. The ornithological Icarus. *Pater, ait* looks like an imperfect recollection of Ovid's *pater o pater, auferor inquit* (*Ars* 2.91).[45] But what of 'the hawklike man'? In two of the three passages quoted the hawklike man is equated with Daedalus, though there was in fact nothing hawkish about Daedalus. There was something hawkish, however, about another character who occurs later in the *Metamorphoses*. After his transformation into a hawk 'he is friendly to none, fierce to all other birds, and suffering himself makes others suffer too' (11.344–5). That man, before his transformation, had the name Daedalion. Joycean scholars will probably tell us that the modulation from Daedalus to Daedalion represents a deeply significant unconscious association of ideas. Perhaps it does. But in ordinary mortals it would simply be called a slip.[46]

And now, political ideology.

Bischof, ich kann fliegen
Sagte der Schneider zum Bischof.[47]

'Bishop, I can fly,'
Said the tailor to the Bishop.
'Look, here's the proof.
Just watch me try!'
He climbed with two things
That looked like wings
To the high high church's roof.
The Bishop didn't stay there.
'It's nothing but a lie,
A man's not a bird,
No man will ever fly,'
Said the Bishop of the tailor.
'The tailor is dead,'
Said the people to the Bishop;
'A silly affair;
His wings were torn and tattered,
And now he lies there shattered
On the hard hard city square.'
'Ring bells from the steeple;
It was nothing but a lie;
A man's not a bird;
No man will ever fly,'
Said the Bishop to the people.

The nucleus of the poem lies in the fact that on 30 May 1811, a tailor called Berblinger jumped from some scaffolding on the Eagle Bastion in Ulm in an attempt to fly across the Danube. He was pulled out of the river and subjected to the usual ridicule. Brecht, who grew up in that area, has given the incident an ecclesiastical setting (the cathedral) and an anti-clerical twist (the Bishop is not only a complacent reactionary but he hears of the tailor's death with something akin to pleasure). Unlike the anti-Christian villain Simon Magus, the tailor is presented as an anti-Christian hero who dies in the cause of progress. Significantly Brecht prefixed to the poem the date 1592, thus bringing the tailor into line chronologically with two other heroes on whom he was writing at the time – Francis Bacon and Giordano Bruno.

From a very different background, but equally fervent in his opposition to fascism, was Lauro de Bosis, whose play *Icaro* won a prize at the Olympic contest in Amsterdam in 1928. A translation appeared in 1933 with a foreword by Gilbert Murray. The work, which recalls the form of a Greek tragedy, contains a number of original variations. Icarus' flight, for instance, is a solo effort, and his fall is described in a messenger-type speech. The play ends with the following reflection:

> dovunque al mondo cuore umano arda
> d'ansia e d'amore, contro i fati armato,
> sempre, non visto, Icaro lo guarda.

> Wherever in the world a human heart
> burns with desire and love, defying fate,
> always, unseen, will Icarus take its part.

A few years later, De Bosis was to pay a more impressive tribute to Icarus. As he could not risk returning to Mussolini's Italy, he acquired an aeroplane and learned how to fly. On 3 October 1931 he flew over Rome scattering anti-fascist leaflets. I am not aware that he was shot down, as Michael Grant states; he may well have crashed into the sea; certainly he never returned.

Like any instrument of power, the myth was also available to the other side. Gabriele D'Annunzio did not grow up as a fascist (he was born in 1863) but he became one later and ended up as Mussolini's most famous, or infamous, henchman. Early in this century he published a collection of poems entitled *Alcione* (1904), which contained a long dithyramb on Icarus. When writing it, D'Annunzio claimed to be tormented by Icarus' ghost. 'He was my soul; he was my very body; he was the anger I felt at being a man without wings; he was my yearning to fly.'[48] Tormented or not, D'Annunzio altered the myth in the direction of a morbid and sometimes grotesque sensationalism. The manufacture of the model cow is described; and Icarus, who is fascinated with Pasiphae, is present at the coupling. Next, after a bloody fight with an eagle, he offers it as a sacrifice to the sun, hoping to gain permission to enter the sky. The rest of the narrative follows Ovid, though at ten times the length, and ends with a prayer for a glorious Icarian death.

When aeroplanes first appeared, D'Annunzio spent hours in the company of Blériot. Now in his forties, he became a pilot, and subsequently took part in a number of air raids. (One cannot deny him courage.) By now he had attained the status of a Nietzschean superman – literary celebrity, irresistible Don Juan, fervent patriot, valiant warrior, and comrade of the Duce. Yet to some of his contemporaries, and to most later critics, there has been something irredeemably false about almost everything he did. Small, bald, and unprepossessing, he was at the same time vain, priapic, sadistic, and totally humourless. Scholars like Mario Praz, who have studied his writing, assure us that much of it is derived from people only slightly less decadent than himself.[49] His energy and fluency were not matched by any notable intellectual insight. It is significant that in his treatment of our myth Daedalus plays a very subordinate role, dwindling into a kind of fictional odd-job man. No doubt D'Annunzio felt that he did not carry any emotional voltage to match that of his glamorous son. If we think of the country and the period in which D'Annunzio lived, we can see that his charisma, like Mussolini's, satisfied a thirst for heroic glory based on a widespread sense of mediocrity. That thirst, combined with that sense, is a worrying phenomenon, not peculiar, alas, to the Italy of the 1930s.

Finally we come to the area of psychology. A few years ago an article by Henry A. Murray appeared, entitled 'American Icarus'.[50] From the author's clinical observations it emerges that the Icarus type is finicky about his food as a child, likes climbing trees and building model aeroplanes, imagines his own death and enjoys watching his mother's grief; has fantasies about urinating from the sky upon the bodies of women, is prone to 'ascensionism' (i.e. the wish to be tall, walk on water, and so on), to 'cynosural narcism' (sic), i.e. a craving for attention, and to 'precipitation', i.e. 'a consciously or unconsciously desired calamitous descension' (sic). All that seems suitably bizarre; in fact some of it sounds like a case history of D'Annunzio. Whether the diagnosis of the Icarus-complex has any therapeutic implications remains unclear. No doubt we shall be told. In the meantime one thinks of the way in which the myths of Oedipus and Narcissus have been 'psychologised' in the last hundred years.

In literature the most elaborate example of the psychological approach to Icarus is the novel *Birdy* by William Wharton, which was made into a successful film in 1985. It is an interestingly constructed book in which the sane but verbally impoverished Al acts as a foil to his highly abnormal friend, who has always cherished aspirations to birdhood.[51] He once sewed feathers on his long johns and made a cap with a beak; he constructed wings and eventually took off with the aid of Al's bicycle above a 40 ft drop, without fatal results. His fascination with birds eventually becomes morbid as he succumbs to sexual fantasies. Then, as a result of some appalling experiences in Vietnam, he becomes locked into this avian world. When the book opens, he is in a military mental hospital, and Al is trying to cajole him back into sanity. He gets little response, but the reader is admitted to Birdy's inner thoughts, which turn out to be conceptually quite sophisticated, revealing a genuinely informed interest in ornithology. Although the ending is unsatisfactory, *Birdy* is an original book, an impressive twentieth-century conflation of Daedalus and Icarus.

In these two essays I have tried to draw attention to some of the more interesting forms taken by the myth. It has entered most of the major genres and served a wide variety of purposes. Together or separately Daedalus and Icarus supplied a model to the Renaissance *uomo universale*; they were treated with reserve by the eighteenth-century man of good sense, admired by the Romantic and embraced by the decadent. More recently they have provided symbols for the unfettered artist; they have been seen as an inspiration by communist and fascist; and followed unconsciously by the mentally deranged. Daedalus and Icarus must surely be amongst the most profound and the most perennially apposite of all myths. It has always been capable of assuming new shapes and answering new needs; and by its constant and yet changing relevance it has helped us to write our own cultural history.

4

OVID THE CRUSADER

C. W. Grocock

Bobbing along in the wake of the better-known and more frequently studied of the Latin accounts of the First Crusade which are gathered together in Riant's monumental collection, the *Recueil des historiens des croisades*, is a work which has hitherto received little attention, the *Historia Vie Hierosolimitane*, written probably in the first decade of the twelfth century by a certain Gilo of Paris. Unlike its more famous contemporaries such as the *Gesta Francorum* and the accounts written by Robert the Monk or Raymond of Aguilhers, this work is in verse, comprising five books of hexameters in a mixture of leonine and end-rhyme, and with some sections not rhymed at all. It also has one short section and a prologue penned in elegiac couplets. The poem tells the story of the Crusade from the arrival of the Christian forces at Nicea to the capture of Jerusalem itself. At a later date (probably c. 1128) an anonymous continuator made substantial additions to Gilo's work, adding four complete books which recount the events of the 'Peasants' Crusade' and the Franks' journey through Europe to Constantinople, as well as Baldwin's exploits in Edessa and a visit by part of the Frankish forces to Egypt.[1]

Despite Gilo's own protestations in his prologue (which will be examined in some detail later), he probably wrote this epic while he was still quite young; at the end of the whole poem he appends two verses which indicate at which stage of his life he wrote the work:

> hec ego composui, Gilo nomine, Parisiensis
> incola, Tutiaci non inficiandus alumnus.

I, Gilo by name, an inhabitant of Paris and the renowned offspring of Thusey, have written these verses.

By 1119, Gilo was no longer an inhabitant of Paris, but a member of the celebrated monastic community at Cluny. We can only surmise that prior to this he had been a student, and had perhaps held some minor benefice; the precise date of his entry to Cluny is not known. However, it seems that he had been there long enough to have built up something of a reputation for himself, for he went to Rome early in 1120 in the entourage of Pope Calixtus II after Calixtus had visited the monastery. By November or December 1121 Gilo had been elected Cardinal-Bishop of Tusculum, and at Rome he produced another work, the *Vita Sancti Hugonis Abbatis Cluniacensis*, apparently at the Pope's request.[2]

Gilo's subsequent career brought him to the land which he had vividly described in his poem on the Crusade; among many other varied missions on which he was employed as a kind of ecclesiastical trouble-shooter, he visited the Holy Land as a papal legate in 1127, performing a successful mission of reconciliation.[3] After 1130, however, he sided with Anacletus II in the schism with Innocent II; he acted as Anacletus' legate in Aquitaine in 1134–6, though by this time he had been discredited and removed from office. His friends (including Peter the Venerable[4]) did their best to persuade him to be reconciled to the 'victorious party' of Innocent; and there is some flimsy evidence to support the suggestion that he may have bowed to their pressure and was indeed reconciled before his death (probably 1142).

This brief sketch of Gilo of Paris' life and career subsequent to the composition of his epic on the First Crusade raises questions about what sort of man he must have been, and what kind of education had shaped his character and intellect; he was erudite enough to have received the commission for the *Life* of Hugh of Cluny, and he also appears as a skilled career diplomat in international ecclesiastical affairs, perhaps in a similar capacity to the later and more familiar figure of John of Salisbury. The delicate missions with which he was entrusted suggest that he was well versed in the arts of persuasion and debate, and this skill is illustrated by the carefully worded letter that he wrote to Bernard of Antioch, his *Life* of St Hugh of Cluny, and, by no means least, his epic on the First Crusade.

Although evidence for education at this period is sketchy, it is fair to assume that the elementary instruction Gilo would have received was not unlike that described by John of Salisbury, *Metalogicon* 1.24, as being given in Bernard's grammar school in Chartres; part of the curriculum here was made up of the learning of passages by rote, and verse composition (features of Latin education not unknown in the English public-school tradition). Before approaching such classics as Virgil, Gilo would have almost certainly begun his studies in Latin literature with the *liber Catonianus*, a collection of very varied works which together made up a standard schoolboy's reading list in the Middle Ages. Its 'final conformation, which is not found in any MS older than the thirteenth century but is likely to have come into existence in the previous century...included Cato, Theodulus, Avianus, Maximianus, the *Achilleid* and the *De Raptu Proserpinae*'.[5] It is not impossible that Gilo may also have enjoyed advanced education in the *ethnici*, or pagan authors, and the liberal arts, such as John of Salisbury enjoyed (cf. his account in *Metalogicon* 2.10).

From this we might fairly assume that many of the conclusions drawn by scholars writing about the twelfth-century renaissance ought to be confirmed in Gilo's epic – particularly with reference, for the present study, to Ovid. According to Reynolds and Wilson, 'Vergil, Horace, Ovid, Lucan, Juvenal,

Persius, Cicero, Seneca, Sallust were the staple diet of the twelfth century';[6] and Franco Munari's exuberant analysis of the emergence of Ovid in the twelfth century illustrates his importance for the medieval writers of that time as a stylist:

In this society, whose eyes turned with more and more longing to the charm and splendour of worldly things, in this society, which for the first time for many centuries gave a place of importance to women and to human love, in this society, which did not yet think seriously of shaking the principles of faith, but which despised worldly pleasure less and less, in this society Ovid, the lover and seducer, Ovid, the man of the world, who lived a life of pleasure at civilisation's high point, Ovid, the master of poetic form, appeared in all his glory, and set out on a victory parade that can have few parallels in the history of western culture. Dawn broke on the *aetas Ovidiana*.[7]

The origins of this *aetas Ovidiana*, and of the twelfth-century renaissance as a whole, have been adequately stated elsewhere,[8] and there is no need to go over them again in detail here. It is worth recalling, however, that by comparison with the twelfth century, little had been known of Ovid in earlier periods; in the Carolingian court circle of poets, Modoin had been given the nickname 'Naso', and Theodulf of Orleans had imitated Ovid's elegiac couplets; but other prominent figures of the Carolingian renaissance such as Einhard and Lupus of Ferrières hardly mention him. In Peter Godman's recent edition of Alcuin's poem on the bishops, kings and saints of York, only one Ovidian reminiscence is noted (from the *Heroides*). It was the growth of the cathedral schools, and the socio-political developments of the late eleventh and early twelfth centuries which created the seed-bed in which the study of Ovid and other poets was able to flourish. 'The Carolingian age had been, in Traube's phrase, *aetas Vergiliana*; now begins the *aetas Ovidiana*. Economic development has encouraged the lust of the eye and the pride of life, and turned men's thoughts to the varied interests of the world.'[9] What *is* significant for the present study from the overall consensus of opinion is the probability that Ovidian influence ought to be noticeable in Gilo's poem. Amongst other authors, Ovid would have formed an integral part of Gilo's reading and training in grammar and literature, and this ought to be evident from his style and also in reminiscences: R. W. Hunt, for example, asserts that 'there are hundreds of tags of classical verses in medieval writers',[10] and some at least ought therefore to be traceable in Gilo if the general opinion about the twelfth century being the *aetas Ovidiana* is to hold true. L. D. Reynolds concisely sums up the evidence:

In the twelfth century...the circulation and influence of Ovid's poetry increased dramatically. Minor works such as the *Ibis*, *Nux* and *Medicamina Faciei Femineae* emerge from obscurity and take their place beside the longer-established compositions...Ovid's entry into the ranks of standard authors (a position he retained through the Renaissance and beyond) can be clearly traced in the treatment accorded his poetry in the most active centre of twelfth-century classical studies, the valley of the Loire...even the less edifying erotic poetry occasionally found its way into the schoolroom.[11]

Ovidian influence on love-poetry written in the twelfth century has been dealt with at length by Peter Dronke[12] – but what of epic? In an epic written by a Christian, a man later to become a bishop, and written on an avowedly religious theme, could Ovid be enlisted as a Crusader to serve the Christian cause? To Gilo's poem we now turn for an answer.

By far the greater part of Gilo's poem, consisting as it does of heroic speeches, descriptions of fighting and deeds of derring-do, sieges, and the like, shows much more obvious affinity with the works of Virgil, Lucan and Statius, than with Ovid. As might be expected, Gilo draws widely on these authors, as well as on the later poets Claudian, Prudentius and Sidonius; but there are a number of reminiscences from Ovid, especially from the *Metamorphoses*. When considering the work of any medieval poet and his sources in the classical tradition, it is useful to bear in mind that no one poet such as Ovid would have held a unique place in his consciousness. Indeed, in view of the breadth of medieval reading of later Latin authors (compared with that of a twentieth-century classics undergraduate, for example) it is remarkable that as much Ovidian influence as is apparent in Gilo does show itself alongside that of Virgil and the other writers of epic.

The traces of Ovidian influence detectable in Gilo are very varied. In an analysis of the kinds of borrowings found in medieval writers, Peter Dronke discerns three different types of reminiscence:

First, (there are) unconscious borrowings – elements that would form part of the poetic *koine* of a well-read author, expressions he would use instinctively in certain situations, without focussing on their classical context, because his education had made them second nature. At times such an unconscious borrowing may be scarcely detectable from a mere coincidence...second, there is conscious borrowing, ranging from unassimilated adaptation of classical phrases to the most individual and sophisticated transmutations of them. Third, there is a range of explicit quotation, where the classical borrowing is meant to be seen as such by an educated audience.[13]

Many of the quotations in Gilo may well derive, it should also be noted, from a reading of *florilegia* rather than of the full text; but it can be argued that Ovid is Ovid, whether studied whole or in 'select portions'. Without doubt, the *florilegia* were an important means whereby the writers of the twelfth century became acquainted with classical authors, and in them, according to Ullman, 'Ovid is more extensively represented than any other poet'.[14]

Similarities to Ovid in Gilo's poem which perhaps correspond to Dronke's idea of a 'poetic *koine*' are quite frequent (of course, Ovid was not the only poet to contribute to this common pool of poetic ideas, and in some of the phrases listed similarities to other authors may be noted). At Gilo 4.37 the phrase *sed tamen* is also found in *Am.* 2.13 (14). 5; in Gilo 5.208, *protinus* begins the verse, as it does in *Met.* 1.128; *nec mora* begins both Gilo 4.221 and *Met.* 1.717. Gilo 4.266 recalls *Met.* 11.670 with its reference to *Tartara* (the *Metamorphoses* was the 'who's who of the ancient world' for the medievals, as

Curtius put it[15] – it formed the principal source of their knowledge of classical myth and cosmology). Gilo 7.423 shares the phrase *per inane* with *Met.* 9.223, and the *Parthus* of Gilo 8.422 is styled *fugax*, as is the case in *Rem.* 155.

More obvious examples of borrowings from Ovid which fall into this category are Gilo 4.239 *iunctis...bubus* (= *Met.* 14.3); 5.125 *de culmine montis* (also found at 7.170; = *Met.* 12.337); 5.251 *de culmine montis* (also found at 7.170; = *Met.* 12.337); 5.251 *ferus hostis* (= *Met.* 1.185 and *Tr.* 2.77); 5.292 *cava saxa* (= *Am.* 3.6(5).45); 7.116 *vultumque severum* (= *Am.* 3.4.43); 7.259 *excipit ictus* (= *Met.* 12.375); 7.298 *ossibus ossa* (= *Met.* 11.707, and also *Her.* 12.122); 7.318 *sub imagine* (= *Met.* 8.824); 7.378 *vires effundite totas* (= *Met.* 1.278 *vires effundite vestras*); 7.448 *hastilis lancea lenti* (= *Met.* 8.28 *adductis hastilia lenta lacertis*); 8.265 *amor immoderatus habendi* (= *Met.* 1.131, *amor sceleratus habendi*). The moral value of some of Ovid's statements was not lost on the medievals who used his work for teaching in the schools, to such a degree that Bernhard Bischoff could assert 'already in the eleventh century the Christianization of Ovid was begun'.[16] In Gilo 9.36 *verba precantia* seems to be a favourite phrase of Ovid's: *Met.* 9.159 has *verba precantia flammis*; *Met.* 14.365 reads *verba precantia dixit*, and *Her.* 11.69 has *precantia verba*. At Gilo 9.301, *sua munera* = *Met.* 9.390.

Turning to Dronke's second grouping of reminiscences, 'conscious borrowing', we find at Gilo 7.309ff a very similar image to that used in *Met.* 8.823ff. The picture in Ovid is of Erysichthon being lulled to sleep:

> Lenis adhuc somnus placidis Erysichthona pennis
> mulcebat: petit ille dapes sub imagine somni
> oraque vana mouet dentemque in dente fatigat   825
> exercetque cibo delusum guttur inani
> proque epulis tenues nequiquam devorat auras.

The gentle God of sleep was soothing Erysichthon peacefully with his wings; in the vision of his sleep he made for a feast, but moved only his empty jaws and ground tooth on tooth; he swallowed hard, cheated by this insubstantial food, and uselessly gulped down empty air instead of good fare.

Gilo's image here is very compressed compared with that in Ovid:

> ora movent pueri matresque vocant morientes,
> aera pro solitis epulis aurasque terentes.   310

Infants moved their mouths and called their dying mothers, grinding on breaths of air instead of their usual food.

The expression may be cramped because of the rhyme-scheme (this is deliberately abandoned in the last book, at the start of which Gilo declares that he will abandon attempts to titillate the reader with rhetorical tricks and rhymes). The contexts of the images in the two poets are of course quite different; there is no attempt to link the pathetic infants champing at the air with the picture of Erysichthon, but the imagery is the same in both. Further evidence that the passage was in Gilo's mind is provided by the near-quotation from 824 of the passage from Ovid at 7.318, a little further on in Gilo's work.

At four points in Gilo's poem there are reminiscences of Ovid which might be classed together under the heading 'borrowings with gross violation of context'. At Gilo 4.145, *singula quid dicam?* comes very close to *Am.* 1.5.23, *singula quid referam*, where Ovid is listing all the details that make a girl attractive. Gilo uses the phrase here, and later at 5.190, purely as a stylistic device. Its original erotic context (quite out of place in a Christian epic, and it is unlikely that Gilo is using the phrase tongue-in-cheek) is completely lost. In the same way Ovidian phrasing becomes purely a matter of style at Gilo 8.90–1, where the erotic statement from *Am.* 3.14.24, *inque modos venerem mille figuret amor* becomes *nec simplex via mortis erat, quia mille necantur/mille modis*. Rhetoric and mannerism are to the fore, and in this Gilo conforms to the poetical canons of his time. An even more glaring example of a phrase taken out of its original context comes in Gilo 9.269–70, where the threat from *Am.* 2.8.27–8,

> quoque loco tecum fuerim quotiensque, Cypassi,
> narrabo dominae quotque quibusque modis.

> I shall tell your mistress, Cypassis, in what places I was with you, and how often, and what many and various ways...

is adapted to fit into lines of apology on the poet's part:

> dicere longa mihi mora finem prospicienti
> quotque quibusque modis breue tempus comparat hostis...

> As I look towards the end of my work it would delay me greatly to tell what many and various ways the enemy made ready in a short time...

Such violations of context may not suit our twentieth-century notions of borrowings from earlier works, but the poetry of any given period needs to be judged in relevant terms. Gilo shows here how much more emphasis was placed on style than on context or implication in medieval poetry. Gilo takes phrases from an erotic context and 'cleanses' them as he incorporates them in his Christian theme, following Jerome's argument based on the instructions given in Deuteronomy 21.22.[17] Finally, the phrase *hec ego composui* found at Gilo 9.375, which is part of the poet's two-line *envoi* to the poem as a whole, is taken from *Am.* 3.15.3, *quos ego conposui*; Gilo demonstrates his fondness for Ovid by ending his poem on a distinctly Ovidian note.

As will be seen from the above citations, most of the reminiscences of Ovid in Gilo are from the *Metamorphoses*, save for some 'choice' examples from the *Amores*; as we shall see when we come to examine the prologue to Gilo's poem, this work seems to have been one with which Gilo was very familiar. This fondness for the *Metamorphoses* is hardly surprising, since from its form and content it was an excellent model for an epic poet. The same is in fact the case with the later (and much more famous) medieval Latin epic writer, Walter of Châtillon: Walter's work contains many more classical reminiscences than Gilo's, and a reading of it shows him to have been overall a superior poet; but the proportions of reminiscences from each of Ovid's works in Books 1–5 of his *Alexandreis* (taken from the *apparatus fontium* of Colker's edition[18]) are similar to those in Gilo: *Amores* 31; *Ars* 28; *Remedia* 12; *Heroides* 41; *Fasti* 58; *Ex Ponto* 24; *Tristia* 22; *Metamorphoses* 275. A number of the reminiscences from the *Amores* are found in the prologues to the books of Walter's epic, rather than in the main body of the text; as we shall see, this is also the case with Gilo.

The 32-line prologue to the poem, which is found only on one side of the manuscript tradition, is written in elegiacs; in view of the fact that Propertius was little known, Martial little understood, and Tibullus read only in the *florilegia* (where he owed his inclusion to the popularity of Ovid in any case[19]), Ovid was the classical model for elegiacs *par excellence*. That he served as such for Gilo is evident from the prologue itself:

> hactenus intentus levibus puerilia dixi
> materia puero conveniente levi.
> nec Turno dedimus carmen, nec carmen Achilli,
> sed iuvenis iuveni carmina multa dedi,
> materiamque gravem penitus mens nostra refugit   5
> et levibus nugis dedita tota fuit.
> etas mollis erat teneris et lusibus apta,
> quecque gravant mentem ferre nequibat ea.
> ausus eram, memini, de bellis scribere: sed ne
> materia premerer, Musa reliquit opus;   10
> nam quamvis modicas mea ludere cymba per undas
> non dubitet, magnas horret adire tamen.
> nunc anni surgunt et surgere carmina debent;
> tempora cum numeris conuenienter eunt.
> iam, positis remis, velo concussa per equor   15
> evolat ex humili littore pulsa ratis.
> errat ut ille rotam qui per declivia motam
> nititur ut teneat cum rota missa ruat,
> sic miser immundum qui non vult perdere mundum
> errat; dum sequitur quod ruit, obruitur.   20
> ergo quisque moram, quia mundus habetur ad horam,
> pellat, et hoc querat quod mora nulla terat.
> detineat fundus nullum, domus optima, mundus,
> quin querat lucem suscipiendo crucem.
> Christus precessit, Christo victoria cessit: 25
> crux quam sustinuit nostra medela fuit.
> ergo lege pari qui Christum vult imitari
> subdat cervicem, suscipiatque vicem.
> securi pugnant qui sub tali duce pugnant;
> huic qui pugnabit dux bonus era dabit.   30
> vere securi pugnant quia sunt habituri
> eternam requiem perpetuamque diem.

Up to now I have spoken of childish matters, my mind set on things of no substance, with subject-matter fitted to a trifling boy. I wrote no poem for Turnus, no poem for Achilles, but many poems as one youth to another, and my mind shrank utterly from serious subjects and was wholly given over to nonsense and trifles. My age was tender and suited for playfulness, and it could not stand anything that weighed heavily on the mind. I had dared, I recall, to write about wars, but lest I be overwhelmed by the subject, my Muse abandoned the task; for though my little boat is not afraid of skipping over the gentle waves, it shudders to approach the great breakers. Now my years advance, and my poems must advance too; my time of life goes well with my verses. Now with oars laid aside my craft is driven by its sail over the seas, and flies from the low-lying shore.

As he errs who struggles to hold back a wheel set in motion down a slope, when the wheel gathers pace, so errs the wretch who will not forsake the unclean world: he is ruined while he pursues what is doomed to ruin. And so let every man shake off his hesitation, so that he may be reckoned pure at that hour, and seek that which no length of time eats away. Let no man's farm, his fine house, the things of the world, hold him back from seeking the light by taking up the cross. Christ has gone before, and the victory has fallen to Christ: the cross which he carried was our healing. Therefore let him who wishes to imitate Christ on equal terms bow his neck and take up the cross in his turn. Those who fight under such a leader fight in safety; that good leader will repay the man who fights for him. Truly they fight in safety because they are destined to possess eternal rest and the light of day forever.

The reader is immediately aware of Ovidian inspiration in matters of style and also in direct quotations, at least in the first half of the prologue, which is divided into halves of exactly equal length, 16 verses each. The first half gives an account of Gilo's earlier activity as a poet, when he was a mere youth (1–8); he admits to having tried to write on weighty matters, but did not persevere with it (9–12). Lines 13ff lead in to the second half of the prologue, which demonstrates the religious motivation behind Gilo's present project, the writing of an epic on the recent campaign to wrest Jerusalem from Islam.

Lines 1–16 show close similarities to the three poems which begin the three books of the *Amores*, while not copying them slavishly, and making use of no direct quotation longer than the half-line *ausus eram, memini* in 9 (= *Am.* 2.1.11). These verses point more to an intimate knowledge of these three poems, and of Ovid generally, than to a knowledge of him gleaned from short excerpts or even single lines used as *sententiae* in the schools. In these lines from the prologue we find a skilful reworking of many of the ideas and themes found in *Am.* 1.1, 2.1 and 3.1, and they reveal Gilo to have been a poet of considerable creative prowess.

In 1, *hactenus* is used in the same position as in *Am.* 2.11.16 and 3.1.31, as well as *Met.* 5.250 and 13.700 (it is also found in this position in other classical authors, such as Virgil, *Georgics* 2.1, and in the late Latin poet Alcimus Avitus, 5.1). The prologue opens with a reshaping of the theme of the poet's embarking on a work, only to find his efforts thwarted, which is found in the three poems from the *Amores*: in Ovid, failure to compose an epic is due to the intervention of a god (he becomes the slave of Cupid), and only in *Am.* 3.1 does he declare, at the prompting of the personified Tragedy, that he will attempt writing in another genre (69–70). Gilo on the other hand adopts a moral stance: for him, his failure to write an epic is a fault of immaturity (1–2, 5), and he explains his writing many poems *iuvenis iuveni* at that time on the grounds of the wayward stage of development as a man at which he then was (7). His failure to write epic is due to human frailty, not divine intervention, and unlike Ovid he makes no attempt to defend his having written them. In the second verse of the prologue, *materia...conveniente* has clear similarities with *Am.* 1.1.2, *edere, materia conveniente modis. Puero levi* recalls *levioribus* in *Am.* 1.1.19. Gilo then reveals that he has not attempted any epic theme after the classical model: *Turno* clearly denotes the *Aeneid*, and *Achilli* the *Achilleid* of Statius. In this Gilo is at one with Ovid in *Am.* 2.1.29, *quid mihi profuerit velox cantatus Achilles?* The feeling here is Ovidian, but the phrases have been reshaped to become Gilo's own rather than having been lifted wholesale from the master and pasted together. This is also true of 5–8, where Gilo protests that his youthful spirit shunned *materiam gravem* (this corresponds to the *gravis stilus*, as opposed to the *mediocris* and the *humilis*; these categories of style, which the medieval poets derived ultimately from Cicero and from the *Ad Herennium* 4.8, are explored in depth by Faral in his study *Les arts poétiques du XII* et *XIII* siècles.[20] There is an oblique reference to the *stilus humilis* in v. 16 of the prologue).

In 5–7 are echoes of *Am.* 1.1.19, *nec mihi materia est numeris levioribus apta; teneris* is an epithet found in *Am.* 2.1.4. The important difference between Gilo and Ovid is Gilo's emphasis on his own weakness and culpability in not writing on serious matters; Ovid (tongue-in-cheek, as so often) protests that Cupid has prevented him from doing so (*Am.* 1.1.23–24, and also *Am.* 2.1), and thus is guiltless in the matter. The poet's protestation that he cannot meet the demands made of him is a commonplace in medieval writing,[21] and occurs elsewhere in Gilo. The start of 9, *ausus eram, memini,* is taken from *Am.* 2.1.11; the next verse recalls *materia premis ingenium* from *Am.* 3.1.25, *accipe dixit opus,* from *Am.* 1.1.24, and more strongly *Musa moveret opus,* from *Am.* 3.1.6. Once again, Ovidian ideas are reworked by Gilo; whereas Cupid is a tyrannical ruler as far as Ovid is concerned, Gilo's *Musa* is portrayed as adopting an attitude of mercy and grace towards him: he finds that she acts in his favour by abandoning his work and effectively putting an end to his struggles.

The metaphor of the ship, which occupies 11–16, is a commonplace in classical, late Latin, and medieval literature.[22] Among classical antecedents there is again a parallel with Ovid, *Ars* 3.25–6, *nec tamen hae mentes nostra poscuntur ab arte;/conveniunt cumbae vela minora meae* ('Such attitudes are not demanded by my art, however; smaller sails suit my craft).[23] As was the case earlier in the prologue, Gilo does not follow any source slavishly, but borrows colours to create a fresh image. His metaphor is finely worked and well sustained over the six lines from 11 to 16.

Further Ovidian echoes to be noted in these lines are a faint reminiscence of *Am.* 1.1.27, *sex mihi surgat opus numeris,* in 13–14, *nunc anni surgunt* and *tempora cum numeris;* 14 also recalls *Am.* 1.1.19, cited above in connection with 2 and 7 of the prologue, and it is echoed in *Her.* 15.6, *carmina cum lyricis sim magis apta modis.*

In the first half of the prologue, therefore, Ovidian influence, and especially influence from the three poems *Am.* 1.1, 2.1 and 3.1, is clearly observable: in addition to phrases taken without much alteration from Ovid there is obvious imitation in phraseology and style. Gilo evidently knew his Ovid – and in view of Reynolds's observation, cited above, that the erotic poems found their way into the schools only gradually, it seems possible that he became familiar with these from his private reading rather than from his education. In the 16 lines we have been considering here, Gilo appears as one of those authors who 'looked upon the Roman writers and especially the authors of school texts, the *auctores,* as teachers from whom he could acquire a standard of writing, who presented him with the rules of literary technique and awoke his creative imagination. But they were close to his heart, and he lived with them as friends.'[24]

When we come to examine the second half of the prologue, we find an entirely different poetical world. In turning from the frivolous poems he had written earlier to the weighty and serious matter with which he was about to deal, Gilo clearly desired to illustrate his 'change of heart' not only through the sense of the words he used, but also through the very style of his verse. Ovidian reminiscences of any kind are absent; the only borrowings in the latter half of the prologue appear in 26, and these are from Prudentius, *Cath.* 10.83. and Fulgentius, *Aet. Mundi* 13.23 – impeccable sources for an upright Christian poet! The imagery in this section is biblical rather than classical, and furthermore, while the metrical patterns in 1–16 are distinctly Ovidian in their use of dactylic rhythms in the pentameters, and there is no use made of rhyme, in 17–32 the metre becomes heavier, with more spondees in the pentameters, and a corresponding shift in the hexameters (17 spondees and 15 dactyls in 1–16, 22 spondees and 10 dactyls in 17–32). The most striking difference between the two halves, however, is that at 17 we are plunged into leonine-rhyming elegiac couplets. The rhyme adds more weight to the verses and reinforces the desired sense of seriousness. Doctrinal and moral content, not Ovidian elegance, are Gilo's main criteria in writing this half of the prologue.

Gilo's 'change of heart' with regard to his poetry recalls the letter that Peter of Blois wrote (*Ep.* 76) to a poet whom he accused of 'introducing the habits of the gentiles to the sanctuary of the Lord'. Peter, who wrote amatory verse in his youth, became an archdeacon later in life and, like Gilo, felt compelled to renounce his earlier pursuits (his poem *dum iuventus floruit* is a splendid illustration of this change of heart[25]). R. W. Southern says of Peter that 'at some point in his career – though not quite as early as he says – he began to write in a *different style* on moral and ecclesiastical subjects. But the abhorrence with which he speaks of his earlier pursuits was a very late development' (my italics).[26] Gilo strikes a similar pose, several decades earlier, and as with Peter, his tendency to avoid classical style and phrasing in the second half of his prologue is also a pose, as the evidence from the main body of the poem shows. The relish with which he handles Ovidian themes and language in the first half of the prologue hardly serves to strengthen the moralising protestations of the second half, and the impression is created that if he does leave behind his earlier interests in poetry, it is with regret.

As has been stated above, the main body of Gilo's poem is written in hexameters, save for a single short passage which, like the prologue, is penned in elegiac couplets. This comes at the end of the fifth book of the 'combined' work of Gilo and his anonymous continuator, and recounts an event that took place during the temporary truce agreed between the Christian and Moslem forces at the siege of Antioch. One Gualo, an otherwise unknown knight, had gone wandering through the city by himself, and was set upon and killed by some unknown assailants in what the poet regards as a callous act of treachery. The passage in question describes the reaction of Gualo's wife Humberga on hearing of her husband's fate:

> audiit ut funus Humberga decens et Hugonis
> filia, nupta prius comitis, tunc nupta Gualonis,   430
> palluit atque genas secat unguibus illa protervis
> et sustentatur matrum stipata catervis.
> dextra comas lacerat; sed que lacerat laceratur,
> subtilisque manus subtili crine secatur.
> exanimemque diu vox pressa dolore relinquit,   435
> sed tandem voci via vix laxatur et inquit
> 'tantane sustinuit Deus infortunia genti
>   occurrisse sue, plus inimica mihi?
> occubuitne decus Francorum, maximus hostis
>   hostibus, ille meus, spesque salusque suis?   440
> languet morte gravi bello non languida dextra,
>   languet et occubuit vir Gualo, vita mea.
> me miseram! non obsequium miserabile feci
>   vir, tibi; cum caderes, compariter cecidi.
> hei mihi! non fovi, non clausi, non ego lavi   445
>   os, oculos, vulnus, veste, manu, lacrimis.
> lux mea, cui moriens morituram deseruisti?
>   ut tecum morerer dignior ipsa fui.
> tu mihi tu certe memini iurare solebas
>   te vitaturum cautius insidias.   450
> sed quam non poterat gens perfida demere bello
>   est sublata tibi vita beata dolo.
> an sine te vivam patris a patria procul absens?
>   absque viro vivet femina castra sequens?

figite me quibus est pietas, opponite telis 455
  Parthorum miseram, mors mihi pena levis,
mors mihi pena levis si iungar morte Gualoni,
  si non sim Turco preda futura truci.'
hos levat Evrardus frater solamine questus
  et reprimit blanda voce graves gemitus. 460

When the worthy Humberga heard of his death – she was the daughter of Hugh, and had earlier been the wife of a count, but was then the wife of Gualo – she grew pale, scratched her cheeks wildly with her nails, and was held up by the bands of ladies round about her. Her right hand tore at her hair, but in hurting she hurt herself, and her graceful hand was cut open by her graceful hair. For a long time her voice was suppressed by her grief, and left her, lifeless, but eventually the path of her speech was loosened just enough for her to speak: 'Has God allowed such great misfortunes to afflict his own people, misfortunes even more hateful to me? Has the glory of the Franks perished, the greatest of enemies to his enemies, my own husband, hope and salvation for his own? The right hand that was not idle in war lies idle in grievous death; my husband Gualo, my life, lies still and is slain. Alas, poor me! I have done no service of pity for you, husband; when you fell dead I likewise fell. Ah me! I have not wiped your mouth with my robe, nor closed your eyes with my hand, nor washed your wounds with my tears. O my light, for whom have you left me in death, me who must also die? I was more worthy to die with you myself. You used – I remember it well – you used to swear to me that you would be wary and very careful of ambushes. But your blessed life, which this treacherous race could not take away in war, has been taken from you by a trick. Am I to live without you, far away from the land of my father? Shall a woman live, following the camp without a husband? You who know your godly duty, strike me down! Stand me against the Parthian spears, death is a slight pain for me, yes death is a slight pain for me if in death I am joined with Gualo, if I am not to be enslaved by the savage Turks.' Her brother Evrard comforted these laments with soothing words, and speaking sweetly he put an end to her deep sobbing.

The elegiacs begin at the start of Humberga's speech; their use here indicates that Gilo felt this metre was especially suitable for her lament, rather than the narrative epic hexameter which is used for the rest of the work. Of all the models Gilo might have had in mind for such a speech as this, the one which most obviously fits the situation is Ovid's *Heroides*, and in the brief examination of the passage undertaken here attention is focused on this collection of poems, although there are in it some reminiscences from other sources. That the *Heroides* were appreciated in Gilo's time is shown by the exchange of letters between Paris and Helen, written by Baudri of Bourgeuil, which was based upon them.[27]

Humberga's actions on hearing the news of her husband's demise follow a pattern for expressing grief found in both classical and biblical literature. She scratches her face (431), grows pale and faints (431–2) and tears her hair (433). The actions in 431 can be compared with those of Canace in *Her.* 11.91–2, *tunc demum pectora plangi / contigit inque meas unguibus ire comas* (cf. also 433 in Gilo), and with Medea's in *Her.* 12.153,

> protinus abscissa planxi mea pectora veste,
> tuta nec a digitis ora fuere meis.

Straightaway I tore my robe and beat my breasts, and my cheeks were not safe from my fingers.

Laniata capillos also recalls Ariadne in *Her.* 10.15–16. The paradox in 433 owes something to the rhetorical tradition of late Latin as well as to Ovidian style, and the same is true of the *annominatio* of *subtilis...subtili* in 434.[28] The speechlessness due to grief seen in 435 is paralleled by Sappho's portrayal in *Her.* 15.110–11. The outpouring of grief itself begins with the elegiac section which starts with the alliteration in 436, leading in to more *annominatio* in 441–2, the latter of which finds echoes in many poems in the *Heroides*, such as (to choose but one example out of many) 19.65, *me miseram! brevis est haec et non vera voluptas*. The exclamation *me miseram* is also found at 19.121 and 19.187; its use here is an obvious one in the portrayal of Humberga's suffering.

Further *annominatio* in 444 precedes some more reminiscences and echoes of Ovid in 445: another exclamation, *hei mihi*, is to be noted at *Her.* 9.145, 12.112, and 13.7; a similar sentiment to that depicted here, though in a different context, is also seen in Hermione's lament, *Her.* 8.93–4:

> non ego captavi brevibus tua colla lacertis
> nec gremio sedi sarcina grata tuo.

I have not embraced your neck with my slender arms, nor like a burden you found pleasant sat on your lap.

A similar idea is also found in Ariadne's lament to Theseus, *Her.* 10.119ff, though here the roles are reversed, and it is the abandoned Ariadne who sees herself dying with no one to comfort her:

> ergo ego nec lacrimas matris moritura videbo,
> nec mea qui digitis lumina condat, erit?   120
> spiritus infelix peregrinas ibit in auras,
> nec positos artus unguet amica manus?

So shall I not see my mother's tears as I die? Will there be no one to close my eyes with their fingers? Will my unhappy ghost go about in foreign breezes, will no friendly hand lay out my limbs and anoint them?

Any overtly Ovidian sentiment here in Gilo's poem is obscured by the distinctly un-Ovidian word order in 445 and 446; Gilo employs a device known as *versus rapportati*, a rhetorical trick of which medieval poets were very fond.[29] The idea expressed in 447 (again making use of *annominatio* in *moriens morituram*) is also found in *Her.* 3.61, *ibis et o! miseram cui me, violente, relinques?* The desire to be united in death with the beloved is also common in Ovid (cf. *Her.* 3.63ff), as is the reminiscence of the past in 449. The phrase *tu mihi tu certe memini* is taken from the *Amores* 2.10(11).1, though its context there is decidedly different. The remainder of 449 has some kinship with *Her.* 10.73, *tum mihi dicebas 'per ego ipsa pericula iuro'*; 450 recalls *Her.* 1.44, *at bene cautus eras et memor ante mei*, as well as *Her.* 3.53, *tu mihi, iuratus per numina matris aquosae*, and 13.65, *Hectora...caveto*. More similarities, this time to *Her.* 1.50, *virque mihi dempto fine carendus abest?*, 10.59, *quid faciam? quo sola ferar?* and 10.64, *quid sequar? accessus terra paterna negat*, can be noted in 453, which in its initial draft (preserved only in one manuscript) read *quid faciam procul a patria, procul a patre degens?* Perhaps some ribald retort to this rhetorical question from one of Gilo's audience, suggesting what she might do far from her father and her fatherland, prompted the change! Similarly the second half of the couplet, which first read *quid faciet fragilis femina castra sequens?* was altered to the reading given above in the text, with equal alliteration in both versions. The question 'what shall a helpless woman following the camp do?' might have raised an eyebrow or two, and was certainly not conducive to maintaining the serious tone which Gilo clearly wanted to come across in his work. One other similarity in this verse should also be noted, this time to Virgil, *Ecl.* 10.46.

Humberga's statement that she died with her husband, though she continues to live on, is closely paralleled by Alcyone's lament in *Met.* 11.700ff, and is again to be seen in the *Heroides*, for example at 1.50 (quoted above), and in 10.75–6:

> vivimus, et non sum, Theseu, tua, si modo vivit
> femina periuri fraude sepulta viri.

I live on, Theseus, and I am not yours – if a woman buried by the deceit of her husband does live.

In the same way Humberga's desire to be killed rather than to live on apart from Gualo is paralleled by the statements in *Her.* 2.139–42, and especially 140, *traiectam gladio morte perire iuvat*; by 9.146, *impia quid dubitas Deianira mori*; and by 10.88, *quis vetat et gladios per latus ire meum?* The repetition of *mors mihi pena levis* is also Ovidian, found in the (disputed) *Her.* 20.92–3 as well as elsewhere in Ovid. There may also be a slight echo here of *Met.* 10.698, *poena levis visa est.* 458 has the same force as *Her.* 10.89, *tantum ne religer dura captiva catena.*

The influence of Ovid is apparent here less than it was in the prologue in so far as direct quotations are concerned, though it is still extremely evident from the style in which these verses from Gilo are couched, and in the sentiments expressed. Many of the 'vague reminiscences' noted might no doubt be due to the 'collective consciousness' of twelfth-century poets and the impact on the poet's mind of regular reading and quotation of classical authors. Gilo's stature as a poet is actually reinforced by this: far from being a mere plagiarist, he makes use of only a few direct quotations and still maintains a high level of imitation, illustrating his admiration and affection for the works of his *auctor*, Ovid.

To conclude, and to answer the question posed at the start of this brief study of Gilo's work, there is indeed evidence for Ovidian influence on the poet's writing in it, even though his epic is on an extremely un-Ovidian theme. In the main body of the text, the evidence for this consists for the most part of 'tags' from Ovid, with some traces of Ovidian influence in Gilo's imagery. The borrowings here illustrate the predominantly rhetorical nature of Gilo's use of his sources: style, rather than allusion to context, was what he was aiming at. In the passage on Humberga, the Ovidian element again for the most part takes the form of stylistic imitation, with a few more obvious allusions and quotations; but it is in Gilo's prologue that we see the closest imitation of Ovid, and most especially of the *Amores*. Gilo follows the rhetorical traditions of his time, but he is not constrained by them, and in the prologue he demonstrates convincingly that he could as it were 'change gear' and write verses that were not based on classical models, if he desired. Such a sense of 'stylistic propriety' with regard to the use he makes of Ovid suggests that despite the rhetorically orientated tradition of twelfth-century writing within which he wrote, Gilo was not insensitive to the type of verse in which such an *auctor* ought to be employed. As is the case with Walter of Châtillon, Gilo's borrowings from Ovid in the main body of his poem are mainly from the *Metamorphoses*, with a few phrases taken from other works. There are many other reminiscences in Gilo, of Virgil, Lucan, Statius, and the other writers who formed part of his literary 'staple diet', as much as Ovid did; but all in all, and especially in the elegiac sections, Gilo's use of Ovidian language and ideas confirms Ludwig Traube's designation of this period of literary history as the *aetas Ovidiana*. Gilo's work illustrates how in the latter part of the eleventh century, Ovid emerged from the obscurity in which he had languished in earlier times to join the other classical poets as a revered, imitated and loved *auctor*. More than this, through Gilo (though one cannot cease to wonder what he would have thought of the prospect), Ovid became a crusader.

5

CHAUCER AND OVID: A QUESTION OF AUTHORITY

Helen Cooper

Mixtaque cum veris passim commenta vagantur
milia rumorum.   *Met.* 12.53–4

Thus saugh I fals and soth compouned
Togeder fle for oo tidynge.   *House of Fame* 2108–9[1]

CHAUCER AND OVID were both superb story-tellers. Chaucer drew liberally
on Ovidian narratives throughout his career, from his rewriting of the tale of
Ceyx and Alcyone in his earliest poem, the *Book of the Duchess*, to his version
of the metamorphosis of the crow in the Manciple's Tale. He used not only the
Metamorphoses but the *Heroides* and the *Fasti*,[2] borrowing stories, allusions
and aphorisms. Much of his knowledge of classical myth and legend derives
from Ovid, and he pays tribute to the greatest of classical story-collections in
a passage that may once have been intended to open the greatest of English
story-collections.[3] It may therefore seem perverse to set as epigraph not a
story but an allegory; but the lines from Ovid's account of the dwelling of a
personified Fama offer a way, not only into Chaucer's *House of Fame*, but into
his attitudes to literary authority and to poetry itself.

Chaucer was first compared to Ovid in his own lifetime by Eustache
Deschamps, and the comparison was more fully developed (and indeed decided
in Chaucer's favour) by Dryden; but Chaucer himself seems to have been fully
conscious of the ground they shared, and on occasion he explicitly invites
comparison with the earlier poet.[4] The Ovid Chaucer inherited was not however the Ovid of the twentieth century, nor of the Restoration. The points of
similarity between the poets that spring to mind most readily now – wit, good
humour, urbanity (not least in matters of sex), humaneness – were not the
qualities for which Ovid was most prized by medieval readers. To them he was
thinker as well as poet: a fine rhetorician, but also both philosopher – hence
Chaucer's use of Ovidian *sententiae* – and theologian, though that was one
aspect in which Chaucer had unusually little interest. He was also taken as a
master in matters of love (as distinct from mere sex); but there is little evidence
that Chaucer knew the love poems at first hand. He describes Ovid as 'Venus
clerk' (*HF* 1487), and allows the Wife of Bath's first husband a copy of 'Ovides
Art' (*CT* III.680), but apparent Ovidian influence on Chaucer in this area seems

71

to owe more to cultural conditions, or to the *Romance of the Rose* as intermediary, than to specific debt. Above all, Ovid was an *auctor*, an authority, and the classical poet most widely read, glossed and admired in the fourteenth century. Chaucer makes more extensive use of him than of any other Roman poet, Virgil included; but his use was critical, not subservient. He did not accept *auctoritas* on trust, and in several places indeed plays off Ovid against Virgil to undermine the master-poet of Western cultural tradition, most strikingly in his retelling of the story of Dido. His description of the dwelling of Fame shows his inspiration by Ovid at its fullest; but even that paradoxically underlines his independence, for he includes within the province of this most untrustworthy of personifications not only rumour and reputation but the telling of tall stories, story-telling in general, and, deriving from all those, literature and historiography. Literary authority, like Fame itself, is compounded of truth and falsehood; and Ovid's unlimited capacity for spinning fables, his interpretations of stories at odds with other authoritative versions, and the medieval practice of taming his unregenerate paganism and libidinousness into orthodox Christian morality by ingenious allegorisation, combined to make him not only an ideal literary model but an ideal focus for questioning the whole nature of literary activity.

That Fame should be the focus of this process is inherent in the way it had come to be understood by the fourteenth century.[5] Its universally accepted etymology, *a fando*, i.e. *a loquendo*, from speaking, connected it with language in all its forms. Ovid's Fama is the recipient of all speech and the source of all rumour, true or false. In Book 4 of the *Aeneid*, itself a key text for the earlier part of the *House of Fame*, *fama* is both Dido's good name and a personified evil monster that spreads rumours intermingling, like Ovid's, false with true (170–95, 321–2). Chaucer divides the concepts of renown and rumour off from each other; and poetry he sees as belonging primarily with the idea of fame as renown, since poets uphold (literally, on the pillars of the palace of Fame) the fame of the subjects they celebrate. But poetry too consists of words, which all alike come to Fame's dwelling; and poets can do no more than record what is known of men's actions, and that is itself under the arbitrary control of Fame. The poets and historians in her hall are quarrelling among themselves, especially over the history of the Trojans – that same history that provides the occasion for the discussion of *fama* in both Ovid and Virgil, and over which, as Chaucer demonstrates in Book I of his poem, they themselves are at odds. Chaucer's Fame is as unreliable as Ovid's Rumour: her decisions to accord glory, infamy or oblivion bear a completely arbitrary relationship to desert.

Ovid portrays a single dwelling of Fama, set on a mountain-top midway between air, earth and sea, to which all sounds come and from which *milia rumorum*, thousands of rumours, true and false, alike emanate. Messages are passed from mouth to mouth among the crowds who fill the place, and grow in the telling. To match his splitting of the concept of fame, Chaucer provides two dwellings, and each draws something from Ovid. His Fame lives, like Ovid's, on a high rock at the junction of air, earth and sea (*HF* 843–52, 1115–30: Chaucer's rock is however made of ice). His house of Rumour is set in a valley below this; it shares with Ovid's dwelling of Fama the crowds who pass on messages in a gigantic game of Chinese whispers, the thousand entrances and exits, the inextricable mixture of false with true, and the jumbled list of conflicting rumours. Ovid describes how

> illic Credulitas, illic temerarius Error
> vanaque Laetitia est consternatique Timores
> Seditioque recens dubioque auctore Susurri   12.59–61

Here is Credulity, here rash Error, groundless Joy and Fears in a state of alarm, new-born Sedition and Whisperings of unknown origin;

Chaucer gives a much longer list of 'rounynges and of jangles' of every variety 'of love, of hate, acord, of stryf', of *transmutacions* and *accident* (*HF* 1960–76). Most famously, the house of Rumour, in one of its many additions to Ovid (along, that is, with its being constructed of multicoloured wickerwork, revolving continuously, and being 60 miles long), contains among its bearers of 'tidynges' shipmen and pilgrims telling stories. For the poet of the *Canterbury Tales*, at least, Rumour as well as Fame could be turned into material for poetry.

This process follows almost inevitably from Chaucer's treatment of the whole subject, for although he separates the dwellings of Rumour and Fame the two refuse to remain conceptually separate. Before the airborne Geoffrey ever reaches Fame's palace he can hear the noises from it,

> full of tidynges,
> Bothe of feire speche and chidynges,
> And of fals and soth compouned   *HF* 1028–30

– precisely the attributes he will also ascribe to Rumour. The quarrelling authorities stress that the material of poetry is at the mercy of opinion. The notion has already been insinuated in Book I of the poem, before any mention has been made of Fame's house, when the narrator–dreamer finds himself in a temple of Venus where the walls are painted with what sets out as the story not just of Aeneas but of the *Aeneid*; but Ovid, in the form of Dido's Epistle from the *Heroides*, gradually subverts the retelling. The opening Virgilian declaration of intent is qualified into subjectivity:

> I wol now singen, yif I kan,
> The armes, and also the man...   *HF* 143–4

and as the events of Carthage begin to be seen from the Ovidian perspective, any sense of reliable authority, or of the possibility of reconstructing historical fact, dissolves into the insubstantiality of rumour, of one opinion, one voice, against another, with no possibility of validation. One can footnote sources:

> Rede Virgile in Eneydos
> Or the Epistle of Ovyde;   *HF* 378–9

but when it comes to the writing of fiction, any writer can claim equal authority with an *auctor*, and fame, in its arbitrariness of record, has no more authenticity than dream, which may likewise be false or true:

> As me mette redely: (dreamed)
> Non other auctour alegge I. *HF* 313–14

The *House of Fame* has gained recognition in recent years as an approximation to Chaucer's own statement of poetic theory – or perhaps a better way of putting it would be as his exploration of the problems of writing poetry. What it suggests is a very different interpretation of *soth* and *fals* from that proposed by conventional literary theory of the Middle Ages, in which the untrue fictional fable was the cover for the moral truth contained within. 'Fable' was frequently used as a synonym for 'lying' in Middle English and French, but fiction was to moral as the shell to the kernel or the chaff to the grain. The idea was commonplace, and is mentioned by Chaucer on several occasions with a casualness that demonstrates thorough familiarity with the concept on the part of both himself and his readers. There is the Nun's Priest's

> Taketh the fruyt, and lat the chaf be stille, *CT* VII.3443

or the Parson's more ascetic rejection of fiction as falsehood,

> Why shoulde I sowen draf out of my fest, (fist)
> Whan I may sowen whete, if that me lest? *CT* X.35–6

To the fourteenth century, the *Metamorphoses* was the key example of fabulous material that could be demystified to produce Christian doctrine, and commentaries that sifted the wheat from such unpromising-looking chaff abounded. What stands out in Chaucer's use of Ovid is his wholesale rejection of this tradition. Ovidian stories can have morals, certainly – they are frequently given by Ovid himself; but given the choice between story and gloss, fable and truth, Chaucer goes straight for the fable. In this respect at least, Chaucer's Ovid is curiously modern in comparison with the moralised Ovids so prevalent in his century.

It was almost impossible to read Ovid in the Middle Ages without some sort of commentary, but when Chaucer can be found using a gloss, it will almost always be a point of fact – for the identification of an allusion and so on. He did make use of the mythographic tradition that used Ovid as its focus, and which is exemplified by Pierre Bersuire's *Ovidius Moralizatus*;[6] but Chaucer stresses the aspects of this tradition that have most to do with astrology and the planetary ordering of the world, and which therefore reflect more of fourteenth-century ways of understanding the cosmos than of understanding Ovid. The attempts that have been made to demonstrate his acquaintance with the *Ovide moralisé*, the 70,000-line French octosyllabic version of the *Metamorphoses* composed in the early fourteenth century which brings the task of Christianising Ovid to its culmination, have produced only exiguous evidence.[7] What would appear to be the most striking parallels may be mediated through Machaut, whose *Jugement dou Roy de Navarre*, *Dit de la Fonteine amoureuse* and *Livre du voir Dit* did draw on the *Ovide moralisé* and were in turn used by Chaucer for his own versions of the stories of Ariadne, of Ceyx and Alcyone, and, possibly, of Phoebus and the crow.[8] Other apparent similarities to the *Ovide* could derive from glosses to Latin manuscripts of Ovid's works or result from simple coincidence of phrasing in retelling the same stories.

The one thing that emerges unequivocally from such source studies is Chaucer's distance from the whole moralising tradition. The approach that can see in Ovid's dwelling of Fama an allegory of the Holy Scriptures, or that can compare Midas' ass's ears (used in an *exemplum* by the Wife of Bath) to the mitres of hypocritical bishops and cardinals,[9] is an infinite distance from Chaucer (though it is interesting none the less that the Wife's retelling of the Midas story comes within a hundred lines of her attack on the religious hypocrisy of friars[10]). However Chaucer may have understood the twice-repeated principle borrowed from St Paul, that 'al that is writen is writen for oure doctrine', it was not in the same way as the author of the *Ovide moralisé*, who uses the text in his opening couplet and manages to make doctrine the very point of fable. Commentators may have attempted to make profane texts respectable through allegorisation from the *Metamorphoses* to the *Orlando Furioso* and beyond, and some recent scholars have attempted to do the same with Chaucer; but he remains obstinately the poet of literal narrative. The nature of his debt to Ovid bears witness to the boldness of that decision. However intermingled the original texts may be with other sources, Chaucer's adaptations of Ovidian stories consistently show a deliberate choice in favour of the story and the meanings that can be developed within the narrative itself, and against using Ovid as evidence for the Christian structure of the moral universe.

Chaucer's Ovid, then, is the Ovid of narrative; but there is an interesting pattern to his borrowings and divergences that helps to define his attitude to his predecessor. His borrowings occur within two main areas. The first of these has to do with tale-telling: Chaucer takes over not only the dwelling of Fama but the revealing of the secret of Midas' ears and the crow's punishment for scandal-mongering. His other predilection is for stories of women in distress that could be developed for pathos, and Ovid could provide abundant material in this line; curiously, Chaucer's extensive quarrying of the *Heroides* runs counter to his interest in the processes of tale-telling, for he converts the heroines' recounting of their own stories into direct narrative. His most striking divergence from Ovid is his refusal to countenance the idea of human metamorphosis into the less than human. A crow may turn black, but at the conclusion of the stories of Ceyx and Alcyone, Nisus and Scylla (*LGW* 1907–21) or Philomela and Procne we are told nothing of the transformations that are Ovid's excuse for telling the stories at all.

Such omissions sound as if they ought to be in keeping with Chaucer's position in the medieval Christian world, but they do not necessarily have that effect. To the sufferers whom Ovid allows an after-existence in changed shape, Chaucer gives only continuing grief or the bluntness of death: of Alcyone, for instance,

'Alas!' quod she for sorwe,
And deyede within the thridde morwe.   *BD* 213–14

It is, of course, extremely difficult to follow a pagan beyond death – Chaucer is very cagey about the ultimate destination of the souls of Troilus and Arcite – but in the instance of his handling of the story of Alcyone in the *Book of the Duchess*, the matter goes beyond the problem of pagans. Ceyx is drowned, and Morpheus is sent by Juno to take up the dead body, appear to Alcyone in her sleep and speak to her in Ceyx's voice to tell her of his death. Alcyone's response, quoted above, is death within three lines as well as three days. The story is read by the narrator before he falls asleep, and the overt excuse for the retelling is to give him the idea of praying to Morpheus for sleep – the sleep in which he will have the dream that forms the main substance of the poem. That dream itself, however, mirrors in inverted form the story he has just read: it is a dream, not of a wife who has lost her husband, but of a knight, 'clothed al in blak', who has lost his lady. Within the fiction of the poem the possibility is kept open that the dream was inspired by the reading, just as in the *Parliament of Fowls* the possible link between dream and reading is explicitly mentioned; but the actual cause of Chaucer's devising the whole poem was the death of Blanche, Duchess of Lancaster, first wife of John of Gaunt, and the poem functions both as an elegy for her and, in an imaginative and unparalleled way, as a *consolatio* for the bereaved husband. Neither elegy nor consolation follow conventional patterns. Even pagan elegies (Virgil's fifth eclogue is perhaps the best-known example) frequently offer the prospect of an afterlife for the deceased as a comfort to the living; in Christian elegies this element becomes almost universal. The *Book of the Duchess* is a remarkable exception. There is no more suggestion of an afterlife for the lady White than for Alcyone; the knight may not die, but he is left at the end metaphorically 'as ded as stoon' (1300).[11] If there is any afterlife for the lady within the fiction of the poem, or any consolation for the bereaved lover, it lies simply in the celebration of her through his recollecting her in the imagination.

This does not mean that Chaucer was in any doubt as to the truth of Christian resurrection, or about Blanche's ultimate destination. The decision to ignore such considerations is a poetic and humanist one. Its effect is to give the suffering of loss its full weight, with no attempt to mitigate the grief of the bereaved by considerations of the state of those who have passed to happier things. It is not, strictly speaking, a Christian way to approach death, though it is not heterodox: it does put man and his sufferings, not God and His Providence, in the centre of the picture. The eulogy of the lady White spoken

76

by the man in black also becomes the *raison d'être* of the work – a poem within the poem, and to which all the rest serves as frame. As such, it claims a central function for poetry within human experience much deeper and more direct than the customary medieval interpretation of literature as the handmaid of ethics.

There is nothing in Ovid quite comparable with this, but that Chaucer can do it at all is, I think, directly due to his reading pagan literature, and above all to his reading of Ovid. It is a humanist approach to both literature and experience, and if the term seems anachronistic, the inspiration and the results are as close to the processes of later humanism as they are distant from the anti-imaginative paradigms of the tradition of Ovid moralised.

The Book of the Duchess does not carry this humanist emphasis to the point of scepticism, but the potential is there, and in the Knight's Tale it is realised. The occasion is, again, one that owes a great deal to Ovid, and this time to the Ovid of the mythographers as well as the classical one. The portrayals of the temples of Mars, Venus and Diana serve to make the case, already articulated by Palamon and Arcite, that the universe is governed not by divine justice or prescience but by an arbitrary or hostile fate. Chaucer was not drawing much from Ovid at first hand in his descriptions of the temples of Venus and Mars – the mythographic tradition and the main source of the whole tale, Boccaccio's *Teseida*, are the principal intermediaries – but the temple of Diana, not described by Boccaccio, does owe more to Ovid, and in one particular it is of crucial interest: it contains portrayals of the only exceptions to Chaucer's avoidance of human metamorphosis. Callisto, 'turned from a womman til a bere', is there, Daphne transformed into a tree, Actaeon 'an hert ymaked' (*CT* I.2056–65). The metamorphoses make literal the images of man as blind beast used by the despairing lovers (I.1177–8, 1261, 1308); and although Theseus' final speech insists on a Boethian reading of the universe that asserts a providential cosmos, the irruption of these gods into the superficial order of the courtly world opens up frightening vistas of a very different reading of experience. That these pagan gods are figures for actual planets and their influences, and therefore with a literal power even within the Christian world, underlines the threat they pose. The Christian answer was to stress the supremacy of God's will above all planetary tendencies, and to insist that man was only a little lower than the angels. The metamorphoses in the temple of Diana insist that man is convertible into beast, not through the abuse of free will but through the workings of an arbitrary or malignant fate.

A similar scepticism lies behind the Ovidian borrowings of the *House of Fame*. The author of the *Ovide moralisé* takes the God's-eye view and turns *fama* into *logos*, 'l'Escripture'. Chaucer does the opposite, stressing the provisional and insubstantial nature of words without any morals drawn about Babel or fallen language. The Scripture of the *Ovide* is the ultimate authority; the *auctores* of the *House of Fame* are shown to be the spokesmen for an arbitrary Fame whose relationship to truth is completely random. Authority is reduced to the level of rumour, 'fals and soth compounded'. The result is close to the incipient humanism of the *Book of the Duchess*: an insistence on the centrality of individual experience, on personal responsibility and the primacy of the imagination:

> I wot myself best how y stonde;
> For what I drye, or what I thynke,   (undergo)
> I wil myselven al hyt drynke,
> Certyn, for the more part,
> As fer forth as I kan myn art.   *HF* 1878-82

Soth is not to be located in the factual content of poetic art (which is untestable), nor in an external or transcendent principle of truth (which the poem avoids altogether); but this does not mean that art becomes an impossibility. Chaucer's mastery of the fallible narrator, brought to its culmination in the multiple voices of the *Canterbury Tales*, serves precisely to exploit the fallibility of literary language, the speech that is Fame's province.

The two major Ovidian narratives of the *Canterbury Tales*, the Wife of Bath's inset story of Midas and the Manciple's tale of the crow, take the problem of the unreliability of language further. In both these stories, the *tidynges* that are being told are true: Midas does have ass's ears, Phoebus is indeed a cuckold. Some things are, however, much safer kept hidden, even if they are true. The Wife of Bath, with her paradoxical relish for everything antifeminist, transfers the revelation of Midas' secret from his barber to his wife, so that she can comfortably conclude, 'We kan no conseil hyde' (III.980). She adds,

> The remenant of the tale if ye wol heere,
> Redeth Ovyde, and ther ye may it leere,   III.981-2

but what is provided by the untold 'remenant' is the fact that it is the reeds that announce the secret to the world; as the Wife has told it, 'we wommen' are left with all the responsibility for tattling. The story does, however, stress the same idea that is expressed by placing Fame's dwelling where all sound will come to it, for there can be no such thing as private speech:

> 'Biwreye me nat, thou water, with thy soun,'   (betray)
> Quod she; 'to thee I telle it and namo.'   III.974-5

To speak at all is as treacherous a process as *tidynges* themselves are unreliable.

The attack on language, speech and report in the Manciple's Tale is mounted on a much broader base and extends across the whole tale. Now it is not only *tidynges*, tale-telling, that comes under scrutiny, but words themselves, for the very choice of vocabulary can falsify. The difference between calling a dishonest wife a 'lady, as in love' or a 'wenche' or 'lemman' is one of class, not morality:

> Men leyn that oon as lowe as lith that oother.   IX.222

The crow's revelation to Phoebus of his wife's infidelity is couched in the bluntest of words, but the fact that he is a messenger of truth does not save him, for Phoebus, repenting his first anger, accuses him of lying. If the truth value of *fama*, reputation, tidings, is random, it is as easy to mistake the true for the false as the false for the true. The safest way out is, in a formulation that recalls the *House of Fame*, to

> be non auctour newe
> Of tidynges, wheither they been false or trewe.　　　　　IX.359–60

That this might entail the entire rejection of fiction is a consequence taken up in the next, and final, section of the *Tales*, the Parson's Prologue.[12]

This might seem a very un-Ovidian conclusion to draw from an Ovidian story if it were not that it follows so consistently from the Chaucerian version of Ovid's *Fama*. The shape of the Manciple's Tale indicates a process of selection and variation from the original story made independently of influence from any other versions he may have known.[13] His alterations all tend towards the same end. Major features Chaucer omits, such as Coronis' name and Phoebus' saving of her unborn child, Aesculapius, are irrelevant to his shaping of the story around the issue of language. The protagonist in the *Meta-morphoses* is a raven, not a crow, but inset within the raven's story is the warning given by a crow against the dangers of speaking even the truth – *ne voce pericula quaerant* (2.565) – and Chaucer transposes the birds along with moral. Phoebus repents of killing his wife not, as in Ovid, because the punishment was too severe, but because he no longer believes the crow's 'false tale' (IX.293). It is Phoebus who teaches the bird to speak in the first instance, and the punishment that Chaucer stresses is less the Ovidian metamorphosis from white to black than that Phoebus 'refte hym al his song', leaving him no longer capable either of speaking or of singing but only of crying 'agayn tempest and rayn': the artist is reduced to weather forecaster (which, one might add, suggests an equally random relationship of false to true). Phoebus' *mynstralcie* too is stressed more than in Ovid, and so is his 'breaking' of it at the end; and it is worth recalling that it is Apollo who is invoked as god of poetry to preside over the dwellings of Fame and Rumour in the last book of the *House of Fame*. The Manciple's Tale leaves Phoebus devoid of music and believing falsehood, the crow deprived of song and speech for telling the truth, and the audience subjected to a lengthy harangue on the dangers of *janglyng* or of using the tongue at all, with the parenthetical exception only of prayer.

Fals belongs to two semantic fields, expressed by its antinomies of *soth*, which refers to the correctness of fact, and *trewe*, which relates to moral qualities. On a number of occasions, and not least when he is dealing with Ovidian materials, Chaucer moves across from one concept to the other. Phoebus believes his wife to be *trewe* (IX.275) and therefore accuses the crow of falsehood. The treacherous lovers of the *Legend of Good Women* regularly hide their lack of *trouthe* in false words: Theseus, Jason, Demophon, and, as in the *House of Fame*, Aeneas, are all condemned in these terms. The opening of the Legend of Dido is instructive for its extraordinary movement from apparent reverence for the highest literary authority to its subversion, paralleling the treachery of the man who was supposedly the greatest hero of Western culture:

> Glorye and honour, Virgil Mantoan,
> Be to thy name! and I shal, as I can,
> Folwe thy lanterne, as thow gost byforn,
> How Eneas to Dido was forsworn.
> In Naso and Eneydos wol I take
> The tenor.   *LGW* 924–9

Neither Virgil nor Aeneas emerges from such a formulation with his *glorye*, his *fama*, intact, thanks to Ovid's rival authority that sets out Aeneas' treachery. Chaucer lays equal stress on undermining the good name of other so-called heroes, not least Jason:

> Yif that I live, thy name shal be shove
> In English that thy sekte shal be knowe!
> Have at thee, Jason! now thyn horn is blowe!   *LGW* 1381–3

The 'horn' sounds very like Aeolus' black trumpet in the *House of Fame*. By contrast, he is concerned to stress how his heroines deserve a good reputation, whatever slander their 'name' may have suffered. Commentaries on the *Heroides* divided up the heroines as instances of legitimate, illicit or incestuous love – examples, that is, to be imitated or avoided;[14] Chaucer takes no examples from the last group (in the Man of Law's Introduction, indeed, he rejects the very idea of writing such dreadful stories as that of Canace), and tends to subject all the rest to a moral flattening that favours the women at the expense of the men. Hypermnestra's virtue is correctly stressed, in terms of the commentators, but characters such as Medea and Scylla (who appears in glosses to the *Heroides* as well as in the *Metamorphoses*) are seen as victims and pass uncondemned. In those legends where Chaucer is using the *Heroides*, he takes the women at their own valuation, by-passing the trumpets of Fame and ignoring the potential fallibility of literary authority in favour of accepting the make-believe of truthful speech. The mode of narration, however, changes, from complaint to direct narrative. The heroines are allowed brief laments, but the rest of their stories is presented as fact, in a remarkable break from Chaucer's normal practice of mediating his narratives through unreliable voices or the uncertainties of dream. The women are *trewe*, and that moral stability is converted into acceptance of their words as *soth*. It is the men who are false, and whose words cannot be trusted.

The process is interesting; the results less so. Plain fact (or plain fiction) does not make great poetry, especially for Chaucer. The *House of Fame* was certainly written before the prologue of the *Legend*, and presumably before the legends themselves, so he must have been aware of all the problems he was ignoring; and when he alludes to the *Legend* in the *Canterbury Tales*, the Ovidian frame of reference he uses suggests a much more sophisticated approach to narrative and the writing of poetry. The Man of Law complains that Chaucer has used up all the good stories, 'mo than Ovide' (*CT* II.53–80). He goes on to liken himself, in his lack of inspiration,

> To Muses that men clepe Pierides –
> *Methamorphosios* woot what I mene.   92–3

The reference seems to be to the daughters of King Pierus who challenged those other Pierides, the Muses themselves, to a singing-contest (not altogether unlike the story-competition in which the Man of Law finds himself) and were changed into chattering magpies.[15] That the true and false Muses share a name is an irony that may well not have been lost on this master of the surrogate narrator. Chaucer is the ventriloquist behind the Man of Law: the poet can function as both Muse and magpie. The last verse-tale of the collection inverts the pattern, as it ends with the god of poetry and a chatterbox crow both shorn of music and song, and Chaucer and the Manciple alike apparently renouncing the speech that constitutes *fama*.

What matters in the *Canterbury Tales*, however, is not the final rejection of voice, fiction, fable, but the stories themselves: the tumbling metamorphoses of narrative material into myriad genres and tones, humour and pathos, earthy and sublime, the humdrum and the edifying and the noble.[16] Chaucer and Ovid are two of the greatest story-tellers of all time. The narrative brilliance of their major works depends largely on their willingness never to adopt an immutable point of view, to allow the multifariousness of experience and style its own languages, to distrust the teller and to trust the tale.

6

LESSONS FROM THE GREAT CLERK: OVID AND JOHN GOWER

Bruce Harbert

multi poetae fecerunt multas poeses inducentes homines ad delectationes carnales, sicut poeta Ovidius.

> Many poets have made many poems enticing men to carnal pleasures, such as the poet Ovid.[1]

THIS DISAPPROVING REMARK of the fourteenth-century English friar John Ridevall is typical of the attitude of many during the Middle Ages. Not only Ovid's eroticism, but also his pagan religion and the questionable conduct of many of his characters made him a suspect author. If he was to be read without danger, his meaning had to be shown to be other than the apparent one. So the medieval Ovid came to his readers disguised beyond recognition, encrusted in an integument of allegorisation, whether in marginal notes, commentaries, or vernacular adaptations. Hence another fourteenth-century Englishman, John Gower, could call him by a title as inapposite to modern ears as 'the grete clerk Ovide', transforming the ardent lover, the man-about-town, into a wizened, retiring and boring, if blameless, scholar, on the pattern of Chaucer's Clerk of Oxford. Such is the received view, and there is truth in it.

It was, however, possible to take one's Ovid neat in the Middle Ages. Nobody provides fuller evidence of this than Gower.[2]

In his *Vox Clamantis* (hereafter VC), a Latin verse complaint against the social evils of his day, of a total of over 10,000 lines, more than 500 are taken from Ovid. This practice, which to us looks like theft, has precedents in some of the earliest Christian Latin poems, the centos, poems on Christian subjects made up of lines taken from classical authors. Sometimes Gower simply transfers one of Ovid's lines to his own poem, such as *labitur occulte fallitque volatilis aetas* (swift age slips secretly and deceptively away); Ovid had used this line twice, once in the *Amores* (1.8.49) to encourage the young to make the most of their good looks, and once in the *Metamorphoses* (10.519) when recounting the growth from childhood to maturity of Adonis. Gower incorporates the line into a warning that conversion to a virtuous life should not be postponed (7.471). Lines or phrases are sometimes adapted, as when *augent secreta furores* (secrecy increases passion) from the *Remedia Amoris* (581) becomes *loca secretos augent secreta dolores* (secret places increase secret sorrows) as Gower wanders alone and afraid during the Peasants' Revolt (1.1459). The effect can be comical, as when Ovid's advice to give rein to love when it cannot be mastered, *dum furor in cursu est, currenti cede furori* (when passion is in full flight, let it run its course) becomes a voice from heaven warning Gower against active opposition to the rebellious peasants (*Rem.* 119 cf. *VC* 1.2029), but few readers will have known Ovid well enough to spot the irony, and clearly Gower did not intend that they should do so.

In comparison with Ovid, the *Vox Clamantis* makes heavy reading indeed, and its interest is less in showing any skill on Gower's part as a writer than in offering us insight into him as a reader. He drew on every part of Ovid's work. We cannot know how Gower recalled the lines he used, whether he had them by heart (which in an age more dependent on the ear and memory and less on the eye for the transmission of literature would be more feasible than in our own) or whether he used some written aid to memory. The familiarity with Ovid – the whole of Ovid – that the *Vox Clamantis* reveals is of an order that must be rare in any age.

Most of the *Vox* consists of a satire on the orders of society taken one by one. In the books where he criticises the clergy the rate of Ovidian borrowing is low; in Book 3, on the legal profession, as few as two per cent of the lines are taken from Ovid. When he comes to write about the knights, Ovid has more to offer him. He criticises them for their amorous failings, and here his rate of borrowing rises to over seven per cent, the majority of the borrowed lines coming from the *Amores, Ars Amatoria* and *Remedia Amoris*.[3]

Gower was convinced that his was an age of decline. He found the same conviction at the beginning of the *Metamorphoses* in the passage that looks back to the Golden Age, (1.89–112), and in the Book of Daniel (2.31–45) where Nebuchadnezzar sees a statue with a head of gold, breast of silver, belly of bronze, legs of iron and feet partly of iron and partly of clay. Daniel explains these as representing the reign of Nebuchadnezzar and the kingdoms that are to succeed it, each being worse than the last. Gower alludes to this statue in Book 7 of the *Vox Clamantis*, but instead of making his own age the age of gold as Daniel does, he follows Ovid in placing the golden age in the past (5–8). His own age he sees as that of iron, to be followed soon by the age of clay. Here Gower has used Ovid to help him reinterpret scripture. He does take lines from the passage on the age of gold in *Metamorphoses* 1 to help him, but he does more: he is here adopting an Ovidian theme.

Gower's view of his own age was confirmed for him in 1381, while he was writing the *Vox*, by the Peasants' Revolt. Being in London at the time, he witnessed the riots, which led him to write a new section and set it at the beginning of the *Vox* as Book 1, the most vivid part of the poem, in which he describes the riots and his own place in them. He strongly disapproved of the rebels, who seemed to him to have lost the use of reason and so to have become no more than animals:

Ovid and John Gower

qui fuerant homines prius innatae rationis
brutorum species irrationis habent.

Those who had previously been men, gifted with inborn reason, now have the appearance of irrational beasts. (1.177–8)

He describes the mob as a horde of wild asses, bulls, boars, dogs, foxes, cats, domestic birds, flies and frogs. He calls on various earlier authors to help him: the section on the flies and frogs draws on the story of the plagues of Egypt in the book of Exodus, that about the asses on the *Speculum Stultorum*, a twelfth-century Latin beast-fable. The idea of creatures who are half man and half beast was familiar in Gower's day from fables, both Latin and vernacular, and from visual art in misericords, gargoyles and manuscript illumination; particular beasts were associated with particular vices, the sly fox, the lecherous goat and so on. But the pre-eminent literary model for stories of men becoming beasts was, of course, Ovid's *Metamorphoses*.

Gower does not take over many of the metamorphoses from Ovid, not surprisingly since Ovid's characters are not usually transformed into base animals, though he does recall the transformation of Hecuba into a dog, briefly narrated by Ovid in his account of the aftermath of the Fall of Troy. (1.442 cf. *Met.* 13.567–75). Rather, he draws on Ovid's menagerie for comparison with his own: the bulls of Colchis are likened to the men-become-bulls in Gower's vision, the dogs of Actaeon to the men-become-dogs (1.263–4 cf. *Met.* 7.104–10; 1.445–6 cf. *Met.* 3.204–52). Like Ovid, Gower gives his dogs names, but his are English ones – Cutte and Curre (1.395). The section where men become swine borrows many lines from the hunt of the Calydonian boar in *Metamorphoses* 8 (1.321–40 cf. *Met.* 8.281–419).

In Book 1 the rate of Ovidian borrowing rises to over twelve per cent. It does not cease with the passage on the beasts. Gower goes on to describe the burning of the priory of St John at Clerkenwell, drawing on Ovid's account of the burning of the temple of Vesta (1.933–6 cf. *Fast.* 6.439–42). The violence is represented as a storm, for the description of which he draws on the storms in Ovid's stories of Deucalion and Pyrrha and Ceyx and Alcyone (1.1623–35 cf. *Met.* 1.264–82; 1.1653–94 cf. *Met.* 11.480–523). The mob becomes a sea-monster, modelled on that in the story of Perseus and Andromeda (1. 1717–21; cf. *Met.* 4.689–707).

The ending of Book 6 reveals the frame of cultural reference within which Gower moved. Lamenting the corruption of his age, he says that all the good characters have disappeared, leaving only the bad ones: Elisha the healer has given way to avaricious Gehazi, Paul has become Saul again, Achilles has been succeeded by Thersites, Socrates by Epicurus, Alexander by Croesus, Trajan by Nero, Cato the just judge by Pontius Pilate, Pyramus and Thisbe by Jason and Medea. Scripture, ancient history and mythology here come together. Similarly, in Gower's reading Ovid takes his place alongside scripture, a twelfth-century

85

versification of the Bible called *Aurora* by Peter Riga, the *Pantheon*, (a historical poem by Godfrey of Viterbo), the beast-fables of the *Speculum Stultorum*, and other collections of stories.

There is no conception of Ovid as a 'classical' author belonging to a distinct category. We may compare the vision in Chaucer's *House of Fame* of Homer sharing with medieval writers such as Dares and Geoffrey of Monmouth the task of 'bearing up' the fame of Troy (1464–76). But Gower's reading, if it was deeper in Ovid than Chaucer's, was not so wide in the ancient authors generally. There is no indication that he had extensive knowledge of any Latin poet except Ovid. Although he knew of Virgil, and included stories about him in the *Confessio Amantis* (5.2031–224; 8.2714–17), he does not use any lines from Virgil in the *Vox*, even in his description of a city in chaos, where *Aeneid* 2 might have come in useful. Ovid was his master, and as he borrows more and more from Ovid we find his work, even the original passages, becomes better not worse. Ovid is now not merely a quarry for Gower, but an inspiration.

After the *Vox Clamantis* Gower began the composition of his long English poem, the *Confessio Amantis*. Like the *Metamorphoses* it is a collection of stories, but its framework could not be more different from Ovid's. It is a confession made by Amans, a lover, to Genius, the priest of Venus. The medieval confessional was as much a place of instruction as of confession, and in Gower's poem there is more of the former than of the latter. Genius, often at the prompting of Amans, instructs him concerning the Seven Deadly Sins and their subdivisions. This had been the subject of Gower's French poem, the *Mirour de l'Omme*, as well, but this time the sins involved are those committed against love. Many of the stories used by Genius to illustrate his teaching, about 40 in all, are from Ovid. Narcissus is given as an example of pride, because he was too haughty to love, Polyphemus of envy because he begrudged Galatea's love for Acis. When treating Sloth, Gower praises Pygmalion as one free from this vice, because his beloved came to life through his own efforts; the section on Sloth also contains the story of Ceyx and Alcyone in a digression on dreams, since it was in a dream that Alcyone learnt of Ceyx's death (4.2927–3131).

In this combination of the amorous and the ecclesiastical, which has a precedent in the *Roman de la Rose*, there is neither cynicism nor salaciousness: the aim of the poem is not to condemn the sins of lovers, but to explore the springs of human action and invite sympathy for the innocent. The sins Gower hates most are those committed against love, particularly sins of violence. Faults that come from love are treated with compassion for they spring from the strength of love, the most powerful force in human life:

> love is of so gret a main
> that where he takth an herte on honde,
> ther mai nothing his miht withstonde.   (6.90–2)

Ovid and John Gower

The root of human sin is the tendency for passion to overcome reason, turning men into beasts like the peasant rebels in the *Vox Clamantis*. This is the philosophical theme that runs through the *Confessio Amantis* and binds it together, just as in the *Metamorphoses* the Pythagorean philosophy that all is subject to change, explicated by Ovid towards the end of his poem, retrospectively gives a certain unity to the series of stories of change that has preceded.

In the Prologue to the *Confessio* Gower again describes Nebuchadnezzar's statue, interpreting it after Ovid, as in *Vox Clamantis* 6, as an image of the decline of the world (585–662). Despite this historical pessimism, Ovid had concluded his poem with praise of Augustus. In his first recension Gower follows this lead and ends the *Confessio* with praise of Richard II. Later, the vicissitudes of the reign led him to revise the end of the *Confessio* so that the second recension ends on a note of warning rather than praise.

Had Gower wished to translate Ovid as closely as possible, he might have chosen a different metre, his octosyllabic couplet offering little scope for rendering Ovid's elaborations. Chaucer had incorporated some passages of translation from Virgil and Ovid in the same metre in his early *Book of the Duchess* and *House of Fame*, but for more extended translation, in the *Legend of Good Women*, he began to develop the five-stressed line which has served well for translation of hexameters from Greek and Latin up to our own day. For his early work Chaucer had earned from his French poet contemporary Eustace Deschamps the title 'grand translateur'. By the time Gower came to write the *Confessio Amantis*, *Troilus and Criseyde* was complete, and the *Canterbury Tales* well under way: Chaucer's command of the five-stressed line had reached its height. Gower used this metre in French in his *Fifty Balades*, in the English *Praise of Peace*, and in his Supplication at the end of the *Confessio*. These show that he could write competently in that form, but for the bulk of the *Confessio Amantis* he retained the octosyllabic. He set out not so much to translate as to remould, and this he does boldly.

He will omit large sections of Ovid's narrative, or severely compress it as when Midas finds that what he touches turns to gold. What Ovid takes twelve hexameters to say, Gower sums up in two brief lines:

> The Ston, the Tree, the Lef, the gras,
> The flour, the fruit, al gold it was. (5.277–8)

He can also expand, as when the well-known line of Horace, perhaps the only one Gower knew, *parturiunt montes, nascetur ridiculus mus* ('the mountains are in labour to bring forth a ridiculous mouse') becomes a story occupying 32 English octosyllabics (7.3553–75 cf. *Ars Poetica* 139).

To form a picture of how the medieval reader saw Ovid we need to take into account not only the allegorising commentaries mentioned earlier but also the use of Ovid's poetry as the basis for rhetorical exercises in Latin. One such poem[4] expands 41 lines of Ovid's story of Pyramus and Thisbe into 186, of which 46 are devoted to describing and praising the beauty of Thisbe:

> Flos Asiae nituit, rerum rosa, balsamus orbis,
> naturae speculum, virginitatis apex.

She shone forth as the flower of Asia, the rose of all things, perfume of the world, mirror of Nature and summit of maidenhood.

Nothing goes unmentioned, even what cannot be seen:

> pectora, mamma, latus, venter, femus, ilia, lumbi,
> brachia, spina, genu, crura pedesque latent.

Her chest, her breasts, sides, stomach, legs, loins, thighs, back, knees and feet are hidden.

The art of rhetoric taught not only embellishment and expansion but also précis. An English MS of rhetorical poems and treatises from the early thirteenth century contains a group of poems retelling myths from the *Metamorphoses*, some in highly condensed form. The flight and fall of Phaethon are narrated in a single couplet:

> munere patris agit currus; ducis error in ima
> ducit eos, quorum sauciat aestus humum.[5]

Because of his father's generosity he drove the chariot, and the driver's error drove it towards the earth, so that its heat wounded the ground.

With such exercises the medieval Latin poets flexed their muscles: this may have been one of the ways in which Gower learnt his familiarity and freedom with Ovid.

French models as well as Latin must be reckoned with in Gower's formation as a poet, particularly since his own first major poem, the *Mirour de l'Omme*, is in French. An allegorical treatise on the vices and virtues, it runs to nearly 15,000 octosyllabic couplets in Anglo-Norman. Through this exercise he must have learnt the fluency and plasticity in handling the form that he shows when he comes to write in English. He used an Old French romance, the *Roman de Troie* by Benoît de Sainte-Maure, to supplement Ovid as a source for the story of Medea in the *Confessio Amantis*, and there is evidence that he used the *Ovide moralisé* in the same way for other stories. The French romances favour psychological introspection and analysis, and though Gower does not often follow them in their love of soliloquy he does show a tendency to concentrate more on the state of mind of the characters and less on the external world than Ovid.

The octosyllabic couplet is also the metre of many of the Middle English metrical romances. In general less sophisticated and courtly, more rustic in sensibility than the French romances, they were composed to be recited to an audience rather than read privately. Their stock-in-trade is the adventures of knights and the marvels of the world of *faierie*. Gower's adaptations of Ovid show affinities with this native tradition as can be seen, for example, in the tale of Actaeon. Ovid begins the story by describing the sacred valley where Actaeon is to discover Diana bathing in a brief but elaborate rhetorical set-piece beginning *vallis erat*, an example of the *locus amoenus* topos. After this description, the arrival of Actaeon is recounted. Gower, by contrast, introduces the valley as seen through the eyes of Actaeon (1.333–78 cf. *Met.* 3.138–252).

> On his hunting as he cam ride,
> In a Forest al one he was:
> He syh upon the grene gras
> The faire freisshe floures springe...

Actaeon has become the questing knight of medieval romance, and the narrator travels with him, as in Malory or many a verse-romance, seeing the world from his point of view, stumbling upon marvels with him so that the narrative retains an atmosphere of suspense and adventure. The stock epithets – 'grene', 'faire', 'freisshe' – are characteristic of oral poetry. Actaeon continues to discover the scene, through his ear as well as his eye. Gower has softened the landscape, making it more like his native Kent by changing the valley into a clearing and substituting birdsong for the sound of a waterfall:

> He herde among the leaves singe
> The Throstle with the nyhtingale
> Thus er he wiste into a Dale
> He cam, wher was a litel plein,
> All round aboute wel besein
> With buisshes grene and Cedres hyhe.

The focus narrows for the great surprise:

> And ther withinne he cast his yhe.
> Amidd the plein he syh a welle,
> So fair ther myhte noman telle,
> In which Diana naked stod...

The effect is simple but haunting: one thinks not only of Ovid but of the magic wells of medieval legend and the sacred wells of medieval religion.

Finally, in addition to Latin, French and English models, the influence of the Bible must be borne in mind. As has already been mentioned, scripture and Ovid are fused in Gower's treatments of Nebuchadnezzar's statue. The tale of Arion shows a similar process. Ovid's Arion is able to subdue nature and the beasts with his music, but not men: indeed, it is men who bring about his destruction (*Fast.* 2.83–118). According to Gower, Arion made peace among men as well: his transformation into a constellation is not narrated. Gower concludes the Prologue to the *Confessio Amantis* with a wish for a modern Arion to reconcile the various orders of society (1053–75). The vision of universal peace,

> The Hinde in pes with the Leoun,
> The Wolf in pes with the Moltoun....
> As wel the lord as the schepherde,

surely owes something to the promise of peace on the holy mountain of God in Isaiah as well as to Ovid: 'The calf and the lion and the sheep shall abide together and a little child shall lead them' (11.6).

The freedom with which Gower remodels Ovid can be well seen in the variety of his adaptations of episodes of transformation. In some cases a metamorphosis is simply omitted from Ovid's story, such as Midas' acquisition of ass's ears or the removal of one of Achelous' horns after he has become a bull and its transformation into a cornucopia. Sometimes Gower will furnish a metamorphosis with an explanation that it does not have in Ovid. The unnatural transformation of Teiresias into a woman is represented as fit punishment for his unnatural behaviour in striking a pair of mating serpents. The flower into which Narcissus is transformed blooms in winter which is against the *kinde* (nature) of flowers as Narcissus' pride was against the *kinde* of man (5.141–332; 4.2045–134; 3.373; 1.2355–8).

Acis' transformation into a spring, by contrast, accords with his nature, for it is fresh as he was fresh in love. Philomela, Procne and Tereus each have their nature more fully revealed when they are changed into birds: the shy Philomela to a nightingale which stays hidden in the woods, the forthright Procne into a swallow which loves to frequent the town, gossiping and complaining about her husband, the violent Tereus into a lapwing (not Ovid's hoopoe, a rare bird in England), proverbial for its unfaithfulness and wearing a crest 'in token that he was a knight' in accordance with his violent behaviour. When Lycaon becomes a wolf, that merely reveals his savagery more clearly, as Ovid had already implied. When the cruel Anaxarete becomes a stone statue, Gower presses home the moral by adapting the story so that her unhappy lover Iphis is buried beside the statue and an inscription warns that he was too soft and she too hard. The poet is not so strict with himself when complaining of his own beloved's unresponsiveness: she is Medusa, he says, and has turned him to stone (2.185–97; 5.5943–6047; 7.3367–9; 4.3648–84; 1.550–6).

The black colour of the crow is attributed to Cornix's preference 'To kepe hire maidenhede whit / Under the wede of fethers blake' rather than accede to Neptune's advances and, while white with pearls without, be black within (5.6207–11). The story of Leucothoe has a curious twist: in Ovid she is changed into an incense-tree, but Gower has her changed into a flower called 'gold' which is governed by the Sun, presumably the sunflower, appropriately for one beloved of Apollo. Here he is conflating the myth of Leucothoe with that of Clytie, which immediately follows it in the *Metamorphoses*, perhaps influenced by a MS of Ovid that read *aurea* for *turea* (CA 5.6776–83 cf. *Met.* 4.252–5 and 266–70). One metamorphosis Gower invents entirely: Phyllis, having killed herself for love of Demophon, is transformed into a filbert-tree, which still bears that name to shame Demophon (4.861–72).

Gower's treatment of Ovid's scenes of transformation also shows how independent he is of allegorisations of Ovid. There is good evidence that he used both the Old French *Ovide moralisé* and the Latin *Ovidius Moralizatus* of Pierre Bersuire since he incorporates into his narratives at several points details found in them but not in Ovid.[6] But he steers well clear of their interpretations of the myths.

For Bersuire,[7] Alcyone represents the Christian soul, Ceyx Christ, his ship the Cross. When the soul considers Christ dead she must cast herself upon him in the sea, that is the bitterness of penitence and confession, be renewed with him in the resurrection and ascension, and put on the likeness of a bird, rising up and flying in contemplation, in fulfilment of the words of the psalm 'Your way is in the sea and your paths in many waters' (Ps. 76.20). Gower contents himself with explaining that Alcyone has given her name to the halcyon-bird (4.3120–3).

The *Ovide moralisé* offers several explanations for the story of Apollo and Daphne, some pure rationalisations: the river Peneus has many laurels alongside it and the sun (Apollo) makes them grow, or Daphne was a girl who died fleeing her lover and was buried under a laurel-tree. Alternatively, Daphne is virginity fleeing corruption, changed into a laurel because it is evergreen and never bears fruit; or else Daphne is the Blessed Virgin, who was the laurel with which the Son of God crowned himself by taking up residence in her body. Gower takes one hint from among these possibilities: Daphne is changed into a laurel because it is evergreen, a sign that she will always remain a virgin and Apollo fail of his desire (3.1713–20).

The story of Pyramus and Thisbe was a favourite subject for rhetorical exercises: one medieval Latin remodelling of it has been mentioned already, and five more survive.[8] Augustine in *De Ordine* tells how he has sought to dissuade a pupil from 'holding conversations' with Pyramus and Thisbe, which may refer to rhetorical exercises or perhaps to daydreams. There is a reference from the twelfth century to a Breton lai of 'the courtly Thisbe of ancient Babylon', and a substantial Old French version of the story survives both independently and incorporated into the *Ovide moralisé*. There is also a Middle High German version. The rhetoric of the mechanicals' play in *A Midsummer Night's Dream* is Shakespeare's comment on the tradition of using this story as a vehicle for displays of rhetorical brilliance. Gower's recasting of the tale shows how radical he can be in handling his source.

Several features from Ovid are omitted entirely: the opposition of the lovers' parents to their love which has the effect of increasing their passion, their speeches through a hole in the wall that divides their houses, the mention of Ninus' tomb, their dying speeches, Pyramus' brief revival as Thisbe discovers his body, the change of colour of the mulberry when stained with Pyramus' blood. Ovid had treated the story as a canvas for the application of his rich embroidery of speeches, similes and other devices. Gower strips much of this away to concentrate on human feelings and the additions he makes serve to focus attention more on the central characters, less on their surroundings (3.1331–494 cf. *Met.* 4.55–166).

According to Gower, the hole in the wall through which Pyramus and Thisbe communicate, which Ovid says had gone unnoticed *per saecula longa* (for long ages), was not there until they made it. This he attributes not so much to their own resourcefulness as to the power of love compelling them:

> For love is evere of such a kinde
> And hath his folk so wel affaited,
> That howso that it be awaited,
> Ther mai noman the pourpos lette.

Throughout, they are shown as subject to forces larger than themselves. When Thisbe leaves the town by night to meet Pyramus, in Ovid we seem to hear the hinge squeaking on the door of the house (*versato cardine Thisbe / egreditur* – 'the hinge turns and Thisbe goes out'); Gower prefers a more general effect that emphasises Thisbe's smallness:

> This maiden, which desguised was,
> Al prively the softe pas
> Goth thurgh the large toun unknowe.

An atmosphere of menace builds up. When Thisbe reaches the tree where they are to meet, she sees a lion 'in his wilde rage' kill a beast, eat it, and seek a drink 'with his blodi snoute', before finding the wimple she has dropped: 'and he it hath todrawe, / Bebled aboute and al forgnawe'. Gower has made this scene more frightening, as in Ovid the beast is a lioness who has already eaten, and the mauling of the veil is narrated with one verb, *laniavit*, not three. Gower completes this section with a new simile showing Thisbe's fear. Again Gower has softened and anglicised the landscape: in Ovid Thisbe's hiding-place is a cave, in the *Ovide moralisé* and in Gower it is a bush:

> And Tisbee dorste noght remue,
> Bot as a bridd which were in Mue,   (confinement)
> Withinne a buissch sche kepte hir clos
> So stille that sche noght aros;
> Unto hirself and pleigneth ay.

Ovid's Pyramus, discovering Thisbe's bloody veil, decides at once to kill himself: '*Una duos*' inquit '*nox perdet amantes*' ('One night', says he, 'shall be the end of two lovers'). In Gower he is not so much resolute as panic-stricken. One line tumbles into another with a frequency of enjambement unusual for Gower, as if the octosyllabics were bursting with Pyramus' feelings, and he wrings his hands like an attendant in a Gothic representation of the Crucifixion:

> Cam nevere yit to mannes Ere
> Tidinge, ne to mannes sihte
> Merveile, which so sore aflihte

A mannes herte, as it tho dede
To him, which in the same stede
With many a woful compleignynge,
Began his hands forto wringe,
As he which demeth sikerly   (certainly)
That sche be ded...

As often, Gower replaces Ovid's direct speech with indirect, but before Pyramus dies, he speaks three lines claiming that, as he has been the cause of Thisbe's death, his suicide is reasonable:

'I am cause of this felonie,
So it is resoun that I die
As sche is ded be cause of me.'

The effect of this is ironical, since Pyramus has so plainly lost his reason. This recalls Gower's constant theme that loss of reason is the cause of sin.

Thisbe on her return is similarly overcome and swoons. When she recovers, Gower gives her an unusually long speech, entirely independent of that in Ovid, on the cruel power of love as personified by Venus and Cupid:

O thou which cleped art Venus
Goddesse of love, and thou, Cupide,
Which loves cause hast forto guide...   (hast)
Helas, why do ye with ous so?

When she has spoken, the weeping Thisbe embraces Pyramus' body until sorrow overcomes her wits and she falls on his sword almost without knowing what she is doing.

Although Gower seems to have used the *Ovide moralisé* for this tale, he uses nothing of the moralisation there offered, according to which Thisbe is the soul, Pyramus Christ, the lion the devil, and the change of colour of the mulberry the staining of the Cross with Christ's blood in the Passion. Gower in fact omits the staining of the mulberry entirely, leaving the focus at the end of the tale on the dead lovers. The result of the story is to evoke our sympathy for the couple. Their sin is *folhaste*, a subdivision of Wrath, the subject of Book 3 of the *Confessio*, in which their story comes. There is no question of moral Gower condemning them as suicides.

Ovid's Medea has two sides to her character, the lover and the witch. The lover is uppermost in the first part of the story, until Jason and Medea elope to Iolcus. The witch comes to the fore with the spells she works for the rejuvenation of Aeson.

Gower follows this pattern, but for the first half he does not use Ovid as his direct source, turning instead to the version of the legend in the twelfth-century *Roman de Troie* by Benoît de Sainte-Maure. Benoît had greatly expanded the narrative, especially the development of the relationship between Medea and Jason, so that 158 hexameters in Ovid became 1360 octosyllabics in Benoît.

Gower is less expansive: he reduces Benoît by about half, but follows him in adapting the story to the conventions of medieval romance. Events at Colchis are carefully timed and dated, lasting four days and four nights. The nights are all medieval insertions into the legend, for Ovid tells us nothing of them. They enable Gower to concentrate more on the development of the relationship between Medea and Jason (5.3247–926 cf. *Roman de Troie* 703–2062).

The days are filled with court ceremonial. The king welcomes Jason as a celebrity on his first arrival and entertains him to a banquet. When he returns with the fleece, Medea watching him from a tower like the Lady of Shalott, the king greets him, he takes a herbal bath and a snack, and goes to meet the king and his knights in the parliament, where every man makes a speech about him before supper. This is highly conventional, of course, and yet Gower shows his independence of romance conventions in keeping his narrative brief. Many romances delight in elaborate set-piece descriptions of the details of court life. For Gower the court is merely the setting for his main focus of interest, relationships between human beings.

It is during the night that these chiefly develop. The first night, Jason and Medea having met, each lies awake thinking of the other. Jason comes to a resolution that

> he wolde ferst beginne
> At love, and after forto winne
> The flees of golde.

On the second night, as they have arranged, a maid comes from Medea to Jason to lead him to her chamber while Hercules keeps watch in Jason's chamber. Medea brings out an image of Jupiter in front of which Jason swears to marry her. A maid then helps them undress, after which 'thei hadden bothe what thei wolde'. Medea then tells Jason of the perils he will have to undergo to gain the fleece. The medieval authors have transferred into this pillow-dialogue all the details that Ovid gives in the narrative of the following day. They part reluctantly, Medea swooning. Jason catches up on his sleep for part of the morning, and then sets out on his adventure. When he returns with the fleece, Medea greets him formally and would have kissed him but for *schame* (modesty). She sends a maid to learn how he has fared and, learning that the news is good, kisses her instead. There is a celebratory banquet that evening at which Medea and Jason sit together and agree that Jason shall come to her at night,

> and thanne of other thinges
> Thei spieke aloud for supposinges.   (to avoid suspicion)

Jason waits until everyone is fast asleep and then goes to Medea's chamber to find her awake and a maid ready to assist him.

> And he with alle haste him spedde
> And made him naked and al warm.
> Anon he tok hire in his arm.

Ovid and John Gower

This is the poet whom Chaucer called 'moral Gower': so much for the clichéd contrast between hot-blooded antiquity and the prudish Middle Ages. In Ovid there is no such development of their relationship: all the sex is in Medea's head, and the most we know of Jason's response is the cold *promisitque torum* when he is trying to enlist her help in winning the Golden Fleece.

Once Jason and Medea have eloped from Colchis on the fourth night, Benoît's story ceases. Gower was still interested, however, and so he turned to Ovid as his direct source for the rejuvenation of Aeson (5.3927–4186 cf. *Met.* 7.159–293). This appealed to a love of magic which Gower also shows elsewhere in the *Confessio* and which was common in the romances. In this section, a catalogue of Medea's magic practices with no exploration of human relationships, Gower follows Ovid unusually closely, like an alchemist holding a book in one hand while filling his cauldron with the other. Nonetheless, Gower makes some omissions, notably Medea's long boast concerning her magical achievements in the past, and adds some touches of his own. When Medea begins her spell, Gower conjures up that atmosphere of silent menace that is distinctively his:

> Al specheles and on the gras
> Sche glod forth as an Addre doth. (glided)

He describes his Medea as *faie*, that is, possessed of magic powers. She is not so spectacular or outlandish as her counterpart in Ovid, at one point more a crazed farmwife than an exotic sorceress, when she runs up and down making bird-noises:

> Sometime lich unto the cock,
> Sometime unto the Laverock, (lark)
> Sometime kacleth as a Hen.

There is a delicate human touch added by Gower when, having made her preparations, she takes Aeson in both her arms to make him sleep. Gower takes Medea's side and asks what more could a woman do to show her love than Medea did for Jason. It is Jason who is the villain: the tale is told to show

> what sorwe it doth
> To swere an oth which is noght soth.

If this seems a flimsy peg on which to hang so long and complex a story, Gower offers another motive, *novellerie*, that is, novelty, for narrating the motive of Aeson. The plain fact is that he was fascinated, as so many have been before and since, by the story itself. When Ovid's story came to an end he turned to a moralised Ovid, either in French or in Latin, as source for Medea's murder both of Jason's new wife Creusa by the gift of a poisoned mantle and of her own two sons by Jason in front of their father.[9] This is narrated briefly, with no relish for the horror. Gower still had Ovid before him, for he says that Medea then went 'Unto Pallas the Court above', a mistranslation of Ovid's *Palladis arces*, that is Athens.

Still Gower's interest in the legend did not fail, for the lover now asks Genius how it was that the Golden Fleece came to Colchis in the first place, and Genius replies by telling the story of Phrixus and Helle as found in the *Ovide moralisé*, but with details from an unidentified source.[10] Gower's handling of the legend of the Golden Fleece shows how he can use several authors, Ovid and his derivatives, and still remain independent of all of them in making his own version.

Ovid has been submerged, even dismembered, at the service of Gower's own poetry. He is never mentioned except in passing, usually when named as an authority for a tale or an opinion: no stories are told about him. Consequently, we can only form a sketchy view of what Ovid meant to Gower. In the *Mirour de l'Omme*, he reproaches himself for composing foolish love-songs in his youth and resolves to amend his ways. In those days the amatory poems will surely have appealed to him, though by the time he wrote the *Mirour* itself he had grown grave enough to choose the epithet 'sage' (wise) for Ovid.[11] The fantastic visions of the *Vox* reveal an affinity with the vivid drama of the *Metamorphoses*. The mode of narration of the *Confessio* is so different from Ovid's that Gower seems by this stage to regard Ovid's poetry as little more than raw material, to be manipulated and transformed without regard to its origin. There remains, however, one point of contact.

At the end of the *Confessio* the poet reveals what he has so far hidden, that he is old and therefore unsuited for love (8.2350 ff). Venus appears and heals him of his unrequited passion for his lady, giving him a set of black beads inscribed in gold *Por reposer*. This scene has the effect of a palinode, implying a withdrawal from the world of love and undercutting the moral judgements that have been offered during the poem. Similarly, Chaucer's Troilus rises above the world at the end of the poem to see his sufferings for Criseyde as insignificant. Chaucer's models for his palinode had been Macrobius and Boethius. Gower's, perhaps surprisingly, is Ovid.

The persona of the bewildered poet unable to face the turmoil of life around him and so choosing withdrawal had appeared before in his work, in *Vox Clamantis* 1.1359 ff., where he flees London, seeking refuge in woods and caves from the Peasants' Revolt. At one point he begins to think the time for his death is at hand (although in fact he still had some 20 years to live), and exclaims:

> Heu! mea consueto quia mors nec erit mihi lecto,
> depositum nec me qui fleat ullus erit.　　　　　　　　(1.1535–6)

Alas that my death will not even be in my customary bed, nor will there be anybody to weep for me at my burial.

These lines are adapted from *Tristia* 3.3.39–40, Ovid's letter to his wife in which he includes his own epitaph. Gower borrows extensively from this and other poems of Ovid's exile as he broods on his solitude. We have here the germ of the persona Gower creates for himself at the end of the *Confessio*.

Ovid and John Gower

The dejected, resentful Ovid of the *Tristia* and *Ex Ponto* is often forgotten by those who think of him chiefly as Venus' clerk. Genius speaks of Ovid in very different terms:

> To the lovers Ovide wrot
> And tawhte, if love be to hot,
> In what manere it scholde akiele. (grow cool)
> (4.2669–71)

This lesson Gower found not only in the *Remedia Amoris*, but also in the late poems. Genius goes on to counsel the lover:

> Forthi, mi Sone, if that thou fiele
> That love wringe thee to sore,
> Behold Ovide and take his lore. (4.2672–4)

At the end of the poem he takes that advice. Just as conjugal fidelity comes to be valued more highly by Ovid in the late poems, so Gower at the end of the *Confessio* reserves his highest praise for four faithful wives of antiquity, Penelope, Lucrece, Alcestis and Alcyone (8.2621–56). He himself took a wife in his old age in 1398 after the *Confessio* had been finished. Faithfulness and tranquillity mean more to an old man than the fires of youthful passion. Many have learnt this lesson, but few can have learnt it from Ovid.

7

ORIGINAL FICTIONS: METAMORPHOSES IN *THE FAERIE QUEENE*

Colin Burrow

THE *Metamorphoses* tells the story of mankind from the creation to the Roman Empire. It shows how man was created and how he changed from a victim of the gods' lusts to a being with independent strength. It dwells with loving detail on human procreation, on the nourishment of children, and zealously tells of the world's population by this new energetic creature. Ovid coaxes mankind through the formation of families, households, states, and finally the pinnacle of human perfection, the Roman Empire. The poem is a hymn to the liberation of man and to his eventual control over the world.

Of course the poem is not at all like this; but this is how one might imagine it to be if one were given a summary account of its structure as a poem coming down *ab origine mundi / ad mea...tempora* ('from the origins of the world to my own times', *Met.* 1.3–4). The poem would be a cosmogony like Book 5 of Lucretius' *De Rerum Natura*, which tidily gives a causal explanation for every stage of its transition from the creation to the civil man of Athens – the pinnacle of human skill (1457). The *Metamorphoses* as it is – a collection of stories, some etiological, some simply fabulous, some concerning gods, others about the founders of cities, others still about the heroes that founded Rome – fails obligingly to fill its historical shape with a causally coherent account of how the creation with which it begins became the Empire with which it ends.

This deliberate disparity between local content and wide-scale structure makes the poem one which is singularly powerful because singularly in need of revision. The opening cosmogony, the historical scheme and the discourse of Pythagoras in Book 15 on the universality of change all suggest a world which is a process of burgeoning mutability where one thing generates another. Yet most of the stories which make up the poem radically cut against the sort of world which its structure suggests. People seem not to play any part in the underlying process that the shape and philosophy of the *Metamorphoses* suggests must be going on. Indeed, by the end of the poem we are left with an Empire full of people and a big, aching question: where do they all come from? Scarcely any children are produced from married union between human beings: Ceyx and Alcyone are married and of fertile age, but childless until they are changed into birds. Medea kills her children. Tereus eats his son. Among the friendly old people in the poem Baucis and Philemon are apparently without

99

offspring, and when Pyrrha and Deucalion are told to repopulate the world they start not by amorous embracements but by throwing stones over their shoulders. Is the world populated by people produced from the rapes of the gods? From Iphis-like lesbianism? From Pygmalian union with stones? The poem is an extraordinarily tense mixture of the generative and the perverse. And Ovid is not interested in reconciling them.

All the elements of Ovid's poem which do not quite add up were features emphasised by different writers in the generation immediately before Spenser. Just before the period of the erotic epyllion, the genre which is commonly thought of as *the* mode of Ovidian imitation in the Renaissance, Ovid was quite commonly moralised in the manner established by medieval readers and exegetes of the poem.[1] But also all those elements – cosmogony, metamorphosis, the discourse of Pythagoras, the historical scheme – which modern critics often regard as Ovid's way of giving a superficial gloss of unity to a mishmash of myths were seen by many as fundamental to the poem and as together making up a general vision of the nature of the universe. Golding in the Epistle prefixed to his translation of the poem (1567) saw in the *Metamorphoses* a unified vision of universal changefulness (9–16):

> Fowre kynd of things in this his worke the Poet dooth conteyne.
> That nothing under heaven dooth ay in stedfast state remayne.
> And next that nothing perisheth: but that eche substance takes
> Another shape than that it had. Of theis twoo points he makes
> The proof by shewing through his woorke the wonderfull exchaunge
> Of Goddes, men, beasts, and elements, to sundry shapes right straunge,
> Beginning with creation of the world, and man of slyme,
> And so proceeding with the turnes that happened till his tyme.

Georgius Sabinus, who wrote the only full-blooded allegorical commentary on the poem which was published in England in the sixteenth century, also regarded Ovid as in part a historian, and saw the creation as *Prima & maxime admiranda Metamorphosis* ('the first and most miraculous metamorphosis'), part of the general theme of the poem.[2] This way of reading Ovid as a poet with a historical and cosmological vision of all things changing existed at the same time as a common belief that the ungenerative forms of sexuality which often led to metamorphosis were images of bestialising vice and *exempla* of what to avoid. Lyly cites various examples of Ovidian sexuality and concludes 'these are set down that we viewing their incontinencie, should fly the like impudencie, not follow the like excesse'.[3] These sorts of reading provide, in potential at least, the interpretative framework for a recognition of the full paradox of Ovid's poem: how man simply does not fit in with what Charles Tomlinson calls 'this universe of fecund change'.[4]

The bulk of Ovidian imitation in the Renaissance shows no real sense of this paradox. *Hero and Leander* and the genre it spawned of the erotic epyllion takes Ovid as somewhere between a Doctor of Wit and a Doctor of Love and virtually ignores the general theme of Change. The elegists loved him for his love. And the Italian epic poets who had most influence on Spenser felt slightly embarrassed by the theme of metamorphosis. Ariosto kept quite tightly within the bounds of Virgilian and Homeric metamorphosis: Astolfo is changed into a tree in imitation of Polydorus; Alcina's lovers are changed to animals and stones after dallying with her Circean charms; and Astolfo makes ships from leaves as Aeneas makes ships from nymphs[5]. His Ovid could be Chaucer's Ovid, the source of complaints made by deserted women and of a general sympathy towards Dido figures in his imperial romance.[6] Tasso is still more rigorous; he has the stock of decorous transformations, with the addition of a first person account of metamorphosis into fish which owes much to Ovidian descriptive techniques. But despite his theoretical defence of metamorphosis in his *Discorsi*, he cut this episode when refashioning the *Gerusalemme Liberata* into the *Conquistata*.[7] Spenser's predecessors in the epic romance (and this is particularly true of Ariosto) take from Ovid an ethos of love: immediate pursuit of beautiful women and the psychological states that result from being frustrated in this pursuit make up the central actions of *Orlando Furioso* and the rebellious sub-plot of Alcina in *Gerusalemme Liberata*. Ariosto and Tasso are so vastly different from Spenser partly because their poems do not contain the Ovidian landscape of nymphs fleeing from lecherous gods and consummating their flight in metamorphosis; rivers do not have their own gods, streams and stones do not have histories which express their nature, and change of form is not a continuing part of the metaphysical environment of the poems. But they accept the Ovidian ethos in a way that Spenser, for all his Ovidian landscapes, very deliberately does not.

The first metamorphosis in *The Faerie Queene* occurs in Book I when Redcrosse is found by Duessa next to a spring; they have a brief row:

> Vnkindnesse past, they gan of solace treat,
>   And bathe in pleasaunce of the ioyous shade,
>   Which shielded them against the boyling heat,
>   And with greene boughes decking a gloomy glade,
>   About the fountaine like a girlond made;
>   Whose bubbling waue did euer freshly well,
>   Ne euer would through feruent sommer fade:
>   The sacred Nymph, which therein wont to dwell,
> Was out of *Dianes* favour, as it then befell.

> The cause was this: one day when *Phoebe* fayre
>   With all her band was following the chace,
>   This Nymph, quite tyr'd with heat of scorching ayre
>   Sat downe to rest in middest of the race:
>   The goddesse wroth gan fowly her disgrace,
>   And bad the waters, which from her did flow,
>   Be such as she her selfe was then in place.
>   Thenceforth her waters waxed dull and slow,
> And all that drunke thereof, did faint and feeble grow.[8]

101

Or is it a metamorphosis? Perhaps an original fiction is a better name for it, since it is a digression not so much about change of shape as about the etiology – the origins – of the well. It represents a version of Ovid's story of Salmacis and Hermaphroditus without the metamorphic union of Hermaphroditus with the Nymph which, in Ovid, eventually leads to his prayer that the well be made enervating. Spenser is interested in the continuities between places and states of mind: he modifies a detail from the description of Salmacis (4.302–4) in order to explain the nature of the waters:

> nympha colit, sed nec venatibus apta nec arcus
> flectere quae soleat nec quae contendere cursu,
> solaque naiadum celeri non nota Dianae.

A Nymph inhabits it, one who is no good at hunting, who does not bend the bow nor compete in races; but who alone of all naiads is not a familiar of swift Diana.

In Ovid this is something of a dummy-run etiology: it looks initially as if the spiritual nature of the Nymph will explain the spring's properties, as so often in the *Metamorphoses* original nature continues in the changed form.[9] In Spenser this continuity is explicit: Diana causes the quality of idleness to diffuse into the waters and makes the place an expression of the Nymph's original nature. But initially – and this is why the passage is a brilliant piece of imitation – the description of the fountain and its surroundings does not seem to be a prelude to an etiological myth at all. It is simply a glade deeply infused with liquid delights: Redcrosse and Duessa '*bathe* in pleasaunce', the heat is 'boyling' and summer too is 'fervent' – boiling etymologically. The spring itself placidly bubbles:

> Whose bubbling waue did euer freshly well

and invites us to dabble in its syntax. 'Waue' might almost replace 'well' as its verb with 'well' and 'freshly' idly doubling their adverbial force and 'bubbling' a gentle verbal noun. Even 'freshly' has in it the faintest undercurrent of delightful verbal inactivity with 'well' as its adverb. Like the rest of the scene the line turns liquid and invites leisured pause as verbs and adverbs flow into one another. At this point the etiological phrase with which Ovid introduces the tale of Salmacis (4.287) is particularly apt:

> causa latet, vis est notissima fontis.

The origin is hidden, the power of the fountain is well known.

The power of the well suffuses everything around it; but as yet both knight and reader have no sense of the cause or meaning of this delightful ease. And when the cause – the explanatory etiology – is revealed ('The cause was this...') it initially appears as nothing more than a lazy irrelevance telling why Diana was angry with her Nymph; an anecdote for a summer's day with no connection to the main plot at all. It is only at the end of the digression that Spenser reveals he is using the word 'cause' with a play on the Ovidian sense of 'etiology'.[10] The last line comes as a terrible shock:

> And all that drunke therof, did faint and feeble grow.

The etiological fiction casts a rather alarming light on the lazy listlessness of the preceding stanza by telling the moral history of the waters; but even the moral explanation is at first hard to recognise as an explanation. Redcrosse, for whom 'causa latet', the etiology is concealed, is idly absorbed into the metamorphic liquidity of the scene. In a quiet acknowledgement of the union of Hermaphroditus with the Nymph in his subtext Spenser makes him into a liquid being 'Pourd out in loosnesse on the grassy grownd'.[11] The metamorphosis of the original is here, but has been transformed to the most delicate hint about the idle stasis that follows from the servitude of Redcrosse to Duessa.[12] The metamorphic motif has been transformed into an inconspicuous underlying process of moral transition.

This concealed metamorphic fiction is a subtle device for showing how inconspicuously sin transforms without ever quite making itself felt as a sin. It enables Spenser to moralise a landscape by telling its history; but it also represents an important *formal* borrowing from Ovid. It is hard to think of any poet writing in English before Spenser who has such complete control over narrative sequence as to be able to give a burst of historical explanation and then return to the main narrative sequence at the point where he left off. Chaucer, for example, uses almost every kind of digression except the etiological flashback. Spenser's interest in the relationship of story and place may have been aroused by Italian myths of locality like Boccaccio's *Ninfale Fiesolano*,[13] but the casual and confident movement into the past is something he learnt from Ovid, and which English poetry learnt from him. Streams and rivers in an early topographical poem like Churchyard's *Worthines of Wales* never have any historical or ethical significance, whereas in works influenced by Spenser like E.W.'s *Tameseidos* human qualities – grief and chastity – fuse quite willingly with the landscape in metamorphic and etiological fictions.[14] And in Drayton's *Poly-Olbion* the metamorphic union of human qualities (usually chastity) and landscape is commonly told through flashbacks into historical origins. By using the narrative device that Spenser learnt from Ovid, Drayton infuses his rivers with an anthropomorphised significance and historical depth which before Spenser they never had.[15] The Ovidian intimation that objects and places are charged with human history begins to play a significant part in English writing after Spenser had naturalised the etiological narrative form.

There is a lot of emphasis on the chaste origins of streams among Spenser's imitators; and this probably derives from the second etiological fiction in *The Faerie Queene*. This occurs in the middle of one of the knottiest interpreters' cruces in Book II. Guyon and the Palmer hear the scream and lament of Amavia, whose husband Mordant has died after drinking of a well. He had previously been cursed with death by Acrasia 'So soone as Bacchus with the Nymphe does lincke' (II i 55). Amavia stabs herself and dabbles her child's hands in her gore, then dies after telling them her story. At the start of Canto ii Guyon attempts to wash the babe's hands in the water of the well, but mysteriously the blood will not come off. The Palmer offers the etiology of the well by way of an explanation (II ii 5–8):

> But know, that secret vertues are infusd
> In euery fountaine, and in euery lake,
> Which who hath skill them rightly to haue chusd,
> To proofe of passing wonders hath full often vsd.
>
> Of those some were so from their sourse indewd
> By great Dame Nature, from whose fruitfull pap
> Their welheads spring, and are with moisture deawd;
> Which feedes each liuing plant with liquid sap,
> And filles with flowres faire *Floraes* painted lap:
> But other some by gift of later grace,
> Or by good prayers, or by other hap,
> Had vertue pourd into their waters bace,
> And thenceforth were renowmd, and sought from place to place.
>
> Such is this well, wrought by occasion straunge,
> Which to her Nymph befell. Vpon a day,
> As she the woods with bow and shafts did raunge,
> The hartlesse Hind and Robucke to dismay,
> *Dan Faunus* chaunst to meet her by the way,
> And kindling fire at her faire burning eye,
> Inflamed was to follow beauties pray,
> And chaced her, that fast from him did fly;
> As Hind from her, so she fled from her enimy.
>
> At last when fayling breath began to faint,
> And saw no meanes to scape, of shame affrayd,
> She set her downe to weepe for sore constraint,
> And to *Diana* calling lowd for ayde,
> Her deare besought, to let her dye a mayd.
> The goddesse heard, and suddeine where she sate,
> Welling out streames of teares, and quite dismayd
> With stony feare of that rude rustick mate,
> Transformd her to a stone from stedfast virgins state.

As in the earlier Spenserian metamorphosis the change is brought about by Diana, who makes the Nymph's emotional state physical; and as in the secondary moral metamorphosis of Redcrosse to a waterish thing, the change is the culmination of a general trend in the descriptive language: '*Welling* out *streames* of teares...*stony* feare'. Her final state is the conclusion of an internal process which begins before metamorphosis. But is her change desirable, or is it like that of the Nymph in Book I, an expression of a failing? Features of Spenser's metamorphosis recall Daphne's and Arethusa's,[16] but the only trans-

Metamorphoses in *The Faerie Queene*

formation of a chaste woman into a stone in the *Metamorphoses* (14.757–8) is that of Anaxarete, whose stony chastity is expressed in her eventual form:

> paulatimque occupat artus,
> quod fuit in duro iam pridem corpore, saxum.

Little by little the stoniness that was already in her hard body ['pectore', heart, in some texts] took possession of her limbs.

Anaxarete was by no means a pleasant creature. As Sandys put it, summarising the main Renaissance view of this loveless Nymph: '*Anaxarete*, converted into a statue of stone for her cruelty; By which is represented the hardnesse of her heart...'.[17] Spenser's version of the metamorphosis is cleaned up rather: Diana 'Transformd her to a stone from stedfast virgins state', yet the result is a bountiless well. The Nymph's waters kill Mordant in fulfilment of the prophecy when mingled with the wine which (presumably) he has already drunk; and because of its peculiar history of chastity her stream does not clean Ruddymane's hands. The action of the passage retains the faintest tincture of the deadly purity of its origins in Ovid: Anaxarete by her chastity causes the death of Iphis as this chaste metamorphosis contributes to the death of Mordant and the continuing stain on Ruddymane. The quality of mind which Spenser's Nymph possesses – laudable chastity or punitive insensibility (the two qualities have an irresistible association in Spenser's imagination[18]) – produces a kind of water quite different from that which the Palmer describes 'Which feedes each liuing plant with liquid sap'. It has a cold purity set apart from Spenser's Nature (II ii 9):

> Lo now she is that stone, from whose two heads,
>   As from two weeping eyes, fresh streames do flow,
>   Yet cold through feare, and old conceiued dreads;
>   And yet the stone her semblance seemes to show,
>   Shapt like a maid, that such ye may her know;
>   And yet her vertues in her water byde:
>   For it is chast and pure, as purest snow,
>   Ne lets her waues with any filth be dyde,
> But euer like her selfe vnstained hath been tryde.

The only thing that this maid ever conceives is old dreads: it is a superb image of permanent retrospective terror becoming unearthly purity. The Palmer clenches the etiological explanation by

> From thence it comes, that this babes bloudy hand
> May not be clensd with water of this well...

The emphasis falls on '*this* well': others without this extraordinary history of abstinence might work rather better.

The standard interpretation of this episode – initially suggested by Winstanley[19] – is that 'the bloody-handed babe stands for mankind which from its infancy has been infected by original sin';[20] and Fowler, interpreting Faunus

105

as concupiscence, writes 'The nymph's metamorphosis signifies that through concupiscence man's original, rationally ordered virtue is lost'.[21] The whole interpretation makes Spenser a comfortably orthodox Calvinist, aware that Article IX of the Church of England states that original corruption in the form of concupiscence is present 'Yea, in them that are regenerated'. The only thing wrong with it is that the stream does not fail to clean Ruddymane's hands because of original sin – not directly at least – but (paradoxically enough) because of original *virtue*: 'For it is chast and pure, as purest snow...' There are iconographical paradoxes here too. Ficino and Comes, two major Renaissance sources of mythology and philosophical lore, both state that nymphs are mythical embodiments of generation.[22] Yet this Nymph chastely flees from the wood god and so resists the generative function which was usually assigned to her breed. Her waters abstemiously resist mingling with Acrasia's wine – and the tempering of wine with water was a traditional emblem of temperance. It is extremely odd that an author who was immersed in traditional iconography and mythical lore should make an emblematic figuration of temperance prove deadly in a Book that is *about* Temperance;[23] just as it is odd that a figure of generation should be so completely unfruitful.

The suspicion that there may be something wrong with this Nymph is also supported by the imagery of the passage. The significant opposition of the well at the literal level is not to 'rationally ordered virtue' but to the generative waters that well from Dame Nature's 'fruitfull pap' and which, in a suggestively sexual procreativity, 'Fill with flowres dame *Floraes* lap'. On the level of fable the Nymph embodies a purity that cannot sustain or create life. At the end of Book II Guyon meets unbridled lustfulness in Acrasia's Bower; at its beginning he encounters an image of uncompromising virtue which blends into insensibility, something which Spenser equates with the origins of man's fallen nature. Spenser's mythic configuration of the fall is far more of an original fiction than is commonly acknowledged. It is a myth about how an imbalance of the relations of the sexes – a violent grasping in the male, a chaste fearfulness in the female[24] – is the direct origin of the continuing stain on human nature.

Spenser is here less an orthodox Calvinist than a writer deeply under the influence of Medieval Naturalism. This ethical tradition holds (essentially at least) vice to be that which is deleterious to human existence and virtue to be the temperate performance of those activities which are necessary to life, like eating, drinking and sex:

Nature, however, attaches pleasure to activities necessary to human life. And for this reason the order of nature requires that man enjoys pleasures of this kind insofar as they are necessary to human life, for the preservation of individuals or of the species. If someone therefore flees pleasure so much that he neglects those which are necessary to conserving nature, he commits a sin.[25]

Complete refusal to do those things which are necessary to life is a sin against nature. It is easy to see that this ethical tradition deriving from Aristotle is not likely to give unqualified approval to a virtue, like virginity, which is intrinsically opposed to the continuation of life. Virtues which depend on abstinence are very hard to explain in terms of a mean between two extremes equally incompatible with life according to nature, and so are in danger of being identified with insensibility – the vice of not taking enough pleasure in order to stay alive. Aquinas makes a piece of special pleading for virginity, denying that it is a vice of defect on the grounds that it allows one to spend more time contemplating God.[26] But Spenser was deeply steeped in works of the Naturalist tradition, like Alain de Lille's *De Planctu Naturae*, in which sexual generation is *the* main object of human life.[27] This colours his myth, and makes it a remarkable piece of synthesis: male concupiscence is the ultimate cause of the indelibility of Ruddymane's stain, but the cold reactive virginity in which it results is the efficient cause.

It has been debated for a rather tediously long time whether Book II is concerned with a pagan view of virtue as consisting in a mean between extremes in a manner that disregards Christian ideas of sin and corruption, or with a more or less explicitly Calvinist theology.[28] The action and rhetoric of this episode *are*, I suggest, concerned with a Naturalistic ideal of virtue as a mean; so much so that the indelible stain on Ruddymane (which does indeed distinctly suggest original corruption) has its origins in narrative examples of excess and defect. Original corruption is represented as deriving from the absence of a temperate mean in sexual conduct which could unite us with the burgeoning forces of Nature: excessive cupidity in the male leads to total abstinence in the female, and the combination is death-giving. Unlike his imitators in the fluvial etiological form Spenser does not regard virginity as an unqualified good – in *Comus*, for example, the Severn can assist the lady because of its perfect chastity.[29] But the resistant virginity of Guyon's Nymph has no such beneficial effects: her terrified purity resists absorbing the stain on Ruddymane, and her waters help kill Mordant. Spenser's substitute for the fall – and it is a substitute rather than a conventional refiguration – is a story about the origins of an unfruitful insensibility opposed to the ideal of natural procreation.

Spenser's aim in using Ovid in *The Faerie Queene* is to develop a form of sexuality which connects human generation with the burgeoning processes and uncorrupted cycles of the natural world. This aim is worked through sequentially. The main version of Ovid in Book I is a tale of lazily deliquescent submission of male to female; that in Book II a preliminary exploration of one form of sexual abstinence in which male dominance results in female frigidity. In Book III, however, Spenser works to fashion an antitype of the frustrated and ungenerative sexuality of the *Metamorphoses*. The Book contains four episodes involving metamorphosis which are arranged chiastically; there are two tapestries, one in the Castle Joyeux showing the love of Venus for Adonis, the other in Busirane's Castle showing the metamorphosed loves of the Gods as they pursue reluctant women.[30] These two versions of corrupt Ovidian sexuality – which adhere closely to the main events of Ovidian stories and are represented in the Ovidian form of tapestry *ecphrasis* with great emphasis on the deceitful artifice of the medium – frame the metamorphoses of the Garden of Adonis and of Malbecco, which are stories which have undergone a sea-change in the transition from Ovid to Spenser. The tapestries are the kind of pictorial borrowing which earlier critics rather tended to assume was the full extent of Spenser's debt to Ovid.[31] But the most significant fact about them is that they represent two forms of sexual dominance, by the female and by the male: the most direct representations of Ovidian love in the poem are put on display as exemplary images of what Britomart must avoid in the castles which mark the beginning and the end of the Book of Chastity.

The privy dalliance of Venus with Adonis depicted on the walls of Malecasta's castle (III i 35) recalls directly the language of the Redcrosse knight's idle afternoon with Duessa and suggests that Spenser is working to create an Ovidian nexus of themes and styles in his poem:

> Now making girlonds of each flowre that grew,
> To crowne his golden lockes with honour dew;
> Now leading him into a secret shade
> From his Beauperes, and from bright heauens vew,
> Where him to sleepe she gently would perswade,
> Or bathe him in a fountaine by some couert glade.

The similarity of vocabulary ('girlonds...shade...bathe') is noted by Hamilton; and these points of contact between two Ovidian moments show again that Spenser has taken more than content from Ovid. This method of linking episodes with similar themes by similar vocabulary is typical of the *Metamorphoses*.[32] The passage also has the same whiff of the timeless as the previous one. The repeated 'Now' followed by timeless participles suggests not a listed sequence but a conflation of different actions into a single timeless present of amorous dalliance. The casual alternatives 'Where him to sleepe she gently would perswade, / Or bathe him in a fountaine by some couert glade.' link rather more intimately if we remember Redcrosse's idle well; bathing in a well like that is tantamount to sleeping. And if we remember Hermaphroditus, the insouciance of the syntax becomes rather alarming; is the pronoun 'him' in 'bathe him' reflexive, or the object of a transitive verb? and is Venus *persuading* Adonis to bathe or is she bathing him herself? Adonis is gently reduced to an equivocal passivity in which his agency is fused with that of Venus. Again the imitation retains the faintest hint of the metamorphic union of Hermaphroditus and Salmacis related in the subtext.

But Book III also contains an original fiction. In between these two images of seamy Ovidian love represented in a deceptively artificial medium there is an etiological fiction, which develops a mythical formulation of ideal generation through Ovidian story types. The Garden of Adonis is so often read as an independent Spenserian set piece that critics and readers forget how the poet manipulates it into his narrative (and this is part of a general neglect of the ways in which Spenser uses narrative form). This central image of the underlying process of creation is set into the poem by the narrative time sequence which I have already suggested was one of Spenser's principal debts to Ovid. The whole of Canto vi is an etiological myth in a newly vital sense: it is an account not of the origins of a well of idleness or of frigid abstinence, but of a person, Belphoebe.[33] It is a very pointed modification of the original fictions about contamination in Books I and II into a form that represents the generation and birth first of Belphoebe and then of all matter.

The first phase of this generative original fiction is a story about how Chrysogonee (Golden Born) conceived her daughters (III vi 6–7):

> But wondrously they were begot, and bred
>   Through influence of th'heauens fruitfull ray,
>   As it in antique bookes is mentioned.
>   It was vpon a Sommers shynie day,
>   When *Titan* faire his beames did display,
>   In a fresh fountaine, farre from all mens vew,
>   She bath'd her brest, the boyling heat t'allay;
>   She bath'd with roses red, and violets blew,
> And all the sweetest flowres, that in the forrest grew.

> Till faint through irkesome wearinesse, adowne
>   Vpon the grassie ground her selfe she layd
>   To sleepe, the whiles a gentle slombring swowne
>   Vpon her fell all naked bare displayd;
>   The sunne-beames bright vpon her body playd,
>   Being through former bathing mollifide,
>   And pierst into her wombe, where they embayd
>   With so sweet sence and secret power vnspide,
> That in her pregnant flesh they shortly fructifide.

Despite Spenser's acknowledgment of a source in 'antique bookes', this passage gives a deeper resonance to the concept of an original fiction: it has no Ovidian origin or any evident source at all. Indeed, if Ovid had told the story it would have involved the preventative metamorphosis, the rape, or at least the unorthodox penetration of Chrysogonee (along the lines of Danae) by Apollo. Noon time by a pool is a dangerous moment for Ovidian Nymphs.[34] Spenser's transformation of the Ovidian mode is generated not by Ovid himself but from the metamorphic nexus he has developed through his own earlier etiological fictions: again he is using the Ovidian technique of self-allusion. Chrysogonee is a remodelling of Redcrosse's idle Nymph, who was also overcome by weariness on a sunny day; but there is no unyieldingly chaste and wrathful Diana to metamorphose her. She is also a virginal reworking of the Venus of Malecasta's tapestry, who was by a pool (irreligiously) 'from *bright heauens* vew' rather than (modestly) 'farre from all mens vew'. Venus' waters in which Adonis bathed were also filled with flowers (III i 36):

> She secretly would search each daintie lim,
> And throw into the well sweet Rosemaryes,
> And fragrant violets, and Pances trim...

She tries to make him idly and thoughtfully remember her and be faithful to her by a little judicious doctoring of the waters: Rosemary is for remembrance, as Ophelia says, 'Violet is for faithfulness', and Pansies (*Pensées*) imply both thoughtfulness and, via their other name, Love in Idleness.[35] Chrysogonee's flowers of love and fidelity are not added to the well; they simply follow her nature and are there: 'She bath'd *with* Roses red, and violets blew'. And unlike Redcrosse or Adonis, this Nymph is not transformed into the weakness of Hermaphroditus nor does she become idly servile; she conceives spontaneously in a fertile transformation of Ovid's Hermaphroditus myth in which one sex does the procreative work of two. Like the Virgin Mary she conceives without pleasure and gives birth without pain (III vi 27). Spenser is making a myth of redemption, and it involves dropping the whole spectrum of Ovidian loves – male pursuit and chaste resistance, or female dominance – as well as metamorphosis, the principal means by which Ovid concludes his tales about deviant sexuality. Yet Spenser's main image for redeemed nature is hermaphroditic spontaneous generation, a way of conceiving that unites human procreation with the burgeoning produced by nature's pap.[36] And to represent this (III vi 8–9) he turns again to Ovid:

> Miraculous may seeme to him, that reades
> So straunge ensample of conception;
> But reason teacheth that the fruitfull seades
> Of all things liuing, through impression
> Of the sunbeames in moyst complexion,
> Doe life conceiue and quickned are by kynd:
> So after *Nilus* invndation,
> Infinite shapes of creatures men do fynd,
> Informed in the mud, on which the Sunne hath shynd.

> Great father he of generation
> Is rightly cald, th'author of life and light;
> And his faire sister for creation
> Ministreth matter fit, which tempred right
> With heate and humour, breedes the liuing wight.
> So sprong these twinnes in wombe of *Chrysogone*...

This is the closest Spenser gets to a paraphrase of Ovid. He uses the account in the *Metamorphoses* (1.416–25) of the origin of animal life, but he transforms it from a unique past event into a continuing present process:

> Cetera diversis tellus animalia formis
> sponte sua peperit, postquam vetus umor ab igne

percaluit solis caenumque udaeque paludes
intumuere aestu fecundaque semina rerum
vivaci nutrita solo ceu matris in alvo
creverunt faciemque aliquam cepere morando...

The earth spontaneously bore other animals with differing forms, after the old moisture grew warm with the fire of the sun, and the slime and wet marshes swelled with the heat. The fruitful seeds of things, nourished in the burgeoning soil as in a mother's womb, grew and eventually took on a form.[37]

When recalling this passage Spenser reversed the priorities of his original. He makes the passage a scientific gloss on what happens during conception, rather than following Ovid by using the growth of a child in the womb as a throwaway illustrative simile ('*ceu* matris in alvo...') for the genesis of animal life after the flood. The result, the inside out version of the Ovidian cosmogony in which all natural processes are made subordinate descriptions of the human miracle of generation in the womb, is the most significant version of Ovid in *The Faerie Queene*. Through the story of Chrysogonee Spenser brings together the two sides of the *Metamorphoses* that are so extraordinarily divergent: the changeful, blooming, unstoppable material world of the more philosophical sections of the poem is put into the space where one would expect a rape or a sterile metamorphosis. The myth is Ovid redeemed, a tale that suggests the incarnation of Christ through the medium of a birth that is perfectly linked to the ideal generative forces of nature and is without a shade of Ovidian sexual corruption. Belphoebe's origin blossoms out through the Ovidian allusion into the origins of life on earth and through the religious allegory into the origins of human atonement: like Golding and Sabinus, Spenser recognised that cosmogonic poetry and metamorphic poetry are part of the same enterprise. Only he was able to synthesise them.

I Ie achieves his resolution of the two divergent sides of Ovid in an etiological flashback. This is far more than a formal device for ordering material: it is a key imaginative shape in which to develop his original vision of human sexual nature. Spenser takes us back through a particular origin into the core of things, and by recessing this mythic representation of ideal generation into the past he gives the whole fiction a special sanctity:

The true character of mythical being is first revealed when it appears as the being of origins. All the sanctity of mythical being goes back ultimately to the sanctity of the origin...By being thrust back into temporal distance, by being situated in the depths of the past, a particular content is not only established as sacred, as mythically and religiously significant, but also justified as such.[38]

The original fictions of Canto vi, the myth of Chrysogonee and the Garden of Adonis, have just this recessed sanctity given them by their temporal relation to the main narrative. They are also the most complete transformations of Ovid in Spenser. Adonis himself, part of this excursion into origins, is massively changed from his Ovidian counterpart. In the *Metamorphoses* the story of

Venus and Adonis is told by Ovid's Orpheus as the last of his tales of amorous frustration which reflect his own loss of Euridice: he ends his catalogue of disappointment with that of Venus herself.[39] Spenser transposes this myth from the centre of Ovid's vision of infertility to the heart of his own world again by fitting the burgeoning eternal changeful side of Ovid into the place of final metamorphosis. From a mythic figure of frustration Adonis becomes an image of eternal life.[40] He is not finally transmuted, but is permanently changing (III vi 47):

> for he may not
> For euer die, and euer buried bee
> In balefull night, where all things are forgot;
> All be he subiect to mortalitie,
> Yet is eterne in mutabilitie,
> And by succession made perpetuall,
> Transformed oft, and chaunged diuerslie...

In the birth of Belphoebe and the Garden of Adonis Spenser resolves the curious disparity between Ovid's image of human sexuality and his overall vision of the world as ceaselessly processual. Significantly enough, this fusion is achieved far back in the period of origins, in the biggest etiological flashback in the poem. Spenser gains confidence in transforming Ovid the further back he progresses towards the origins of things; his imagination works best when it is going backwards.

Malbecco is the only figure in *The Faerie Queene* to be transformed before our eyes in a narrative sequence that goes forwards: all the other metamorphoses and quasi-metamorphoses in the poem are digressive explanations of a state of affairs that has already been encountered in the main narrative. He has been cuckolded by Paridell; his wife has subsequently joined the lustful Satires; he also loses his money, which Trompart has dug up and stolen. At this point he goes mad and rushes off (III x 55–7):

> High ouer hilles and ouer dales he fled,
>   As if the wind him on his winges had borne,
>   Ne banck nor bush could stay him, when he sped
>   His nimble feet, as treading still on thorne:
>   ...
>
> Still fled he forward, looking backward still,
>   Ne stayd his flight, nor fearefull agony,
>   Till that he came vnto a rockie hill,
>   Ouer the sea, suspended dreadfully,
>   That liuing creature it would terrify,
>   To looke adowne, or vpward to the hight:
>   From thence he threw himselfe dispiteously,
>   All desperate of his fore-damned spright,
> That seem'd no helpe for him was left in liuing sight.
>
> But through long anguish and selfe-murdring thought
>   He was so wasted and forepined quight,
>   That all his substance was consum'd to nought,

> And nothing left, but like an aery Spright,
> That on the rockes he fell so flit and light,
> That he thereby receiu'd no hurt at all,
> But chaunced on a craggy cliff to light;
> Whence he with crooked clawes so long did crall,
> That at the last he found a caue with entrance small.

Upton wrote of Malbecco's metamorphosis 'he is turned into a monstrous fowl...',[41] which pushes one of Spenser's suppressed metaphorical metamorphoses rather too far towards physical definiteness. The language drifts him there, with his light fall and his crooked claws, but the metaphors fit a desperate figure of skin and bone, whose fingers are long and bony from starvation and desperate clawing at the rock rather than a 'monstrous fowl'. But then there is a faint suggestion that he is growing wings in

> High ouer hilles and ouer dales he fled,
> As if the wind him on his winges had borne...

'His winges'; whose? The construction aligns this fluttering flight with two Ovidian metamorphoses. Daedalion becomes suicidal when his daughter is burnt (11.336-7):

> iam tum mihi currere visus
> plus homine est, alasque pedes sumpsisse putares...

At that moment he seemed to run with more than human speed, and you might have thought his feet had taken wings.[42]

Spenser does not need to introduce the illusion of growing wings by 'you would have thought', but makes the language lightly hint at an unheralded transformation. Yet there is also a powerful overlay of another suicidal Ovidian hero whose metamorphosis (also into a bird) is preceded by his body wasting away. The metamorphosis of Aesacus fits into the imaginative shape of the Malbecco episode rather more closely than that of Daedalion. He too has lost his love (11.791-3):

> furit Aesacos, inque profundum
> pronus abit letique viam sine fine retemptat.
> fecit amor maciem...

Aesacus goes crazy and dives headlong into the sea. He tries again and again without end to find the way to death. Love made him thin...[43]

This image of deathless desperation with the body wasting into nothing has another element that draws it to the interconnection of concerns behind Malbecco: Aesacus was a historical merchant, say Sabinus and Sprengius, who lost all his wealth and sought it desperately in the sea.[44] As a parallel to the Malbecco story this episode and its gloss is not very close; but it may well have given Spenser an outline of concerns which could coalesce into a new story about a man who wastes to nothing after losing his love and is driven to an unattainable suicide by the loss of his money.

The Ovidian parallels which are to the forefront of Spenser's mind at this point in the story explain Upton's misreading: Spenser's text is extraordinarily sensitive to the fate of Malbecco's predecessors who *are* turned to birds. Malbecco is a brilliantly confusing mingle of possibilities. His flight is given no simple motive until he arrives at the cliff: a jumble of impulses cause it – despair, avarice, wretchedness, an unspecified fear – and it is underwritten by metamorphic possibilities provided by the Ovidian stories. This moment before Malbecco's change is full of centrifugal opportunities for the eventual metamorphosis: he could become a monstrous fowl, Fear, or a second Despaire. Then (III x 58) a peculiar detail comes in: Malbecco suddenly loses the idea of committing suicide, and

> Resolu'd to build his balefull mansion,
> In drery darkeness, and continuall feare
> Of that rockes fall, which euer and anon
> Threates with huge ruine him to fall vpon...

The previous description does not quite prepare us for the easy-going allusion to *that* rock. Presumably it refers to the cliff: OED sense I for 'rock' (common in the sixteenth century) is 'A large rugged mass of stone forming a cliff, crag, or natural prominence on land or in the sea'. But the familiarity of the reference becomes a bit more explicable if we are thinking as much as Spenser is about Gascoigne's *Adventures of Master F.J.*:

he fortuned (sayling aloane by the shoare) to espy a rock, more than sixe hundreth Cubits high, which hong so suspiciously over the seas, as though it would threaten to fall at everye litle blast: this dyd *Suspicion* Imagine to be a fit foundation whereon he might build his second Bower.[45]

Spenser's allusion to that rock (which Alpers finds so odd that he has to invent a new rock to fit it, and Hamilton says in a puzzled way that it 'may be the cliff itself', and then in desperation 'or the rock may be simply the roof of the cave': neither seem to have looked the word up[46]) is glossed by the story of Suspicion. It is the cliff in his original – though an inferior version of it, since Gascoigne's phrase '*as though* it would *threaten* to fall' is more appropriately inexplicit than Spenser's blatant '*Threates* with *huge* ruine...'. Gascoigne's rock teeters on the edge of teetering, and needs the nervous imaginative prod of 'as though' to set it rocking: only if one is suspicious does it seem unsteady. But the familiarity of this allusion marks how Spenser is shifting sources away from Ovid; the Gascoigne–Ariosto passage starts to dominate his mind and modify his landscape. As it does so Malbecco ceases to be the splendidly decaying imperfect fusion of motives and sources which he embodies during his flight. He loses the suicidal birdlike overlay that Daedalion and Aesacus have given him, and he becomes fixed (III x 60):

> Yet can he neuer dye, but dying liues,
> And doth himselfe with sorrow new sustaine,
> That death and life attonce vnto him giues,
> And painefull pleasure turnes to pleasing paine.

There dwels he euer, miserable swaine,
Hatefull both to him selfe, and euery wight;
Where he through priuy griefe, and horrour vaine,
Is woxen so deform'd, that he has quight
Forgot he was a man, and *Gealosie* is hight.

Malbecco's despairing immortality answers the continuing fertility of Adonis and may owe a little to Aesacus' eternal pursuit of death, but it is not Ovidian. Metamorphosis into an abstraction is not something that ever happens in Ovid. And the particular abstraction that Malbecco becomes does not have an Ovidian continuity between narrative motives and eventual condition; it is continually surprising. It does recall his earlier nature as a jealous husband, but it completely fails to continue the weird centrifugal variety which he became during his Ovidian madness and which immediately precedes the change. It recalls Gascoigne's Suspicion, who 'became of a suspicious man, *Suspicion* it selfe'.[47] Spenser has fallen under the charm of someone else's original fiction: the story of Suspicion as it is told in Gascoigne begins with the abstract quality of suspicion and tells the tale of the personification's origins in an etiological digression from a novel about love intrigues. As a result the tale always knows that it is going towards a final change into an abstraction. But in Spenser Malbecco is not *simply* a 'daemonic agent' obsessed by a single idea that sucks the vital juice out of him and turns him into an allegorical figure;[48] there is a stage in his history at which he could become almost anything from a bird to Feare or Despaire. Malbecco's transformation is unique in *The Faerie Queene* for happening forwards; it is the only metamorphosis in the poem which does not start with the state of affairs with which it ends, and as a result Spenser has to find an ending which fits the dynamics of the tale. He does not quite succeed: the metamorphosis into an abstract quality marks a final capitulation to one of his sources which does not develop the decaying intertextual vitality of Malbecco's flight.

Yet this final subservience to one of his sources is appropriate. The episode is not one of Spenser's original fictions, where time moves backwards towards origins, and it does not have the bold novelty which so often accompanies this narrative movement. It is also thematically centrifugal: Malbecco moves away from the centripetal images of fertile love and generation which are at the core of *The Faerie Queene*, since he runs desperately towards the sexual isolation of Jealousy rather than *back* towards procreation. The zone of bleached abstraction which he enters is distinctive not for literary and sexual freshness, but for stale dependence on other texts and desperate self-absorption. Spenser's unoriginality at the end of this tale brilliantly chimes with its subject: Malbecco has run out from the poem's original area of sexual and imaginative growth. And the poet is left searching in the original fictions of other writers for a way to finish him off.[49]

The whole history of the poem suggests that Spenser was not very good at going forwards or at reaching endings.[50] *The Faerie Queene* is unfinished, and, as with the tale of Malbecco, it is difficult to conceive any image that could enclose all the jumble of directions, the fusions of philosophies, the tangle of models and motivations that radiate from the forward process of its narrative. Since Ovid gives the poem a narrative form that enables it to proceed backwards rather than forwards and provides the raw materials for fertile vistas of eternity, it is rather surprising that the poem as we have it ends with its most consistently Ovidian passage. It has long been recognised that the 'Mutabilitie Cantos' are a fabric of Ovidian matter;[51] but no one has ever found it surprising that the poem should end with Ovid.

The main story of the Cantos – Mutabilitie's presumptuous ride to heaven in search of sovereignty – recalls features of the presumptuous ride of Phaethon on his father Apollo's chariot. But Spenser also brings into the Cantos all the aspects of the Ovidian nexus that have been the subject of this essay. The etiological motif and the corresponding narrative form of the historical digression provide the theme and structure of the long inset story about how Faunus spied on Diana as she bathed and how her anger at him caused the Irish countryside to be full of wolves and robbers. The opening of the digression goes straight into an Ovidian *locus*, Diana and her Nymphs bathing in a secluded grove.[52] There is a change, however, from the previous associations of Diana's entourage with perfect sexual purity: she goes to Arlo hill (VII vi 39)

> With all her Nymphes enranged on a rowe,
> With whom the woody Gods did oft consort:
> For, with the Nymphes, the Satyres loue to play and sport.

This sportive mingling of nymphs with the wood gods is a new feature in the Ovidian nexus; and there is no suggestion that they are furtively breaking chaste vows,[53] there is just an easy familiarity between the sexes which is quite different from the desperate flight of Guyon's Nymph from the wood god Faunus. This is not a place of infertility like that represented in Book II; rivers here immediately suggest associations with marriage. Molanna, the stream in which they bathe (VII vi 41) is so beautiful

> For, first, she springs out of two marble Rocks,
>   On which, a groue of Oakes high mounted growes,
>   That as a girlond seemes to deck the locks
>   Of som faire Bride, brought forth with pompous showes
> Out of her bowre, that many flowers strowes:
>   So, through the flowry Dales she tumbling downe,
>   Through many woods, and shady coverts flowes
>   (That on each side her siluer channell crowne)
> Till to the Plaine she come, whose Valleyes she doth drowne.

Again details from Spenser's Ovidian nexus are transformed: the two rocks from which the stream springs are a rejuvenated recall of the double-headed stone of Guyon's stream ('Lo now she is that stone, from whose two heads, / As from two weeping eyes, fresh streames do flow,' (II ii 9)); and the shady 'girlond' of foliage that surrounds Redcrosse's well is transformed by simile into a bridal chaplet. Diana's chastity is rather out of place in this landscape which twinkles with desired weddings and hints at the continual union of Fauns and Nymphs. It is because this is a landscape in love that Diana is exposed to the greedy eyes of Faunus, since the final temptation which he uses to persuade Molanna to give him a glimpse of the goddess is the offer of a lover (VII vi 44):

> There-to hee promist, if shee would him pleasure
> With this small boone, to quit her with a better;
> To weet, that where-as shee had out of measure
> Long lov'd the *Fanchin*, who by nought did set her,
> That he would vndertake, for this to get her
> To be his Loue, and of him liked well...

The whole stanza is full of love 'out of measure', as Faunus' eagerness for Diana leads him to produce seven feminine rhymes in a row – a number of syllables beyond the measure of the line unsurpassed anywhere else in the poem. Arlo hill is a world on holiday, full of fast-talking hucksters and amorous possibilities. Even when Faunus manages to see Diana naked (he gives himself away with a giggle which is typical of the mood of the episode) things do not change very much. Certainly when the goddess and her Nymphs catch Faunus things do not change in a metamorphic sense (VII vi 50):

> At length, when they had flouted him their fill,
> They gan to cast what penaunce him to giue.
> Some would haue gelt him, but that same would spill
> The Wood-gods breed, which must for euer liue:
> Others would through the riuer him haue driue,
> And ducked deepe: but that seem'd penaunce light;
> But most agreed and did this sentence giue,
> Him in Deares skin to clad; and in that plight,
> To hunt him with their hounds, him selfe saue how he might.

Actaeon is metamorphosed into a stag and torn apart by his own hounds where Faunus is just given a good run.[54] Richard Ringler notes the absence of metamorphosis and concludes from it that 'Spenser feels [it] is an impossibility in Nature's universe...'.[55] Like most critics writing on Ovid in the 'Mutabilitie Cantos' he forgets the rest of the poem: Guyon's Nymph is turned to a stony wellspring, and Malbecco certainly undergoes some form of change. It is not that Spenser regards metamorphosis as impossible, but that he does not want its finality here. Or more particularly, he does not want *death* here: the whole tone of the episode calls for a joke metamorphosis, and the whole tendency of the counter-Ovidian argument in the poem leads towards a final benign metamorphosis transformed. The tale of Actaeon is unusual in Ovid for ending with the complete destruction of its hero rather than his perpetual fusion with the natural world. Spenser's version of it is modified by his primary imaginative drive: life must continue;

> Some would haue gelt him, but that same would spill
> The Wood-gods breed, *which must for euer liue.*

Faunus, like Adonis, cannot die, since he supports the continuing generation of a whole breed of creatures 'which *must* for euer liue'. As in the episode of Chrysogonee, generative perpetuity overrides metamorphic destruction.

Molanna too survives the judgment of Diana. Like the previous Water Nymphs in the poem, she remains true to her origins after her change – but her original features were not chastity or sloth but bridal freshness (VII vi 53):

> They, by commaund'ment of *Diana*, there
> Her whelm'd with stones. Yet *Faunus* (for her paine)
> Of her beloued *Fanchin* did obtaine,
> That her he would receiue vnto his bed.
> So now her waues passe through a pleasant Plaine,
> Till with the *Fanchin* she her selfe doe wed,
> And (both combin'd) themselues in one faire riuer spred.

The stones do not matter very much. This river's original desire is to marry, and she achieves this desire despite Diana and remains, not a wellspring of idleness or an unbountifully chaste stream, but part of the fertile landscape of Ireland. The Ovidian landscape of the 'Mutabilitie Cantos' has completely absorbed the transformed Ovid of Belphoebe's birth. It maintains at least the underlying pulse of vitality even after Diana has transformed the landscape (VII vi 54–5):

> Nath'lesse, *Diana*, full of indignation,
> Thence-forth abandond her delicious brooke;
> In whose sweet streame, before that bad occasion,
> So much delight to bathe her limbes she tooke:
> Ne onely her, but also quite forsooke
> All those faire forrests about *Arlo* hid,
> And all that Mountaine, which doth over-looke
> The richest champian that may else be rid,   (seen)
> And the faire *Shure*, in which are thousand Salmons bred.

> Them all, and all that she so deare did way,
> Thence-forth she left; and parting from the place,
> There-on an heauy haplesse curse did lay,
> To weet, that Wolues, where she was wont to space,
> Should harbour'd be, and all those Woods deface,
> And Thieues should rob and spoile that Coast around.

When there is a chaste Nymph to be transformed into a stone Diana's metamorphic powers work without resistance to produce an object outside fecundity. But here she works against the landscape: metamorphosis has become a capricious (and rather superficial) vandalism opposed to the underlying fertility which has become a part of Spenser's Ovidian nexus. This fertility is beyond Diana's ken. In the original fictions in Books I and II she was able to transform the effects of water and to save her Nymphs from Faunus, but here the salmon-breeding stream, Faunus, Fanchin and Molanna continue to breed and marry despite her. Ireland's woods and coasts may be full of wolves and thieves, but the underlying pulse of the vital is not destroyed. Her departure is Diana's loss: she foregoes 'all that she so deare did way'. The version of Ovidian change-fulness – generative perpetuity – which Spenser has worked through the poem to create by gradually modifying a core of Ovidian motifs is in these Cantos an established part of the natural scene. Although it is not an antidote to meta-morphosis it is a counterthrust to its finality. This world has mercy impregnated in it by the need for life to go on. And that is the main foundation of Spenser's last original fiction.

Spenser's use of Ovid covers more or less every possible variety of imitation and indebtedness. He borrows motifs and locales from the *Metamorphoses*. He also makes great use of two Ovidian techniques for forming a variety of material into a long poem, the etiological flashback and the use of recurrent descriptive detail in order to confirm thematic continuity. Yet he is wilfully uninfluenced by Ovid's version of the ungenerative sexual hostilities and mis-directions that cut human beings off from the productive cycles of universal change. Indeed, as I have argued here, he uses precisely those formal devices which he learnt from Ovid as a means to create an original alternative to this way of regarding sexuality: a string of etiological narrative digressions con-nected by common motifs develops a counter-Ovidian vision of the unstoppable vitality of the landscape and the figures in it. Elements in this changing sequence of Metamorphoses need to be thought of as part of an unfolding revelation of universal benignity, which in its later phases, the birth of Belphoebe and the 'Mutabilitie Cantos', intimates that there is an original and perpetual fecundity in human amorousness which is more primitive and deep-seated than original corruption.

8

OVID AND THE ELIZABETHANS
Laurence Lerner

THOMAS CAREW in his famous 'Elegy upon the Death of the Dean of St Pauls, Dr John Donne' (first published 1633) describes the vices from which Donne rescued English poetry, and which after his death will now recur:

> But thou art gone, and thy strict laws will be
> Too hard for libertines in poetry.
> They will repeal the goodly exiled train
> Of gods and goddesses, which in thy just reign
> Were banished nobler poems, now, with these,
> The silenc'd tales o'th'Metamorphoses
> Shall stuff their lines, and swell the windy page...   (61–7)

At a first glance, this looks an accurate prediction: only the previous year, in 1632, George Sandys had published the second complete translation of the *Metamorphoses* into English. Carew may even have had Sandys in mind; though since he published a verse tribute to Sandys five years later, on the occasion of his divine poems, that would have become an embarrassment. But the goodly exiled train never returned with the same vivacious abundance they enjoyed in the sixteenth century, just as Sandys's translation, competent and succinct as it was, never attained the popularity of Arthur Golding's lively but clumsy fourteeners, first published in 1567, and reprinted six times within Shakespeare's lifetime.

But more important than Carew's prediction is his opinion: that mythology was a vice from which Donne had saved poetry. Any creative innovation in poetry will make what went before seem a windy page, and one can see why Donne's wit had that effect on the taste for myth and legend; but windy imitation of metaphysical conceits palls sooner than gods and goddesses, and the sixteenth-century love for Ovid is not in itself more vicious than the nineteenth-century love for Keats – and indeed must have felt liberating in a similar way. Just as the Romantic enthusiasm for Keatsian particularity involved a rejection of Augustan abstractions, so the Elizabethan discovery of Ovid involved detaching the stories at least partly from the heavy weight of moralising they had generally carried in the Middle Ages. How far this was done is a disputed question. Some scholars emphasise continuity, and insist that the *Ovide moralisé* survived vigorously into the seventeenth century; others see the Renaissance Ovid as freed from the medieval habit of reading for the allegory. It is not easy to decide. Both Golding and Sandys are moralisers, and both added commentaries to their translations. Golding's is the more naive, consisting either in simply naming the theme or emotion found in the story, or in tacking on a moral simple and implausible enough to please Alice's duchess; occasionally there is a touch of syncretism that finds a parallel to Christianity in the pagan myths. Sandys is much more sophisticated, taking his view of mythology mainly from Bacon, and showing his delight in multiple levels of reading: 'But why may not this fable receive a double construction?' he writes of the Actaeon story, 'Those being the best that admit of most senses'.[1] For practical purposes, however, what mattered most may be the simple fact that both left the text free of their glosses: Golding added an allegorising Epistle, and a Preface to the reader that is Puritan in content but syncretist in tone; Sandys added an elaborate prose commentary after each book. Both left the reader free to enjoy his Ovid if he wished, and many readers did.

There is one preliminary problem in discussing the presence of Ovid in sixteenth-century poetry: the difficulty of detecting it. If you absorbed Ovid, not perhaps with your mother's milk, but at any rate with your schoolmaster's rod, you – and your readers – might not know when you were using him. And if your literary taste included what Braden calls 'the sheer urge to flaunt',[2] the presence of a classical original might be something you would go out of your way to declare, or even to invent. We are better able to appreciate this than our more Romantic grandparents: Eliot and Pound reintroduced the idea of *imitatio* into our literary taste, and Harold Bloom has even suggested that the true subject of a poem is previous poetry. To hinder oversimplifying, I here invoke Thomas Nashe's scorn for those who 'feed on nought but the crumbs that fall from the Translator's trencher' and vaunt 'Ovid's and Plutarch's plumes as their own';[3] but far commoner was the claim that an admired poet was the modern Virgil or Ovid. Everyone knows Francis Meres's claim in 1598 that 'the sweet witty soul of Ovid lives in mellifluous and honey-tongued Shakespeare',[4] and the same compliment was paid to Daniel, Drayton and even Chapman.

Is Milton, for instance, drawing on Ovid when *Lycidas* (1637) moves from the death of Edward King to the death of any poet by describing the murder of Orpheus:

> What could the Muse herself that Orpheus bore,
> The Muse herself for her enchanting son
> Whom universal Nature did lament...? (58–60)

In *Amores* 3.9 (on the death of Tibullus) Ovid wrote:

> quid pater Ismario, quid mater, profuit Orpheo,
> carmine quid victas obstipuisse feras? (21–2)

What did his father or his mother profit Ismarian Orpheus, or his ability to conquer and freeze wild beasts with his song?

The whole poem develops the same train of thought as this paragraph of *Lycidas*: but what does it mean to point this out? Certainly it does not mean that *Lycidas* is an academic exercise, for the presence of Ovid in no way diminishes the emotional intensity; and does it mean that the reader must identify the imitation and include that knowledge in his reading? This will clearly depend, as Milton would have been the first to grant, on who the reader is.

A more extended example could be Shakespeare's Sonnet 140. In *Amores* 3.14 Ovid tell his mistress that she need not be virtuous, but must pretend to be so:

> quae facis, haec facito: tantum fecisse negato
> nec pudeat coram verba modesta loqui. (15-16)

Go on doing what you do; just tell me that you haven't done it, and don't be ashamed to speak modestly when in my presence.

Shakespeare gives the same advice:

> Be wise as thou art cruel; do not press
> My tongue-tied patience with too much disdain,
> Lest sorrow lend me words, and words express
> The manner of my pity-wanting pain.
> If I might teach thee wit, better it were,
> Though not to love, yet love to tell me so;
> As testy sick men, when their deaths be near,
> No news but health from their physicians know.
> For if I should despair I should grow mad,
> And in my madness might speak ill of thee.
> Now this ill-wresting world is grown so bad
> Mad slanderers by mad ears believed be.
>   That I may not be so, nor thou belied,
>   Bear thine eyes straight, though thy proud heart go wide.

There is no explicit reference to Ovid, and no line of the original is so well known as to suggest itself unprompted. It is not even clear that the poem would be enriched by an awareness of the original: the opposite might be truer, since Ovid's poem is set in a context of miscellaneous love poems, and Shakespeare's is one of a series that are obviously making the same reiterated points to the same woman, and therefore imply more clearly a particular situation. It is true that all the *Amores* appear to be addressed to Corinna, but the link this provides is often little more than a name, whereas one of the most striking qualities of Shakespeare's sonnets to the woman is the ghost of narrative that inhabits them: the repetitiveness and intensity seem to imply a strongly autobiographical source, yet the narrative details are never spelt out. It is as if the reader already knows them, or is being teased by the fact that he is not going to be told.

Yet Shakespeare must have known the *Amores*. What we are looking at is then the handling of a source – or the rehandling of a common tradition. We can certainly use Ovid's poem as a starting point – perhaps the best starting point – to establish exactly what Shakespeare's poem is doing. Once we do this, two differences appear: that Ovid is more explicit sexually, and that Shakespeare shows far more rhetorical complexity, and far more careful control of tone. Ovid does not hesitate to spell out the details of infidelity – rubbing thighs, varied postures, the shaking of the bed – and in her presence he sees not simply the evasive glance but the love bites on her neck (*collaque conspicio dentis habere notam* 34). In contrast, Shakespeare's sonnet is a cry of pain at her lack of love, not a prurient dwelling on her sexual exploits. Yet that she has been unfaithful is not left in doubt: no. 137 makes this quite clear, but still without details – a general image ('be anchored in the bay where all men ride') expresses his disgust. Sexual details are only inserted when they can be used for puns or other verbal ingenuities: he is contented 'to stand in thy affairs, fall by thy side'.

An elaborate fascination with rhetorical devices informs Sonnet 140 as it informs all these sonnets. Thus in 'Though not to love, yet love to tell me so', the second 'love' can be either an infinitive or a vocative; just as in 'might speak ill of thee'. 'ill' could be the object of 'speak' or an adverb ('slander thee'; 'speak as I should not'). There is a constant traffic in slight ambiguities, the alternative meanings being usually very similar, but creating an effect of shifting connotations. Since the whole poem is poised on the edge of fierce irony (culminating in 'belied'), the verbal effect is of the poet being in consummate control on one level, and helpless before shifts of meaning on another – an exact parallel to the fact that he is helpless as a man and in control as a poet. How relaxed about it all Ovid seems by comparison.

Shakespeare's 'sugared sonnets among his private friends' had been written by 1598: these sonnets to the woman are not sugar but wormwood, and may have been written later. Marlowe's translation of the *Amores* was not published until 1600, but Shakespeare might of course have known the work earlier, either by reading it in Latin, or by Marlowe's translation being circulated too among private friends. There is no external evidence for the common view that Marlowe wrote it when still a student, but it is clumsy enough to suggest no great experience in writing verse. Take for instance two of the most brilliantly suggestive of the poems, 1.4 and 1.5. In the former the poet attends a banquet with his mistress and her husband, and instructs her how to send secret signals:

> cum tibi succurret Veneris lascivia nostrae,
> purpureas tenero pollice tange genas. (21–2)

Intensely jealous, he begs her not to let her husband fondle her, nor to reveal what happens when she returns home with him. In 1.5, the poet describes a sexual encounter with Corinna on a hot afternoon: it is one of the most delicately erotic of all the *Amores*, moving from the shadows of the darkened room, through the advent of Corinna, clad in a light tunic which he pulls off (*nec multum rara nocebat*: 'it was so thin that it did me little harm', or 'that its loss did her little harm'? – the ambiguity is almost Shakespearian) to an enthusiastic outburst about her body (*quantum et quale latus! quam iuvenale femur!*: 'what a flank – and how much of it! and what a youthful thigh!') and so to a concluding litotes: *cetera quis nescit*? ('who doesn't know the rest?')

Marlowe botches a good deal in these two poems. Ovid's instruction to touch her cheek with her thumb when she thinks about their pleasures (above) becomes a line that is awkward to the point of puzzlement: 'Thy rosy cheeks be to thy thumb inclined'. Ovid's neat complaint that the husband can demand of right the pleasures that he enjoys in secret (*quod mihi das furtim, iure coacta dabis* 4.64) loses its rhetorical balance without even becoming idiomatic: 'But force thee give him my stol'n honey bliss'. Much of Marlowe's clumsiness may derive from his care to turn each line of the original into a line of English verse, and his version has had its staunch defenders – most interesting of them, perhaps, Lee T. Pearcy, who remarks 'the Ovid translations do not succeed; but their failure dazzles', and claims that Marlowe sometimes uses latinate word-order to imply a suppositious original (a 'second, ghostly Latin text') not actually in Ovid.[5] And occasionally he finds a line that strikes exactly the right note, and the translation turns not only into English, but into the ease of the accomplished versifier:

> saepe mihi dominaeque meae properata voluptas
> veste sub iniecta dulce peregit opus.   (47–8)

> I and my wench oft under clothes did lurk
> when pleasure moved us to our sweetest work.

Marlowe hardly ever rises to this, but there are neat touches in 1.5 as well. The ambiguity of '*nec multum rara nocebat*' is admirably retained ('being thin, the harm was small'), and the last line, when Ovid wishes '*proveniant medii sic mihi saepe dies*', catches the tired note of contentment very well through its one slightly amused polysyllable: 'Jove send me more such afternoons as this'.

But for the true English imitation of the sweet (or sour) and witty Ovid, we should turn to Donne's *Elegies*. Here are many of the Ovidian themes, brilliantly recaptured: impassioned praise of nakedness ('To his Mistress going to bed'), or the vivid torturing of the unfortunate husband of 1.4 (in Donne he has become a more groteque figure):

> We must not, as we us'd, flout openly,
> In scoffing riddles, his deformity;
> Nor at his board together being sat,
> With words, not touch, scarce looks adulterate.   (*Elegy* 1.17–20)

Here too we find one of the most brilliant versions of the love–war parallel. This widespread topos goes back to Horace as well as to Ovid (*Ars Amatoria* 2.233ff; *Amores* 1.9), who works out the parallels with some care:

> pervigilant ambo, terra requiescit uterque;
> ille fores dominae servat, at ille ducis.   (7–8)

> Both do without sleep; each lies on the ground; the one goes forth to serve his mistress, the other the general.

But Ovid's poem seems tame compared with Donne's vitality. Donne spends little time establishing the analogy, but leaps into a survey of the wars going on all around:

> Sick Ireland is with a strange war possessed
> Like to'an Ague, now raging, now at rest... (20.13–14)

Then, turning to love's war, Donne rehearses the commonplace analogy with wit and a kind of verbal passion:

> Here let me war; in these arms let me lie;
> Here let me parley, batter, bleed, and die.
> Thine arms imprison me, and mine arms thee;
> Thy heart thy ransom is, take mine for me.
> Other men war that they their rest may gain,
> But we will rest that we may fight again. (29–34)

Perhaps the most vivid of all the Elegies is no. 16, which begs his mistress not to disguise herself as a page and follow him like a Shakespearian heroine:

> By our first strange and fatal interview,
> By all desires which thereof did ensue,
> By our long starving hopes, by that remorse
> Which my words' masculine persuasive force
> Begot in thee, and by the memory
> Of hurts which spies and rivals threatened me,
> I calmly beg... (16. 1–7)

The mounting movement of this opening must always have seized readers; today, the line we are most likely to single out is the fourth. The speaker may beg rather than command, but his language has the assertiveness we now think of as masculine. What Donne takes from Ovid may be above all his masculinity: masculine cynicism, masculine power, masculine brilliance. The love–war analogy may not simply be a chance for striking analogies, it may be a view of love that belongs to men rather than women (even when the woman is the warrior, the poem is still written by a man). To say all this has now ceased to be a compliment: there is an unawareness of the sensibility of the other that converts brilliance into a kind of bullying. It is not easy to know just what the ramifications of this observation are. Does it apply to all love-poetry? If not, which are the feminine love-poems? They will not simply be those written by women. And can we see it as a virtue in Donne (or Ovid) that instead of disguising their masculinity as worship or compliment, they flaunt it so openly? These wonderful opening lines are active not passive, self-centred not considerate, brilliant not patient. Would Donne be as good a poet if he listened more?

The Ovid who mattered most to the sixteenth century was not the love-poet but the mythographer, and the *Metamorphoses* is both his most important and his most influential poem. There had been verse collections of myths before

Ovid, and the idea of using metamorphosis as a unifying thread had been used before him. If one asks what is common to all myths, the most likely answers today would emphasise death and immortality, natural processes and man's relationship with nature. Compared with these, metamorphosis seems almost quaint, and we can ask how seriously Ovid took it: certainly some of the metamorphoses, unmentioned till the end of the story, are cursory; but the terse is not necessarily the trivial. Ovid's version of the Narcissus story runs to nearly 170 lines, of which only the last two tell us

> nusquam corpus erat, croceum pro corpore florem
> inveniunt foliis medium cingentibus albis. (3.509–10)

His body had disappeared; and instead of a body, they found a yellow flower encircled with white petals.

This is very similar to the brief metamorphosis at the end of Shakespeare's *Venus and Adonis*, though Shakespeare expands the two lines to four, and then adds a simile to circle back to Adonis:

> By this the boy that by her side lay kill'd
> Was melted like a vapour from her sight,
> And in his blood that on the ground lay spill'd,
> A purple flower sprung up, checkered with white,
>   Resembling well his pale cheeks and the blood
>   Which in round drops upon their whiteness stood. (1165–70)

To see how much this is still in the spirit of Ovid, we can contrast the very different metamorphoses of Marston and Lodge. In *The Metamorphosis of Pygmalion's Image* (1598), Pygmalion caresses Galatea and takes her to bed while she is still marble, begging her to turn into flesh; this removes all element of surprise, and so removes all sense of the numinous; in its place we have sexual perversion – which Marston makes worse by refusing, at some prurient length, to describe what happened after the change.

In *Scylla's Metamorphosis* (1589) Lodge has an equally damaging change. Whereas in Ovid Scylla is changed into a monster by the baleful magic of Circe, who also loves Glaucus, Lodge removes Circe (and also the changing of Glaucus into a sea-god) and causes Scylla merely to melt away as she laments her hopeless love: again the mystery has gone, and we can see that saving the metamorphosis for a sudden sharp ending may be the most powerful way to introduce it.

If metamorphosis is not merely quaint, what is its significance? Nature after all has its own metamorphoses: pupation, hatching, birth. The changes into flowers, stars or birds that form the climax of so many myths can be seen as an invitation to find apparently magical changes in our own life-cycle. For a story of seduction, rape or even happy consummation to conclude with the magic of metamorphosis can act as a reminder of mystery: the mystery of those natural processes we are tampering with. That blood should empurple a flower, that Daphne should become a tree or Arethusa a spring: that the act of sex should change a woman's shape, that the pains of childbearing should produce a new life or a blow from a stone should end one, even that a grub should turn to a pupa, then to a butterfly. Need the second list seem stranger than the first?

Sex, generation and death are clearly the areas of human metamorphosis, and these are the themes of the Elizabethan epyllion. A story of sexual love can include or (more probably) end with happy fulfilment; it is more likely to contain frustrated, sublimated or perverted sex. This need not mean that the story itself is perverted: it is the nature of narrative that fulfilment can be implied through the treatment of shortcomings and indirection, and in Ovid they are not always easy to distinguish. Even the same images can imply either. Take for instance, the hermaphrodite, an obvious image for frustration or displacement: Spenser uses it in one of his most splendid passages of fulfilled love (so successful a passage that he felt obliged to cut it out when he decided that the story was to continue instead of ending there):

> Had ye them seen, ye would have surely thought
> That they had been that faire Hermaphrodite,
> Which that rich Roman of white marble wrought
> And in his costly bath caused to be site,
> So seemed those two, as grown together quite. (*FQ* III xii 46)

It is time now to turn to the epyllia themselves, and especially to the two most famous of them, written at almost exactly the same time, Marlowe's *Hero and Leander* and Shakespeare's *Venus and Adonis* (no one is sure which influenced which). The Hero and Leander story comes from the *Heroides*, where the lovers exchange letters full of conceits and antitheses: Leander is exhausted, then sees the fire on Hero's tower and says *meus ignis in illo est* (18.85). Hero does and does not want Leander to swim to her through the dangerous water (*Me miseram! cupio non persuadere, quod hortor*: 19.187). Marlowe's poem owes little to these elegant variations, and suggests rather the rich narrative world of the *Metamorphoses*.

The central effect of *Hero and Leander* derives from its blend of the magnificent and the ironic, the rich sensuousness and the knowing amused commentary. On the one hand we have:

> as she spake
> Forth from those two tralucent cisterns brake
> A stream of liquid pearl, which down her face
> Made milk-white paths, whereon the gods might trace
> To Jove's high court. (I. 295 ff)

And on the other the amused disdain of Marlowe's double rhymes:

> By this sad Hero, with love unacquainted,
> Viewing Leander's face, fell down and fainted. (II.1–2)

Since much of the magnificence is lavished on the persons of the lovers, it is worth observing how differently they are described. The lines on Hero's tears are in fact untypical, since there is little description of her body and much of her clothes: it is not only Hero but also the coral she wears which blushes. Leander spends far more of the poem naked than she does, and his body is lovingly handled by Neptune and (verbally) by Marlowe (who had after all said, if Baines is to be believed, that all who love not tobacco and boys are fools[6]):

> His body was as straight as Circe's wand;
> Jove might have sipped out nectar from his hand.
> Even as delicious meat is to the taste,
> So was his neck in touching, and surpassed
> The white of Pelops' shoulder. I could tell ye
> How smooth his breast was, and how white his belly,
> And whose immortal fingers did imprint
> That heavenly path with many a curious dint
> That runs along his back...   (I.61ff)

This is not the poetry of cherry lips and swansdown neck, but a self-conscious toying with the pleasures of analogy, and with the resources of myth as signifier. Some of the details seem deliberately mischievous: why should the wand whose straightness is invoked be Circe's, if not to flout the usual association of Circe *moralisée* with vice and depravity? And the next line tells us that Leander had a finer and cleaner hand than Ganymede (who used a cup when serving), and thus has homosexual implications. The most extended touch of homosexuality comes in the advances made by Neptune when Leander is swimming, and is one of the deftest passages in the poem:

> He clapped his plump cheeks, with his tresses played,
> And smiling wantonly, his love bewrayed.
> He watched his arms, and as they opened wide
> At every stroke, betwixt them would he slide
> And steal a kiss...   (II.180ff)

The elegance of this resides, of course, in the way it hovers between a literal description of Neptune's homosexual advances, and a figurative description of the way the swimmer's body slides through the water: Neptune is mocked for his infatuation, and at the same time celebrated because he is caressing Leander's body just as the poetry is. And the view of myth implied is, for once, not that of metamorphosis. Here the mythological theme is not magic and mystery, but nature itself. Golding has touches of this view: in his *Epistle* he explains the story of Deucalion in naturalistic terms:

> And forbecause that he and his were driven a while to dwell
> Among the stony hills and rocks until the water fell,
> The Poets hereupon did take occasion for to feign
> That he and Pyrrha did repair mankind of stones again.   (507–10)

This is a crude version of what Marlowe does much more subtly. Regenerating mankind from stones means that the survivors lived among the rocks; Neptune's sexual advances means that the water caresses your body.

There is then less direct description than we might at first think; and there is also less straightforward characterisation. It is easy to point out (and several critics have) that the characters of the lovers are not consistent: Leander is at one moment a polished seducer, at another is sexually naive, Hero is by turns innocent, eager, spiteful and helpless. But to expect coherence of characterisation is to push the poem into a straitjacket it refuses to wear: it is richer to see it as exploring alternative views of love, the lovers shifting as they fit into these. Three views of sexual love have been traditional in European poetry, and all three are found here. Love as a game, in which deception, delay and pleading are in themselves enjoyable, is central to the *Amores*, and Marlowe plays the game well:

> Like untuned golden strings all women are,
> Which long time lie untouched, will harshly jar.   (I.229–30)

Love as war can be explored in the same playful spirit, but can also be taken seriously as an image for the exploitation of women, as Marlowe does in a sudden strong, even frightening couplet:

> So that the truce was broke, and she alas
> (Poor silly maiden) at his mercy was.
> Love is not full of pity (as men say)
> But deaf and cruel where he means to prey.   (II.285ff)

Finally there is love as mutual delight, and love-poetry as a celebration of that joy: Marlowe puts this at the climax, and it is difficult to know whether to call that Ovidian or not. The *Ars Amatoria* does prefer the pleasure to be mutual, but its remorselessly masculine and even cynical perspective prevents any true concept of mutuality, beyond the merely physiological. Looking at his poem as a whole, we might feel the same about Marlowe, but when *Hero and Leander* does shed its masculinity, it achieves a tenderness unknown to the Ovid of the love-poems:

> And now she wished this night were never done,
> And sighed to think upon th'approaching sun.   (II.301–2)

If then we place the ambivalence of love at the centre of the poem, we shall not much mind its inconsistencies. Indeed, to enter Venus' temple is immediately to be shown a central inconsistency. The mosaics we find there would belong in Spenser's House of Busyrane, where all the gods are shown as victims of Cupid, degraded by their passion; but in Marlowe's description there is no moralising:

> There might you see the gods in sundry shapes,
> Committing heady riots, incests, rapes:...
> Jove slyly stealing from his sister's bed
> To dally with Idalian Ganymede.   (I.143ff)

Looking after this temple is a priestess vowed to chastity: what could be more paradoxical? Leander does not hesitate to point this out, and to call Hero a 'holy idiot'. Yet the paradox of 'Venus' nun' makes sense. Sexual delay and reluctance are necessary preliminaries to sexual initiation, and the depth of the reluctance may determine the intensity of the eventual delight.

There is no direct evidence that Marlowe regarded his poem as a fragment, though it does of course leave the story unfinished. When Chapman continued it he divided it into two, added four more sections, and called them sestiads (playing of course on 'six' and 'Sestos'). Chapman's version has little of Marlowe's sensuous splendour, and none of his irony; it has a good deal of melodrama, a good deal of moralising, including italicised 'sentences' and a reproach from Ceremony, and is full of laboured conceits, some of them among the commonplaces of Elizabethan poetry:

> If then Leander did my maidenhead get,
> Leander being myself, I still retain it. (III.359-60)

Fuller's anecdote of Shakespeare and Jonson describes how Jonson 'like a Spanish great galleon...was built far higher in learning', and Shakespeare like an English man of war 'could turn with all tides, tack about and take advantage of all winds by the quickness of his wit and invention'.[7] It may be unfair to Jonson, but it is an admirable description of the difference between Chapman and Marlowe.

Three years before his completion of *Hero and Leander*, Chapman published *Ovid's Banquet of Sense* (1595). This very strange poem describes how Ovid hid in the Emperor's garden to spy on Julia, his daughter, and saw Corinna bathing. The delight of beholding her naked is described at great length under the heading of each of the five senses in turn. Hearing, smell and sight are satisfied while he is still hidden; he makes himself known to her to beg a kiss (taste), but is interrupted before he can have the pleasures of touch. The subtitle, *A coronet for his Mistress Philosophy*, is hardly Ovidian, and the poem is a twisted piece of Renaissance neoplatonism. It claims to lift us from the level of body to that of soul, but the claim involves a central confusion: the senses are celebrated for their spiritual effect, and those who do not enjoy them are dismissed as 'mere flesh'. The confusion is so great that Frank Kermode has suggested that the poem condemns Ovid, showing the collapse of his soul into bestiality. This is certainly untenable, because of the close resemblance between the narrative voice and Ovid's own self-defence. There is no way of rescuing Chapman from his confusion, but it is built out of many of the commonplaces of Renaissance art and thought. A naked woman can be an emblem of the soul, and the spiritual is often treated by Donne as if it were a refinement rather than a rejection of the sensuous. The ladder of analogy underlies much of the poem's imagery:

> Sweet sounds and odours are the heavens, on earth
> Where virtues live, of virtuous men deceased... (325-6)

– and the elitism of the preface is certainly platonist:

The profane multitude I hate, and only consecrate my strange Poems to these searching spirits, who learning hath made noble and nobility sacred.

This very un-Ovidian poem comes so close, at moments, to exposing absurdities in the flesh–spirit analogy, without ever turning into parody, that we can call it, in modern parlance, a deconstruction of the doctrine.

Yet Chapman too has his occasional Ovidian touches. Into *Ovid's Banquet* he slips a stanza that could come from the *Ars Amatoria* (11.433–441: 'Attempts and not entreats get Ladies' largess'); and in his *Hero and Leander* there are a couple of extra metamorphoses. In the 3rd Sestiad Leander's perspiration sprinkles the earth and leaves a 'snowy foam' from which the 'first white roses spring'; in the 5th, Adolesche is for no particular reason changed into a parrot. And we are given our full share of digressions: virtually the whole of the 5th Sestiad is taken up with the tale of Teras: lovers change hearts, Hymen disguises himself as a girl, maids are captured by robbers, there are extended similes, numerology, a wedding and its consummation – a farrago of the truly Ovidian and of the Elizabethan Ovid.

Francis Beaumont's *Salmacis and Hermaphroditus* (1602) is more truly Ovidian. Ovid's version of the story comes in *Metamorphoses* 4.285–388, and is straightforward enough (though itself an insert): Salmacis falls in love with the beautiful youth Hermaphroditus and tries to rape him, he resists, and she wraps herself so tightly round him that they are turned into a single person, *nec femina nec puer*. Most of the 100-odd lines are taken up with Salmacis' dislike of hunting (she was the only Naiad *non nota Dianae*), with the beauty of Hermaphroditus, and above all with his athletic struggles to preserve his virtue from her. Beaumont's poem (nine times the length of Ovid's version) both elaborates details and inserts extra stories. To begin with he anticipates the story by having Diana fall in love with (and throw herself at) Hermaphroditus before the Diana-like Salmacis appears on the scene, and Jove falls in love with Salmacis – which unleashes an elaborate digression in which Jove visits Astraea's palace and finds Venus plotting against her husband Vulcan: the digression performs an elaborate arc before it rejoins the story, as does the even more elaborate second digression in which Mercury steals Apollo's chariot wheels. Beaumont also uses the story of Narcissus, an obvious parallel, and frequently invoked:

> Remember how the gods punisht that boy
> That scorn'd to let a beauteous nymph enjoy
> Her long wisht pleasure   (703–5)

– an Ovidian sentiment that is not in Ovid. Indeed, since Hermaphroditus and Salmacis are hardly ever named, it is easy to drop into assuming that we are reading about Narcissus and Echo.

Ovid and the Elizabethans

In the end, Mercury and Venus are persuaded by their son to bestow a magic power on the stream, that any man who bathes there shall suffer the same fate, and be changed into a hermaphrodite. In Ovid we are told that they stain the water with baleful power; in Beaumont:

> His parents harkened to his last request,
> And with that great power they the fountain blest.   (919–20)

Is 'blest' careless, or ironic? Or is Beaumont writing with a high degree of self-consciousness, so that the fountain is blest because it yields so much narrative?

Digressions are one of the most prominent features of the epyllia. There are tales within tales in the *Metamorphoses* itself: many of the myths in Book 4, for instance, are inserted into the story of Bacchus and the daughters of Minyas. But the Elizabethans took up the device with enthusiasm, inserting elaborate and invented stories with the most casual of excuses. Beaumont's two lengthy digressions are probably his most inventive passages, and the blending of the story with the Narcissus–story can also be seen as a kind of assimilated digression. Marlowe's one elaborate digression is perhaps even more extravagant: to explain the unsurprising 'fact' that the Fates hate Cupid, he inserts the elaborate story of Hermes and the nymph, the theft of nectar from Hebe, and the banishing of Jupiter. This too, but in a very different sense from Chapman – more conscious and more mischievous – can be seen as a deconstruction of the aetiological myth.

Why is digression so important in these poems? To make up a myth is both to accept and to make fun of its explanatory power. Myths are not personal but transmitted, yet the individual who makes up his own is breaking the rules in a way that responds to what myth has given him. Picking at random a tiny detail that hardly needs explaining, then constructing an absurdly roundabout explanation, most of which does no explaining, and tacking on the final detail as cursorily as a metamorphosis – all this is to mock, but in a way that reinforces the power of what is mocked.

Here is a very different kind of digression:

> Imperiously he leaps, he neighs, he bounds,
> And now his woven girths he breaks asunder;
> The bearing earth with his hard hoof he wounds,
> Whose hollow womb resounds like heaven's thunder.
> (Shakespeare, *Venus and Adonis* 265–8)

At the point in his epyllion where we might expect one of Venus' previous adventures, or an elaborately invented explanation of why she loves Adonis, Shakespeare gives us the sexual eagerness of Adonis' horse – 11 stanzas of it, and, later in the poem, when Venus urges Adonis to hunt something safer than the boar – a hare for instance – we get six stanzas about the hare. What makes these digressions unusual is not their length, but the fact that they are not stories. The epyllion is above all a genre devoted to narrative, normally to

133

narrative about the gods; its paganism looks away from nature to myth or (as Coleridge unkindly put it when preferring Hebrew poetry to Greek), for the Greeks 'all natural objects were *dead* – mere hollow statues – but there was a godkin or goddessling *included* in each'.[8] It is not in such poetry that we would expect to find the Wordsworthian variety of natural appearances, or a Hardyesque love of minute particulars:

> If I pass during some nocturnal blackness, mothy and warm,
>   When the hedgehog travels furtively over the lawn,
> One may say 'He strove that such delicate creatures should come to no harm.
>   But he could do little for them; and now he is gone'.   ('Afterwards')

Yet in *Venus and Adonis* we do find something very similar:

> By this poor Wat, far off upon a hill,
> Stands on his hinder-legs with list'ning ear,
> To hearken if his foes pursue him still...
> Then shalt thou see the dew-bedabbled wretch
> Turn, and return, indenting with the way.   (697–9, 703–4)

Shakespeare too was a man who used to notice such things. Or (to put it differently) Shakespeare demythologises: in the very act of telling us about the godkins, he looks at the natural objects direct.

Venus and Adonis also undercuts the myth by its treatment of Adonis, struggling to resist the insistent advances of (I cannot better C. S. Lewis's description) a 'flushed, panting, perspiring, suffocating, loquacious creature' who 'is supposed to be the goddess of love herself'.[9] Poor Adonis, embarrassed and petulant, wants only to get on with his hunting:

> 'Fie, fie,' he says, 'you crush me; let me go,
> You have no reason to withhold me so.'   (610–11)

Was Shakespeare the first to invert matters in this way? The only precedent specific to this story is Titian's painting (Pl. 4), where a very brisk-looking Adonis (much more masculine and athletic than Shakespeare's!) is tearing himself away from the clutches of an importunate Venus; but there are precedents for aggressive female wooers and timid youths – an inversion of the dominant convention of the importunate youth and the reluctant maiden that there must have been considerable psychological pressures to devise. Hippolytus is one, and (as we have seen) Salmacis and Hermaphroditus, and more immediately there is Lodge's *Scylla's Metamorphosis* (1589), which can claim to be the first English epyllion. Lodge's demanding female produces rhetorical antitheses and abstract nouns in droves, but has none of the overwhelming physical presence of Shakespeare's:

> With this she seizeth on his sweating palm,
> The precedent of pith and livelihood,
> And trembling in her passion, calls it balm,
> Earth's sovereign salve to do a goddess good:
>   Being so enrag'd, desire doth lend her force
>   Courageously to pluck him from his horse.   (25–30)

Ovid and the Elizabethans

It is all great fun – and not, in its burlesque, unusual. Marlowe was not the only Elizabethan to mock at the story he was telling: it is almost standard practice in the epyllion. Sometimes, as in the Pyramus and Thisbe story in *A Midsummer Night's Dream* or in Nashe's prose parody of *Hero and Leander*, we are given mere mockery; more common is a blend of the comic and celebratory, as we find, in their very different ways, in *Hero and Leander* and in *Romeo and Juliet*, where mockery enriches the mocked. And in *Venus and Adonis* too, that fleshly and loquacious goddess is able to shift imperceptibly into the tender or the richly sensuous:

> Full gently now she takes him by the hand,
> A lily prison'd in a gaol of snow,
> Or ivory in an alabaster band:
> So white a friend engirts so white a foe. (361–4)

Ambivalence is central to Elizabethan mythology. The culture itself must have demanded ambivalence: where belief is Christian and education is classical, where the authors offered as models are all telling lies, there must be a sense in which the reader both does and does not accept the authority of learning. Syncretism is of course the standard device for dealing with this situation, and the retelling of myths led to a special variety of syncretism, in which there is an amused scepticism at these old-fashioned stories (that of course derives from Ovid himself) as well as sheer enjoyment of them. Those who mock most are also those who enjoy most.

So that is the pagan stuffing of old idols from which Donne 'rescued' English poetry! Donne owes his twentieth-century popularity, more than anything, to the belief that sensuousness and wit are compatible, that a poem can both mock and celebrate its subject. By this criterion, the Marlowe of *Hero and Leander*, the Shakespeare of *Venus and Adonis*, to say nothing of the Ovid who lies behind them, could easily be metamorphosed into the sons of Donne.

9

OVID'S NARCISSUS AND SHAKESPEARE'S RICHARD II: THE REFLECTED SELF

A. D. Nuttall

SHAKESPEARE'S RICHARD II is the most elaborately Narcissistic of his heroes. In this essay I propose to explore first the kinship and then the difference between Ovid's story of Narcissus in the third book of the *Metamorphoses* and Shakespeare's play. More particularly I shall be concerned with the startlingly complicated things great poets can do with mirrors.

Richard II is presented by Shakespeare as the anointed king whose power is violently usurped by Bolingbroke. At the same time, he is shown as egoistical, capricious and strangely prone to turn his own situation into a story, so that, with a certain excess or overflow of consciousness, he seems to understand everything about current events except the fact that they are really happening. In Act III, Scene ii, when news reaches the king of the falling-away of his supporters, Aumerle puts the practical question, 'Where is the Duke my father with his power?' (143). Richard simply brushes the question aside:

> No matter where – of comfort no man speak:
> Let's talk of graves, of worms, and epitaphs...
> Our lands, our lives, and all are Bolingbroke's
> And nothing can we call our own but death,
> And that small model of the barren earth
> Which serves as paste and cover to our bones.
> For God's sake let us sit upon the ground
> And tell sad stories of the death of kings:
> How some have been depos'd, some slain in war,
> Some haunted by the ghosts they have deposed,
> Some poisoned by their wives, some sleeping kill'd,
> All murthered – for within the hollow crown
> That rounds the mortal temples of a king
> Keeps Death his court, and there the antic sits,
> Scoffing his state and grinning at his pomp.   (III ii 144–5, 151–63)

It is a tremendous speech, richly redolent of the dark, doom-laden world of the Histories – the sort of speech that finds its way into anthologies. But as long as we treat the speech as merely an especially splendid example of the sort of thing that goes on in these plays we are making a mistake – oddly enough, a *logical* mistake. Anthologies abolish context, but in listening to this speech we need to be especially alert to context if we are to feel the real weirdness of Richard's words. That is why I included what an anthologist would exclude, Aumerle's urgent question.

It is not that Richard is responding in a manner which we, outside the fiction, can construe as poetical. He is himself enjoying the poetry, the literary flavour, as if he were one of us, a spectator of the action rather than a leading participant. We need to spell this out in elementary terms. Shakespeare's plays are for the most part written in verse, but the characters, within the fiction, are not normally aware that they are speaking verse. Similarly they are allowed a measure of poetic linguistic richness seldom if ever found in ordinary discourse, but this poetry is the poet's, not theirs. With Richard, however, this convention, normally secure, seems to slip. In traditional Shakespeare criticism he has been called variously 'the poet king' and 'the player king', in an attempt to register the fact that the logical division between the real world of the spectator and the fiction of the play is spectrally repeated *within* the fiction, so that Richard can strut to and fro, 'appreciating' the spectacle as though he were a spectator. The effect is of course necessarily fugitive, with a smell of perversity – even of schizophrenia – about it. For, within the play, Richard really is the king, really is about to be deposed, really is to die. He relishes 'as poetry' what is indeed poetry for us but is for him mere, imminent fact. Thus his speech is not an ordinary specimen of the way people talk in Shakespeare's Histories. Rather it is, so to speak, doubly literary. Shakespeare has his doomed king deliberately evoke all the fallen princes of *The Mirror for Magistrates* with a separate consciousness of language and atmosphere. It is indeed the world of the Histories, but it is that world distilled for us by an oddly aloof Olympian consciousness. At the same time (and here lies the peculiar force of the play) Richard is not Olympian, not detached. He is about to die in his own poem. The face he contemplates as if it were a picture is his own face. And all this is – very slightly – mad.

There is a sense in which Richard is more realistic than those around him. The help desperately sought by the practical Aumerle is not to be had. Richard clairvoyantly perceives what is coming towards him, but he distances it, pluralises it, generalises it by seeing it as image rather than reality. Indeed there may be a further subtlety whereby Shakespeare suggests that Richard's antici- patory, artistic sense of the way the plot is going may actually help the events to occur. As a playwright masterminds the episodes of a play Richard master- minds and perhaps, to a certain extent, creates his own undoing. His adversary, Bolingbroke, is psychologically underdrawn. Where Richard has a reduplicated consciousness, Bolingbroke seems conversely to lack full consciousness of what he is doing, to be much less of a purposive agent than a plot-summary would suggest. It is Richard who defines Bolingbroke's acts as rebellion, as usurpation. Bolingbroke seems merely to move, mutely, into spaces vacated for him – with elaborate and ironic art – by Richard. When we come to the great scene of deposition we find that it is Richard who presides over his own dethronement.

Ovid's Narcissus and Shakespeare's Richard II

It is, as Walter Pater said,[1] an inverse ritual, an upside-down coronation, and Richard relishes the element of literary paradox in this.

Nevertheless, although we may allow a certain prophetic realism and even a degree of self-destructive historical efficacy to Richard we still feel that, in all the brilliant displays of self-awareness, he is somehow not aware for most of the play of the real Richard. It is as if, in order to be conscious of the self, we must to some extent objectify the self, and a self which has been turned into an object is no longer, truly, a self. In the act of introspection the real self will be that which is doing the introspecting, and that which is being introspected will be some sort of image. Hence the correlation in Richard's nature of a centripetal introspective impulse with a centrifugal tendency to turn everything, even his own death, into a remote, contemplate-able image. All of this is remarkable both as art and psychology. We need to remember that Shakespeare is not able to build on a pre-existing foundation of subtle interior characterisation in novels. There is much here that is being done for the first time in English literature. But it seems possible that in older civilisations material which we address directly in psychological language was explored – often with an astonishing though uncontrolled subtlety – through myth. The latent analogy between much mythological narrative and some psychological explanations became explicit when Freud began freely to borrow from Greek sources: Oedipus, Electra and – of course – Narcissus.

We have isolated as central to Richard's nature the co-existence of self-regard and self-projection. These terms are highly abstract, redolent of the polysyllabic twentieth century. If we try to re-express the thought in *image* terms we shall find that there is one image which immediately conveys the required tension: the mirror.[2] The face in the glass is oneself and yet not oneself, a mere projected image. This lies at the heart of the Narcissus story. Shakespeare never mentions Narcissus in *Richard II* and I doubt whether he even so much as thought of him when forming his conception of the protagonist. In his early poems Shakespeare shows that he associates Narcissus with self-love, beauty and paradoxes of freedom and possession. Thus he writes in *Venus and Adonis*,

'Is thine own heart to thine own face affected?
Can thy right hand seize love upon thy left?
Then woo thyself, be of thyself rejected;
Steal thine own freedom, and complain on theft.
 Narcissus so himself himself forsook,
 And died to kiss his shadow in the brook'   (157–62)

where 'Steal thine own freedom' shows the young poet throwing off, in joyous rivalry, a Shakespearian answer to the Ovidian paradox *inopem me copia fecit* (*Met.* 3.466). In *The Rape of Lucrece* he writes,

Whereat she smiled with so sweet a cheer
That had Narcissus seen her as she stood.
Self-love had never drown'd him in the flood.   (264–6)

The only[3] other place where Shakespeare refers to Narcissus himself is *Antony and Cleopatra*:

> Hadst thou Narcissus in thy face, to me
> Thou wouldst appear most ugly.   (II vi 96–7)

But the Ovidian story of Narcissus and Echo is powerfully evoked by Juliet's words,

> Bondage is hoarse, and may not speak aloud,
> Else would I tear the cave where Echo lies,
> And make her airy tongue more hoarse than mine...
>
> (*Romeo and Juliet* II ii 160–2)

Shakespeare has remembered how Echo, despised, wandered among caves.[4] Ever since R. K. Root's study[5] which set the tone for the twentieth-century reassessment of Shakespeare's classical learning, most scholars have been aware that Ovid was an engrossing influence on Shakespeare. Nor was his knowledge confined to Golding's version. Even the grudging J. A. K. Thomson concedes that 'Undoubtedly he read a certain amount, perhaps a good deal, of Ovid in Ovid's words.'[6] T. W. Baldwin sums the matter up when he writes, 'Ovid was Shakespeare's master of poetry...No other poet ancient or modern receives such attention.'[7] More generally, Ovid was of all the classical poets, the one who most nourished literature in the sixteenth century.[8] Moreover the first English translation from the *Metamorphoses* in the sixteenth century is a version of the Narcissus story – Thomas Howell's *The fable of Ovid treting of Narcissus*, five years before Golding's translation.[9]

Yet, while all this is true, Shakespeare makes no use of Ovid in building the character and situation of Richard II. There are only two hints to the contrary – and they are faint indeed. The first is a certain Ovidian sensuousness in his description of the rising pallor driving the blood from the King's cheek in II i 118. We may compare with this Ovid's description of Narcissus' complexion, '*in niveo mixtum candore ruborem*', 'mingled red with snowy white' at *Metamorphoses* 3.423 and the comparison at 483–6 of his bruised skin to fruit – apples and grapes – flushing as they ripen (we may further remember that 'face', a word of power in *Richard II*, is to figure later in Cleopatra's allusion to Narcissus). But the likeness is fugitive and certainly cannot be securely identified as an Ovidian allusion. The second hint of Ovidian influence comes in the words of Bolingbroke at IV i 292–3:

> The shadow of your sorrow hath destroy'd
> The shadow of your face.

Compare with this *Metamorphoses* 3.434: *ista repercussae quam cernis, imaginis umbra est.* ('What you see is but the shadow of a reflected form.')[10] It is just possible that *repercussae*, despite the fact that it here means 'reflected', could have suggested to Shakespeare the idea of a *shattered* image. Again, however, because the idea is commonplace we cannot be sure that an allusion was intended. It is better to confess that we are dealing not with a matter of direct, specific influence but with a powerful literary analogy. Richard is Narcissus, not by allusion but by his nature. And the matter is clinched by the mirror.

As the reflection in the pool is at the heart of Ovid's story, so the reflection in the glass is at the heart of Shakespeare's play. When the moment of deposition comes, Richard calls for a mirror:

> Give me that glass, and therein will I read.
> No deeper wrinkles yet? Hath sorrow struck
> So many blows upon this face of mine,
> And made no deeper wounds? O flatt'ring glass,
> Like to my followers in prosperity,
> Thou dost beguile me! Was this face the face
> That every day under his household roof
> Did keep ten thousand men? Was this the face
> That like the sun, did make beholders wink?
> Is this the face which fac'd so many follies,
> That was at last out-fac'd by Bolingbroke?
> A brittle glory shineth in this face,
> As brittle as the glory is the face,
>   [Dashes the glass against the ground.]
> For there it is, crack'd in an hundred shivers.
> Mark, silent king, the moral of this sport,
> How soon my sorrow hath destroy'd my face.   (IV i 276–91)

It is then that Bolingbroke, 'the silent king', tells him that the shadow of his sorrow has destroyed the shadow of his face.

It is time we turned to Ovid. Narcissus, Ovid tells us, was the son of a nymph, Liriope, who was raped by a river, Cephisus. Teiresias the seer predicted that Narcissus would reach maturity only *if he never knew himself* (Met. 3.348). Already we have water and perilous self-knowledge. Narcissus reached his sixteenth year, a boy of astonishing beauty, attractive to both males and females but responsive to neither (353–5). Like Hippolytus in Euripides' play he seems to have preferred hunting. He was driving deer into his nets when Echo (another nymph) saw him and fell in love with him. Echo still had a body (she became a disembodied voice shortly afterwards) but, as now, could utter no words of her own, but could only repeat the last sounds she heard (359–61). She is, notice, an '*auditory* mirror'.

This gives Ovid an opportunity for some brilliantly mannered writing in which the last sounds of Narcissus' refusal are translated, in the mouth of Echo, into a profession of love: 'I'll die before I'll let you have me', says Narcissus and Echo answers, 'I'll let you have me':

> 'ante' ait 'emoriar, quam sit tibi copia nostri'
> rettulit illa nihil nisi 'sit tibi copia nostri.'   (391–2)

141

Because of this rejection Echo pines away in a curiously fundamental manner, leaving nothing but the voice, still weakly echoing, clinging to existence (there was a stage when the voice came from a skeleton and then the skeleton dislimned, the bones leaving the voice and becoming simple stone (396–400), just as Narcissus himself is turned to marble at 419 – the poetry oscillating between images of fluid insubstantiality and hard substance).

One expects Echo to curse Narcissus but that is not quite what happens. The narrative seems to slip sideways for an instant and then to continue (402–6). Thus Narcissus mocked Echo, Ovid says, and thus he mocked other nymphs and young men, and one of *these* prayed that Narcissus himself should love and be frustrated. Nemesis heard and granted the prayer. Narcissus, worn out by heat and the chase (of deer, of course) comes to a lonely, sunless pool and lies down to drink from it (413–16).

> dumque bibit, visae conreptus imagine formae
> spem sine corpore amat, corpus putat esse quod umbra est.
>
> (416–17)
>
> As he drinks, seized by the image of a shape,
> he loves a bodiless hope, thinks that body which is shadow.

Ovid's mirror, we find, is not metal or glass but water and in the primal world of the *Metamorphoses* it may be presumed that it is the first reflection Narcissus has seen. He must actually *mistake* the face for another's. He is now subjected to the beauty which has already enslaved everyone else (424).

Ovid's Latin now begins a kind of dance, shifting from active to passive voice and back:

> se cupit inprudens et, qui probat, ipse probatur,
> dumque petit, petitur pariterque accendit et ardet.
>
> (425–6)

In his folly he desires himself, he who does the appreciating is himself the one who is appreciated, even while he pursues he is pursued, equally he kindles the fire and is the flame which burns (36 words of English for 15 of Latin!).

This matching of active and passive, with its inner absurdity, corresponds to the mismatch of subject and object which we found earlier in Richard's introspection. Ovid magically closes a gap which we know cannot be closed. The object is the subject. But that which introspects is never identical with that which is introspected and, in like manner, Narcissus cannot really love, find or touch the person he sees. The marriage of active and passive is *too* perfect – too close to be a real marriage while, in another way, the parties can never be joined at all. These may seem rarefied paradoxes for a classical poet but they are pursued with almost Euclidian pertinacity in the lines which follow.

What we find in a mirror image is a reciprocity too perfect, too immediate for love. Even as one stretches out one's hand to embrace the image does the same and the embrace is prevented. Fingertip touch and perhaps a kiss – strangely cold – is possible, though even here one seems to encounter not so much a body as a dividing film, *exigua prohibemur aqua*, 450, 'we are kept from one another by thin water'. In Virgil frustrated embraces (with ghosts, dreams and the like) are conveyed by the formula *ter conatus...ter frustra*, 'three times he tried...three times in vain' (*Aen.* 2.792–3; 6.700–1). In the perverse world of Ovid frustration is instead conveyed by a too docile responsiveness, so that instead we find the apparently fulfilling formula, *quotiens...totiens*, 'as often...so often':

> cupit ipse teneri!
> nam quotiens liquidis porreximus oscula lymphis,
> hic totiens ad me resupino nititur ore. (450–2)

He longs himself to be embraced. For as often as I reach out with my lips towards the shining waters, so often he strains towards me with upturned face (mouth).

Notice how Ovid has modulated the voice of the infinitive to the passive – *teneri*, 'to be embraced' where we might have expected an active 'embrace' (as in the Virgilian formula). This brings out the special frustration of Narcissian love-making, for what is lacking is the touch of someone other than oneself. At most one can only, in a minimal fashion, touch; one cannot be touched. As at the erotic level, so at the level of consciousness: the self can perceive but cannot be perceived. Each frustration echoes the other (at which point we should note that Echo figures in this myth, as it were, by right). *Resupino*, which I rendered 'upturned', is good. We must not forget that the mirror of Narcissus is horizontal because it is the surface of a pool. Narcissus hangs over the loved image, which is supine beneath him.

Ovid pursues the thought further in the lines which follow:

> cumque ego porrexi tibi bracchia, porrigis ultro;
> cum risi, adrides; lacrimas quoque saepe notavi
> me lacrimante tuas; nutu quoque signa remittis
> et, quantum motu formosi suspicor oris,
> verba refers aures non pervenientia nostras.
> iste ego sum! sensi; nec me mea fallit imago:
> uror amore mei, flammas moveoque feroque.
> quid faciam? roger, anne rogem? quid deinde rogabo?
> quod cupio, mecum est: inopem me copia fecit. (458–66)

When I stretch out my arms to you, forthwith you stretch out yours; when I smile, you smile back; then too I have many times seen tears on your cheeks when I was weeping. I nod and you nod back! And I strongly suspect from the movement of those beautiful lips that you are uttering words in answer, words which never reach my ears. I am that you! I have felt it, I am no longer deceived by my own image. I am burned in the fire of self-love. I stir the flames and endure them. What shall I do? Am I to court or be courted? Why in the end shall I court at all? What I desire is here, with me. My very wealth has made me poor.

'I am that you' is an attempt to convey as literally as possible the almost untranslatable *iste ego sum*. Here Ovid brilliantly exploits the character of *iste*, a pronoun with no exact English equivalent. It is 'a demonstrative of the second person' normally applied to objects associated with the person addressed, a mixture of 'that' and 'your'. Here it expresses very directly the frustration of the whole endeavour: it is as if Ovid can no longer say *tu*, 'you', because there is no clear Other to address; at the same time, however, there is certainly an object, of a kind, associated with an apparent Other Person: the image, after all, is manifestly there; hence *iste*. But – finally – even that is identical with the observer: *iste ego sum*, 'I am that you'.[11]

The suppleness and wit of Ovid's management of language are remarkable. The correlation, 'when...then' implies that the events described are happening at the same time; but sentences are themselves uttered in time and a presumption of consecutiveness easily creeps in. Consider the simple word, 'and'. Logicians and grammarians used to say that the word 'and' carried no temporal force until someone innocently asked whether 'She got married and had a baby' had the same meaning as 'She had a baby and got married'. So in the Latin the simultaneous movements of the image can be construed for a moment as responses (I have related this to the fact that sentences are uttered in time but I suspect that even in *perception* with its near-instantaneous process something of the same sort can occur, and that Ovid knows this: a person looking at his image in a glass can, as his attention shifts from himself to the image, fall momentarily into the error of thinking that that which he *notices* later actually *happened* later). Ovid's artfully patterned lines toy with this structure of action and response and then acknowledge that it must vanish: it is not that he who courts will be courted in turn. Rather there is no space for courtship at all (I translated *quid deinde rogabo* as 'Why in the end shall I court at all', but the phrase could also be rendered word for word 'What in the end will I be courting?' or 'What in the end shall I be asking for?'). This leads to the breathtakingly clever *inopem me copia fecit*, which I translated, a shade desperately, as 'My very wealth has made me poor'.[12] Lovers have always talked of union with the beloved. Ovid invites them to consider that *real* union would kill their love, would starve it. To give the converse paradox one might say that love thrives on the separateness of the beloved; annihilate that and love dies in a kind of immediate surfeit. And so Narcissus prays to be separated from his own body, '*O utinam a nostro secedere corpore possem*' (467) and adds, '*votum in amante novum: vellem, quod amamus, abesset!*' ('Strange prayer in a lover! I want the absence of the thing I love.') Remember here how Plato played on paradoxes of wealth and poverty in the *Symposium*, 195A–203D. Agathon, the airy poet in that dialogue, was asked to describe love and answered that love was beautiful and happy; Socrates gently corrected him: love, he explained, is poor and hungry, for love in all its richness is a kind of lack. But of course to take away that hunger would be to abolish love and so, in another sense, to *impoverish* human nature (now the *other* metaphor of wealth takes over).

Oscar Wilde said wickedly, 'To love oneself is the beginning of a life-long romance'.[13] Ovid asks, more brutally, 'But how exactly do you make love?' The word *copia*, 'wealth', picks up the earlier exchange with Echo,

'ante', ait, 'emoriar, quam sit tibi copia nostri'
rettulit illa nihil nisi 'sit tibi copia nostri'   (391–2)

which I translated, '"I'll die", he said, "before I'll let you have me"', and she answered nothing, but "I'll let you have me"'. The only way, perhaps, to bring out the repetition of *copia* (which gets lost in an idiomatic version) is to use the words 'possess' and 'possession'. At 391 Narcissus must say 'before you shall possess me' while at 466 he must say 'possession has made me poor'. We must not forget that we are watching the fulfilment of a curse. Although the curse was not in fact laid on him by Echo there is a symmetry in the way Narcissus is reduced to something resembling Echo's strangely restricted mode of courtship. She could say what the other said, and nothing more. At last Narcissus breaks out in a fit of weeping and – marvellous touch – his tears as they fall in the water blur the image (475). Richard wilfully smashed the image of his face; Narcissus inadvertently destroys the vision by the mere physical effect of his grief. He calls out to it to stay and pleads that he may at least be allowed to go on gazing. There is something faintly perverse about the word *alimenta*, 'food' in line 479:

liceat, quod tangere non est,
adspicere et misero praebere alimenta furori!   (478–9)

Let me look at what I cannot touch
and provide food for my unhappy passion.

It is as if he is settling for voyeurism (compare Shakespeare's line in *As You Like It*, 'The sight of lovers feedeth those in love', III iv 57). He convulsively beats his white breast until it is flushed with bruises and then, as the water grows smooth, he sees this too and is further enflamed by love until he can bear no more (480–90). The perversity is now, perhaps, stronger still ('auto-sado-masochism'?) but by no means impossible where Ovid is the author.

The fate of Narcissus thus mirrors the fate of Echo, with whom in a strange manner he is reunited. His body wastes away, becomes insubstantial. As he cries 'Alas' Echo hears him and answers, as her nature bids, 'Alas' (496). Before, when he refused her, the joke was that his very rejection ended with words which, on her lips, proffered love. Now the words of Echo and Narcissus merely coalesce; they are the same and utter nothing but sadness. At last (at 501) he says 'Goodbye' and she, with the mirror's simplicity, answers, 'Goodbye'. Echo became mere voice, Narcissus little more than image. Such are the loves of the shadows, united only in grief and valediction. Narcissus has found a pitying, auditory mirror. But the symmetry is still flawed. He continues really to love only himself. Echo, a true native of Mirror Land, can really love Narcissus, and does so still. It is as if, all the time, whatever it was that shimmered in the pool wanted to love Narcissus. Narcissus dies but even in the Underworld is tormented by the face he glimpses in the River of Death (505). No body could be found to place on the funeral pyre, but only a flower with white petals surrounding a yellow centre.

Sufflaminandus sum, which is as much as to say, these are wild thoughts and should be curbed. 'Is it likely', I may be asked, 'that Ovid could be writing about self-knowledge or introspection?' Certainly the late medieval and Renaissance commentaries do not interpret the passage in this way. I concede at once that it is most unlikely that Ovid would do such a thing but in this case, I submit, he has done it. Ovid began his story with the prediction of Teiresias: Narcissus, he said, would reach a ripe old age so long as *he never knew himself* (*si se non noverit*, 348). Since, as we all were shown, he met with an untimely death it follows as the night the day that his death is involved with self-knowledge. What is not so clear is that such self-knowledge is to be construed in terms of philosophic 'knowledge of the *nature* of a person or thing' rather than in terms of simple acquaintance. When the artless Cyclops tells Galatea how he saw himself in a pool, he says *certe ego me novi*, 'Surely I know myself' (*Met.* 13.840). The passage as a whole is parallel and – quite clearly – carries no suggestion of profound self-exploration. But then the parallel is rather a variation on the Narcissian theme than a direct repetition of it. Although the Cyclops is not a full inversion of Narcissus (he does not shudder, as we might expect him to, at his own shaggy appearance) we are certainly given a much less intense, more purely comic version of the encounter with the image. Where Narcissus falls fatally in love with what he sees, the Cyclops simply *likes* the image:

> placuitque mihi mea forma videnti.
> Adspice sim quantus (13.842–3)

I liked my shape when I saw it. Look how big I am!

In the Narcissus episode the reference to self-knowledge acquires an extra resonance from being spoken by a prophet and directly linked with impending death, so that it is difficult to exclude an association with the oracular 'know thyself!' (where 'know' must of course bear the 'deeper' sense). Ovid himself adds at lines 349–50 that the sequel confirmed the seer's prediction and goes out of his way to comment on the novelty, or oddity of Narcissus' passion (*novitasque furoris*). Jacobus Pontanus[14] in what has been called 'the greatest of the Renaissance Ovids'[15] remarks on the strangeness and difficulty of the prediction (since self-knowledge is commonly commended as a good in antiquity) but explains that the problem is resolved if we take self-knowledge to be, in this case, knowledge of one's own physical beauty. This explanation is repeated over and over again in Renaissance handbooks. George Sandys in his Excursus on the third book of the *Metamorphoses* comments, 'As strange as obscure; and seeming contradictory to that Oracle of *Apollo*: to know a mans selfe is the chiefest knowledge. The lacke hereof hath ruined many: but having it must ruine our beautifull *Narcissus*: who only is in love with his own perfection.'[16] The explanation is altogether too limp for the tense, witty poetry Ovid has given us. Sandys is right to remind us of the traditional words, 'know thyself'. What happens in the third book of the *Metamorphoses* is that Ovid, having half-invoked the notion of serious self-knowledge, immediately subjects the idea to a dexterous erotic parody, in which the simpler notion of knowledge-as-acquaintance is after all employed. The effect of the parody is not, however, to trivialise the material but has, on the contrary, a real philosophic sting of its own. The way he points the story is to stress constantly the difference between image and substance and also the impossibility of introducing normal subject–object relations when observer and observed are one. The introduction of the erotic theme into this subject–object failure has immediate and brilliant consequences. G. Karl Galinsky, in his admirable study of the *Metamorphoses*, stresses both the *novitas furoris*, 'new species of passion' and the 'psychopathological' character of this episode.[17]

I do not suggest that Ovid thought to himself, 'Self-knowledge is a systematically frustrated enterprise; the moment you look you disturb the data – I'll write a story to illustrate that', as if he were some early Heisenberg of philosophical psychology, though such thoughts *did* occur, quite explicitly, to Romans before the time of Ovid (Cicero says in the *Tusculan Disputations* that 'Know thyself' means 'Know thy soul' and goes on to link the difficulty of knowing one's soul with a paradox of visual perception: the eye can see everything but itself).[18] In Ovid's case I would rather guess that sheer wit and the live hexameters under his hand carried him into a series of immensely fruitful analogies which he himself could scarcely have formulated in more explicit terms. It is often so with poets. The linking of the self-knowledge theme with the posing of the question, 'What would *real* union with the beloved be like?' hurls him willy-nilly into paradoxes of identity.

All this may seem tenuously related to Shakespeare's Richard. Certainly Ovid does things Shakespeare does not attempt (notably in the field of erotic implication). Conversely Shakespeare for his part does more with the mirror itself, when he makes the glass in Richard's hand into a recalcitrant truth-teller *resisting* a pre-existent self-image in Richard's own mind. Richard, romanticising and extrapolating into the future as usual, expects to see on the glass a ravaged countenance but instead he is confronted by a young and healthy face. 'No deeper wrinkles yet?' he says in only half ironic disappointment (IV i 277). He smashes the glass in a fit of histrionic pique, because it presents too optimistic a picture. As he does so he slips into a careless idiom, 'How soon my sorrow hath destroy'd my face' (IV i 291) and Bolingbroke steps in swiftly: 'The shadow of your sorrow hath destroy'd the shadow of your face'; in other words, 'That is not your face which lies broken on the floor; it is a mirror, a mere image; and – for that matter – the sorrow wasn't real either; it was play-acting'. Bolingbroke senses that Richard's grip on the distinction between

147

metaphor and literal truth is slipping. In Ovid, on the other hand, the reflection does not affront or contradict a self-image which Narcissus had previously formed. That is partly because we are in the world of myth, not drama. Ovid will not present self-love or self-consciousness as a compact psychological phenomenon having certain social and political consequences. Rather as a mythographer he will explore with his story the inner character of self-knowledge in a quasi-allegorical manner. Once we grasp this we shall see that the reflection Narcissus sees presents *him* also with an obstinate truth: self is self is self. There is nothing to say and nowhere to go. Love, thought, truths, sentences will not form within the congealed block of mere identity. Without *relation*, we are loveless, speechless, witless. Even the notion of self-consciousness, insofar as it has real content, demands an artificial splitting of the individual.

This indeed is common to Shakespeare and Ovid. Richard, in order to look at himself, needs, so to speak, to place himself at arm's length. This he first does by turning himself into a richly coloured body of *stories*, as we saw, and by 'orchestrating' his words and actions artfully, as poets or actors do. Then, at the high point of the play, he feels the need for something sharper, brighter, and calls for the glass. Then, as we have seen, Shakespeare contrives his brilliant discrepancy between the image presented and the earlier fictive images projected or privately entertained by Richard. Hippolytus has already been mentioned in this essay as a mythic analogue to Narcissus. We can now link him with Richard. At the crisis of suffering in Euripides' *Hippolytus* the protagonist expresses a sudden need to be able to look at himself:

εἴθ' ἦν ἐμαυτὸν προcβλέπειν ἐναντίον
cτάνθ', ὡc ἐδάκρυc' οἷα πάcχομεν κακά.　　　　　(1078–9)

[Literally] Would that it were possible for me,
having stood opposite (myself), to look at myself,
at how I weep at the kinds of evils I am suffering.

Barrett in his commentary on the *Hippolytus* explains these lines by suggesting that Hippolytus is ashamed of weeping and therefore is led to express the 'rather odd wish' that someone else might do the weeping for him.[19] This note is both linguistically and critically inexact. Like Pontanus before him Barrett refuses to attend to the notion of *looking* and, in particular, at looking at oneself. Meanwhile it is by no means clear from the Greek that the other self should do the weeping. What the other self is asked to do is watch. The element missed by Barrett is, precisely, the element of Narcissism.

I said earlier that *Richard II* was a great exploratory achievement, perhaps the first such exploration in English literature. I was in fact careful to say 'English' because Euripides' *Hippolytus* was nagging at the back of my mind. Indeed – though we cannot be sure of this because so much Greek drama is lost – it may be that Shakespeare's *Richard II* and Euripides' *Hippolytus* are curiously parallel feats: that Shakespeare had to repeat for himself the discovery of Euripides. The thought continues, after *Richard II*, in *Julius Caesar*: Brutus, another tensely introspective figure, is tempted by Cassius with the words, 'Tell me, good Brutus, can you see your face?' (I ii 51). Meanwhile in *Richard II* Shakespeare shows us that, as long as the projected self is a matter of free fiction, as when Richard tells romantic stories of the death of kings, he is not directly confronting his fate or himself at all, and when the image he sets before himself *really* closes with the fact (the mirror image, this time) it dissatisfies him. Indeed, as in Ovid, it frustrates the elaborate gestures of self-love and self-glorification Richard would like to perform. Richard soon falls back into the old manner but for a moment he was seriously disturbed, and therefore smashed the glass.

I have drawn an analogy between two studies of self-love, but it would be wrong to assume, in works as rich as these, that there will not be endless differences which escape the net. Richard was relieved when the image was broken, Narcissus was distraught. Looking at one's own face is not the same thing as introspection though it can serve as an emblem for introspection. Thus, while Ovid makes the docile image in the pool express the impossibility of a neutrally objective introspection, Shakespeare's play with the glass allows a more social, public, practical form of self-knowledge to show for an instant before it is crushed by the King. For Richard could actually have learned something very much to the point by attending to the physical facts presented in the glass. Indeed the truth he almost grasps could be called a psychological truth, though it has little to do with straining to see into the darkness of the soul. I do not wish to imply that Ovid and Shakespeare were proto-behaviourists, denying the reality of an inner world. One can remember one's thoughts as well as one's actions and one can be aware of them as they occur; what one cannot do is to take a hard look at them in process, because to do so involves shifting the very apparatus of thought and so altering the *datum*. The thought you would look at becomes the thought which is looking. This nightmarish, doggy docility of the mind is caught in Ovid's lines. When Narcissus longs for distance he longs for that of which Richard, poet-like, is master, but a self so distanced is not really a self at all.

In his *Vanity of Dogmatizing* Joseph Glanvill wrote,

It's a great question with some what the *soul* is. And unless their phancies may have a sight and sensible palpation of that more clarified subsistence, they will prefer infidelity itself to an unimaginable *Idea*. I'le only mind such, that the soul is seen, as other things, in the Mirrour of its effects, and attributes: But, if like children they'll run behind the glass to see its *naked face*, their expectation will meet with nothing but vacuity & emptiness. And though a pure Intellectual eye may have a sight of it in reflex discoveries; yet, if we affect a grosser touch, like *Ixion* we shal embrace a cloud.[20]

Alice in *Through the Looking-Glass* actually passed through the great glass above the Victorian chimney-piece into a counter-world, but that was only a logician's game. Narcissus stared impotently at the film of water which seemed to divide him from his love – not a wall, not a mountain, not an ocean, he says, but a little water (448–50). Yet to break through would be to destroy the object. Here too the expression reflects a certain paradox of vision. The image in a glass, construed as a person, will seem to be twice as far away as the surface of the glass; this encourages us to say that the glass lies between us and it. But in fact the image is located in/on the glass; the film of water debars Narcissus not by intervening between him and his desire but rather by its very fragility. If he touches the image, by so much as a fallen tear, it will be taken from him.

We have been contemptuous of Ovid for too long. The Latin poet who ran constantly in Shakespeare's thoughts was not Virgil but Ovid. Indeed, as we have seen, the English Renaissance was nourished and schooled by Ovid. His fault – and I must confess that I find no difficulty at all in forgiving it – is that he is not always (Arnold's word) *serious*.

IO

ILLUSTRATING OVID

Nigel Llewellyn

> Look, why do you think we remember
> The swan-upping of Leda, or Io's life as a cow
> Or poor virgin Europa whisked off overseas, clutching
> That so-called bull by the – horns? Through poems, of course.
> (*Amores* 1.3.21–4)[1]

I

SOME OF OVID'S LISTENERS might not have found these words amusing.[2] Artists might have thought it a poor joke that it was the words of his verse not the form of their images that would transmit the stories to posterity. This mocking of their countless efforts over the last two thousand years ignores, if it does not deny, the complexities of narrative art. But not all artists would have suffered, for not many of them would have read the love poems. Their staple was the *Metamorphoses* which has come to be called their Bible[3]. Together with Holy Scripture, Homer and Virgil it was the source for most of the visual art produced until the later eighteenth century.

We should not take for granted the relationship between the artists and these texts. The translation of word into image or set of words into a series of images was a practical transformation which required a theory. Ovidian art shows how two components determine our capacity to recognise a text from the images depicted: first, the form of the text itself and second, the artist's adaptation of its contents to supply a programme for the picture.

Ovidian subject-matter is extremely common, but artists did not always make the same reading of Ovid. The study of 'Jupiter and Europa' at the end of this essay is intended to illustrate this variety. In fact, the relationship between artists and a particular text is subject to few universal laws. The *Metamorphoses* is certainly familiar – perhaps more to the consumers than to the producers of the art – but this would not always have been to the artist's advantage. To aid initial identification, artists would have benefited from the fact that the viewers would know the stories illustrated; recognition did not usually necessitate captions.[4] But those viewers would also have expected textual subtleties, such as word-play, and have been familiar with narrative structures and strategies hard to translate into a visual format. Amongst essays such as those in this book, primarily concerned with linguistic aspects of Ovid's

151

work, it is worth making the point that in medieval and early modern Europe most of the artists producing Ovidian pictures were illustrating a text which they could not read in the original Latin. Artists who illustrated the Bible faced analogous difficulties. For this reason if no other, a painter or sculptor's transcription from text into image was always a complex process. We might draw an analogy with the modern commercial artist commissioned to produce an advertisement for some technology which he does not fully understand. Usually artists coped with Ovid by relying on the iconographic tradition or linguistic intermediaries such as translations or accounts by word-of-mouth. They also depended upon the sounds of the spoken stories which they expected to be echoing still in the minds of their viewers, who were mostly better read. The adaptation of the text from one medium into another demanded a process of reinvention. Many painters and carvers thus became 'poets'.

As a result of its complexities – the stories within the stories must have presented particular problems – artists were obliged to adopt illustrative strategies which would reduce or adapt the *Metamorphoses*. Such simplification was not always approved of as it gave the impression that the higher status of words over images within Western culture was being challenged: Borghini's harsh view of Titian (see below) was a case in point. Textual fidelity was achieved by means of the vernacular translations which the artists used to overcome their insufficient understanding of the Latin original. The education of artists did not normally allow them access to texts in such languages. In due course we shall note the contributions of Nicolas Poussin and Rubens, but few earlier artists could have read Ovid,[5] and fewer still have had the scholarly approach of Piranesi (1720–78) who quoted parts of the *Metamorphoses* in his theoretical work *Parere su l'Architettura*.[6]

Sometimes artists were able to ignore the poetry altogether, so conventional were the subjects loosely describable as Ovidian, a category including most mythological art with classical subject-matter. The convenient familiarity of much Ovidian material also appealed to the patrons, who often seem to have been uninterested in the complicated textual origins of the pictures they paid for. In his plans for the suburban Villa Madama, outside Rome, Cardinal Giulio de' Medici was characteristically relaxed. His only worry was over social propriety. He told a correspondent that he did not care what subjects his painter, Giulio Romano (1492 or 1499–1546) treated as long as they were recognisable. Ovid, he wrote, would do as well as anything else if the scenes were interesting, but the Old Testament would have to be avoided as this source was reserved for the use of the Pope.[7] The inability even of the educated elite always to recognise Ovidian subjects is borne out by a comment passed in 1598 on Titian's *Bacchus and Ariadne* (Pl. 8): 'a picture of square format, by the hand of Titian in which Laocoon is depicted'.[8] Workshop conventions in the form of pattern-book formulae, of the sort which were used for the attributes of the saints and other religious iconography, must have been worked up for much Ovidian iconography. The poet's treatment of a story such as 'Venus and Mars' (*Met.* 4.171ff) was not very interesting for artists as there were no props or setting to speak of.

Throughout the early modern period, the argument about the merits of Poetry, Painting, Music and other arts was a standard topic of humanistic discourse. The debate led to texts and images being given a relative priority, a feature of art theory which formed an important social circumstance for visual art. I have been talking about artists as if they were somehow dominated by the text, as if they were obliged to get their pictures or sculpture 'correct' in some relation to it. I have assumed and left unchallenged a hierarchy which locates words above images. Perhaps the very notion of priority offends our liberal construction of 'the arts' as a series of modes of discourse each with an equal part to play. This view certainly runs counter to the evidence of many manuscripts where exactly the same visual configuration is used to illustrate several different texts or episodes in the text.[9] The examples offered by Schapiro give us a clear idea of the domination of texts over both the work and reputation of the visual artist.

2

This short essay has two modest objectives: first, to survey the history of Ovidian illustration and give some idea both of the range of problems set to artists and of the solutions they have offered in response;[10] second, to look at one of the more popular themes – the 'Rape of Europa' – as treated by a handful of artists to show how painters can properly work in the spirit of Ovid without necessarily always having to follow every word of his poetry. The bibliography appended to the notes will suggest more possibilities for those with the energy and resources to explore this enormous subject.

But first some thoughts on the intellectual steps required of the artist prior to making a picture after Ovid. As with any complex text, illustrating the *Metamorphoses* demands that some theory of the narrative image be adopted. Consider the problem a painter faces in tackling any of the best-known transformations amongst the 15 books of the poem. One obvious solution is to accept the burden of the iconographic tradition. But such a step did little for the reputation of the visual arts, something with which artists became more and more concerned from the Renaissance adoption of humanism as an art theory to the codification of academic practice in the later eighteenth century. The social and economic status of artists rose according to their capacity to show their successful emulation (in both technique and production) of literature. Stories, even those in the *Metamorphoses*, are experienced as a linear narrative, and Ovidian art had to adopt practices to accommodate this fact.

Before the invention of the cinema, the visual adaptation of a written text had to be organised episodically. With a linear narrative such as Ovid's, the moment chosen for illustration might well have to make reference outside itself in order to be comprehensible,[11] and the spectators' capacity to recognise the participants in a scene might require explanation beyond the picture-frame. For example, in Plate 14 we know that Jupiter must feature because the eagle hovering above is his sign, despite the fact that his master's normal appearance is hidden from us by his transformation. Few artists seek to catch the moment of transformation: Plate 11a is an exception. Time, before or after an event, poses great problems for the artist given only one picture to fill. Captions can include essential additional data, but the traditional polemic centred on the Horatian phrase *ut pictura poesis*[12] reminds us of the pressure on visual artists to remain independent of text in order to secure their intellectual status as equal practitioners to the writers of those texts. Captions suggest the inadequacy of the image; illustrations to texts are taken as signs of the infectious potency of the text.[13]

These observations should determine our expectations of narrative art. From the point-of-view of its own development, art history has sought quality of execution rather than the exposition of meaning. Yet without a sense of signification we cannot understand the narration in a narrative picture whatever its 'quality'. The theory of narrative painting and the relationship between text and image has recently gained considerable attention, a development symptomatic of art history's search for methodologies – in this case structural linguistics – closer to those of the social sciences. This theory argues that the basic conventions of representation, vital if a narrative is to be 'read' accurately, determine the positioning of elements in a picture as they do units of verbal language within grammatically controlled sequences. For example, conventions like progressive and regressive colour, scales of light and shade and structural pairs such as broad/narrow, high/low, centre/margin can all direct the eye in a sequence of moves within the picture-frame. Size or scale relates to a clear hierarchy of semiotic value.[14] From this intellectual current come certain concepts which can be applied to the 'reading' of mythological narrative art: for example, synchronic analysis, which describes the scanning of the picture from left to right as if reading,[15] or the necessity for combining incidents (altering or compressing time) in so-called continuous narrative (see Pl. 16).

These theoretical aspects of picture-making can help us understand Ovidian illustration, whereas the game of searching for pictorial equivalents to the text gets us nowhere. The identification of sources has been the practice of the iconographers and has therefore become the main field of enquiry amongst art historians treating narrative art. Such procedures demonstrate what art history owes to the philological training of the discipline's founders. But their effort is misplaced: few painters compose with a copy of the text propped up by their easel.[16]

If the full treatment of text consigns the picture so easily to the low status of what Schapiro calls a 'mere token',[17] we might ask why artists have bothered with Ovidian art? Two reasons come to mind. One – patronage – is virtually a universal condition of most art produced before the later nineteenth century, and the other is specific to narration. The main stimulus for the creation of almost all visual art, including narrative, came not from artists but from patrons. The consumers made the choice of subject, not the producers. Until relatively recently, art was an economic product which resulted directly from a contractual arrangement between artist and patron. Ovidian art was usually large, expensive and bespoken. This social fact underpins a second, which refers again to the relative status of text and image. Given the priority normally accorded to words, the status of pictures could be elevated if they could be associated with words by taking prestigious texts as their subject-matter.

In addition to helping the visual arts approach the accomplishment of literature, Ovid's *Metamorphoses* supplied subject-matter which was suitable in two other important ways: the potential for moralising and the potential for decoration. The lines should not be drawn too sharply between these two objectives, and there were not necessarily any great, adverse tensions in early modern art between what, in a materialist age, we might wish to describe as two mutually exclusive functions. In the Middle Ages it was Ovid's capacity to write poetry capable of bearing a sustained moral exegesis that excused its reputation for licentiousness: exquisite landscape settings and naked bodies writhing in sexual pleasure had, somehow, to be excused. In later art, it is tempting to ignore the fact that Ovidian pictures are telling stories capable of such moralising and treat them entirely as objects of pleasure. Ovidian pictures were history paintings, and it was the role of history to interpret, perhaps with the help of some light entertainment. The problems which can arise when this instructive role is forgotten will be explored in the brief study of Europa and the portrayal of her abduction. In general, we must expect to find the twin impulses of instruction and decoration behind every image discussed.

3

The art of the poet's own day shows the irrelevance of seeking an exact text in Ovid for every Ovidian image. The *Metamorphoses* is a new compilation of stories that were mostly well established. A Roman observer's identification of the subject-matter in a contemporary landscape fresco or figurative floor mosaic would not necessarily lead to the location of the textual equivalent in Ovid's verse. On an empirical, statistical level, if we survey Roman art, there is no marked increase in 'Ovidian' subjects following the publication of the text.[18] Many of the poet's stories were well known, and the pictures went with the stories rather than with his version of their telling. The Europa mosaic from the apsed *triclinium* of *c.* AD 330 of the villa at Lullingstone (Pl. 12) is a simple image and adduces a text from outside Ovid altogether.[19] Without knowing the first book of the *Aeneid*, the caption would be meaningless. It reads:

> Invida si ta[uri] vidisset Iuno natatus,
> Iustius Aeolias isset adusque domos.

If envious Juno had seen the bull's swimming, more justly would she have gone to Aeolus' home.

Ovid's account of the story, which we can imagine echoing in the minds of the picture's first viewers, introduces a second text which increases dramatically the moralising potential of the same image. The allusion to Virgil suggests that it is not only the injustice of Juno's *vendetta* against the Trojans but also Jupiter's promiscuity and Europa's naivety which are referred to as part of a world of allusion beyond the poem itself. The choice of the caption would not have been with the artist, and it is doubtful whether he would have even understood the reference.[20] As in any other narrative art our unravelling of signification in Ovidian illustration is possible only if we understand the work's reception and the expectations of its original audience. The audience – and we are part of it – therefore completes the meaning of the work of art, and the construction of meaning is not the business of the artist alone. We can perhaps draw a parallel between this Ovidian picture from the Roman world and devotional subjects in Christian art. Often these are only very loosely related to the Gospel narrative: for example, the *Pietà* or the 'Rest on the Flight into Egypt'.

In Roman art there are many examples of Ovidian subjects but few works which we can satisfactorily link to specific passages from the *Metamorphoses*. Mythological subjects were popular for wall paintings, and, judging from the ratio of landscape to figures in those that remain, they were usually considered decorative rather than didactic.[21] During the Middle Ages this ratio was reversed and the principal way in which Ovidian stories could be expected to survive as subject-matter was by adopting a clear moralising function.[22] The manuscript tradition, often described by the generic title the *Ovide moralisé* after the enormous early fourteenth-century French poem, relied on an allegorical treatment of the text which offset the *risqué* nature of some of the stories told in it.[23] The illustrations encouraged the reader to substitute the values familiar from Christian ethical instruction for the supposed standards of pagan antiquity.[24] The patrons of the manuscripts in this tradition presumably expected the illuminations to strengthen the text's contribution to the synopsis of pagan and Christian thought that was the great work of medieval scholarship. Dante's transformation of Virgil is perhaps the most revealing example of this tendency. The *Ovide moralisé* illustrations are partly classical revival, but more concerned to depict the pagan gods and goddesses as kings, nuns and other contemporary figures of exemplary virtue.[25]

Two illustrations (Pls. 7a and 7b) from this tradition stress the contemporary relevance of the image. A small picture from the *Ovide* MS now at Lyons shows a moment from the story of Argus, soon to be killed by Mercury, on Jupiter's orders (*Met.* 1.668–721). The scene described by Ovid is here transformed into a medieval idyll with Mercury dressed in a stocking cap and carrying a set of bag-pipes surrounded by an unlikely breed of amiable, minute sheep. The goats and reed-pipes of the original poem have disappeared as have the hundred eyes of Argus himself. The medieval tradition of illumination was a direct antecedent of the woodcuts included in the earliest printed versions of the *Ovide moralisé*. Colart Mansion's edition, printed at Bruges in 1484 with 34 cuts, from which our plate is taken, again makes extensive reference to contemporary culture as a means effectively of moralising the readers.[20] Here we see Mars, furious as the god of war, in fifteenth-century armour, whip in hand, mounted on a crude chariot and accompanied by a wolf. Behind him, the cityscape is unmistakably medieval.

This didactic tendency in medieval illustrations of Ovid was not rejected in the early modern period. Indeed the capacity of texts to exemplify patterns of behaviour and the need for higher painting to emulate such texts was a key principle in the humanist theory of art developed in fifteenth-century Italy. Alberti's theoretical manual *De Pictura*, in circulation in Florence in the early 1430s, stressed the need for painting to develop a new sort of picture – the *istoria*.[27] His description of what later academic theory regarded as a genre of subject-matter forms the basis of what has come to be known as the history painting. Alberti wished painters to become what has been called 'professional visualisers' of stories, which would exert some influence for moral good on the minds of their audience.[28] In fifteenth-century Florence, these stories were mostly religious, but Alberti – a professional Latinist – cites a classical subject (an allegory of Calumny originally painted by the ancient artist Apelles) as suitable for the *istoria*.[29] By the end of the century, mythological scenes, amongst them stories from Ovid, were treated as part of *istoria* joining a category of traditional subject-matter for larger, serious pictures. The medieval exploitation of Ovid as a moraliser was thus taken up once again under a humanistic guise. All the visual arts, from tapestry design to garden land-scaping, used classical subjects to make didactic statements by means of allegory, and Ovid was prominent as a source.[30] But mythology was not always didactic. 'Rapes of Europa' appear on ivory casket-covers of the ninth century, as reliefs on metal dishes made at Augsburg *c.* 1700, on a fireback from Hampton Court Palace and on a faience ewer of the 1490s, as well as in innumerable two-dimensional painted and printed versions.[31]

Most of the pictures illustrated in this volume come into the category of the history painting, the early modern theory of which demanded both textual fidelity and a moralising intention. In cultures where criticism was self-consciously neoclassical artists could find their history paintings censured for not subjecting the image to the text. Titian's *Venus and Adonis* (Pl. 4) suffered an attack of just this sort from the Florentine Raffaello Borghini who fussed about the exact time of day suggested by the lighting and the figure-poses in the picture as incompatible with Ovid's text.[32] Titian would not, perhaps, have felt much threatened by such views, and most of his audience seem to have been unconcerned about such pedantry. However Borghini's scholarly attention, although it represented academic interest in reviving the ancient rhetoric of the *ecphrasis* and despite its concentration on a tiny point of textual exegesis, flattered the intellectual pretensions of visual art. Perhaps more than any other artist Titian was able to paint Ovidian pictures without a slavish dependency upon Ovid's text.[33] The Venetian tradition, within which he was trained, developed the *poesia*, which came to be regarded as a challenge to the intellectual supremacy of the Florentine *istoria*. Titian's famous mythologies, painted for Philip II of Spain, now hanging in various galleries across Europe, were described by their creator as *poesie*, which we should take to mean a poetic recreation of the mood one might find in a poem. The Venetian *poesie*, often Ovidian but sometimes also Christian, were not illustrations to texts as such but rather visual texts supplied directly by the painter; exercises in poetry without verbal signs. The *poesia* sometimes combined elements from different textual sources.[34] This relative independence from text has always been held against the *poesia*, and has, since Vasari, become a way of placing all Venetian painting beneath that of the Florentine and Roman schools in terms of the relationship between text and image as laid down by neoclassical theorists and sympathisers.

By the seventeenth century, so the historiography of art has it, two factions had evolved, led by Rubens and Poussin and the flags of 'colour' and 'drawing'. Both artists were expert painters within the mythological tradition and both realised that their reputations depended partly on their capacity to render myths on a level of sophistication which approximated that reached by the poets. Their pictures had, therefore, to work as narrative, allegory and decoration. Rubens' *Venus and Adonis* of *c.* 1635 (Pl. 5) tells the same story (*Met.* 10.519–59) as the painting by Titian, and indeed his picture makes many formal references to that work then part of the Royal Collection at Madrid, which Rubens knew well.[35] But, unlike Titian, Rubens expected his audience to interpret details in such stories allegorically. Here the undone quiver at Venus' feet denotes the Discord which will follow the parting of the lovers.[36]

Rubens's studio produced many pictures on Ovidian themes but only one series devoted entirely to the *Metamorphoses*. Given its huge scale, it is perhaps to be expected that the cycle undertaken to decorate a royal hunting lodge outside Madrid – the Torre de la Parada – would depend heavily on the formulae provided by printed, illustrated editions.[37] Literally dozens of myths were treated in the project which was under way by November 1636, and of these it has been calculated that 41 were Ovidian narratives.[38] The Torre de la Parada cycle occupies an interesting place within the development of history painting, for Rubens consciously avoided subjects already well established within the canon and those he had already treated himself. It is also clear that the cycle was not intended to function as a narrative sequence, for the pictures were not even hung in textual order. The idea that the text might dominate the hanging-sequence was probably rejected either for formal, decorative reasons or because it would have been at variance with the didactic theory of the history painting whereby the artist was encouraged to exploit the full range of expression and experience suggested by the text. The slavish following of the words was more often left to the book illustrators.[39]

Poussin's Ovidian paintings are the visual traces of a profound interest in ancient poetry and philosophy. These scholarly endeavours were encouraged by the circle of patrons who supported him in Rome in the 1630s, among whom was Cassiano del Pozzo who directed him to Ovid. The Louvre *Echo and Narcissus* (Pl. 6) has been dated *c.* 1627[40] and was in the French Royal Collection by the 1680s. By this latter date, Poussin's work was regarded as exemplary in neoclassical art theory and the model for academic practice. As early as 1623 the artist was illustrating Ovid for the Italian poet Giovanni Battista Marino[41], and his drawings for this project are now in the Royal Library at Windsor.[42] The series tends to avoid the supernatural and stress the psychological tensions and drama implicit in the myths. Italian poetics of *c.* 1600 regarded Ovid's works as vehicles for allegory, and Narcissus (*Met.* 3.339–510) symbolised the barrenness of self-love not at the level of physical reality but in metaphorical opposition to the theme of fertility which characterises so many Ovidian myths. Poussin, like other artists, was always attracted by the variety of allegorical or psychological potential in Ovid.[43] His period of greatest interest in the poet (up to *c.* 1633) also coincided with his greatest formal interest in Titian.[44] His pictures ask us to note formal references as well as literary citations to enrich the allegory. Venus mourning Adonis quite properly conjures up a reminiscence of the Lamentation over the Dead Christ, and thus functions powerfully as a didactic version of the text.

Throughout his Ovidian phase, Poussin took care to be elegiac not merely erotic. This stance was compatible with the academic theory that the history painting should appeal to the viewer via the senses but go well beyond sensuality to stimulate the intellect. For reasons the Victorians well understood, Ovid could be made an object of suspicion in the eyes of the theorists. Inevitably illustrations which stressed corporeal and temporal transformations were sometimes criticised as too sensual. Bernini's *Apollo and Daphne* (Pl. 10b) is essentially an exercise in the catching of a physical moment.[45] The *concetto* the sculptor illustrates from *Metamorphoses* 1.452–567 is that of a dialogue of touch and response.[46] The text is especially sensual in its treatment of this story: as she flees, the wind bares Daphne's limbs; as he approaches, Apollo's breath touches the hair on the nape of her neck. The moment chosen is the crucial one as transitory sensations are recorded on the faces of the two protagonists. Daphne turns in horror at Apollo's touch (she is unaware of her physical change), while her face already shows some of the blankness of wood. There is nothing here of the smug expression sometimes given Daphne as Apollo is deprived of his wishes and her virtue left intact.[47] The god is shown chasing still but amazed at the transformation only he, as yet, has noticed. This play between joy and bitterness was the theme of a distych attached to the statue's plinth by its patron, Cardinal Scipione Borghese, already cited in the Introduction to this volume.[48]

The concentration upon the moment of transformation is entirely forgotten in the rapturous rendering by Gérôme (Pl.10a) of a scene from the myth of Pygmalion (*Met.* 10.243–69). This illustrates the academic tradition of Ovidian subject-matter which endured well into the modern era.[49] Despite the philosophical play on the nature of deception in art that can be made in the retelling of this story, Pygmalion's reactions are solely physical and Gérôme's picture makes full use of the snow-white skin of the ivory statue – emblematic of virtue in opposition to the 'many faults' of the Propoetides – posed here like Venus for whom it substitutes.

Bernini's sculpted group was purchased by an aristocratic patron as an addition to his display of works of art. The collection included ancient marbles,[50] and an early biographer noted the artist's conscious rivalry with these ancient works.[51] The group was part of an interior, decorative scheme, and intended to be viewed at an angle from a single point upon entering a room of modest size.[52] Ovid was overwhelmingly popular as a source for art collected to be displayed. For example, an entry in the inventory of the Venetian collector Marcantonio Michiel, dating from the first years of the sixteenth century, mentions 'Un Europa rapita sopra un bue', and values it at eight ducats, the most expensive of the many bronzes listed.[53] In the eighteenth century, Ovidian subjects were rather self-consciously included in British landscape paintings to elevate the status of what were essentially decorative works. Richard Wilson's formal model was Claude Lorrain, and recent scholarship has demonstrated that classical subject-matter had an essential ideological significance for his work.[54]

The mixture of decorativeness with a narrative interest in transition is also apparent in a huge Ovidian painting by Luca Giordano (Pl. 9).[55] Showing one of the scenes most rarely illustrated – *Perseus and the Companions of Phineus* from *Metamorphoses* 5.1–235 – the picture was probably hung in a reception room in the Palazzo Balbi, Genoa. It was painted *c.* 1680 by an artist whose career shows how important was a facility with Ovidian myth if painters were to achieve success in the higher genres. As with Bernini's *Apollo and Daphne*, technical virtuosity has been called upon to convey the transition of form: in the sculpture, flesh to wood, here, flesh to stone. Giordano uses colour (which Bernini regretted was unavailable to a sculptor), and shows to the left Perseus' adversaries undergoing metamorphosis, their stony limbs contrasting with the flesh tones of the hero positioned to the right of centre.

Art theory demanded that a history painting take a moment, extract it from the linear narrative and use the subject to impress the intellect with its moral gravity. But such pictures were still obliged to amaze and entertain by their manual dexterity. Inevitably, the sense of sight had to be stimulated. Titian, Correggio and other painters were criticised for their choice of erotic subject-matter which worried church authorities.[56] But twentieth-century critics have often taken the iconography of Titian's Ovidian *poesie* to be symbolic not erotic.[57] In assessing these judgements we have to recall the strength of the contemporary sense of propriety or decorum which was used to control the reception of pictures in early modern culture. We should also understand how the delicate image of the picture in its historical setting can be shattered by its relocation in a museum or by its reproduction as a photographic plate in a book.

Neoclassical critics applied the theory of decorum to Ovid's poetry, and we should apply it to Ovidian pictures. For example Dryden thought Ovid's habit of introducing wit into harrowing or pathetic situations a mark of his poor taste. Most of Ovid's amorous stories included such combinations of lust and poignancy. Each conquest has a victim. Many modern observers experience parallel discomfort, and question whether the eroticism so typical of Ovidian mythological painting belongs in art. With Old Masters, a partial resolution of this conflict can be achieved by considering the original location of the pictures, which could be curtained if desired. Correggio's tall, slender *Jupiter and Io*, now in Vienna (Pl. 11a), must, from its shape alone, have been intended to fit within some decorative scheme.[58] The rhetorical notion of decorum would determine its location in some appropriate place: many such Ovidian pictures were for private chambers or bedrooms. *Io* is about the sensuality of Jupiter's transformation out of the cloud and the ensuing coupling. Correggio's image is intended to display his virtuosity in barely suggesting the god's hands and face, and leaves the beholder of the picture, who knows the myth (*Met.* 1. 568–600) to comprehend what would otherwise be left inexplicable. It is almost certainly inappropriate to seek a moralising intention in such a work.

Correggio's paintings never quite achieved the sustained influence so often exerted by Titian, but at various points in the history of taste his reputation as a mythological painter has been very high. His works were concerned to stimulate private sensuality rather than supply public homilies through allegory, and Correggio's subtle rendering of myth was specially appreciated in early eighteenth-century France. The stately decorative schemes of the Grand Siècle[59] gave way to more intimate works making fuller play of the erotic charge that could be elicited from ambiguity. Boucher's renderings of the myth of Europa will return us to this theme, but meanwhile Watteau's *Judgement of Paris*

(Pl. 11b) shows clearly how these artists mobilised the sensitivity exemplified by Correggio's *Io*.[60]

Watteau's small picture, painted so rapidly that some have referred to it as a 'sketch',[61] employs familiar devices to increase the erotic potential of Paris' choice of sensual beauty (Venus) rather than virtue or wisdom (Juno or Minerva). The central figure of Venus, seen from the rear, plays on the erotic potential of voyeurism. Once again, it is the assumed participation of the viewers of the picture which completes its meaning. We can only imagine what it is that Paris sees, but the contrast between Venus' silky flesh and the hard, reflective metal of Minerva's shield is displayed in what is clearly an attempt to set up a tantalising juxtaposition of tactile sensations. This scene reminds us that Ovid is not the only source of mythological subject-matter for early modern painters. They were aware of the erotic potential in what is surely a tale mostly about bribery and lust which Ovid did not include. In illustrating the scene, Watteau entirely forgot the moral basis of choice in favour of erotic stimulation, and in so doing gave later critics the excuse to place him outside the neoclassical, theoretical tradition by then entirely dominated by history painting as the superior moralising genre.

4

We saw above how artists took subjects from authors like Ovid partly to elevate the status of painting. Ironically more recent views of Ovid have concentrated on his lack of seriousness. Compared with Virgil, his work seems like story-telling for its own sake. Certainly nineteenth-century critics tended to be sceptical about Ovid's moral potential, and they concentrated on the disturbing sensuality of so much of the *Metamorphoses* and by implication of the pictures taken from it. The Goncourt brothers were unusual in their celebration of such traits:

> And there is indeed a resemblance between these two painters of decadence, between these two masters of sensuality, Ovid and Boucher. A page of the former has all the brilliance, the fire, the style and the appearance of a canvas by the latter...[62]

The Rape of Europa (*Met.* 2.836–76 and 4.103–7) was hard to gloss within the didactic tradition, but it retained its popularity throughout the early modern period. Indeed, by the mid-eighteenth century, critics were starting to get bored with it. An anonymous pamphlet of 1749 attacked the artists whose work had been shown in the Paris *salon* of 1747 for their choice of tired themes unrelated to modern life.[63] Boucher's *Europa*, now in the Louvre, is summarily dismissed: 'The "Rape of Europa" isn't that a bit worn thin?'.[64]

We have already seen how an ancient rendering of the myth (Pl. 12) was made, and we should return to it to note the characteristics of the Lullingstone mosaic and thereby establish the long tradition within which Boucher is work-ing.[65] The setting for the figures is very simple: white for the sky and blue for the sea. Red outlines are given to all the figures including a pair of playful *putti* to complement the two protagonists. Europa rides expressionless. The only suggestions made about the manner of her journey we take from her veil, which is puffed out by the speed of the bull and from her attacker who is shown leaping above, rather than over, the waves. The face of the bull shows what has been described as 'fatuous' gratification.[66] The standard of the drawing is such that it might be hard to countenance an interpretation, but it shows that the ancient iconography of Europa included a tradition whereby eye-contact was set up between bull and viewer. This device has important psychological implications for the interpretations of the pictures.[67]

The four early modern renderings of the scene grouped together here (Pls. 13–16) take different moments from the narrative, but they have in common their rejection of the ancient reliance upon bare essentials for story-telling. Some elements do remain – the flying drapes (Pl. 13) and the interest in establishing a relationship between viewer and Jupiter (Pls. 13 and 14) – but the pictures all employ subsidiary characters. These figures have many functions. They increase the potential fidelity of the scenes to Ovid's account (*Met.* 2.836–76); they register the scenes as taking place in the world of myth, not that of reality and, finally, they carry out the demands of history painting by using the tableaux thereby created to give the fullest possible perspective on human action and suffering. In this respect these pictures are within the spirit of Ovid's poem without necessarily being entirely accurate transcriptions of his words. Artists created pictorial glosses on the text and sometimes used other texts to help them do it. Titian is known to have used Dolce's translation of Ovid of 1553 which perhaps supplied the painter with a few extra narrative details.[68]

In this group of pictures a variety of narrative structures are employed. Veronese's painting, if placed alongside those 50 or so lines of Ovid's verse, presents us with an exciting degree of agreement. He gives us the geographical setting: the sea-shore and the pyramid suggestive of Phoenicia.[69] All the actors mentioned in the text are here, for example, the young girls of Tyre. The *putti* are ever-present assistants at acts of Ovidian love. Veronese also gives us three stages of the narrative: Europa lured onto Jupiter's back, the amble down to the sea and the moment of abduction. The visual priority within the picture's composition matches this sequence. Largest and nearest happens first; then we move back into the picture as we read through the text. It is the continuous narrative system of the woodcut illustrative tradition. But the drama and pathos sometimes central to illustrations of Europa are here rejected in favour of a theatrical, almost courtly presentation of the story.[70] There is none of the action of Titian or the irony and dissembled wickedness we shall see in Boucher. Why? Critics have often blamed the painter's lack of talent but the answer surely lies in the control exerted by decorum. Veronese's picture was painted at the behest of an aristocratic patron – a member of the Contarini family – for the Anticamera of the Sala di Collegio in the Ducal Palace at Venice. It was, therefore, a painting for official, if not fully public consumption, more decorative than intellectual in its appeal, a work of show not of psychological subtlety.

Subtlety is exactly what most critics have looked for in Titian's late *Europa* (Pl. 13) sent to Philip II of Spain in the early 1560s, by which time Titian had been supplying these *poesie* for high-ranking, European patrons for almost 40 years. Despite the many attempts by ingenious iconographers to seek and locate allegorical significance in this picture, the documentary evidence tells against such a reading. Titian takes the moment in the story which immediately follows the last of the three stages illustrated by Veronese. By now we are far out to sea, as at Lullingstone, the *putti* are enjoying the fun and Europa is hanging on for dear life. The ancient motifs of swirling drapes and eye-engagement with Jupiter are re-employed.

Such has been the furore over discovering both textual sources outside Ovid and complex allegorical significance within the picture that its basic character has largely been ignored. Like most of the *poesie* sent to Philip, sexual suggestiveness plays a major part in Titian's decision to compose his picture in the way he has. Not only does Europa's pose in the Boston picture convey the physical discomfort of her journey, it is also the means of displaying her body, of making her available to the viewer's gaze, something that Titian has Jupiter understand better than most modern art historians. There is some evidence to suggest that Titian used a particular translation of Ovid,[71] but his is not a scholarly telling of the story. His term *poesia* bears the same relation to 'story' that Ovid's poetry does to the ancient stories that were his sources. Titian's *poesie* were not text-related as directly as Alberti's *istorie* were obliged to be.

The final two paintings in the group are by Boucher (Pls. 14 and 15), and they illustrate an earlier point in the myth, that same moment given priority by Veronese (Pl. 16). Boucher's academic training encouraged him to resist continuous narrative and observe the unity of time, just as Poussin did in his drawings made more than 100 years before. Rather than show us what finally happens, Boucher relies on our knowledge of Ovid to complete the meaning of his chosen moment, and as a consequence his pictures become intense and demanding exercises in the psychology of sexual conflict far removed from the vapid pastorales we first might see. In this respect, Boucher's earlier picture is perhaps more successful than that later version singled out by the anonymous critic of the 1747 *Salon*.

The earlier picture, now in the Wallace Collection (Pl. 14), is one of a set of large mythologies painted to decorate the billiard-room of the patron, a mason called Derbais, when the artist was about 30 years old and had just returned from Italy. It acts both as decoration and instruction. It is within the tradition of the Italian *istoria* but aims to satisfy the contemporary French interest in the nature of love. The picture shows how Ovid can always be made topical by a good enough illustrator. Here, as in so much of the work of Watteau which Boucher had spent several years of his apprenticeship engraving, the main interest lies in deception as the prelude to love, or less coyly to sex. Boucher's theme is not the gallantry shown by Veronese or Titian's rough and tumble but the malicious trickery which Jupiter's disguise allows him to perpetrate. The bull's eye is once again the focus for our analysis.[72] He knows we know the story, and he knows we know what will soon happen. However, Europa and her handmaidens are ignorant, as Ovid puts it:

> Until the princess dared to mount his back,
> Her pet bull's back, unwittingly whom she rode.   (*Met.* 2.868–9)[73]

But there are other participants in the scene placed around and above the 'centre-fold'. Here Boucher has broken with the tradition established by the Lullingstone mosaic. These are beings of the world of myth and party to the transformation but they are unseen by Europa and her 'real' band. Above the omnipresent *putti* launching an arrow at the victim; the eagle, symbolic of Jupiter's might, and, to the lower left, personifications of the stream that trickles off-stage down to the sea. These last, with the eyes of mythical beings, are able to spot the heavens above them suddenly crowded and their expressions show their realisation that something is afoot. But the full story is reserved for us, Ovid's readers, who can see the irony of Jupiter's situation heightened by the juxtaposition of eagle and flowered garland: symbols of power and abandoned dignity. As Ovid puts it:

> Ah, majesty and love go ill together   (*Met.* 2.846–7).[74]

The act of physical violence about to be perpetrated on the innocent girl is not referred to in the Wallace Collection picture, but is perhaps suggested in the later Louvre version by the dramatically lowering sky and the distant coasts of Crete just glimpsed on the horizon.[75] This picture comprised Boucher's entry in a history painting competition organised by the French state and was judged a preeminent work amongst the 11 works submitted.[76] Just as the critics have usually concentrated on Titian's *Europa* as allegory not sex object, Boucher's pictures are rarely discussed in terms of the physical abuse (rape) which will take place but rather of what is assumed to be the artist's approval of the abduction that precedes it.[77] Here too Boucher lets the full drama creep up on us. The figures are more clearly arranged than in the earlier picture: mortals to the left; immortals to the right and above; the main protagonists in the centre. The lower right is an area especially dense in the signalling which sets, once noticed, an electric charge through what seems initially to be such an innocuous scene. Jupiter has been ridden 'slowly, slowly down the broad dry beach' (*Met.* 2.868), planted his hooves in the surf and made contact with his servants, the Nereids and Tritons, who are duty-bound to assist his designs. Above, the *putti* prepare the canopy to mark what will become both an abduction and a triumph, for Europa was to give her name to one third of Ovid's world in reward for her humiliation. With the *putti* is the eagle, always bad-tempered and apparently disapproving of the indecorous disguise of its master.[78] One of the *putti* is preparing a carpet saddle for Jupiter's victim on her ride into history, but to the right one small gesture shows both the inexhaustibility of Ovidian subjects for picture-making and the crassness of the anonymous critic who was presumably seduced by the luscious but traditional, formal qualities of the painting into missing its bitter play on human frailty. For one of the Tritons makes a gesture of silence, familiar both to us and Boucher's first viewers from many French paintings of this period,[79] and is seen by one of Europa's hand-maidens. This communication crosses the boundary between mortal and immortal worlds. Another girl, carrying flowers for Jupiter's garland, appears wary of the *putto* that by all accounts she, a mortal, should not see.

Far from being a hack exercise on a familiar theme, Boucher's later *Europa* exemplifies the potential of Ovidian illustration realised by imaginative artists working within the classical tradition. All four pictures convey the genuine passion underlying the familiar myths recounted in the *Metamorphoses* sometimes only trivialised by illustrators. The intimations of tragedy might need to be exposed, but these pictures cannot be understood without such a process. The greatest Ovidian illustration is *poesia* not *istoria* let alone *devozione*, but the most Ovidian *poesie* do not ask the viewer to read the picture as an accurate transcription of the text into a visual language but make a reading of the story. Such works are adaptations or versions not illustrations in the literal sense.

We can end with an adaptation at which Ovid himself might have laughed a good deal louder than the artists faced with the quotation with which we started:

> As once the poets, so now let the painters
> Inscribe their works: Ovid was my guide.   (*Ars* 3.811–12)

II

DRYDEN AND OVID'S 'WIT OUT OF SEASON'

David Hopkins

I

ONE OF THE OLDEST and most persistent charges which has been levelled against the Ovid of the *Metamorphoses* is that the poet trivialises his depictions of pain, anxiety and suffering by prolixity, by a callous impassivity, and by displays of tastelessly inappropriate wit. Again and again in the poem acts of violence and destruction are treated by Ovid with fanciful playfulness, and characters in the extremity of distress are made to burst into puns, epigrams or strings of obtrusive rhetorical figures. This habit, it is alleged, reveals Ovid's essential frigidity and frivolousness, his lack of sensitivity to human suffering and his 'Alexandrian' weakness for the display of his own verbal brilliance, whatever the demands of his subject.

The first recorded instances of such criticisms occur in the work of a commentator who had known Ovid personally. In his *Controversiae* the elder Seneca (who had been an eye-witness of the poet's declamations in Arellius Fuscus' rhetorical school[1]) commented on Ovid's propensity to proliferate to a fault the brilliant verbal formulations of which he was so fond. The example which Seneca cites is taken from an incident which Ovid narrates in *Metamorphoses* 13, and which had been one of the subjects of Euripidean tragedy. Troy has fallen, and the Trojan women are now prisoners of the Greeks. The ghost of Achilles has appeared and demanded the sacrifice of Polyxena, Hecuba's daughter. The ritual slaughter has been performed and Hecuba is lamenting her lot. Achilles when alive, she says, had killed her sons and laid her city waste. Now, when she had finally thought herself safe from his malign power, the Greek hero has spoken from the grave to wreak yet more havoc on her family:

> cinis ipse sepulti
> in genus hoc pugnat.

Even the ashes of the buried man fight our family.

This comment, says Seneca, would have sufficed to convey Hecuba's sentiments eloquently and pointedly, but Ovid has the Queen go on: *tumulo quoque sensimus hostem* ('We have felt our enemy, even in his grave.')...and on – this

167

time with a grisly fancy and a display of obtrusive alliteration: *Aeacidae fecunda fui.* ('I was fertile – for Achilles.') Seneca comments:

Aiebat autem *Scaurus* rem veram: *non minus magnam virtutem esse scire dicere quam scire desinere.*

[The orator] Scaurus was quite right in saying that to know how to stop is as important a quality as to know how to speak.[2]

Quintilian, too, criticised Ovid for being *lascivus* ('extravagant', 'frivolous') in the higher genres of poetry, where more seriousness was required, and for being *nimium amator ingenii sui* ('unduly enamoured of his own gifts').[3] And the younger Seneca, in his *Naturales Quaestiones*, commented, in the course of some speculations of his own about the destruction of the world by flood, that Ovid had, characteristically, ruined his own portrayal of the flood, undercutting those parts of his description in which he had effectively conveyed the grandeur and momentousness of the scene by descending *ad pueriles ineptias* ('to childish silliness'). In depicting the wolf swimming among the sheep and the lions carried along by the waves, Seneca remarks, Ovid had exercised his imagination in ways which were irrelevant and distracting, rather than restricting his tone and treatment to an appropriately grave solemnity.[4] He had thus made the flood seem paltry and absurd: *Non est res satis sobria lascivire devorato orbe terrarum* ('To make the annihilation of the world a subject for frivolity shows insufficient seriousness').[5]

The criticisms of Ovid voiced by Quintilian and the two Senecas were re-echoed, with minor additions and shifts of emphasis, down the centuries, so that, for example, Adrien Baillet's compilation of Renaissance and seventeenth-century *testimonia* on Ovid in his *Jugemens des Savans* (1685–6) consists, for the most part, of Roman sentiments re-expressed in modern terms. Ovid's works, say the critics cited by Baillet, for all their *esprit* and *facilité*, lack *règle* and *mesure*, and abound in *des jeunesses, le mauvais goût, les faux brillans* and *les superfluités.* The Roman and Renaissance criticisms of Ovid were reinforced by Romantic demands for 'seriousness', 'pathos' and 'sincerity' (in all of which Ovid was found conspicuously wanting[6]), and have thus survived to our own century.

The strength and persistence of the Roman objections to Ovid, together with the widespread familiarity with and affection for Ovid's works among educated readers, made it inevitable that Ovid should feature prominently in the critical debates of the seventeenth century about the role which verbal and imaginative exuberance and playfulness might properly play in dramatic, heroic and lyric poetry.[7] These were debates in which John Dryden took a special interest, and to which he made frequent contributions in his critical prose.

In one of his earliest essays, the Dedicatory Letter to *Annus Mirabilis* (1667), Dryden praised Ovid's depictions of his passionate heroines for precisely those qualities which had been denied by many critics, arguing that Ovid is so anxious to produce 'concernment' in the reader for his distressed ladies that

his words...are the least part of his care, for he pictures Nature in disorder, with which the study and choice of words is inconsistent. This is the proper wit of Dialogue or Discourse, and, consequently, of the *Drama*, where all that is said is to be suppos'd the effect of sudden thought; which, though it excludes not the quickness of wit in repartees, yet admits not a too curious election of words, too frequent allusions, or use of Tropes, or, in fine, any thing that showes remoteness of thought, or labour in the Writer.[8]

But by the time he came to write the Preface to Tonson's composite version of *Ovid's Epistles* (1680), Dryden, while still maintaining much of his earlier admiration for Ovid's portrayal of women in love, had moved significantly closer to the 'Roman' view:

the copiousness of [Ovid's] Wit was such, that he often writ too pointedly for his Subject, and made his persons speak more Eloquently than the Violence of their Passion would admit: so that he is frequently witty out of season: leaving the Imitation of Nature, and the cooler dictates of his Judgment, for the false applause of Fancy.[9]

Dryden went on to reiterate the Roman criticisms of Ovid at various points in his later prose, and nowhere more memorably than in the Preface to his last volume, *Fables Ancient and Modern* (1700). There, having expressed a general preference for the poetry of Chaucer over that of Ovid, he remarked:

The Vulgar Judges, which are Nine Parts in Ten of all Nations, who call Conceits and Jingles Wit, who see *Ovid* full of them, and *Chaucer* altogether without them, will think me little less than mad, for preferring the *Englishman* to the *Roman*: Yet, with their leave, I must presume to say, that the Things they admire are only glittering Trifles, and so far from being Witty, that in a serious Poem they are nauseous, because they are unnatural. Wou'd any Man who is ready to die for Love, describe his Passion like *Narcissus*? Wou'd he think of *inopem me copia fecit*, and a Dozen more of such Expressions, pour'd on the Neck of one another, and signifying all the same Thing? If this were Wit, was this a Time to be witty, when the poor Wretch was in the Agony of Death? This is just *John Littlewit* in *Bartholomew Fair*, who had a Conceit (as he tells you) left him in his Misery; a miserable Conceit. On these Occasions the Poet shou'd endeavour to raise Pity: but instead of this, *Ovid* is tickling you to laugh.

If Ovid had been called upon to write Arcite's dying speech in Chaucer's *Knight's Tale*, Dryden speculates,

He would certainly have made *Arcite* witty on his Death-bed. He had complain'd he was farther off from Possession, by being so near, and a thousand such Boyisms, which *Chaucer* rejected as below the Dignity of the Subject.[10]

Dryden here alludes silently to a specific example of Ovid's wit-in-a-serious-circumstance which he had himself recently translated,[11] and endorses the Roman verdict on Ovid to the letter. The 'Boyisms' of the Preface to *Fables* are the direct descendants of the younger Seneca's *pueriles ineptiae*.

It is, however, a striking fact that, in the very translations from the Preface to which these remarks are quoted, Dryden, far from attempting to play down or expunge Ovid's 'Boyisms',[12] renders them with verve, skill and uninhibited relish. As so often, Dryden's stated critical position is in direct conflict with his poetic practice. It therefore seems pertinent to ask what the qualities were in Ovid's witty, playful or aloof handlings of 'serious' situations which undermined Dryden's conscious defences and caused him, when exercising his art, to delight in aspects of the Roman poet's work which, as a critic, he felt obliged to deplore.

Two of the translations in *Fables* offer themselves as appropriate test cases for such an investigation. Modern commentators have been almost universal in their condemnation of the long passage in Book 12 of the *Metamorphoses* which depicts the battle between the Lapiths and the Centaurs, and the terms of the critics' disapproval show them as true heirs of the Roman tradition. The episode has been called 'tedious and otiose', and even 'repulsive'. Critics have seen in it an 'ingenious gruesomeness' and have condemned it for its 'succession of *outré* killings' and its 'lurid and suggestive detail which today is the hallmark of reporting on capital crime in the tabloid press'. Ovid has been thought to have been 'revelling' in this episode 'in ever new ways of imagining how bodies can be mangled, maimed and disintegrated'.[13] Dryden, however, praises the passage strongly, remarking in the Headnote to his complete translation of Book 12 that 'The Fight of *Achilles* and *Cygnus*, and the Fray betwixt the *Lapythae* and *Centaurs*, yield to no other part of this Poet'.[14]

The story of Ceyx and Alcyone from Book 11, unlike the episode of the Lapiths and Centaurs, has been warmly praised by several modern scholars[15] and has been, down the ages, one of the most frequently excerpted and imitated of all the tales in the *Metamorphoses*. But even here the critical verdict has been mixed. Georges Lafaye, the translator of the *Metamorphoses* for the Budé series, charged Ovid with displaying *mauvais goût* in his description of Ceyx's drowning and in Alcyone's lament for her dead husband,[16] and the most recent English commentator on Book 11 has accused the poet of having undercut 'the pathos of his own narrative by pursuing fancy to the brink of the preposterous', of having allowed his interest in 'the setting' to 'distract from the tragedy itself', and of having depicted the last moments of Ceyx 'mercilessly', allowing his 'visual realism'...'to puncture a general effect of dignified pathos'.[17] Yet Dryden's version of the episode shows him to have lavished all his poetic skill on emulating precisely those qualities in his original which are singled out for particular censure by the modern critics.

An examination of Dryden's renderings of these two episodes would thus seem to provide a particularly useful basis for an attempt to comprehend, and by comprehending perhaps to come to share, some of the English poet's pleasure in the distinctively Ovidian handling of violence and pain.

2

Modern scholars have offered various explanations of Ovid's poetic intent in the episode of the Lapiths and Centaurs. Some have seen the passage as having been written out of, and designed to appeal to, the 'lurid curiosity for novel kinds of agony'[18] characteristic of a society whose favourite entertainment was gladiatorial combat. Others have attempted to explain the episode's appeal to the Roman intelligentsia by drawing analogies with the penchant displayed by some twentieth-century sophisticates for 'the spattering of blood and brains and furniture' in the 'Spaghetti Western'.[19] Others, again, have seen the whole of the later books of the *Metamorphoses* as an attempt on Ovid's part to bring his longest poem to an 'Augustan' culmination by concentrating on deeds of arms (an attempt for which, they say, he was temperamentally unsuited, and which therefore failed[20]), or conversely have seen the 'lurid' and 'grotesque' elements in the later books as a deliberate attempt at '*anti*-Augustanism': a parody or *reductio ad absurdum* of epic combat which wickedly subverts the heroic ideals embraced by Augustus and Maecenas.[21] This last group of critics has stressed the obtrusively 'literary' quality of the final section of the *Metamorphoses* – Ovid's deployment for his own very different purposes of subject-matter and language which his audience would immediately recognise from other (chiefly Homeric and Virgilian) contexts. A further group of commentators, while similarly stressing the allusiveness of the later books, has held that this practice constituted, itself, the *raison d'être* of these sections of the poem: Ovid, they say, was parodying, inverting and varying the epic material with which his sophisticated readers were already familiar, his primary intention being to produce a 'purely literary' pleasure and to turn attention onto the virtuosity of the narrator himself, rather than to reorientate his audience's perceptions of the human situations and problems with which epic literature deals.[22]

But none of these responses accounts for the particular kinds of interest and pleasure which Dryden's translation shows him to have taken in the episode. The version clearly demonstrates Dryden's sense of the sophistication and control exercised by Ovid throughout Book 12, a control quite incompatible with neurotic or depraved blood-lust. Dryden does not seem to have detected any ideological purpose in the episode, nor did he make any consistent attempt to apply the passage to the politics of his own day.[23] He would have been little interested in poetry which was designed to display a 'purely literary' virtuosity. And he was not influenced by the allegorical interpretations which had seen the battle of the Lapiths and Centaurs as a solemn warning against the dire effects of wine and lust.[24]

Dryden's version of Book 12 of the *Metamorphoses* has, in fact, received little critical attention. Most accounts of the poet's work pass over the translation cursorily with, at most, a few (usually unenthusiastic) general remarks.[25]

So it would seem necessary at this stage to look at a number of short crucial passages, to establish some sense of the nature of Dryden's engagement with his original at the detailed, local, level. It may then be possible to move to some more general suggestions about his interest in the imaginative potential of Ovid's battle.

The central section of Ovid's Twelfth Book (lines 210–535 in the Latin, 292–705 in Dryden's version) depicts the carnage and destruction which ensues when one of the Centaurs, who have been invited as guests to the Thessalian wedding of Perithous and Hippodamia, attempts to rape the bride. Most of the lengthy passage is taken up with detailed descriptions of the maimings and deaths of various of the Centaurs and their opponents the Lapiths, culminating in the burial under an immense pile of logs of the invulnerable Caeneus, whose metamorphosis into a golden-feathered bird brings the episode to its close. One of the first to be maimed in the conflict is Grineus, a Centaur who has just hurled a huge altar-stone into the midst of the Lapiths, instantly killing several of their number. The Lapith Exadius vows vengeance, and immediately seeks a means of putting his vow into effect:

> He look'd about, where on a Pine were spred
> The votive Horns of a Stags branching Head:
> At *Grineus* these he throws; so just they fly,
> That the sharp Antlers stuck in either Eye:
> Breathless and Blind he fell; with Blood besmear'd;
> His Eye-balls beaten out, hung dangling on his Beard.   (374–9)

Dryden has been especially struck by the ordered precision with which the incident is narrated. The teller in the translation (as in the original) gives the impression of being entirely untroubled as he narrates Grineus' gruesome fate. There is mordant punning in Dryden's characterisation of the antlers' flight as 'just': they effect the desired revenge for Grineus' initial crime and also strike so 'justly' (exactly) that both eyeballs are extruded by the single blow. The effect of clinical, impassive, observation is reinforced by the brisk, businesslike, step of line 377 ('That the sharp Antlers stuck in either Eye'). But the manner of narration is also flexible and leisurely enough to include a beautiful Miltonism ('a Stags branching Head'[26]) to describe the majestic votive offering which has effected the atrocity, and the last two lines of the passage quoted are notable for their obtrusive alliterative patterning which, as well as adding force to the description, simultaneously reminds readers that they are being given not raw uncensored violence but material which has been carefully processed and fashioned by an artist's hand. Here Dryden offers an English analogue of the effect created in the Latin by the patterned deliberateness of Ovid's 'pars...pars' construction:

> Eruiturque oculos. quorum pars cornibus haeret:
> Pars fluit in barbam; concretaque sanguine pendet.   (269–70)

And his eyeballs were gouged out. One of these stuck to the horn and the other rolled down upon his beard and hung there in a mass of clotted blood.[27]

A little after the maiming of Grineus, Aphidas meets his fate:

> Amid the Noise and Tumult of the Fray,
> Snoring and drunk with Wine, *Aphidas* lay.
> Ev'n then the Bowl within his Hand he kept:
> And on a Bear's rough Hide securely slept.
> Him *Phorbas* with his flying Dart, transfix'd;
> Take thy next Draught, with *Stygian* Waters mix'd,
> And sleep thy fill, th'insulting Victor cry'd;
> Surpris'd with Death unfelt, the Centaur dy'd;
> The ruddy Vomit, as he breath'd his Soul,
> Repass'd his Throat; and fill'd his empty Bowl. (435-44)[28]

Here, if anywhere, we might have expected Dryden's translation to show the influence of moralistic readings of the episode as an indictment of drunken abandon. Yet he has followed Ovid in deliberately avoiding any censorious emphasis, and in stressing, rather, the peaceful oblivion of Aphidas' slumber and the consequent painlessness of his death. Though Dryden can incorporate an irony in the adverb used to characterise Aphidas' sleeping – 'securely' (and in Phorbas' exhortation to him to 'sleep' – we might have expected 'drink' – his fill), the central detail around which he clearly thought Ovid had shaped his little scene was the way in which the bowl held in the sleeping Centaur's hand was conveniently at the ready to receive the blood which flowed from his throat at the point of death. Dryden has been struck by the way in which the Centaur's idle and accidental retention of the bowl has now provided a neat and apt receptacle for the 'ruddy Vomit'. The balanced antithesis of his last line mirrors Ovid's precise specification of the 'Vomit's' destination in the Latin ('inque...inque'):

> plenoque è gutture fluxit
> Inque toros, inque ipsa niger carchesia sanguis. (325-6)

and from his full throat out upon the couch and into the very wine-cup the dark blood flowed.

Ovid's treatment had stressed the bizarre incongruity of the event. But he had also observed a number of telling miscellaneous details in the imagined scene. He had noted, for example, the precise materials from which the death-dealing spear had been made. He had reminded readers of the potential pathos of the scene: the Centaur is a *juvenis* (323). A beautiful Greek-derived poetic plural (*carchesia*) had been used to describe the drinking vessel into which Aphidas' blood was disgorged. Even the fabulous origin (Mount Ossa) of the bearskin on which Aphidas lay had been noted. And the whole was shaped into a poetic entity by Ovid (in a way carefully imitated by Dryden) with subtle patterns of assonance and alliteration.

Towards the end of the battle, Ovid interjected a digression depicting 'the Loves and Death of *Cyllarus* and *Hylonome*, the Male and Female Centaur', which Dryden singled out as 'wonderfully moving'.[29] Cyllarus, a particularly handsome Centaur, is loved by Hylonome, a beautiful Centaur 'Maiden'. Both have come to the wedding feast and both now fight side by side. Cyllarus is pierced by a stray spear and dies in the arms of his beloved, who then takes the weapon from her lover's heart and uses it to kill herself.

Commentators have often seen the description of Cyllarus' and Hylonome's love as providing attractive and welcome relief from the lengthy catalogue of slaughters which have preceded it.[30] Dryden responded to this change of mood and pace in Ovid's text, and also discovered in the passage an opportunity to explore one of his favourite poetic subjects – the similarities and differences between sexual love in the human and animal worlds. His initial description of Hylonome (like that in his original) contains lines which, if excerpted, could be taken for an evocation of a beautiful human maiden or a wood-nymph:

> ut sit coma pectine laevis:
> Ut modo rore maris, modo se violâve rosâve
> Implicet: interdum candentia lilia gestet:
> Bisque die lapsis Pagasaeae vertice silvae
> Fontibus ora lavet: bis flumine corpora tingat. (409–13)

so that her long locks are smoothed with a comb; now she twined rosemary, now violets or roses in her hair; and sometimes she wore white lilies. Twice each day she bathed her face in the brook that fell down from a wooded height by Pagasa, and twice dipped her body in the stream.

> For him she dress'd: For him with Female Care
> She comb'd, and set in Curls, her auborn Hair.
> Of Roses, Violets, and Lillies mix'd
> And Sprigs of flowing Rosemary betwixt
> She form'd the Chaplet, that adorn'd her Front:
> In Waters of the *Pagasaean* Fount,
> And in the Streams that from the Fountain play,
> She wash'd her Face; and bath'd her twice a Day. (542–51)

And the couple's life together is even momentarily assimilated, in the English version, to the paradisal bliss of Milton's Adam and Eve:

> With equal Flame
> They lov'd: Their *Sylvan* Pleasures were the same:
> All day they hunted: And when Day expir'd,
> Together to some shady Cave retir'd. (554–7)[31]

Yet in both the original and the English version we are also never allowed to forget that the couple are half-horses. The description of Hylonome quoted above is prefixed in Ovid's text by the proviso:

> Haec & blanditiis, & amando, & amare fatendo
> Cyllaron una tenet. cultus quoque *quantus in illis*
> *Esse potest membris*. (407–9, my italics)

She, by her coaxing ways, by loving and confessing love, alone possessed Cyllarus; and by her toilet, too, *so far as such a thing was possible in such a form*.

Dryden's version, though much gentler, offers essentially the same reminder:

> *Hylonome*, for Features, and for Face
> Excelling all the Nymphs of double Race:
> Nor less her Blandishments, than Beauty move;
> At once both loving and confessing Love.   (540–3)

Here Dryden has been careful to imitate Ovid's *polyptoton* (& *amando* & *amare fatendo*) in his own version ('At once both loving and confessing Love'). The effect works both to reinforce the reader's sense of the intensity and frankness of Hylonome's affections, and simultaneously draws attention to the very incongruity involved in such feelings being displayed by a creature 'of double Race'. The poet makes no attempt to conceal his part in controlling the reader's response.

The constant reminders of the couple's (partial) horsiness allow both Ovid and Dryden to bring an unexpected blend of emotions into play in the reader's mind when the two Centaurs die. We remember, with equal force, the couple's devotion and beauty and the fact that this beauty is one in which 'the Beast was equal to the Man' (531). The vocabulary of Dryden's version exploits the age-old English reverence for equine splendour: Cyllarus has a 'Back proportion'd for the Seat', a brawny 'Chest' and a 'Coal-black' coat which 'shone' 'like Jet' (534–6). At the moment of the couple's death, the English version incorporates two strokes of wit, both of them characteristically 'Ovidian' but neither of them directly prompted by the Latin. When Cyllarus falls, mortally wounded, Hylonome rushes to him,

> And while her Hand the streaming Blood oppos'd,
> Join'd Face to Face, his Lips with hers she clos'd.
> Stiffled with Kisses, a sweet Death he dies.   (566–8)

It is possible to detect a slight raise of the eyebrows in the very deliberateness with which the joining of faces and lips is described. Ovid, at the equivalent place in the original (425) seems, in saying that *animae fugienti obsistere tentat* ('[Hylonome] strove to hold from its passing the dying breath'), to be alluding to the belief that one should catch the departing breath of a loved one with a kiss, and perhaps thus prevent death occurring (since a dying man's expiring breath carried his soul from his body[32]). Dryden redirects the fancy, suggesting that, in her anxiety to smother her lover with kisses, Hylonome was part cause of his death, which, nevertheless, was found sweet by Cyllarus because it was accompanied by her embraces.

The death of Hylonome herself is described thus by Ovid:

> telo, quod inhaeserat illi,
> Incubuit: moriensque suum complexa maritum est.   (427–8)

She threw herself upon the spear which had pierced Cyllarus and fell in a dying embrace upon her lover.

175

Dryden expands the moment considerably:

> In madness of her Grief, she seiz'd the Dart
> New-drawn, and reeking from her Lover's Heart;
> To her bare Bosom the sharp Point apply'd;
> And wounding fell; and falling by his Side,
> Embrac'd him in her Arms; and thus embracing, dy'd.   (572–6)

The double *polyptoton* of the last two lines, plus the conclusion of the paragraph with a triplet plus an Alexandrine, gives Hylonome's end a conspicuously stylised cast. The effect is to concentrate and epitomise the ambivalent impressions which the Centaur-lovers have made from the start. Hylonome dies to a poetical flourish which simultaneously aggrandises and, in its neatly patterned antitheses, distances us from her, allowing the reader to perceive the moment as both an impassioned *Liebestod* and a slightly melodramatic, almost 'hammy', gesture from a creature who is, after all, only *half* human.

A few lines after the suicide of Hylonome, the Centaur Phaeocomes kills the Lapith Phonolenides:

> Codice qui misso, quem vix juga bina moverent
> Juncta, Phonoleniden a summo vertice fregit.
> Fracta volubilitas capitis latissima: perque os,
> Perque cavas nares, oculosque, auresque cerebrum
> Molle fluit. veluti concretum vimine querno
> Lac solet; utve liquor rari sub pondere cribri
> Manat; & exprimitur per densa foramina spissus.   (432–8)

Hurling a log which the combined force of two yokes of cattle could scarce move, he struck Phonolenides a crushing blow upon the head. The broad dome of his head was shattered, and through his mouth, through the hollow nostrils, eyes, and ears oozed the soft brains, as when curdled milk drips through the oaken withes, or a thick liquid mass trickles through a coarse sieve weighted down, and is squeezed out through the crowded apertures.

Dryden translates:

> He threw at *Pholon*; the descending Blow
> Divides the Skull, and cleaves his Head in two.
> The Brains, from Nose and Mouth, and either Ear
> Come issuing out, as through a Colendar
> The curdled Milk: or from the Press the Whey
> Driv'n down by Weights above, is drain'd away.   (585–90)

Ovid's lines have been much criticised. *Res foeda*, commented the editor of the Oxford Variorum Ovid of 1826 dryly, *poterat sine similitudine transmitti* ('The foul event could have been conveyed without a simile'[33]), and the passage has been rejected from some editions of the *Metamorphoses*, one editor finding it 'totally unworthy of Ovid'.[34]

Though one of Dryden's editions informed him that the slaying of Phonolenides did not appear in some manuscripts of the *Metamorphoses*, the poet may have recollected a passage in the *Fasti* where Ovid had used a similar image of whey being squeezed through a wicker-work sieve in the cheese-making process.[35] At any rate, he evidently regarded the simile (suitably tidied up and purged of the slight obscurities which have puzzled scholars) as very much in accord with the general spirit of the Lapiths and Centaurs episode. For there were other moments in Book 12 where Ovid had drawn the reader's attention to the precise physical laws which the processes of destroying living limbs, tissue, features and bones in battle manifest in common with other, apparently totally dissimilar, activities and occurrences in the peacetime world.

Just as, earlier, Ovid (in Dryden's rendering) had likened the 'shriveling' 'crackle' of burning hair to 'dry Stubble fir'd' (386) and to the hissing of 'red hot Iron, within the Smithy drown'd' (390), and had described the firebrand with which Rhoetus had beaten Comoetes to a 'Lever' which 'drives the batter'd Skull, within the Brains' (401), so, here, the poet's attention is on the precise similarity of pressure and texture between crushed brains passing through the apertures of an impacted skull and the manner in which whey is extracted in cheese making. No attempt whatever is made to encourage sympathy or fellow-feeling with the Lapith on whom the action is being performed.

The point has now been reached where it may be possible to make some larger suggestions about the nature of Dryden's interest in the episode of the Lapiths and Centaurs as a whole. It might first be noted that Ovid took much care to establish a particular context for his battle, a context which Dryden, by rendering the whole of Book 12, was able to preserve intact. The story of the Lapiths and Centaurs is told, in a period of respite from the fighting round Troy, by the traditionally garrulous and aged Nestor, for the benefit of Achilles. Achilles in Ovid's narrative is not totally divested of his aura of Homeric heroism, but Ovid's treatment also allows the reader a certain amused delight in Achilles' boyish naiveté, and at the undignified situations in which he finds himself, particularly his exasperated attempts to defeat the invulnerable Cygnus. Nestor's tale, itself told in a legendary past, refers his audience to a yet more distant past (when he was in the second of the three centuries which, according to Ovid, he had lived so far) and deals with semi-mythical creatures in a semi-mythical and remote region of northern Greece. Before the narration of the battle even begins, therefore, the reader has been positioned at several stages removed from the conflict. And the narrative itself is constantly punctuated by reminders that the deaths and dismemberments which we are witnessing are of 'Brutes', 'Monsters' and 'Beasts', not of beings which too closely resemble any which we might expect to encounter in life. As we have seen, moreover, Ovid's style constantly serves to remind us, obtrusively, that we are experiencing a highly fashioned work of art, not attending to anything which could for a moment be confused with the world of day-to-day reality.

An advantage of this elaborate process of verbal and narrative distancing is that, once established, it allows the poet various kinds of freedom and flexibility in his depictions of violent fighting which might not have been possible if his readers' sympathies had been more straightforwardly and whole-heartedly engaged with the emotions and fortunes of the characters in the drama. Ovid's narrative allows readers to entertain thoughts about and attitudes towards human conflict which might not have been possible if human conflict had been his overt subject. We can, for example, focus, in this battle, on the sheer arbitrariness and inconsequentiality of much of what happens once any hand-to-hand fighting has commenced. Freed by his fantastic setting from any pressing obligation to pass moral judgement or to take sides, the poet can concentrate with scrupulous exactness and fascinated attention (but without gloating, or attempting to produce vicarious thrills) on the precise physical processes involved in the disintegration of flesh and bone. He can register the curious resemblances between actions on the battlefield and other actions which the reader has seen or experienced in quite different regions of life. He can see symmetry and shape in actions which, looked at in almost any other conceivable frame of mind, would seem merely chaotic and confused. He can register the potential for beauty and humour and horror at one and the same moment in one and the same action, and his verbal wit and rhetorical patterning can be his means of containing and focusing these paradoxical responses.

The poetic stance adopted by Ovid in Book 12 might thus seem less simple-mindedly callous and less gratuitously tasteless than it appears at first sight. And the positive appeal of such a stance for a poet of Dryden's temperament is not difficult to appreciate. It has always been recognised that Dryden particularly relished poetic situations which enabled him to adopt an oblique, distanced or analytical relation to his subject. And the sceptical attitude towards martial heroism which is such a prominent feature of his later writing[36] may have made him particularly well disposed towards an episode which, though many of its individual acts of violence have their parallels in the *Iliad* or *Aeneid*,[37] tends to concentrate on the ultimate weakness and insignificance of fighting men rather than, like Homer, viewing heroic combat as the moment which simultaneously asserts life's frightening vulnerability and its supreme preciousness and grandeur, or, like Virgil, seeing it as a painful but necessary means to the establishing of a great civilisation.

Yet both Ovid's battle and Dryden's version are still open to serious objections, of a kind similar to those which Dr Johnson levelled against the 'metaphysical' poets:

they...wrote rather as beholders than partakers of human nature; as beings looking upon good and evil, impassive and at leisure; as Epicurean deities making remarks on the actions of men and the vicissitudes of life, without interest and without emotion.[38]

Ovid and Dryden, it can be objected, are using their mythological narrative to affect a godlike superiority to the painful dimensions of earthly life, a more-than-human view of humanity which ignores the poets' own participation and implication in the human condition, and which consequently strikes the reader as sub- rather than supra-human.

Another of Johnson's criticisms of the metaphysical poets can be pressed against Ovid's episode:

Their attempts were always analytick: they broke every image into fragments, and could no more represent by their slender conceits and laboured particularities the prospects of nature or the scenes of life, than he who dissects a sunbeam with a prism can exhibit the wide effulgence of a summer noon.[39]

In the battle of the Lapiths and Centaurs, Ovid and his English translator display an acute eye for the incongruous detail, the strange resemblances 'in things apparently unlike',[40] the bizarre arbitrarinesses of the situation depicted, but these remain opportunist and isolated strokes, never seeming to connect in the reader's mind so that they all appear to emanate from an imaginatively coherent general conception of life. They never, that is, attain what Johnson thought to be the characteristic quality of the best witty imaginings of poets: they never seem 'at once natural and new'.[41]

3

However, the impulse to write about human life from a standpoint in some ways resembling that of a god, looking down on humanity with a broader, more comprehensive, view than human beings can ordinarily attain, is not necessarily coldly sub-human or vainly and self-deludedly presumptuous. On two occasions Dryden published memorable renderings of famous moments in Latin poetry where the poet, or his persona, had imagined the pleasure of rising above the human condition to see it from a larger, and therefore more complete and truthful, vantage-point. Dryden had begun his rendering of the opening of Lucretius' Second Book thus:

> 'Tis pleasant, safely to behold from shore
> The rowling Ship; and hear the Tempest roar:
> Not that anothers pain is our delight;
> But pains unfelt produce the pleasing sight.
> 'Tis pleasant also to behold from far
> The moving Legions mingled in the War:
> But much more sweet thy lab'ring steps to guide,
> To Vertues heights, with wisdom well supply'd,
> And all the *Magazins* of Learning fortifi'd:
> From thence to look below on humane kind,
> Bewilder'd in the Maze of Life, and blind.   (1–11)

And in his version of Pythagoras' discourse from the Fifteenth Book of the *Metamorphoses*, Dryden warmed to the Greek philosopher's desire

> To leave the heavy Earth, and scale the height,
> Of *Atlas*, who supports the heav'nly weight;

179

To look from upper Light, and thence survey
Mistaken Mortals wandring from the way
And wanting Wisdom, fearful for the state
Of future Things, and trembling at their Fate!   (215-20)

The details of the speakers' positions in Dryden's two originals differ considerably. But his versions show that he saw affinities between the Lucretian and Pythagorean desires to look down on mankind not 'without interest and without emotion' but, rather, having attained a comprehensive view of life, encompassing both sympathetic involvement and objectifying distance, in which the pains and glories, follies and pleasures, pathos and comedy, of the human condition could all be given no more and no less than their due, and could thus be contemplated and enjoyed in untroubled calm.

In the fable of Ceyx and Alcyone from Book 11 of the *Metamorphoses* Dryden found an episode in which Ovid had attained such a stance. In this episode, Ovid achieved a perspective on human life which, though freer and larger than many to be found in fiction, is not (like the battle of the Lapiths and Centaurs) vulnerable to the charge that the poet has forsaken his own humanity in the pursuit of an 'analytick' impassivity.

But if the poet's stance in *Ceyx and Alcyone* can be described as (in some ways) 'godlike', it is not that of any of the gods who appear in the episode itself. In his reworking of his sources, Ovid had transformed the tale from one of divine vengeance for impiety into a story in which the gods' part in the affair is altogether more mysterious.[42] Ceyx and Alcyone, in Ovid's version, have committed no crime, and the malignity of the storm which destroys Ceyx seems as strangely arbitrary as the reaction of Juno to Alcyone's prayers of distress, or Somnus' to Iris' request that a dream be sent to inform Alcyone of her husband's fate. Both deities act not out of any sense of duty, justice or compassion, but to rid themselves of their petitioners' tiresome pestering.[43]

Yet the narrator–poet sees beyond the arbitrariness which constitutes one aspect of the gods' activity, to include the beneficence which is also part of their character. For the tale ends not on a note of frustration, dejection or bafflement, but with Ceyx's and Alcyone's beautiful metamorphosis and consequent release from their grief and separation, a metamorphosis which is itself the work of gods, now for a moment as mysteriously merciful as they had previously been indifferent, impotent, or heartless.

If the poet can acknowledge both the arbitrariness and the beneficence of the gods, so can he see his human characters' behaviour in a greater variety of lights than is usual in narrative fictions. This largeness of vision is strikingly noticeable in his treatment of his heroine. Begging her husband not to go on his intended sea-voyage, Alcyone reminds Ceyx of the closeness of their relationship: *Jam potes Halcyone securus abesse relicta* (423). ('Can you now abandon your Alcyone with no thought of her?'). Dryden heightens the pathos and seriousness of her request by having his heroine evoke her marriage in a phrase which had been used by Milton's Adam to characterise his relationship with Eve, the crown of his happiness in Eden:

> Can *Ceyx* then sustain to leave his Wife,
> And unconcern'd forsake the Sweets of Life?　　　　　(19–20)[44]

And when Alcyone begs to be allowed to travel with Ceyx, she is given, in the English version, a tone of ardently romantic insistence:

> Go not without thy Wife! but let me bear
> My part of Danger with an equal share,
> And present, what I suffer only fear:
> Then o'er the bounding Billows shall we fly,
> Secure to live together, or to die.　　　　　(49–53)

Dryden has given a heady flourish to the close, but in a way that also, with unobtrusive irony, anticipates future events. In his fidelity to the precise tenor of Alcyone's request in Ovid, Dryden conveys more of her discreetly intelligent realism, as well as her passion, than is apparent in the more straightforwardly confident (and therefore more than a little self-deluding) romanticism of Charles Hopkins's Alcyone:

> Take me along, let me your Fortunes share,
> There's nought too hard for Love like mine to bear.
> In Storms, and Calms, together let us keep,
> Together brave the dangers of the Deep,
> The grant of this, my flattering Love assures,
> Which knows no Joys, and feels no Griefs but yours.[45]

The sentiments of Dryden's Alcyone are also sometimes voiced with a super-scrupulous exactness which reveals an acute psychological understanding on the poet's part, but which simultaneously allows the reader something approaching a smile at her precision and earnestness. A good example occurs at the moment when she is warning Ceyx about the difficulty which her father Aeolus has in controlling the turbulence of the sea winds. At this point Ovid's Alcyone remarks:

> Quo magis hos novi, (nam novi, & saepe paterna
> Parva domo vidi) magis hoc reor esse timendos.　　　　　(437–8)

The more I know (for I do know them, and have often seen them when a child in my father's home) the more I think them to be feared.

Dryden remembered George Sandys's version:

> These knew I, and oft saw their rude comport;
> While yet a Girle, within my fathers Court.[46]

In his own rendering, he took his cue from Ovid's repetition of *novi* and from the emphatic parenthesis in the Latin, and made the smallest changes in

Sandys's wording to turn Alcyone's remark into an insistent reminder of what, as a child, she had noted down for future reference:

> I know them well, and mark'd their rude Comport,
> While yet a Child, within my Father's Court. (41–2)

Dryden then extended the thought by taking up the hint from Sandys's 'Court' and, in an addition of his own, likening Aeolus' fear of his subjects to that which had been recently experienced by more than one English monarch:

> In times of Tempest they command alone,
> And he but sits precarious on the Throne. (43–4)

But Dryden's momentary likening of the winds to the (in his view) subversive and anarchic forces which had twice shaken the English throne in his own lifetime was not undertaken in any spirit of fear or disgust. Aeolus' impotence is imagined with a relish, and the winds' wayward gusto and malice with a vigour which gives the reader an access to the imagined spectacle which is pleasantly independent of any authorial censoriousness. And we are allowed something approaching a smile at the solemn insistence with which Alcyone makes her point, while simultaneously registering the seriousness of what might be at stake. The poet's sympathies are everywhere at once – with the helpless king, with the headstrong winds, with the desperate wife telling all this in a passionate attempt to prevent her husband's departure:

> Nor let false Hopes to trust betray thy Mind,
> Because my Sire in Caves constrains the Wind,
> Can with a Breath their clam'rous Rage appease,
> They fear his Whistle, and forsake the Seas;
> Not so, for once indulg'd, they sweep the Main;
> Deaf to the Call, or hearing hear in vain;
> But bent on Mischief bear the Waves before,
> And not content with Seas insult the shoar,
> When Ocean, Air, and Earth, at once ingage
> And rooted Forrests fly before their Rage:
> At once the clashing Clouds to Battle move,
> And Lightnings run across the Fields above. (29–40)[47]

Ovid's combination of sympathy and distance can be seen, too, in his treatment of Ceyx. One characteristic touch occurs when, having tried many arguments in vain to persuade Alcyone of the necessity of his voyage, Ceyx eventually prevails by telling her that his journey will only be of two months' duration. Ceyx's breakthrough is likened to a lucky strategy devised by a lawyer to win his case. Hitherto all his arguments have failed:

> Nec tamen idcirco caussam probat. addidit illis
> Hoc quoque lenimen, quo solo flexit amantem. (449–50)

For all that he did not prove his case. He added this comforting condition, also, by which alone he convinced his loving wife.

Dryden and Ovid

Dryden preserved the legal metaphor, so allowing the reader to stand back a little from Ceyx's predicament. While never doubting the genuineness of his affection, we observe him fixed (as human beings so often are) in his own resolve, searching for an unanswerable argument, rather than making any real attempt to face or answer his wife's objections:

> Nor these avail'd; at length he lights on one,
> With which, so difficult a Cause he won. (60–1)

As the couple part, Dryden follows Ovid in allowing us to view the scene both from the vantage-point of the departing ship (it is the land which recedes) and of Alcyone (we also see the boat going down, in carefully defined stages, over the horizon). He also imitates and heightens the orderly cause-and-effect explicitness and balance with which Ovid had described the successive stages of Alcyone's reaction. We are thus able to observe the whole situation, and particularly the Queen's behaviour, with a cool attentiveness:

> The Queen recover'd rears her humid Eyes,
> And first her Husband on the Poop espies
> Shaking his Hand at distance on the Main;
> She took the Sign; and shook her Hand again.
> Still as the Ground recedes, contracts her View
> With sharpen'd Sight, till she no longer knew
> The much-lov'd Face; that Comfort lost supplies
> With less, and with the Galley feeds her Eyes;
> The Galley born from view by rising Gales
> She follow'd with her Sight the flying Sails:
> When ev'n the flying Sails were seen no more
> Forsaken of all Sight, she left the Shoar. (75–86)

Dryden has delicately pointed up the momentary similarity of Alcyone's plight to that of Virgil's Dido, by rendering Ovid's

> vacuum petit anxia lectum:
> Seque toro ponit. renovat lectusque locusque
> Halcyonae lacrymas: & quae pars admonet absit (471–3)

Heavy-hearted she sought her lonely couch and threw herself upon it. The couch and the place renewed Alcyone's tears, for they reminded her of the part that was gone from her

thus:

> Then on her Bridal-Bed her Body throws,
> And sought in sleep her weary'd Eyes to close:
> Her Husband's Pillow, and the Widow'd part
> Which once he press'd, renew'd the former Smart, (87–90)[48]

recalling the moment in Book 4 of the *Aeneid* which he had rendered:

> She last remains, when ev'ry Guest is gone,
> Sits on the Bed he press'd, and sighs alone;
> Absent, her absent Heroe sees and hears. (117–19)[49]

Ovid's evocation of the storm which destroys Ceyx, and his depiction of the shipwreck and drowning itself are, it might be remembered, the sections of the episode which have prompted the most serious objections from modern critics. Here Ovid's wit and fancy, and his adapting to his own purposes of previous literary storm scenes,[50] are exercised to their full extent. As in the earlier descriptions of Aeolus, Dryden aligns Ovid's storm with tempestuous events of a kind experienced in his own century:

> In this Confusion while their Work they ply,
> The Winds augment the Winter of the Sky,
> And wage intestine Wars; the suff'ring Seas
> Are toss'd, and mingled as their Tyrants please. (111–14)

But, as before, the thought of civil strife is entertained in a way that seems closer to appreciative delight than appalled horror. Dryden has extended the hint contained in Ovid's animistic characterisation of the waves as *indignantia* ('aggrieved', 'complaining') to give an exhilarated sense of the way the winds seem to delight in the extent of their tyrannical power over the seas, a power which reduces the vast bulk of the oceans to something which can be 'toss'd' and 'mingled'.

Even more surprising is the poet's attitude when contemplating the storm's effects on its human victims:

> Ipse pavet; nec se, quid sit status, ipse fatetur
> Scire ratis rector; nec quid jubeatve, vetetve:
> Tanta mali moles, totâque potentior arte est. (492–4)

The captain himself is in terror and admits that he does not know how the vessel stands, nor what either to order or forbid; so great is the impending weight of destruction, more mighty than all his skill.

> The Master wou'd command, but in despair
> Of Safety, stands amaz'd with stupid Care,
> Nor what to bid, or what forbid he knows,
> Th'ungovern'd Tempest to such Fury grows:
> Vain is his Force, and vainer is his Skill. (115–19)

Here the antitheses, marked alliteration and *paranomasia* on 'bid' / 'forbid' (all directly imitative of stylistic features in Ovid's Latin), together with the deliberate exploitation of the two meanings of 'stupid' ('stunned with surprise' / 'obtuse') seem, cumulatively, both to evoke the nonplussed exasperation which the captain is feeling and, by their very obtrusiveness, to embody and provoke an attitude towards that exasperation which keeps us at a quizzical distance from the captain's plight.

Dryden's imitation and extension of Ovid's fanciful animism reaches its height at the moment when the waves mount their final assault on the vessel:

> Now all the Waves, their scatter'd Force unite,
> And as a Soldier, foremost in the Fight
> Makes way for others: And an Host alone
> Still presses on, and urging gains the Town;

So while th'invading Billows come a-brest,
The Hero tenth advanc'd before the rest,
Sweeps all before him with impetuous Sway,
And from the Walls descends upon the Prey;
Part following enter, part remain without,
With Envy hear their Fellows conqu'ring Shout:
And mount on others Backs, in hope to share
The City, thus become the Seat of War.   (161–72)[51]

The simile likening the decisive 'tenth wave' to a soldier leading an assault on a city is redeemed from seeming childishly extravagant by the precision and aptness of its fanciful logic. Ovid had attributed to his waves not merely a human will but also competitiveness, envy, vainglory, muscle-power, and tactical skill. Dryden extends the fancy, making the waves, explicitly, 'invaders', evoking their *élan* in the vivid onrush of his verse (167), and imagining the waves overcresting each other as climbing on one another's backs in envious eagerness to enter the city and share the spoils of war.

The inexorable force of a stormy sea (which to a human observer can seem almost wilful in its destructiveness) and the murderousness of looting insurgents could not possibly be enjoyed by anyone whose life was in direct danger from either. But such personal involvement in any hazardous action necessarily produces a certain myopia, a refusal to register aspects of the situation which might be apparent to a more distanced, and therefore in some senses more clearsighted, observer. Ovid's witty analogy allows the reader to entertain the senses in which a turbulent sea and an invading army might be thought of as impelled by a single grand spirit or power, whose anarchic and exuberant vigour can be legitimately conceived in a spirit of appreciative delight rather than merely being deplored or feared.

If Ovid can encourage us to relish a destructive storm, can he also allow us to view the predicament of a drowning man quizzically, without reproaching ourselves after the event for unpardonable callousness? Here are three excerpts from Dryden's rendering of the death of Ceyx:

All *Ceyx* his *Alcyone* employs,
For her he grieves, yet in her absence joys;
His Wife he wishes, and wou'd still be near,
Not her with him, but wishes him with her: (188–91)

But yet his Consort is his greatest Care;
Alcyone he names amidst his Pray'r,
Names as a Charm against the Waves, and Wind;
Most in his Mouth, and ever in his Mind: (214–17)[52]

As oft as he can catch a gulp of Air,
And peep above the Seas, he names the Fair,
And ev'n when plung'd beneath, on her he raves,
Murm'ring *Alcyone* below the Waves:
At last a falling Billow stops his Breath,
Breaks o'er his Head, and whelms him underneath.   (222–5)

Here the diction ('peep', 'gulp'), the pat antitheses which (among other things) seem almost to mimic the bobbing motion of a body in water, and the near-comic potential (combined with great precision) of lines 217 and 190-1 (the latter substantially Dryden's invention) ensure that the reader's reaction to the events is far removed from that of Shakespeare's Miranda in similar circumstances:

> O! I have suffered
> With those that I saw suffer. A brave vessel
> (Who had, no doubt, some noble creature in her)
> Dash'd all to pieces! O, the cry did knock
> Against my very heart. Poor souls, they perish'd.[53]

Yet we perhaps too often underestimate the ease with which what we call 'sympathy', in life and literature, can slide into a self-cherishing sentimentality, and a consequent failure of real imaginative engagement with and attentiveness to the situation we are purportedly contemplating. In any case, the Ovid / Dryden handling of Ceyx's drowning is not one which automatically and consistently excludes feelings at the more tender and pathetic end of the spectrum. These lines follow immediately after the first of the extracts quoted above:

> Now with last looks he seeks his Native Shoar,
> Which Fate has destin'd him to see no more;
> He sought, but in the dark tempestuous Night
> He knew not whether to direct his Sight.
> So whirl the Seas, such Darkness blinds the Sky,
> That the black Night receives a deeper Dye.   (192-7)

The treatment of Ceyx's drowning allows the reader to register many different reactions to the King's death: the ignominy of such a man being tossed like driftwood on the ocean, his part-devoted, part-superstitious, part-selfless, part-desperate obsession with his wife as he goes down, his precarious and pathetic vulnerability to the destructive forces about him.

One commentator on Book 11 spoke for many readers of the *Metamorphoses*, past and present, when he praised the episode depicting the Cave of Sleep for its 'hushed and trance-like' quality, drew attention to the way in which the very sound-patterns of Ovid's verse contribute to that effect, and remarked that 'Somnus...incorporates the very essence of sleepiness in live detail'.[54] Somnus is indeed an embodiment of the repose and release from worldly care which sleep provides. The surroundings of his cave are evoked in Dryden's version with a soothing melodiousness analogous to that which the commentators find in Ovid's original. And when, in Dryden's version, Iris addresses Somnus:

> O sacred Rest,
> Sweet pleasing Sleep, of all the Pow'rs the best!
> O Peace of Mind, repairer of Decay,
> Whose Balm renews the Limbs to Labours of the Day,
> Care shuns thy soft approach, and sullen flies away   (308-12)

Dryden and Ovid

the poet seems to be recalling the desperate yearnings of Shakespeare's Macbeth
for the sacred restorative powers of sleep:

> innocent sleep,
> Sleep that knits up the ravell'd sleave of care,
> The death of each day's life, sore labor's bath,
> Balm of hurt minds,...[55]

But Ovid's godlike inclusiveness of view extends to the gods themselves, and
in this poem Somnus is a figure who also embodies the comic dimensions of
sleep. The very poppies round his cave are 'nodding', both in reverence to the
god, and because they themselves can hardly keep awake. And as he hears Iris'
address, Somnus' chin knocks his bosom in weariness, and his utterances are
punctuated by yawns. As he wakes he (Sleep-as-god) has to 'shake off' himself
(Sleep-as-process). He only accedes to Iris' request to send a dream to warn
Alcyone of Ceyx's death because to do so will allow him to go back to sleep
all the sooner.[56]

It is just after hearing the news of her husband's death that Alcyone is given
what is perhaps the most striking piece of Ovidian word-play in the whole
episode:

> Nunc absens pereo, jactor nunc fluctibus absens:
> Et sine me, me pontus habet. (700–1)

But now far from myself I have perished; far from myself also I am tossed about upon
the waves, and without me the sea holds me.

Dryden finds his own equivalents for Ovid's *ploche* ('*Nunc...nunc*';
'*absens...absens*') and *anadiplosis* ('*...me, me...*'):

> Now I die absent, in the vast profound;
> And Me without my Self the Seas have drown'd. (423–4)

This would seem to be the moment in the poem where one might be most
inclined to pose Dryden's question: 'Were this a Time to be witty?' Indeed,
one commentator has described the lines as 'an Ovidian paradox pursued to
verbal breaking point' and t'the most extreme example of a type of word-play
to which Ovid was addicted'.[57] Yet, in the light of the arguments already
advanced, it is possible to see the lines as something more than a mere exercise
in wanton and unfeeling ingenuity. Ovid uses his rhetorical figures to reassert
the intimate *rapport* between the couple while simultaneously distancing the
reader from Alcyone's grief, allowing us to appreciate at the very same moment
the element of self-absorption and self-regard which is perhaps an inevitable
part of all human expressions of both grief and love. The effect is confirmed a
little later, at the moment when Alcyone first begins to recognise the corpse
floating towards her as that of Ceyx:

187

> quod quo magis illa tuetur,
> Hoc minus, & minus est amens sua. iamque propinquae
> Admotum terrae, iam quod cognoscere posset,
> Cernit. (722–5)

The more she regarded it, the less the deranged woman was in possession of herself. And now it had come close to land, now that it was something she could recognise, she perceived it fully.

> The more she looks, the more her Fears increase,
> At nearer Sight; and she's her self the less:
> Now driv'n ashore, and at her Feet it lies,
> She knows too much, in knowing whom she sees. (460–3)

Dryden has strengthened Ovid's emphasis on Alcyone's greed for knowledge which she already half knows she does not want to possess, a greed which makes her almost forsake her normal personality (she becomes *amens*) only to come to an all too sharp realisation of the position she is now in. The irony is all the more piquant in the light of her determination, only a few lines earlier, to treat the (as yet unidentified) corpse floating towards her *as if* it were Ceyx's, and her exclamation that the unknown wretch is unhappy, 'but *more* [his] widdow'd Wife' (Dryden, 457; my italics).

Yet Ovid's distance from Alcyone's grief in no way detracts from the sense of release and joy which is felt when the final metamorphosis occurs. Since at this culminating moment Dryden has responded with remarkable fullness to the challenge of his original, the passage must be given entire:

> to the neighb'ring Mole she strode,
> (Rais'd there to break th'Incursions of the Flood;)
> Headlong from hence to plunge her self she springs,
> But shoots along supported on her Wings,
> A Bird new-made about the Banks she plies
> Not far from Shore; and short Excursions tries;
> Nor seeks in Air her humble Flight to raise,
> Content to skim the Surface of the Seas:
> Her Bill, tho' slender, sends a creaking Noise,
> And imitates a lamentable Voice:
> Now lighting where the bloodless Body lies,
> She with a Funeral Note renews her Cries.
> At all her stretch her little Wings she spread,
> And with her feather'd Arms embrac'd the Dead:
> Then flick'ring to his palid Lips, she strove,
> To print a Kiss, the last essay of Love:
> Whether the vital Touch reviv'd the Dead,
> Or that the moving Waters rais'd his Head
> To meet the Kiss, the Vulgar doubt alone;
> For sure a present Miracle was shown.
> The Gods their Shapes to Winter-Birds translate,
> But both obnoxious to their former Fate.
> Their conjugal Affection still is ty'd,
> And still the mournful Race is multiply'd:

They bill, they tread; *Alcyone* compress'd
Sev'n Days sits brooding on her floating Nest:
A wintry Queen: Her Sire at length is kind,
Calms ev'ry Storm, and hushes ev'ry Wind;
Prepares his Empire for his Daughter's Ease,
And for his hatching Nephews smooths the Seas.　　　　(470–99)

This passage seems to epitomise the distinctive blend of involvement and distance, pathos and near-humour, psychological precision and extravagant fancy, discretion and daring, which are so characteristic of Ovid's episode. Dryden has responded to those touches in the Latin which evoke the miniature delicacy of the newly metamorphosed Alcyone. Where Ovid had, for Alcyone's leap from the breakwater, used the verb *insiluit*, a word which 'suggests a birdlike movement and so contains a hint of what is to come',[58] Dryden adopted the word 'springs' from his predecessors Sandys and Hopkins, but his combination of this with the phrase 'shoots along' to describe her new-found motion gives a far more vivid impression of her sudden sensation of the lightness of her own body than had been apparent in either of their versions.[59] The touching tentativeness of her flight is equally aptly captured in the 'short Excursions'[60] which she 'tries' (both nervousness and modesty prevent her attempting more ambitious flight), and we are reminded of the agile gracefulness of her movement in the way she 'skims' the seas and hovers 'flick'ring' in her vain attempts to kiss her husband's corpse with her 'slender Bill' and to embrace the body with arms which are now 'tiny' and 'feather'd'. These last touches remind us of both the delicate beauty and the disconcerting awkwardness of her transformation. She can now only emit eerie 'creaking' sounds which are a weird miniaturisation of her former groans of human misery. When Ceyx, too, is transformed, the couple are perceived to preserve in their changed state both the devotion and the sadness they had known in human life. Dryden daringly draws attention to the changed nature of their sexuality in his boldly witty and technically precise 'bill', 'tread',[61] 'compress'd', 'brooding', 'Nest'[62] and 'hatching', but these touches seem to fuse with, rather than merely undercut, the beauty and dignity of the new-formed union. Alcyone is felt genuinely to be a 'wintry Queen', the mother of a 'Race'. In the most daringly witty stroke of all, Dryden makes play with his own Catholicism, in asserting that their transformation, the work of gods far removed from the God of Christianity (Aeolus now seems able to exercise without difficulty the power over his subjects which had formerly eluded him), is 'a present Miracle', a demonstration that, by mysterious means to which only the gods are privy, human grief *can* be transcended and overcome, just as the storms of Winter are transformed into the calm of the 'halcyon days'.

Ovid's refusal to align himself, or the reader, in a position of straightforward empathy with the characters in the drama allows him and us a distance which enables us to see their conduct and thoughts in many different lights – appreciative, critical, quizzical, sympathetic, indulgent, clinical – without any of these predominating. Ovid puts into practice the principle enunciated in a couplet which Dryden inserted into his translation of the story of Cinyras and Myrrha:

> Eyes and their Objects never must unite,
> Some Distance is requir'd to help the Sight. (74–5)

To be allowed to share the poet's large vision has a consolatory, calming effect on the reader. For the mind, as Johnson knew, can only repose on the stability of truth. The Ovidian vision, which allows readers to face, comprehend, and thus enjoy, in a state of untroubled equanimity and delight, a view of human life as simultaneously glorious and futile, dignified and absurd, precious and dispensable, ordered and arbitrary, the care of the gods and of no concern to them at all, at one in its transience with the rest of Nature, with which it is involved in a continuous process of transformation, metamorphosis and flux, is a more adequate attempt to see life steadily and whole, for *all* that it contains, than many apparently more 'serious' literary endeavours. This may go some way towards explaining the endless fascination which, despite a hostile critical press, the best parts of the *Metamorphoses* have continued to provoke down the centuries, to the creation of which Ovid's notorious 'wit out of season' has made such an indispensable contribution.

12

THE *HEROIDES* AND THE ENGLISH AUGUSTANS

Rachel Trickett

In *The Rape of the Lock* occur these lines, the narrator's comment on the deaths of Dapperwit and Fopling in the battle of the beaux and the ladies:

> Thus on *Maeander's* flow'ry Margin lies
> Th' expiring Swan, and as he sings he dies.   (Canto v 61–2)

They are an allusion to the opening lines of Dryden's translation of Ovid's *Dido to Aeneas*, the seventh of his *Heroides*. Ovid's lines run:

> sic ubi fata vocant, udis abiectus in herbis
> ad vada Maeandri concinit albus olor...

and Dryden's translation:

> So on *Maeander's* banks, when death is nigh
> The Mournful *Swan* sings her own Elegie.[1]

By the time he wrote *The Rape of the Lock*, Pope had translated *Sappho to Phaon*, and two years after the final version of his mock epic he would, in 1717, publish his brilliant adaptation of Eloisa's letters to Abelard into the widely popular genre of the Heroic epistle. Ovid's influence on English poetry, from the allegorisations of his stories in the Middle Ages to the profusion of material – style, subject-matter, theme – from the *Metamorphoses* which occurred during the Renaissance, had contracted formally in the late seventeenth and early eighteenth centuries to this particular model of the epistolary monologue.

A general decay of belief in the vital symbolism of myth in this period accounts for the comparative neglect of the *Metamorphoses*, though Garth's 1717 edition of them went into seven more editions in the course of the century. The *Amores*, widely popular in the seventeenth century, had spawned the erotic elegies Restoration Court Wits continued to write as a modernised Ovidian genre, but their appeal was exceeded by that of the *Ars Amatoria* throughout the eighteenth century. Dryden had brilliantly translated the First Book of the *Ars Amatoria* as a piece of witty tongue-in-cheek didacticism which did not supersede the extant version of the poem[2] under the title of *De Arte Amandi* (of which there were seven separate editions between 1662 and 1705) until 1709. This 1709 edition with Dryden's translation, which also included the *Remedia Amoris*, was reprinted 14 times between 1709 and 1799.

The *Heroides* first newly appeared in this period in 1680 as *Ovid's Epistles* translated by several hands. The 1683 edition included Dryden's *Preface Concerning Ovid's Epistles*, and of the 19 reissues of this version in the rest of the eighteenth century, the 1725 edition and all subsequent ones included a translation of the *Amores*. So Ovid's celebration of the sorrows of love and of the pains and pleasures of its pursuit were bound together for eighteenth-century readers. But it was the Heroic epistle, the female tragic monologue, that attracted imitators, not, as in the seventeenth century, the male lover's diary of frustrations and enjoyments.

What was the cause of the popularity both of the form and the substance of these particular Ovidian poems in the eighteenth century? Dryden in his *Preface* writes that it seems that the Epistles are 'generally granted to be the most perfect piece of Ovid', and it seems likely that he is referring to the polish of the elegiac couplet which is so marked in them, and which served as a useful model for the English Heroic couplet with its terse antithetical balance and its pointing. But they were seen, too, as carrying to perfection Ovid's understanding of the nature of love. Dryden continues, 'If the Imitation of Nature be the business of a Poet, I know no Author who can justly be compar'd with ours, especially in the Description of the Passions.' Garth, who draws openly on Dryden in his own *Preface to the Translation of Ovid's Metamorphoses*, writes of Ovid's 'peculiar Delicacy in touching every Circumstance relating to the Passions and Affections', and again:

Ovid never excels himself so much, as when he takes Occasion to touch upon the Passion of Love; all Hearts are in a manner sensible of the same Emotion; and like Instruments tun'd Unisons, if a String of any one of them be struck, the rest by consent vibrate.[3]

'Venus's Clerk Ovyde' retains his position in this period not only as 'love's schoolmaster' in the *Ars Amatoria*, but also, and more importantly, as the sympathiser, the sharer and recorder of women's particular woes. In the *Heroides* he is at once natural and realistic in his portrayal of the psychology of women in love, but also heightened and intense, 'tenderly Passionate and Courtly, two Properties well agreeing with the Persons which were Heroines and Lovers', in Dryden's words. This mingling of an almost intimate naturalism with the convention of high rhetoric made an especial appeal to the English Augustan imagination. The language of pathos and sentiment in the idiom of the complaint, the tirade, the declamatory plea, describes and defines passion rather than attempting to express it by imitation or by dramatic metaphorical intensity. The language of the Heroic epistle, like that of Heroic drama, is a sort of code-language, the reader recognising at once the situation, the character of the woman, and the extreme nature of her feelings. She is torn by a mixed passion, experiencing at one and the same time shame and ardour, despair and hope, anger and submission. Ovid works out many variations on this stereotyped pattern, from the argumentative complaint of his Dido (quite other than the noble reticence of Virgil's queen), to the witty self-exposure of Helen, leading Paris on while she pretends to reject him. Helen is, as it were, at the other end of the scale of the victimised heroines – where Helen is taking the first fatal step to her downfall, they are facing the final consequences of their actions. The conflicting divisions of passion in the tragic heroines, however, though at the opposite extreme are on the same scale of temperament as Helen's innate duplicity.

In each case duality and division are in the very nature of the situation and of the poem, for the balanced antithetical style emphasises them. They appealed immediately to the shrewd observation and the analytic vision of the satirist. In the Introductory Argument to his translation of *Helen to Paris*, Dryden gives an ironic summary of her conflicting emotions and motives:

Helen, having receiv'd the foregoing Epistle from Paris, returns the following Answer: Wherein she seems at first to chide him for his Presumption in Writing as he had done, which could only proceed from his low Opinion of her Vertue: then owns herself to be sensible of the Passion, which he had express'd for her, tho' she much suspect his Constancy; and at last discovers her Inclinations to be favourable to him. The whole Letter showing the extream artifice of Woman-kind. (*Works* 514)

The placing of the opening lines of Ovid's *Dido to Aeneas* in the last Canto of *The Rape of the Lock* betrays Pope's understanding of the popular conventions of love in the literature of his own and the immediately preceding Restoration period. It is the intention of his mock-heroic poem to expose and undermine them. The war of the sexes, an Ovidian motif in the *Ars Amatoria* and elsewhere, is ironically translated into literal terms in Pope's battle between the beauties and the fops – the climax of the poem. The careful placing of the allusion to Ovid puts the false rhetoric of foppery and courtly love-lyric alongside the more sincere rhetoric of the complaint of deserted women. The two dandies, named after characters in Wycherley and Etheredge, recall the world of Restoration comedy, the witty foil to the claustrophobic emotionalism of Heroic tragedy. Pope proposes here, and in all his *Epistles* to women, a middle course between the false glamour of the sex-game and the pathos of women's vulnerability – the lesson of 'good sense' and 'good humour' and the substitution of rational friendship for passion. This wisdom grew out of the two literary extremes of libertinage and unrequited love, and eighteenth-century writers in prose and poetry universally support it. It shares the realism of Ovid's Roman wit without his cynicism, and the sympathy of his pathos without its submission to love's destructive force. Morally and in terms of everyday living it is one of the most attractive of eighteenth-century ideas, but it lacks the immediate appeal to the imagination and the senses which the Ovidian stylisations of love so enduringly possess. In poems like *The Rape of the Lock* and *The Essay of the Characters of Women* the fashionable world retains its dazzle even under the satirist's glass and the haggard ghosts of beauty retain, in every meaning, a haunting presence. Pope himself claimed to find 'breathings of the heart' in his own version of the Heroic epistle, *Eloisa to Abelard*, which suggest the 'sincerity' which was already becoming a prerequisite of 'true' poetry. It was written when he thought he was in love (with Lady Mary Wortley Montagu), and the material, often the precise language and phrases, were taken from the actual letters of Eloise to Abelard which had recently been published in translation. Commending this supremely successful English example of the Ovidian Heroic epistle, Dr Johnson wrote pointedly 'The heart naturally loves truth. The adventures and misfortunes of this illustrious pair are known from undisputed history.'[4] As we shall see, however, Pope was by no means the first to adapt Ovid's limited realism in his treatment of the heroines of myth and literature to actual historical figures.

Earlier than Augustan versions of the *Heroides* had emphasised quite simply the universal nature of the stories and the situations of the deserted girl. As Reuben Brower writes in his *Pope, The Poetry of Allusion*, 'Heroic love in the Ovidian tradition is not a private affair, but a drama played on the stage of history.'[5] Universality of sentiment and experience was emphasised by this, and the status of the heroines already established before Ovid chose them. His characters are the protagonists of well-known stories: thus Chaucer can draw on them in *The Legend of Good Women* as a martyrology, lists of well-known queens, nymphs and noblewomen who have given and lost all for love. The satisfaction of telling such stories lies, anyway, to a medieval author in their familiarity. The interest of the Elizabethan version of the Heroic epistle, however, reveals a further development. Drayton's *England's Heroicall Epistles*, unlike the medieval story versions, retain the form of the letter but concentrate less on the emotion than on the historical circumstances surrounding the love episode. Drayton's poems are an unusual, and unusually successful, experiment with Ovid's genre. His use of actual historical figures rather than mythological heroines adds another dimension and a further complication to the form which tends to draw away from the stereotyped situation.

In his Introduction *To the Reader* Drayton claims to have 'interwoven matters historical' so that not simply 'amorous Humour were handled therein', and something of the detail and vividness of Ovid's style is picked up in the historical references which give a kind of dramatic immediacy to the familiar love rhetoric. Rosamund's Tower and Labyrinth at Woodstock are exploited for poetic effect in both her and Henry's epistles; the city background makes a busy realistic setting for Edward IV's epistle to Jane Shore. Her reply is full of Ovidian overtones – reminiscent more of the *Ars Amatoria* than the *Heroides* as she speaks of the traps set for City women:

> Blame you our Husbands then, if they denie
> Our publique Walking, our Loose Libertie?
> If with exception still they us debarre
> The Circuit of the publique Theatre;

> To heare the Poet in a Comick straine,
> Able t'infect with his lascivious Scene;
> And the young wanton Wits, when they applaud
> The slie perswasion of some subtill Bawd;
> Or passionate Tragedian, in his rage
> Acting a Love-sick Passion on the Stage:
> When though abroad restraining us to rome,
> They very hardly keep us safe at home;
> And oft are touch'd with feare and inward grief,
> Knowing rich Prizes soonest tempt a Thief?
>   What Sports have we, whereon our Minds to set?
> Our Dogge, our Parrat, or our Marmuzet;
> Or once a weeke to walk into the field.[6]

This kind of local colour or atmosphere adds to the circumstantial nature of the historical epistles, while both Drayton's Arguments and his historical annotations show a genuine interest in political situation and manoeuvre.

There is nothing, except his narrative skill, quite comparable in Ovid to this historical as opposed to psychological realism, and no occasion for it. But the local setting as well as the dramatic situation is given a stronger colouring in several of the *Heroides* to emphasise the intensity of the feeling displayed. The violence of the wintry sea, the wailing of the nymphs in the cave where Dido and Aeneas consummate their love as Dido remembers the sound – these are slight touches and scarcely descriptive, but they are atmospheric and intensifying. Ovid took from Virgil the genealogy of heroic love – from Virgil of the *Eclogues* (8.43) – and it is illuminating to compare Dryden's version of each. Dryden's translation of *Eclogue* 8 reads:

> 'I know thee, Love! In deserts thou wert bred,
> And at the dugs of savage tigers fed;
> Alien of birth, usurper of the plains!
> Begin with me, my flute, the sweet Maenalian strains...'[7]

His version of Ovid, more than the original, deliberately alludes to Virgil:

> From harden'd Oak, or from a Rocks cold Womb,
> At least thou art from some fierce *Tygress* come;
> Or, on rough Seas, from their Foundation torn,
> Got by the Winds and in a Tempest born...[8]

Finally Pope in his Pastoral *Autumn* conflates both versions for a powerful definition of heroic love:

> I know thee Love! on foreign Mountains bred,
> Wolves gave thee suck, and savage Tygers fed.
> Thou wert from Aetna's burning entrails torn,
> Got by fierce whirlwinds and in thunder born.   (89–92)

The decor against which this passion is demonstrated is like a mannerist or baroque painting, picturesque, embodying the mood of the declamation – the rocky sea-shore where Ariadne cries for Theseus, the sea that carries Aeneas away from Dido, the chapel which commemorates Dido's murdered husband Sychaeus; these all have a melodramatic effect which takes the place of the symbolic associations of Ovidian description in Elizabethan poetry. Pope learned from these especially in his own version of the form, *Eloisa to Abelard*.

The graveyard imagery of *Eloisa* made an unexpected appeal to Dr Johnson who, as we have seen, entirely approved of the poem:

> The mixture of religious hope and resignation gives an elevation and dignity to disappointed love, which images merely natural cannot bestow. The gloom of a convent strikes the imagination with far greater force than the solitude of a grove.[9]

This mixed passion at least found favour, though it is not so much in the poem a struggle between religious hope and resignation and disappointed love, as between appalling frustration and resignation. Geoffrey Tillotson in his Introduction to the poem in Volume II of the Twickenham edition of Pope has recorded the whole background from Ovid and his translators to the letters of Eloise in Hughes's translation of 1713, with the influence of the popular *Letters of a Portuguese Nun* (1699), and for a sympathetic landscape background Milton's *Il Penseroso*, for mood Crashaw's luxuriant religious eroticism.[10] I find nothing to add to this brilliant and comprehensive survey, but it remains to consider why, as Tillotson observes, the poem retained its immense popularity throughout the eighteenth century but tends to be overlooked or disparaged by the modern reader. His answer is 'Until the modern reader has appreciated the battling contrarieties general and particular, 'classical' and 'romantic', calm and rhetorical passions, he has not begun to respond to *Eloisa to Abelard*.'[11] Such a conflict might seem to be of universal interest, and, though what Tillotson describes as the 'geometry' of the poem and its rhetoric are characteristic not only of the original form in Ovid, but also of the English Augustan poetic conventions, it is still necessary to ask why another technique or form was not found for the same conflict in the nineteenth or the twentieth century.

The poem arouses mixed responses today. Its intensity attracts, its rhetoric repels some readers. We are not used to associating passion with convention; to us it does not read spontaneously. Yet there is no doubt that the subject, the story, the factuality of the events still attract attention, and even move the reader. The Ovidian antitheses –

> Now warm in love, now with'ring in thy bloom,
> Lost in a convent's solitary gloom! (37–8)

are too neatly symmetrical to evoke a post-Romantic response, but the extreme expression of passion, which is of its very nature *disorderly*, appeals more immediately to a modern sensibility:

> I waste the Matin lamp in sighs for thee,
> Thy image steals between my God and me,

> Thy voice I seem in ev'ry hymn to hear,
> With ev'ry bead I drop too soft a tear.
> When from the Censer clouds of fragrance roll,
> And swelling organs lift the rising soul;
> One thought of thee puts all the pomp to flight,
> Priest, Tapers, Temples, swim before my sight:
> In seas of flame my plunging soul is drown'd,
> While Altars blaze, and Angels tremble round. (267–76)

But the whole structure of the poem is symmetrical and formal, and the conflicting contrasts are emphasised by it. The danger is a sort of monotony; we do not doubt Eloisa's struggle between resignation and passion, devotion and rebellion, but we are less sympathetic than even the unsophisticated eighteenth-century reader to the effects of repetition, the opposition of heroic love to conventional religious ideas ('How happy is the blameless Vestal's lot! The world forgetting, by the world forgot...' 207–8) – we no longer believe them, and, as the impassioned language of Eloisa shows that she herself does not, their function in the poem begins to seem artificial. These ideal conventions of retreat, devotion, chastity still had some emotional weight when Pope was writing. A certain literary memory only preserves them for the modern reader, though the sense of genuine conflict, the gloomy decor and the solemnity of a strife between inclination and belief can still move. There is a connection between the Augustan (indeed the Ovidian) conception of Heroic love and the post-Romantic idea of passion, but the latter depends less on the sense of a personal, interior struggle than on the wider conflict of individual necessity and the conventions of decorum in society. The Romantic lover struggles for justification; the Heroic lover more often against an element in his or her own nature. The idea of honour is implicit in the tradition of the *Heroides*, and with it a sense of shame that comes across in *Eloisa to Abelard*, though Pope, the most Romantic of the Augustans, fails to convince the modern reader entirely if only because he is instinctively nearer to the later instinct for rebellion. The Romantic victim or the Romantic rebel conceives of rebellion itself as a virtue, an idea that undercuts the whole Ovidian tradition of inner conflict.

Heroic love, described by Ovid, or portrayed in Euripides whom some thought his master in this art, or copied in cruder form by Seneca in his portrayal of criminal heroines, or adapted from them by Racine and the authors of Heroic tragedy in England (who tended to take over the more recent historical and national examples as in Rowe's *Jane Shore*), is a presentation of extremes of emotion. The effect of this exaggeration is to universalise rather than to particularise the feeling and the heroine who feels it. The art of Heroic rhetoric in such subjects was to strike a balance between universality and the particular. Many modern critics of Ovid (in particular, for instance, Professor W. S. Anderson of Berkeley) have insisted on his originality in transforming the heroines of myth and exemplary history into recognisable women of Augustan Rome whose arguments and complainings introduce an element of wit that

197

preserves them from total dereliction. A deserted woman writing to her betrayer, if she is to carry any conviction in her appeal, must evidently have some skill and some hope. Late seventeenth- and eighteenth-century readers recognised this paradox, but with a deprecating smile at female volubility and arts of persuasion which seems not to change through the ages. Garth even attributes to Virgil a half-satirical appreciation of this characteristic:

Virgil has, through the whole Management of this Rencounter, discover'd a most finish'd Judgment. Aeneas, like other Men, likes for Convenience, and leaves for greater. Dido, like other Ladies, resents the Neglect, enumerates the Obligations the Lover is under, upbraids him with Ingratitude, threatens him with Revenge, then by and by submits, begs for Compassion, and has recourse to Tears.

It appears from this Piece that Virgil was a discerning Master in the Passion of Love: And they that consider the Spirit and Turn of that inimitable Line – Qui Bavium non odit – cannot doubt but he had an equal Talent for Satyr.[12]

We have seen how Dryden considered Helen's reply to Paris an example of 'the extream artifice of Woman-kind', but Professor Anderson, taking a more optimistic twentieth-century view, says:

For my part, I read (Helen's) letter with greater admiration for her and her poet-creator than I do the letter of Dido or her complaining sisters of Heroides, I – xv. It may be that I merely respond more readily to scenes of hopeful love than I do to sentimental pictures of lost love, but I tell myself, at least sometimes, that Ovid has indeed made advances in the way he understands the process by which people do commit themselves to worthwhile feelings regardless of practical considerations and social taboos.[13]

The crucial word here is 'worthwhile', not one which would have recommended itself to Ovid or his imitators and translators. 'Inevitable', 'understandable', 'universal'; but the question of 'worth' is scarcely considered in their view of this ruling passion. When Pope as social arbiter begins to think about worth, he turns his back on the divine madness and the entertaining love-game and proposes a rational alternative. But in writing Eloisa to Abelard he accepted the ancient image of the lover as the victim of 'Venus toute entière à sa proie attachée.' And hers is a levelling experience; Mrs Thrale tells us that the kept women of the town loved the poem and she thought that a good illustration of its power of Nature and Passion. The best example of this view of Heroic love in English is Shakespeare's Cleopatra, who in reply to Iras's plea: 'Royal Egypt, Empress!...' says:

> No more but e'en a woman, and commanded
> By such poor passion as the maid that milks
> And does the meanest chares...
>
> (Antony and Cleopatra IV xv 71–5)

In no other of his plays is there any suggestion that Shakespeare shared the ancient view of love as the divine madness. But here, in Antony and Cleopatra, he faces directly Ovid's problem of reconciling the individual woman with the archetypal victim, and solves it though every artifice of subtlety and poetry of which he was capable. His historical lovers are at once acting out a story of the gods – Venus and Mars – and living through their human experience of heroism, duplicity, fallibility and failure. But, apart from his genius, Shakespeare had the advantage of a form that was flexible and unrestricted except by the five-act structure and the theatrical performance. Poetically he was free to make of this loose convention what he chose.

Ovid's imitators and translators preferred to be bound by the form of the declamation or monologue, but especially, after the Middle Ages, by the convention of the epistle. The idea of a communication – one to one rather than in the convention of soliloquy or monologue, an address to an unseen or unknown audience – conveyed a peculiar intimacy. Ovid makes much of the actual physical fact of writing, of the tablets he inscribes; he makes fun of the whole technique in the *Amores*, the maid delivering wax tablets to her mistress with his messages on them. Even in the *Heroides* he frequently refers to the writer's situation. Dryden's translation of *Canace to Macareus* describes her posture:

> One hand the Sword, and one the Pen imploys,
> And in my lap the ready Paper lyes...
>
> (Dryden, *Poetical Works* 512, 3–4)

Helen in her letter to Paris twice exploits the act of letter writing – first to explain how unused she is to this way of communicating:

> My hand is yet untaught to write to Men:
> This is th'Essay of an unpractis'd Pen
> Happy those Nymphs whom use has perfect made...
>
> (Dryden, *Poetical Works* 816, 139–41)

but by the end she has perfectly sized up the advantages of the art:

> This is enough to let you understand,
> For now my Pen has tired my tender Hand,
> My Woman knows the secrets of my Heart,
> And may hereafter better news impart.
>
> (Dryden, *Poetical Works* 517, 256–9)

Dryden's translation is brilliantly neat in the style of one who had practised so many forms of address – panegyric, prologues and epilogues, epistles to familiar friends and colleagues – that he could exploit effortlessly the convention in which he was working. To compare his translations with Wye Saltonstall's clumsy efforts – though Saltonstall's translations of the *Heroides* were the most popular examples from 1636 to 1695 when Dryden's and others' superior versions overtook them – is to recognise how important to the effect of the genre was sophisticated technique and an instinctive appreciation of the fact of writing itself. As the poet is consciously practising an art, so too is the letter-writer, the heroine. There is a double artifice here which is ruined by floundering attempts like this from Saltonstall's *Helen to Paris*:

> And in a letter thus my mind to shew
> Is a task, I before did never do.
> They are happy that do use it every day,
> To others it is hard to find the way....

(Ovid's Heroical Epistles, Englished by WS. 1636)

The convention of poetic letter-writing, adapted by Ovid from Propertius, was, I believe, the peculiar reason for the popularity of the *Heroides* in the Augustan period in England. Heroic love as such had been celebrated in erotic elegies and in the drama with a full sense of the declamatory passion. But the Horatian epistle had already become one of the most important models for occasional verse, for an easy half-formal, half-intimate, exchange of views and sentiments, the mode in which the Augustans relaxed earlier conventions and provided an opportunity for a wider range of subject-matter and mood. Epistolary writing, too, had been adopted in prose as a more subtle and revealing mode of exposing motive and the sources of emotion. The mingling of psychological realism and convention was a vital concern of poetry from the Renaissance to the Romantic period and only began to lose its urgency as a topic of criticism and a preoccupation of practising poets when a new genre for treating human situations and emotions emerged – the prose fiction, the novel which gradually in the eighteenth century superseded the traditional character interests of poetry and drama. It is no accident that the predominant style of the novel of sentiment and character in this period was epistolary. Richardson's apology for his use of it goes some way to explain both the popularity of the *Heroides* and of the best modern adaptation of this form, *Eloisa to Abelard*, and the reason why, eventually, the prose version superseded the poetic. Richardson's explanation of the advantages of the form in his Preface to *Clarissa Harlowe* might almost be an account of the opportunities of the Heroic epistle for conveying tragic experience:

All the letters are written while the hearts of the writers must be supposed to be wholly engaged in their subjects (the events at the time generally dubious): so that they abound not only with critical situations, but with what may be called *instantaneous* descriptions and reflections...as also with affecting conversations; many of them written in the dramatic or dialogue way.

'*Much more* lively and affecting,' says one of the principal characters, 'must be the style of those who write in the height of a *present* distress; the mind tortured by the pangs of uncertainty (the events then hidden in the womb of fate); *than* the dry, narrative, unanimated style of a person relating difficulties and danger surmounted, can be; the narrator perfectly at ease; and of himself unmoved by his own story, not likely greatly to affect the reader.'[14]

The difference here is that in a Heroic epistle the outcome is not dubious to the reader who knows, in most cases, the conclusion. So that the immediacy of effect in the poem must be achieved by the power of the rhetoric rather than by the dramatic or fictional device of suspense. Eventually the greater capacity of the prose form to engage the curiosity of the reader, its circumstantial realism, its day-to-day rhythm, its opportunities for exceptional subtleties in exploring the motives, admitted and concealed, of all the correspondents, gave it a superiority over the poetic form. Margaret Doody and other critics have indicated how much Richardson owed to the tradition of Heroic drama, and by implication of the Heroic epistle in his treatment, especially, of his tragic heroine Clarissa. With the growing anachronism of the tight rhetoric of the formal poetic epistle, the advantages of the prose form became more apparent. That necessary poise between realism and convention could only be sustained as long as the poetic convention bore some relation to contemporary ways of thinking about the experience of tragic love.

It would be untrue to suggest that the convention decayed rapidly though the very few examples of the Heroic epistle in the mid-eighteenth century suggest that it was no longer a vital inspiration. James Hammond's *Epistles in the Manner of Ovid* in Volume 4 of Dodsley's *Collection* are among the last serious instances; and these have the air of an academic exercise. *Flora to Pompey*[15] is an interesting example of a complex love situation – the heroine complains that her lover has grown tired of her and is offering her to his best friend who has fallen in love with her – which we can already imagine as a subject for a novel rather than a brief poem. Richardson himself was, indeed, the first novelist to deal with the 'triangular' situation at length and very seriously in *Sir Charles Grandison*, and the brief display of conflicting emotions in Hammond's poem seems slack and slight in contrast to Richardson's exploration of the theme. Yet the need for some artifice by which to convey love had not died in the eighteenth century. One of the girls who used the young Richardson as 'secretary' in writing to her lover, he recalls, said to him, 'I cannot tell you what you must say, but you cannot write too kindly'. In his description of these innocent customers, Richardson reveals the desire of the simple women of his own age for some convention they themselves could not master by which to communicate their feelings. But the convention was less and less likely to be poetic.

The truth of Garth's ironic remark that Aeneas like other men likes for convenience and leaves for greater, and that Dido like other ladies resents the neglect and responds predictably, does not change in and after the eighteenth century, but the writer's attitude towards it and his way of expressing it does. A more complicated response to the age-old situation is possible in the new form of the novel. The universal passion which suited rhetorical verse conventions was edged out gradually from literature to other more formal genres – opera, for example, where the skeletal outlines of a simple plot could often contain the pure expression of generalised emotion or tragic simplicity. That it was still possible, however, to accommodate Ovid's vision of the heroine, at once realistic woman and archetypal victim, in the more complex atmosphere of the nineteenth century when the novel had already take over the role of the drama in representing human conflicts and passions, is indicated by the last entirely successful use of the form of the Heroic epistle in English poetry. This is Donna Julia's letter to Don Juan in the first Canto of Byron's poem *Don Juan*, perhaps better remembered for its aphoristic statement of Ovid's implication than any other:

> Man's love is of man's life a thing apart;
> 'Tis woman's whole existence...

Byron, the most Augustan of the Romantics, knew very well what he was doing here. His loose rambling epic – 'fierce wars and faithless loves' the subject (as Ovid's Dido would have seen the *Aeneid*) – owes as much to the picaresque novel, and especially to Sterne, as to the Italian improvisatores and the ancients. It is as allusive as Pope, but in a throw-away, conversational manner which almost admits that the old style of literary consensus is long over. The psychological complexities of the war of the sexes and the Heroic love of the Ovidian epistles is as real in his vision of life as in any earlier poet's. But he sees them as simply realistic. After the idyllic love of Juan and Haidée has been consummated on the sea-shore in exquisitely romantic terms, he breaks off to ask the impertinent question Ovid would surely have seconded:

> But Juan! had he quite forgotten Julia?
> And should he have forgotten her so soon?
> I can't but say it seems to me most truly a
> Perplexing question...

And the reader, perhaps, turns back to Canto I and Julia's Heroic epistle. The theme is Ovidian, the mode original. Byron makes more than Ovid or any later imitator of the *fact* of the letter:

> – I write in haste, and if a stain
> Be on this sheet, 'tis not what it appears;
> My eyeballs burn and throb, but have no tears.
>
> I loved, I love you, for this love have lost
>   State, station, heaven, mankind's, my own esteem,
> And yet cannot regret what it hath cost,
>   So dear is still the memory of that dream;
> Yet, if I name my guilt, 'tis not to boast,
>   None can deem harshlier of me than I deem:
> I trace this scrawl because I cannot rest –
> I've nothing to reproach or to request.
>
> Man's love is of man's life a thing apart,
>   'Tis woman's whole existence; man may range
> The court, camp, church, the vessel and the mart;
>   Sword, gown, gain, glory, offer in exchange
> Pride, fame, ambition, to fill up his heart,
>   And few there are whom these cannot estrange;
> Men have all these resources, we but one,
> To love again, and be again undone.   (Canto I 1534–52)

Neither Ovid nor his imitators had expressed so simply and directly the bare
situation of the heroine. Byron concludes her letter without melodrama, but
with the novelist's objective observation of detail, as intensifying, and yet a
more detached device than the earlier rhetoric of background:

> 'I have no more to say, but linger still,
>   And dare not set my seal upon this sheet,
> And yet I may as well the task fulfil,
>   My misery can scarce be more complete:
> I had not lived till now, could sorrow kill;
>   Death shuns the wretch who fain the blow would meet,
> And I must even survive this last adieu,
> And bear with life to love and pray for you!'
>
> This note was written upon gilt-edged paper
>   With a neat little crow-quill, slight and new;
> Her small white hand could hardly reach the taper,
>   It trembled as magnetic needles do,
> And yet she did not let one tear escape her;
>   The seal a sun-flower; '*Elle vous suit partout*,'
> The motto, cut upon a white cornelian;
> The wax was superfine, its hue vermilion.   (1569–84)

The pathos of this derives from a completely different convention from that
of *Eloisa to Abelard* or of the Ovidian rhetoric of the *Heroides*, though the felt
malice recalls his original. Byron, like his predecessors, avoids the embarrassment of describing the recipient's response. We never hear of Juan's reaction
to the letter, and, after his more romantic affair with Haidée, are confronted
simply by Byron's awkward question. That the question remains is a sign of the
changes in belief and sensibility between the original form and this, its latest
version. Ovid's heroines were already dead or destined to death; Chaucer's
good women rested – if not in theirs, in their author's view – in a charitable
limbo; Pope's Eloisa and her lover were, historically, saved in their monastic
future. Julia simply faces desertion without melodrama, without excess or
crime, without faith. Byron is in this, not only in style but in vision, the most
coolly realistic of all Ovid's followers.

The divided heart, the conflicting passions, the whole psychology of Heroic
love disintegrated with the development of the analytic novel, and the possibility of 'worthwhile alternatives' which Pope recommended and which
modern critics hold on to as a 'realistic' interpretation of the old weeping
acceptance of, or mocking against, love as a kind of madness. There are few
more recent writers, except Hardy, who were bold enough to face the paradox
that Ovid and his successors handled so skilfully. The present serious and
quasi-Romantic obsession with sex precludes a genuine new interpretation of
the old dilemma of love. Perhaps the cool and anxious eighteenth century with
a foot in both camps, the new and the old, was the last period in which Ovid's
powerful yet curiously relaxed image of Eros was, though in its decadence, still

tolerable. Byron's brilliant reassertion of it is, like so much of his best work, unique and individual but characteristic of a backward-looking though yet original genius. Pushkin followed him; the letter scenes in nineteenth-century opera carry their echoes of Ovidian and Byronic pathos. It is still strange, however, that so long a tradition of so universal a topic has, since *Don Juan*, sunk into oblivion. But the reasons for this would demand too long and too perplexed a discussion for this occasion.

13

SOME VERSIONS OF PYGMALION

Jane M. Miller

APART FROM Ovid's own account of the Pygmalion story, there is a different version preserved in the writings of two Christian apologists: Clement of Alexandria[1] and Arnobius.[2] Both are reporting the work of another writer, Philostephanus, who was a pupil and a compatriot of Callimachus. Little of his work remains,[3] but it is known that he wrote accounts of the cities and regions of the Greek world. In particular, he described their foundation legends and the aetiologies of their cults. In one of these works, *On Cyprus*, he narrated the legend of Pygmalion (see notes 1 and 2). Philostephanus was 'a true Callim-achean';[4] both the interest of the Callimachean circle (attested by Callimachus himself, Ister, Apollonius Rhodius) in religious rites and their aetia and the evidence of the few extant fragments[5] alike strongly suggest that Philostephanus' account was an aetion of the hierogamy[6] between the king of the island and its goddess, not merely an obscene incident as suggested by the Christian Fathers.[7]

As Ovid sets the Pygmalion story between two other Cyprian tales (the Propoetides and Myrrha), it seems reasonable to suppose that these two may also have been in Philostephanus. In Philostephanus' version of the legend, Pygmalion falls in love with a statue of Venus but he is not himself the sculptor. Ovid, however, describes the creation of the woman-statue by Pygmalion. He retains the original setting, Cyprus, an island famous for its cult of Aphrodite.[8] Before Pygmalion's story, Ovid briefly narrates the tale of the Propoetides, the first prostitutes. They are turned to stone for 'denying the goddess'. According to Herodotus 1.199 and Athenaeus 12.516a, temple-prostitution was frequently practised in Cyprus as a form of worship and was considered an act of piety. Behaving as a prostitute would not, then, constitute a denial of Venus. Origin-ally (though not in Ovid) the Propoetides, whose story bears a strong resem-blance to that of Cinyras' daughters (Apollodorus 3.14.3–4) must have com-mitted some other crime. As Heinrich Dörrie[9] explains: 'They performed the act, which was required within the temple grounds by the orders of the gods, outside and without orders, undoubtedly for their own profit. In other words, they broke the monopoly which the shrine practised.' The transition from the Propoetides to the Pygmalion narrative is abrupt. Ovid only gradually offers information about Pygmalion. As each new detail is revealed the reader finds he must reassess his interpretation of the tale so far. Thus the story itself metamorphoses, taking on new meaning and significance as it unfolds. An analogous technique has been noted by O.S. Due:[10] a tale shifts its focus as the one following is read and sheds new light on its predecessor. In the case of the Pygmalion episode, the story itself alters as it continues.

The story of Pygmalion has been interpreted as 'a fable of a miracle, of art, of love, and of a better human being'.[11] It offers, in this view, a metaphor for the creative process: the artist creates a perfect work of art which then comes to life. Pygmalion is, alternatively, seen as a good man whose piety is rewarded by the goddess. However, neither of these interpretations takes into sufficient consideration the clear undercurrent of eroticism which runs through Ovid's narrative.

Pygmalion rejects nature's women[12] and creates his own ideal out of ivory. He is obviously a great craftsman for the statue possesses a beauty *qua femina nasci/nulla potest* (*Met.* 10.248–9), which no woman ever born could have. It is noteworthy that Ovid specifically declares this beauty unattainable by any woman born. Aphrodite was the goddess who personified ideal female beauty and was like no woman born in two senses: she was a goddess and therefore supernatural, but she was also born, according to legend, from the sea-spume, not from male and female.[13] The suggestion could be, therefore, that the statue represents the goddess, as in Philostephanus' aetiology.

Once the statue is finished, Pygmalion falls in love with it: *operisque sui concepit amorem* ('and he falls in love with his own work', 249). The word *concepit* is a sexual metaphor, already hinted at by the use of *nasci* in the previous line.[14] This statue is so life-like that Ovid comments *ars adeo latet arte sua* (252: 'in such a way does his art conceal his art'),[15] a phrase which should remind us that the statue is not alive, despite Pygmalion's behaviour towards it. Ovid reiterates this in the following lines:

> miratur et haurit
> pectore Pygmalion simulati corporis ignes.

Pygmalion is full of admiration and burns with love for this semblance of a body.

It is a *simulatum corpus*, not a real body. The use of words like *haurit* and *ignes* conveys vividly the strength of Pygmalion's passion and, when juxtaposed with a phrase such as *simulati corporis*, perhaps also indicates the fleshly quality of his love.

Pygmalion has, against reason, convinced himself of the reality of his creation:

> saepe manus operi temptantes admovet, an sit
> corpus an illud ebur, nec adhuc ebur esse fatetur.   (254–5)

Often he lifts his hands to the work to test whether it is flesh or ivory, nor does he yet admit it is ivory.

Ovid describes how he kisses and fondles it, believing his kisses to be returned and fearing that his fingers may leave bruises on the statue's 'flesh'. Despite his absence from the company of women, Pygmalion proves to be an accomplished lover, following the precepts laid down by Ovid in the *Ars Amatoria* and the *Amores*. He flatters his statue and brings it little presents, just as any lover would court his mistress.[16] Ovid continues to build up the eroticism within the relationship as he describes the great care and enjoyment with which Pygmalion dresses and undresses his beloved.[17] When he writes: *cuncta decent*; *nec nuda minus formosa videtur* (266: 'all these were beautiful; but no less beautiful does she appear naked') these must be Pygmalion's thoughts. This undercurrent of sexuality is maintained as Pygmalion lays his statue on a bed and covers it:

> appellatque tori sociam adclinataque colla
> mollibus in plumis tamquam sensura reponit　　　　　　(268–9)

He calls it the consort of his couch and rests its neck on soft feathery pillows, as if it could feel them.

She is called his *tori sociam*,[18] the partner of his bed. Ovid seems to be indicating a sexual relationship; there are certainly several other examples of stories about men having physical relationships with statues.[19]

Venus is now mentioned for the first time in this episode as her feast day arrives. Ovid thus expands the significance of the story, reminding the audience of the setting and its religious importance. There is also a hint that Pygmalion is more than a simple sculptor as he approaches Venus' altar with his own gift of incense, an act which may imply kingship. Much has been made of Pygmalion's piety and modesty in not daring to ask for the ivory maiden itself (herself?). However, if the statue is indeed a representation of Venus, then his reluctance is understandable. It would have been dangerous blasphemy to ask for the goddess to become his *tori socia*. When Pygmalion returns home, he rushes to his statue's bedside. Ovid no longer calls the artefact an ivory maiden. Instead he refers to *simulacra suae...puellae* (280). This is the second time the statue has been called *puella*, the first being when Pygmalion 'wooed' it: *puella* has a sexual sense and can mean 'mistress'. Horace makes frequent use of it in this way, particularly in the *Odes*, and there are also examples in Ovid and Propertius.[20] The connection with love-elegy is appropriate, especially in the wooing scene.

Having used the word in this elegiac context, Ovid is playing on its dual meaning when it occurs the second time. When the statue is described as *simulacra suae...puellae*, Ovid is suggesting subtly that Pygmalion is using it as a substitute for a mistress.[21] As the statue is also lying on a bed, there are clear sexual overtones to the description. Pygmalion now begins to kiss his statue: *incumbensque toro dedit oscula* (280). *Incumbens* has been translated as 'leaning over' but usually means 'lying on'. Again, Ovid presents an erotic image: Pygmalion actually lying on the bed on the statue to kiss and fondle it. As he does so, the sculptor senses a change in his ivory maiden. He kisses again and touches her breasts with his hands, another indication of an erotic relationship between man and statue.

As the transformation takes place, Pygmalion is caught between joy and doubt. Urgently he tests the statue time and again; *rursus amans rursusque manu sua vota retractat* (288) has been taken to have some religious meaning, *vota* being interpreted as 'prayers'. However *vota* also means 'desires' or 'objects of desire', a reading which changes the sense of the line subtly and makes more sense of *retractat* (as 'handles'). There is now a final revelation about the sculptor's status. He is referred to as *Paphius...heros*, Lord of Paphos. Ovid's Pygmalion is the King of Cyprus. The anachronistic use of *Paphius* (Paphos being named after Pygmalion's son) seems to have distracted critics from giving the word *heros* its full significance. The statue-maiden is now alive. There are obvious parallels between her vivification and human birth, but instead of seeing the light of day and her mother, she sees the light of day and her lover. This birth-image reinforces the view that the statue is, in a sense, the child of Pygmalion, a notion which would have obvious bearing on the Myrrha story. Interpretations such as those of Fränkel, Otis or Griffin are unsatisfactory.[22] There are strong sexual overtones in much of Ovid's narration which tell against the view of the story as one of piety rewarded. His treatment is erotic rather than obscene but a physical relationship between sculptor and statue is implied.

Ovid seems to have remythologised the story reported by Clement and Arnobius. The first element of his narration deals with the story of a man on Cyprus who falls in love with a statue and has a sexual relationship with it. In the second, the man is revealed as Pygmalion, the King of Cyprus, and the statue is Venus, their union being the *hieros gamos* probably described by Philostephanus. The two aspects cannot be divided and are therefore told more or less concurrently.

Dörrie, in his interesting analysis of the Pygmalion theme, argues that Pygmalion cannot be considered an archetype since each generation has responded to it in a different way. However, there are two broad categories into which these interpretations tend to fall: in traditional terminology 'historical' or 'mystical'. Both are present in the *Ovide moralisé*, a medieval French poem dating from the beginning of the fourteenth century which seeks to find Christian and moral truths in the *Metamorphoses* by reinterpreting the stories. The first interpretation put forward in the *Ovide moralisé* (4.356off) is a kind of aetiology expressed in demythologised terms which has clear parallels with the Cinderella story. Pygmalion is interpreted as a great lord who has in his household a serving girl, dirty and uneducated perhaps but nonetheless beautiful. Such a lord might take this girl and groom her until finally she is fit to be his wife. The second interpretation sees the story as a Christian allegory of the relationship between God and his creation, humanity.

Some versions of Pygmalion

The best-known example of a 'historical' appproach to this extremely popular theme is Shaw's *Pygmalion*. The play was very successful from its first production in April 1914 and the metamorphosis of Eliza Doolittle from flower-girl to fake duchess is famous even today, especially after its own metamorphosis into a stage and film musical. Although the play itself is short, the fact that Shaw added a Preface and an Epilogue indicates the consideration he gave to the legend when writing *Pygmalion*.

Shaw chooses to show how a person can be moulded to fit into a completely alien society. This metamorphosis is not achieved without great pain, particularly on Eliza's side. Nor can the experiment be said to be a complete success. The bet was to pass Eliza off as a lady at the ambassador's party and this is done, but Nepommuck, the bogus phonetician, is convinced that she is Hungarian, not English. The reason he gives is that she speaks English *too* perfectly. Note that in Ovid the statue is perfectly, super-humanly beautiful (*qua femina nasci/nulla potest*). Moreover, the change, though impressive, actually makes Eliza unfit for normal life. Once she can speak 'properly' she can no longer be a flower-girl, but neither can she join the social group whose speech she has adopted because she possesses none of the other social graces (or its economic *sine qua non*).

In Shaw's version the ideal woman is represented by Higgins's mother. She is his Venus, so strong and intelligent that he finds all other women lacking. Shaw explains that she is the reason why Higgins is a confirmed bachelor.[23] For Higgins the ideal woman and Galatea[24] are two different characters. His image of ideal womanhood (his mother) prevents him from marrying, just as Ovid's Pygmalion fails to marry because he is haunted by an ideal. Shaw does not end his play with a union between Eliza (Galatea) and Higgins. In the Epilogue he explains at length the psychological realism of the play and its inevitable sequel. He is contemptuous of people who want 'happy endings'. These lengthy explanations of what happens after the end of the play form Shaw's attempt to combat the efforts of the actors, who tried to suggest an eventual union between Higgins and Eliza in their performance. Beerbohm Tree (Higgins) threw a bunch of flowers across the stage to Mrs Patrick Campbell (Eliza) just as the curtain fell, much to Shaw's fury.

Shaw's careful analysis of the personalities of his characters shows that Eliza is bound to marry Freddy, not Higgins. As he observes, strong people are attracted to weak and vice versa. Moreover, Eliza realises that she could never be Higgins's 'nearest and fondest and warmest interest', could never 'obtain a complete grip of him'. Thus she will inevitably turn to Freddy, although her interest in and involvement with Higgins will never cease. Shaw has already emphasised the way parents affect their children's models of what men and women should be (Higgins's idealisation of his mother). Now he observes that the opposite can be true. Eliza's father has provided her with a clear model of the kind of man to avoid in marriage. 'She knows that Higgins does not need her, just as her father did not need her.' Indeed Doolittle is a neat mirror-image of Higgins.

Besides Eliza's transformation, there are two other examples of what M. Meisel calls the 'Cinderella–Galatea motif of transformation and testing' in *Pygmalion*.[25] The lazy, immoral dustman Doolittle becomes a rich Society character who even marries the woman he lives with (another variant of the Propoetides–Pygmalion situation). Freddy's sister Clara, presented throughout the play as a snob and a failed social climber, is changed dramatically, so we are informed in the Epilogue, by her discovery of the writings of H. G. Wells. One character, however, remains steadfastly the same throughout: Higgins.

Just as Shaw separates the theme of metamorphosis from that of the ideal woman (Eliza and Mrs Higgins), he also seems to separate the image of the statue from these other two elements. He ends the Epilogue with a brief discussion of Eliza's attitude towards Higgins after her marriage: 'She has even secret mischievous moments in which she wishes she could get him alone, on a desert island, away from all ties and with nobody else in the world to consider, and just drag him off his pedestal and see him making love like any other common man.' Thus even the statue-motif is reversed. Higgins, the shaper of Eliza, is also the statue-figure himself. Shaw ends the whole work with an epigram which gives an interesting twist to the old legend: 'Galatea never does quite like Pygmalion: his relation to her is too godlike to be altogether agreeable.'

Although not as overtly didactic perhaps as Shaw's version of the legend, W. S. Gilbert's *Pygmalion and Galatea*[26] must be acknowledged as its partial forerunner at least. This play, 'an original mythological comedy', was first produced in 1871 and was a tremendous success. Gilbert uses the old myth to make satirical comments on the Victorian art world. Chrysos (a significant name) is the epitome of the vulgar Victorian 'patron', a man with money and no taste, who measures the value of a piece of sculpture by its weight. His wife, Daphne, is as unpleasant as he is. Her advice to him during the negotiations for the statue of Galatea (modelled by Pygmalion's own wife Cynisca) is as follows:

> Give money for the stone,
> I've heard that it is far beyond all price,
> But run it down; abuse it ere you buy.

Pygmalion will not sell and Chrysos is furious to be refused by a mere artist:

> Confound it – if a patron of the arts
> Is thus to be dictated to by art,
> What becomes of the art patron's patronage?

However, far from teaching Pygmalion a lesson, Chrysos comes to regret ever having seen the statue of Galatea.

Gilbert's Pygmalion is not the misogynist of the Ovidian tale. His wife is very beautiful and the model for all his statues. In fact, the love story of Pygmalion and his statue is transferred to Pygmalion and Cynisca. She was a devotee of Artemis and had promised to remain chaste. However, when she fell in love with Pygmalion, the goddess released her from her vow and at the same time gave her a terrible gift, the power to blind her husband if he should be unfaithful. The ability was also given to Pygmalion, but he is not presented as a character sufficiently jealous ever to have used the awful gift.

The main plot concerns what happens when Cynisca goes away for a few days; Pygmalion has just completed a particularly fine statue of her (Galatea), and when he protests he will be lonely without her Cynisca tells him to regard the statue as her proxy during her absence. The jest misfires when Galatea comes to life. There is also a sub-plot revolving around the courtship of Myrine, Pygmalion's sister, by the soldier Leucippus. All these characters are profoundly affected by Galatea's vivification. Her short life (she becomes a statue again in the final scene; the whole action is set within a space of 24 hours) serves to emphasise the hypocrisy riddling everyday society. She is (selectively) innocent and naive, reacting with total honesty in all situations.[27] As a result she causes embarrassment and confusion. In fact she cannot be tolerated in a 'civilised' society. Her qualities also serve as a contrast to the shortcomings of others, particularly Cynisca. In the end she sacrifices her life and happiness for Pygmalion and teaches the beautiful Cynisca the meaning of pity and love. Gilbert reverses the obvious interpretation of the two characters, it is the statue who possesses the qualities of warmth, kindness and pity, while the woman is cold, pitiless and hard. Galatea's innocence causes many misunderstandings, and Pygmalion is convinced that he is being punished for his presumption in praying for his statue to live. It is clear that she cannot be accepted by society, and her return to stone is the only solution for the other characters' problems. Despite her goodness, honesty and innocence, however, Galatea does learn one thing from her experiences of civilised society – bitterness:

> Nay – let me go from him
> That curse – his curse – still ringing in mine ears,
> For life is bitterer to me than death.

Although there is much comedy in the play, it also has tragic undertones, certainly for Galatea, and attacks a society which claims to prize certain qualities so highly (innocence, simplicity, honesty), yet finds them unacceptable in everyday life.

The 'mystical' aspect of the Pygmalion story seems to have held perhaps an even greater attraction for artists than the 'historical' approach. Above all, in *The Winter's Tale*, Shakespeare deliberately turns away from his source (Richard Greene's *Pandosto*) and creates as the climax of the play a statue scene in which the queen is restored to life. As Frank Kermode points out,[28] the pattern of the last act is determined 'by the need for a double recognition, but nothing at the level of plot required the dramatist to bring Hermione back into the play as a statue.' Why then does Shakespeare choose to do so? The whole of the play is concerned with the theme of Nature versus Nurture, Nature versus Art (preoccupations common to another of Shakespeare's late plays, *The Tempest*). We are shown how Perdita is 'naturally' noble, and how this 'better nature' allows her to rise above her apparently base-born origins. Polixenes gives voice to the general opinion of the time that Art is an agent of Nature which improves it but is not greater than it:

> This is an art
> Which does mend Nature, change it rather; but
> The art itself is Nature.   (IV iv 95–7)

The image of a gardener used in this scene is an interesting one and could be compared with Ovid's sculptor; both improve upon nature.[29] The theme of Nature and Art reaches its climax in the final scene where Hermione, apparently a statue, is vivified. The statue is praised for its 'life' and naturalness but Paulina counters this by warning that the colour is still wet and referring to it as a 'poor image'. Yet to Leontes the statue is more than art. It seems to breathe and see so that, he cries, 'we are mocked with art'. When it moves, that art becomes magic. Finally the statue is revealed as being no mere work of Art but one of Nature. Hermione's beauty and goodness are perpetuated in Perdita. This, Shakespeare seems to say, is an immortality worth having, rather than the frozen perfection of a work of art. The creative power of Nature is greater and a truer conqueror of time than that of mere human intellect.

William Morris, in his *Earthly Paradise*, is also much concerned with the problem of Time's destructiveness and how to achieve immortality. He sets his version of Pygmalion in the month of August, the month of fruition which also marks the end of the 'year's desire'. The story tells of the loss of immortality; the statue loses her chance of eternal life when she is made human. However, her immortality is not to be desired. It is preferable to be human and mortal rather than exist as an inanimate object; that is no answer to the problem of death. Indeed Morris indicates that life is perhaps sweet precisely because it must eventually end. Morris is clear that art, no matter how perfect, cannot replace real life; the statue cannot replace a living girl as an object of love. To convey this, he has to use the elaborate technique of relieving Pygmalion of his unnatural obsession so that it can be replaced by normal human love when the maiden comes to life. In Ovid passion is simply transferred, but for Morris there can be no question of the two objects or the feelings they inspire being interchangeable. The poem ends with the statue-maiden repeating the message that there cannot be pleasure without pain. The only possible path is one of total commitment to life.

Some versions of Pygmalion

Morris's version of Pygmalion is associated with the paintings of his great friend, Edward Burne-Jones.[30] These pictures are particularly good illustrations of the 'mystical' interpretation of Ovid's tale.[31] Burne-Jones is reported to have declared his intentions as a painter thus: 'I don't want to copy objects – I want to show people something'.[32] His yearning for something 'beyond' which he could not reach found a natural expression in the story of the artist who was dissatisfied with the world around him and sought to create his own ideal. Although Burne-Jones expressed great spiritual longing in his pictures, he realised that they represented 'another world' into which he could not pass. A cartoon he drew for a young friend (British Museum, pen and ink, 1883) perfectly illustrates this point. 'The artist attempting to join the world of art with disasterous (*sic*) results' shows Burne-Jones in despair trying to leap into a picture he is painting, only to find himself crashing through it. The Pygmalion series pre-dates the cartoon and seems to explore the opposite possibility, a work of art entering human life.

Burne-Jones was obsessed with the idea of (young) female beauty and would surely have himself considered the problem of the statue's mortality; once she is vivified, her beauty will inevitably fade with age. Art is generally used to transform human, transient loveliness into eternal beauty. This is the task which the painter set himself. Yet in the story of Pygmalion the sequence is reversed. The eternal beauty of the statue, once brought to life, must undergo decay and destruction. Although Burne-Jones calls the final picture in his series 'The Soul Attains', we must not assume that he found in the story a satisfactory answer to his desire for constant beauty in his life. His recurring fantasy about entering the world of art shows the opposite to be true.

The Pygmalion series has been called 'a sequence of thought on human aspiration'.[33] Though suggestive, this analysis does not explain the paintings fully. There is no evidence that Burne-Jones placed any particular importance on 'divine power' in art and such a religious interpretation cannot be substantiated. It is perhaps best to view the paintings as one of the artist's many attempts to express his pursuit of the 'other world', the 'something' he never apparently attained. His spiritual longing, his love of beauty and his ultimate frustration; the Pygmalion story illustrates all these elements.

'Mystical' interpretations of the Ovidian tale abounded in the nineteenth century in particular (for example, Ernest Hartley Coleridge, *Pygmalion's Bride*, Sir Ronald Ross, *Edgar or The New Pygmalion*, Robert Buchanan, *Pygmalion the Sculptor*). Sometimes the story is seen as a Christian allegory, sometimes an exploration of the notion of 'the religion of love', love as a divine experience. Often interpretations were heavily Romantic, emphasising the supremacy of art and the strange attraction of death (Frederick Tennyson, *Pygmalion*, G. E. Lancaster, *Pygmalion in Cyprus*). These sometimes self-indulgent versions form an interesting contrast to the 'historicist' interpre-

213

tations, which generally contained an element of social comment. They are interesting as products of their time but lack the vitality of the Ovidian original. Unfortunately these 'moralistic, intellectual interpretations' (L. P. Wilkinson, *Ovid Recalled* 212) have tended to obscure rather than illuminate the original story, and Ovid's ingenuity and artistic skill are not matched.

14

OVID AND THE NINETEENTH CENTURY

Norman Vance

'It was only in the nineteenth century', claimed Hermann Fränkel in 1945, 'that Ovid's prestige fell as low as it stands today.'[1] The generalisation is plausible, particularly when we consider the deep shadow Homer and revitalised Greek scholarship cast over almost all Latin poetry in this period, but it is not entirely true. It claims too much for the nineteenth century. Critical approval had never been universal even in antiquity and by the middle of the eighteenth century an enthusiasm for Ovid might well seem quaint, not to say misguided. In 1770 the young Goethe found it impossible to convince Herder that the *Metamorphoses* had any merit.[2] On the other hand Ovid continued to be part of what every schoolboy knew, a common starting-point for the study of Latin poetry and part of the general current of thought and feeling expressed by writers and painters. In the early 1800s Benjamin West, President of the Royal Academy, painted a number of subjects suggested by Ovid; in the 1890s another President of the Academy, Lord Leighton, was still finding inspiration in Ovidian themes.[3] Ovid the supreme mythological story-teller and Ovid 'the soft philosopher of love'[4] were no longer regarded in quite the same light but Ovid's cultural status suffered change rather than straightforward decay. From an *arbiter elegantiae* he became a rather raffish *éminence grise*, a valuable imaginative asset with which no one was entirely at ease.

Part of the difficulty in assessing the significance of Ovid in the nineteenth century is that one can never see him on his own. His influence is nearly always mediated, sometimes by old paintings on Ovidian subjects such as Polidoro da Caravaggio's *Andromeda* which haunted the young Browning or Piero di Cosimo's *Death of Procris* which inspired a poem by Austin Dobson.[5] Even without the painters, other poets, translators, commentators and compilers constantly interpose themselves between Ovid and the nineteenth-century reader. Chaucer, Shakespeare and Milton, Natalis Comes, George Sandys and the Revd John Lemprière all cluster round holding up a bewildering array of coloured lenses and more or less distorting mirrors. John Keats pored over a Latin text of Ovid, but he also had Sandys's translation, while Andrew Tooke's *Pantheon* (1698) and Lemprière's indispensable *Classical Dictionary* (1806 edition) were to hand to guide him to particular passages, to narratives and images which had already kindled the imagination of his beloved Shakespeare or Milton. In mythological matters 'We learn from Ovid and Lemprière' as Byron put it, speaking in effect for his generation.[6] As Lemprière's carefully detailed references made clear, Ovid was far from the only available source of information on mythological matters even if he had long been the most important and the most convenient. There were more ancient àuthorities, Greek as well as Latin. The Homeric Hymns, Hesiod and Apollodorus as well as the Greek tragedians and Homer could supply details not found in Ovid which perhaps represented more reliable traditions. The Scottish scholar–poet John Stuart Blackie cautiously supplied two epigraphs for his poem 'Ariadne', one from Ovid's *Fasti* and one from Hesiod's *Theogony*.[7] Tennyson, like Milton in *Paradise Lost*, wrote poetry about Proserpine with Ovid in mind.[8] But Milton's 'fair field of Enna', poetically associated with Eden, planted new blossoms in the Ovidian meadow and in any case Tennyson's principal classical source was the much older Homeric Hymn to Demeter, not known to Milton since the sole surviving manuscript had been discovered in a Moscow stable only in 1777.[9] Tennyson's title, the Greek 'Demeter and Persephone' rather than the Latin 'Ceres and Proserpina', seemed to demonstrate the unimportance of Ovid and Latin sources generally in a mythological poem. Yet without Ovid's version of the story and Milton's imaginative use of it which turned Tennyson's thoughts to Sicilian Enna rather than the Nysian land of the Homeric Hymn the poem might never have been written.[10]

The other problem is the nineteenth-century disintegration of Ovid. The poetry and the poet drifted apart in popular awareness. Ovid the rake, the sophisticated tactician of love's siege-warfare, tended to be separated from Ovid the highly convenient if barely acknowledged source of decorative and sometimes disturbing myths and legends, not to mention Ovid the witty and elegant maker of verses. Needless to say this development blunted sensitivity to the actual poetry. It also had the curious and unfortunate effect of making Ovid simultaneously obnoxious as a personality and almost invisible as a poet. Before considering the influence of the poetry we should perhaps take account of what the nineteenth century made of the man.

Generally speaking he was regarded as a degenerate in a degenerate age, the frivolous author of 'perhaps the most immoral poem ever written'.[11] One is tempted to blame the continuing legend of Ovid the rake on the nineteenth-century enthusiasm for moralising biography as the best way to understand everything. Carlyle had taught that the history of the world was but the biography of great men: David Masson's monumental *Life of Milton* (1859–80) and Edward Dowden's *Shakespeare* (1875) had applied the lesson to literary history and criticism. In this climate it was perhaps inevitable that Ovid should appear as the poet romantically or quite rightly exiled for a wicked book and (probably) for the wicked life that enabled him to write it. Karl Marx and Flaubert found it natural to identify light-heartedly with Ovid the exile without thinking much about Ovid the poet.[12] But Ovid connived at this superficial biographical approach through persistent self-dramatisation. His accounts of his exile created the familiar role of lonely aesthete fallen among Philistines. He assures us that his downfall came about through a poem (the *Ars Amatoria*) and a mysterious *error* (*Tr.* 2.207). It was only human to take the poem for granted and speculate about the error. In the *Amores*, early in his career, he describes what purport to be his own loves. Much later, in the bitterness of disgrace, he lays out for us an attractive version of the volatile (but of course respectable) love-life settling into marriage which had been disrupted by exile (*Tr.* 4.10.65–8). He insists that his life is more moral than his verse (*Tr.* 2.353), but the very insistence has somehow encouraged sceptical gossip. Ovid the scandalous and witty exile, if not exactly 'bad, mad and dangerous to know' as Lady Caroline Lamb said of Lord Byron,[13] still presents himself as a kind of Roman Byron, almost inviting the sort of interest and disapproval, biographical rather than textual, that Byron drew from nineteenth-century readers.

Byron himself rather encouraged the identification. Just as the *Ars Amatoria* was among other things a burlesque of the Latin didactic poem, so *Don Juan* irreverently impersonates the drearily earnest, morally impeccable long poem of the early nineteenth century:

> Now, if my Pegasus should not be shod ill,
> This poem will become a moral model,

he promises. Tongue in cheek the poet virtuously denounces the moral dangers associated with attractively written amatory verse, not only Petrarch, 'the Platonic pimp of all posterity', but Ovid himself (*Don Juan* V i 2). 'Ovid's a rake, as half his verses show him', he informs us, pretending to sympathise with the dilemma of Don Juan's mother as she seeks to provide for her son an education which is both strictly moral and strictly classical. The problem is solved by using heavily expurgated editions with all the indecent passages conveniently collected at the back (I xlii–v). But despite Donna Inez' best endeavours and Byron's stern propriety the story of Don Juan's adventures becomes in a sense Byron's exploration of the art of love,

> of whom great Caesar was the suitor,...
> Horace, Catullus, scholars, Ovid tutor (II ccv).

Affecting the role of worldly, experienced mentor in affairs of the heart, a role Ovid had long since played to perfection, Byron advises moderation in love:

> In short, the maxim for the amorous tribe is
> Horatian, 'medio tu tutissimus ibis'.

It is possible that Byron made a genuine slip, for moderation is an Horatian theme and the expression 'golden mean' comes from an Horatian phrase, but it is much more likely that he expects us to notice that this is an Ovidian tag attributed to Horace to dress up cynical Ovidian shrewdness as Horatian wisdom.[14]

217

It may be coincidence that Julia, Don Juan's first lover, has the same name as the notoriously adulterous daughter of the Emperor Augustus, traditionally if mistakenly identified as the beloved of Ovid and the Corinna of the *Amores*. On the other hand Byron's Julia inspires half-understood passions in a youth 'In feelings quick as Ovid's Miss Medea'.[15] Byron may have known that in the Renaissance the historical Julia had enjoyed undeserved literary prominence as Ovid's *femme fatale*. George Chapman's bizarre neoplatonic poem *Ovid's Banquet of Sense* (1595) had presented Ovid as a hidden observer glutting his senses on the spectacle of Julia bathing and playing upon her lute and Ben Jonson's *Poetaster* (1602) used the dangerous loves of Julia and Ovid as a sub-plot. In the nineteenth century Julia and her equally scandalous daughter, also named Julia, were given a new lease of life as part of the lurid legend of Ovid. The only evidence from antiquity for the Julia–Corinna identification seems to be a casual reference in an elaborate verse-epistle by Sidonius Apollinaris, saintly Bishop of Auvergne in the fifth century.[16] But biographical speculation on this matter was widespread and animated in the nineteenth century and at least one Victorian scholar seized hold of Sidonius to support his particular version of the intricate conspiracy of illicit sex and power-politics, about which Ovid's lips were tantalisingly sealed, which was thought to lie behind his disgrace and exile.[17]

This squalid and extravagant intrigue sounds like the plot of some Victorian sensation-novel, possibly by Wilkie Collins. Browning's novel-in-verse *The Ring and the Book* has some of the same elements, and it makes use of the Ovid legend. Count Guido, a nobleman short of funds, marries a girl for the money which she turns out not to have. Then he harasses her until a young Canon helps her to escape from him, only to be exiled for adultery while Guido takes hired bullies and murders his wife. The setting in seventeenth-century Rome makes references to classical Roman poets natural enough, but the pattern of reference to Ovid gradually emerges as a strategy for establishing guilt by association. Canon Giuseppe Caponsacchi's exile is linked with Ovid's to suggest a common disgrace through sexual misconduct.[18] Chaucer had described Ovid as the clerk of Venus, evangelist of the great god of Love,[19] and Count Guido slanderously sets up Caponsacchi as the same sort of clerk in not very holy orders, suggesting he is better versed in Ovid's *Art of Love* than Aquinas and making out that the murdered Pompilia was his Corinna, a 'gamesome wife', perhaps playing the same sexual games as the Roman Julia (V 1357–9).

But all this is deliberate mystification. The case is finally submitted to the Pope who realises that Caponsacchi and Pompilia are innocent victims of Guido's designs from the beginning. Despite all his efforts they resist transformation into Ovidian sexual conspirators. The impenitent Guido is the true Ovidian, clever and worldly, devoted to exploiting a world of unstable realities and to effecting transformations not through the narrative art of the *Meta-morphoses* but through artful intrigue. His concluding speech alludes significantly to the myths of the *Metamorphoses*, defying the doctrines of the Pope and of at least nominally religious Rome to embrace amoral Ovidian paganism. He sees his end not as the conventional hell or purgatory but 'some such fate as Ovid could foresee'; (XI 2048), turning into a wolf like Lycaon (*Met.* 1.237–9), his savage, wolfish nature finally purged of its meagre dilution of humanity.

Ovid continued to be an important background influence in nineteenth-century literature, but his bad reputation kept him away from the front of the stage. Browning incorporated him into the poetic and dramatic structure of *The Ring and the Book* secure in the knowledge that everyone knew who Ovid was but only a rebel or a reprobate would want to identify too closely with him. George Meredith found this a problem when he tried to retell the Daphne story in the *Metamorphoses* in a sensuously Keatsian poem three times the length of his original. It was not his best or his liveliest work but it hardly deserved the criticism of the High Anglican *Guardian*: 'Ovid is bad enough, but 'Daphne' and 'The Rape of Aurora' in this volume are worse, from their studied and amplified voluptuousness, than anything in the Metamorphoses.'[20] Meredith loved the woods and streams and teeming earth as Ovid had done but after this he was cautious about showing too much direct interest in him. In *The Egoist*, as in so many Victorian novels of contemporary life, Latin quotations sprinkle the narrative and lard the speech of those of good family and education, but while Catullus, Horace and Virgil are frequently invoked Ovid is conspicuous by his absence. Other Roman poets might have lived and loved irregularly, but they had not suffered the final disgrace of exile for lewdness.

But the Victorian reading public could accept that earlier ages had been less censorious in love and literature. In *Henry Esmond* Thackeray alludes to Ovid and other Latin poetry almost as frequently as the eighteenth-century *Spectator* to establish period atmosphere. The English Augustan age in literature which Esmond examines from the sidelines had harked back to the Rome of Augustus and the poets of his era, so there is a special appropriateness in Esmond's adapting Ovid's phrase about merely seeing Virgil (*Vergilium vidi tantum*) in describing his glimpse of the famous Dr Swift (*vidi tantum*).[21] Ovid the rake or cheerful rascal, more tolerated under Queen Anne than under Queen Victoria, supplies the *mot juste* for Thackeray's fictional version of the incorrigible spendthrift Richard Steele. He is made to allude, inexactly, to a famous tag: Ovid's Medea, driven by passion despite her better judgement, manifests an aphoristic moral realism when she sighs

video meliora proboque,
deteriora sequor!　　　　　　(*Met.* 7.20ff; *Esmond* I, chap. 6)

Medea's words have wider implications in the novel: they encapsulate the tension between lofty moral vision and a harum scarum life which Ovid understands and accepts. So do Steele and, to some extent, Thackeray, whatever Victorian public opinion might think. More seriously, Ovid was the poet experienced in love who knew all about deserted women and the shameful experiences of the old mythology: the young Esmond's translations from the *Heroides* and an allusion to the *Metamorphoses* speak eloquently to the situation of the lady of Castlewood neglected by her philandering husband (*Met.* 1.758ff; *Esmond* I, chap. 8).

Thackeray's *Esmond* dramatised the Whig history of Macaulay, and Thackeray's casual allusions to Ovid imply an estimate of Ovid the man not unlike Macaulay's: 'He seems to have been a very good fellow: rather too fond of women; a flatterer and a coward [in exile]; but kind and generous...' Macaulay was less sympathetic to the actual poetry which he thought over-rhetorical and merely ingenious.[22]

Other nineteenth-century critics, even those who liked the poems more than Macaulay, find moral disapproval of the poet 'rather too fond of women' and spineless in exile tempering whatever enthusiasm they might have. The conservative Anglo-Irish man of letters William Preston tried to link moral and aesthetic deficiency by complaining that Ovid was one of the first to spoil

> the pure taste of the *Romans*. He is lavish in flowers and ornaments,
> in sallies of imagination, in conceits and points of wit; in his morality,
> he is most relaxed and vicious...Many of his subjects are licentious,
> many immoral, in the highest degree, and not only scattered passages,
> but entire compositions are such, as are highly offensive to decency,
> and must shock the modest reader.[23]

The implied criterion of Roman taste is a curious blend of rugged virtue of the kind celebrated in the earlier books of Livy and classical simplicity and restraint of the kind imagined by Winckelmann after contemplating Graeco-Roman statues half a century earlier.

Ovid the moral and aesthetic transgressor overshadowed Ovid the poet of wit and fancy for almost all except Walter Savage Landor, whose staunch republicanism and anti-establishment attitudes, a delight to later poets such as Swinburne, gave him a natural relish for transgressors, particularly if they had style. In several of his *Imaginary Conversations* (1824–9, 1853) he makes the Roman Messala and the Italians Petrarch and Vittoria Colonna as well as Landor himself praise Ovid's facility and ingenuity (Macaulay thought only that he was too clever by half), his fertile imagination and his dramatic and rhetorical power particularly in the contest between Ulysses and Ajax in the *Metamorphoses* which, it is claimed, exceeds anything in Virgil.[24]

But one cannot help suspecting that Landor would in any case have felt bound to prefer the poet Augustus exiled to the poet who sang of the glory that was to come under Augustus. Some other nineteenth-century commendations

of Ovid have the same slightly perverse quality. The long war between puri-
tanical public opinion, sometimes labelled 'Mrs Grundy' for short, and the free
artistic expression of the full range of human experience inevitably dragged
Ovid on to the barricades. If Mrs Grundy was going to complain of Sir Richard
Burton's 'plain and literal' translation of the *Arabian Nights*, John Addington
Symonds observed, she ought equally to complain about translations of Ovid
'now within the reach of every schoolboy'. Algernon Swinburne defended
Rabelais against the society for the Suppression of Vice with a similar argument,
ironically recommending the suppression of Ovid and other Latin poets and of
course the Bible in the interests of literary purity.[25]

But Swinburne did not really care for Ovid, according to his biographer.[26]
His classical enthusiasm was for Greece rather than Rome. Where most poets
would write dedicatory verses in the vernacular or, exceptionally, in Latin,
Swinburne dedicated his verse-tragedy about Meleager and Atalanta, *Atalanta
in Calydon*, in 78 lines of Greek elegiacs addressed to Landor. These were
inserted between an epigraph from Euripides and another from Aeschylus, both
alluding to the Meleager legend, to establish expectations of a Greek tragedy
in English.[27] Lyrical choruses which contain some of Swinburne's best poetry,
passages of terse dialogue approximating to the *stichomythia* of the classical
tragedians, and an apparatus of messengers to report much of the action are all
designed to confirm such expectations. But the 'play' is far too long, too florid,
too intemperate and undisciplined and at times too vague to bear much
resemblance to real Greek tragedy. In fact it deserves many of the reproaches
Preston had levelled at the questionably classical Ovid. Interestingly, Ovid
rather than the Greeks supplies the plot. W. R. Rutland suggests that Swinburne
may first have encountered the story in a fragment of Euripides from which he
took one of his epigraphs since this was included in a book he was given when
he left school.[28] This may be so, but the fragment is so small that it could have
done no more than alert him to the existence of the legend. Homer tells the
story in a rather obscure aside, but he offers a Meleager already married to
someone else and makes him die differently: he does not mention Atalanta, so
love for her is not a motive either for slaying the Calydonian boar or for falling
out over the spoil. There is a version of the story in Apollodorus, but this
degrades Meleager to a would-be adulterer by giving him a wife and describing
him lusting after Atalanta. Only Ovid in the *Metamorphoses* proposes an
unmarried Meleager nobly in love with Atalanta, and makes a much more lucid
and coherent story out of it. This is the story Swinburne follows.[29]

In trying to minimise Ovid's importance to *Atalanta* Edmund Gosse observes
that 'The courtly sweetness and scented grace of Ovid' were alien to Swinburne's 'austere and archaic' conception of his story.[30] But this is to read Ovid
through the enchanted confusions of *A Midsummer Night's Dream*, in a sense
the most Ovidian of Shakespeare's plays but comfortably remote from the
frequently harsh and even grotesque pagan universe adroitly reduced to the

continuous narrative of the *Metamorphoses*. It is with this pagan world that the defiantly anti-Christian Swinburne is anxious to identify, and Ovid is his undervalued guide into it. In the Meleager story Swinburne senses a point of access to the grim and remorseless world of savage ritual closely linked with the pitiless processes of nature. In this respect he shares some of the concerns of his contemporaries Max Müller and Andrew Lang, rival theorists of mythic origins. He also intuitively anticipates a few of the conclusions of J. G. Frazer's anthropological studies published not only in *The Golden Bough* but later still in his commentary on Ovid's *Fasti*.[31]

Swinburne's technique in *Atalanta* is to embroider a simple story almost endlessly in sometimes minimally relevant choric odes and descriptions deploying metaphors and images which can be linked with the main action. 'When the hounds of spring are on winter's traces', the first line of the first chorus, introduces an apparently otiose metaphor for the purpose of establishing the atmosphere of the chase or boar-hunt which is the main theme of the work. But the idea of relentless pursuit, of hounding without mercy as Actaeon was pursued, is poetically transferred to the natural sequence of the seasons from which there is no respite. The same chorus chants mellifluously but with a studied callousness that 'the brown bright nightingale amorous/Is half assuaged for Itylus'. The (Homeric) Greek form of the name does not disguise the reference to Itys and one of the most revolting stories in Ovid, Procne's revenge on her husband Tereus by causing him unwittingly to eat his son, Itys or Itylus. Swinburne's poem 'Itylus' treats the story at greater length, alluding to 'The small slain body, the flowerlike face' which there can be no forgetting.[32]

There are far too many flowers in Swinburne, but flowers and fruit and grain grow from the pagan earth. The chorus in *Atalanta* praises the earth

> That hast made man and unmade; thou whose mouth
> Looks red from the eaten fruits of thine own womb,

and Meleager applies this language to his own mother who causes his death. She is unjust and unholy, he feels, and yet like nature herself she commands reverence:

> thou too, queen,
> The source and end, the sower and the scythe,
> The rain that ripens and the drought that slays,
> The sand that swallows and the spring that feeds,
> To make me and unmake me – thou, I say
> ...whence a wheaten ear
> Strong from the sun and fragrant from the rains
> I sprang...   (*Poetical Works* II, pp. 314, 330).

This identification of motherhood with vegetation deity is most explicit, in Swinburne's poem to Hertha (the north-Germanic Earth-mother goddess[33]) and his Proserpine poems. The flowers growing in such profusion in Ovid's

Enna, so closely associated with Proserpine, are clutched to Swinburne's bosom in an exaggerated gesture of self-identification:

> O daughter of earth, of my mother, her crown and blossom of birth,
> I am also, I also, thy brother; I go as I came unto earth.

The earth-mother Hertha identifies with her fruit mankind:

> One birth of my bosom
>   One beam of mine eye;
> One topmost blossom
>   That scales the sky,
> Man, equal and one with me, man that is made of me, man that is I.

In a sense this is all extravagantly romantic commentary on the world of the *Metamorphoses* where humanity can be at one with or pass over into trees and birds and the constellations of the heavens. More particularly it is a commentary on the Ovidian story of Ceres and Proserpine (Swinburne does not use the Greek form of the names) as vegetation myth, anticipating one of the chapters of Frazer's *Golden Bough* some 30 years later.[34] This is as much a defiant act of identification with paganism and a challenge to Christian values of righteousness and compassion as the speech of the villainous Guido at the end of *The Ring and the Book*. Swinburne would have liked to appear a rebel and rascal on the same grand scale.

Yet Swinburne disguised all this ostentatious paganism as unmediated Hellenism and kept Ovid in the background. This was Ovid's usual position at the time. Browning went out of his way to establish an authentically Greek atmosphere in *Balaustion's Adventure* and *Aristophanes' Apology*, going to the length of following the alien-seeming German convention of transliterating Greek names so that Alcestis as she appears in the Latin of Ovid is somehow restored to primitive classical authenticity as Alkestis. But Ovid is solidly present behind this façade. In these poems and many others, particularly *Pauline*, much of the mythological material is quietly borrowed from the *Metamorphoses*. In *Balaustion's Adventure*, for instance, Browning, like Tennyson (and Milton) follows Ovid rather than the *Hymn to Demeter* in locating the rape of Proserpine/Persephone in Sicily.[35]

Apart from questions of moral respectability and revulsion from Ovid the rake there are perhaps two main reasons for this wilful and faintly unworthy suppression of Ovid. In a literary climate still dominated by Romanticism he seemed to be merely facile and he was blamed for being derivative. He was identified not only with Byron but with Pope. Like Pope he was a brilliantly adroit verse-maker. Whatever he wrote turned out verse, he claimed: Pope likewise maintained, in conscious imitation, 'I lisped in numbers for the numbers came'.[36] But Pope was out of fashion, and so was metrical facility. Herbert Paul was not praising Ovid when he remarked, in *The Nineteenth*

Century, that he wrote the *Fasti* to prove he could versify anything.[37] Pope had admired and sought to imitate the neat, cerebral, aphoristic style which could perform miracles of crystallisation and engineer pithy antithesis and word-play in season, and out of it, even in the most passionate despairs of the *Heroides* or the most sublime disasters of the *Metamorphoses*. Not surprisingly, the only satisfactory 'equivalent' English translators had found for the well-turned Ovidian elegiac couplet or hexameter was the iambic heroic couplet of Pope and Dryden, poets condemned almost beyond recovery by Matthew Arnold in the nineteenth century as classics of our prose rather than our poetry.[38] Pope and Dryden, Addison and Congreve and other seventeenth- and eighteenth-century Ovidian translators had been brought together by Dr Samuel Garth in 1717 in a composite translation of the *Metamorphoses* and this had no real rivals throughout the nineteenth century. J. J. Howard attempted a blank-verse *Metamorphoses* in 1807 but this foundered on the rock of the translator's heavy-handed pomposity and his 'attempt to chasten the prurience of his [Ovid's] ideas and his language, so as to fit his writings for more general perusal'.[39] Other attempts, such as the distressed gentlewoman Emma Garland's *Ovid's Epistles, in English Verse* (1842), were competent enough, often using the now old-fashioned heroic couplet, but without the Ovidian sparkle. Some of the most pleasing versions came not from grave scholars or literary personages but from two clever young Oxford graduates, F. H. Hummel and A. A. Brodribb, who were light-heartedly willing to give Byron and Pope their due. For the *Amores* they proposed a four-line stanza with frequent feminine rhyme, in effect a modification of the rapid serio-comic stanza of Byron's *Don Juan*. This worked quite well:

> High deeds of heroes to rehearse
> I thought, in grave heroic measure,
> When Cupid, laughing, clipped my verse,
> And bade me sing of love and pleasure.
>
> Usurping boy! what right has he
> To deal with poets as he chooses?
> I'll start afresh, and let him see
> I'm not his servant, but the Muse's.

Brodribb attempted heroic couplets for a version of the Daphne story from the *Metamorphoses*, with some success: *sic deus et virgo*; *est hic spe celer, illa timore* (lit. 'so [ran] god and maiden, he swift from hope and she from fear')
becomes
> So Daphne fled, so follows Phoebus near,
> The one from ardour swift, the one from fear.[40]

This is the nearest English equivalent to Ovidian wit: it is pastiche Pope. But it is remote both from the studied colloquial roughness and verve of Browning's verse and the humourless, determinedly non-iambic lyricism of Swinburne, not to mention the metrical virtuosity of Tennyson in his singing-robes.

Ovid and the nineteenth century

The Popian Ovid was out of favour not merely for being glib and clever but for being unoriginal, articulating 'what oft was thought but ne'er so well expressed'.[41] After all, more primitive and 'authentic' versions of his material could be consulted in other sources, usually Greek. Greek scholarship and awareness of Greek antiquity had vastly improved from the days of Joseph Spence's *Polymetis* (1747) an elaborate compendium of Greek mythology drawn almost exclusively from Latin sources. From the 1830s onwards British scholars became aware of the important developments in the study of comparative mythology initiated in Germany by K. O. Müller and C. A. Lobek and synthesised in England in the work of R. W. Mackie whose book attracted a review from George Eliot.[42] Behind the Ovidian Venus there loomed not only the Greek Aphrodite and Astarte but the biblical Ashtaroth and the Babylonian Ishtar. The Ovidian Deucalion (described also in the much less familiar Apollodorus) had once rested snugly inside the framework of Bible-based English literary culture as the Graeco-Roman Noah. Reconciling the chronology was difficult but not impossible in a world only six thousand years old. George Sandys and John Milton after him contrived the moral and imaginative alignment of Deucalion and Genesis without dismay. It was known that there was another fragmentary near-Eastern flood-narrative by Berossus preserved in Eusebius, but it was confidently assumed that like the Deucalion story this was a later reflection of the biblical Noah. The confidence was misplaced. In 1872, in Assurbanipal's library in the ancient palace of Sennacherib, King of Assyria, George Smith discovered a clay tablet bearing the tale of Ut-napishtim, a Mesopotamian flood-story forming part of the epic of Gilgamesh. This was much older than the story of Noah in Genesis which presumably derived from it in some way. It was immeasurably older than Ovid, whose Deucalion now appeared very late and literary.[43]

This was only the most striking instance of Ovid's smooth secondariness, his unexciting position near the end of the long chain of tradition. Ever since the eighteenth-century enthusiasm for the 'Gothic' and the shaggily primitive, associated in particular with the ballad-collecting Bishop Percy and the critic Thomas Warton, elegant redaction had been at an aesthetic disadvantage. Ovid told mythological stories more lucidly and dramatically than most of his frequently prosaic or obscurely allusive predecessors, which is why he continued to be drawn on by stealth. But Herder objected that the neatly ordered narrative poetry which had kindled Goethe's imagination was merely derivative from more 'authentic' writers closer to raw nature. Despite Goethe's urgings, he could not accept the *Metamorphoses* as 'natural' by virtue of being a poetic creation and rejected it as a valid vision of reality.[44] Goethe's, however, was not a solitary voice. The great French critic Sainte-Beuve was sufficiently interested in Ovid to consider making him the subject of his important inaugural lecture-series at the Collège de France, though he finally lectured on Virgil instead. Like Goethe, he felt Ovid's poetry was not so much inferior to the work of original geniuses such as Homer and Shakespeare as different in kind: Ovid belonged in a separate category, among the studious writers and careful artists, Cicero and Tibullus or Dryden and Prévost.[45]

Despite Goethe and Sainte-Beuve the view persisted that Ovid was in some sense imaginatively trivial and insignificant because he could not be assimilated to Romantic theories of the poetic. This assessment was all the more perverse since he provided imaginative stimulus for both Wordsworth and Keats, a stimulus which made them uneasy. Like Goethe, Wordsworth encountered Ovid as a schoolboy and recorded how deeply upset he was to find him unfavourably compared to Virgil.[46] The schoolboy enthusiasm for Ovid and the myths he recounted lay dormant for some years but eventually, in *The Excursion*, Wordsworth set out his matured convictions about the value of mythology as the language of the natural imagination. His abiding respect for the emotional and moral strengths of simple country-dwellers led him to praise their fancies which 'exalt/The forms of nature and enlarge her powers', and myth is an outcome of such fancies. The old stories were

> Fictions in form, but in their substance truths,
> Tremendous truths [,] familiar to the men
> Of long-past times, nor obsolete in ours.
>
> (*Excursion* 4.718–62, 847–87; 6.545–8)

The rocks and stones and trees of his own early imaginings had mingled easily with the mythic imaginative landscape of the *Metamorphoses* since despite enormous cultural and topographical differences both poets shared a sense of nature as a living presence and so both retained a sympathy for the animistic universe of the times before either of them when in Schiller's phrase – '*Gab man höhern Adel der Natur*' ('Man gifted nature with divinity').[47] Needless to say, Wordsworth was no Cumbrian Ovid: he was a moralist as well as a dreamer. But Ovid contributed to the substance of his dreams. Proteus rising from the sea and old Triton blowing his wreathéd horn, both probably taken from the *Metamorphoses*, might be part of the outworn creed of the pagan but they belong with the lost vision of nature Wordsworth laments in his famous sonnet 'The world is too much with us'.[48] In *Laodamia* one of the heroines of the *Heroides* is sternly taken to task by the author of the *Ode to Duty*. Though Virgil and Euripides as well as Ovid supply details, the theme of passionate desolation is characteristically Ovidian. Wordsworth begins by letting Laodamia express her despair and her longing to see again 'Her Hero slain upon the beach of Troy'. But he is not content to explore the psychology of desertion for its own sake: the slain Protesilaus returns from the dead but only to admonish his widow to 'control/Rebellious passion', and through disciplining the affections 'by fortitude to seek/Our blest re-union in the shades below.' Lacking such fortitude Laodamia dies of despair when Protesilaus rejoins the shades below. Wordsworth was torn between severity and sympathy

226

in his conclusion to the poem. In earlier editions Laodamia was indulgently admitted to Elysium, the serene region of the happy Ghosts, where she could find her husband. The judgement was gentle upon one 'who so deeply loved'. But some years later this was condemned as 'weak pity' and she was permanently excluded 'as for a wilful crime' from Elysium and Protesilaus, a verdict softened in the next edition to a purgatorial period of separation.[49]

Wordsworth has indecisively mingled Virgilian sternness and pathos with Ovidian emotional rhetoric. Where Ovid's Laodamia merely contemplates the desolations of widowhood, fearing her husband is about to die, Virgil's Laodamia is already wandering disconsolate in the underworld separated in eternity as she had been in life from the hero she had loved.[50] Wordsworth had known youth and passion and was imaginatively sympathetic to the feelings of the moment unallayed by the longer perspectives of contemplative maturity and metaphysics. In his sober middle years, less given to rapture than reflection, 'a bard of ebbing time', he sought to detach himself from the dramatic emotional excess of the old mythological world rendered by Ovid as from an earlier phase of his own development, but detachment was not always easy. His 'Ode to Lycoris', like his 'Laodamia', seeks to assert the mature, rational, prudent Wordsworth over against the younger and more passional self, but the strong pull of passion is what imparts interest and tension to both poems. 'Lycoris', the name he gives to his wife in the 'Ode', was the pseudonym of the beloved of Ovid's fellow-poet Cornelius Gallus, the counterpart to Ovid's Corinna or Propertius' Cynthia, and she is mentioned in this company in the Ars Amatoria.[51] Gallus, like Ovid, had incurred the anger of Augustus and was exiled: by implicitly adopting the role of an Ovidian alter ego and toying with the idiom of the Latin love-elegy Wordsworth shows an unexpected affinity with Ovidian poetry even if the conclusion to his own poem backs away from all this to assert the values of mature common sense and stern morality.

John Keats never reached the reflective maturity of middle age. His fancies lingered more fondly than Wordsworth's in the world of Ovidian myth since there was no long retrospect of years to overshadow it or place it in a context of accumulated experience. As Leigh Hunt observed, his first volume, published in 1817, showed how attentively he had read the passages on myth in The Excursion, published just three years before. The 'Fauns and Dryads' of his poem 'I stood tiptoe upon a little hill' appear in a passage which his friend Woodhouse marked 'Ovid', identifying the nameless figure who pulled aside the boughs to disclose Pan and Syrinx in a richly mythological forest. But in this case at least it was Wordsworth's account of the origin of Pan and the satyrs and nymphs of the ancient countryside which sent Keats to the world of the Metamorphoses.[52] Bacchus in his leopard-drawn chariot, a recurring image in Keats, makes his first appearance in 'Sleep and Poetry' in the 1817 volume, but it was not so much Ovid as Titian's Bacchus and Ariadne, on exhibition in London at the British Institution in 1816, that first enticed him on to Ariadne's

Naxos.[53] But Ovid, encountered directly or indirectly, was not quite enough. Recreating the Ovidian dream-world of the old mythology and celebrating a mythologised nature, the realm of 'Flora and old Pan', could only be an episode in the growth of a poet's mind, Keats tried to convince himself, and he constantly peered beyond it in the direction of the 'nobler life,/Where I may find the agonies, the strife/Of human hearts'. The old enchantment lingered into later poems such as both versions of *Hyperion*, tempered with melancholy and a sense of evanescence, expressed as a vision of a once-bright world 'Far sunken from the healthy breath of morn', its ancient god dethroned.[54] But there were other possibilities for poetry.

The urge to leave Ovidian territory and pass beyond straightforward identification with the oneness of nature to some wider world is present in *Endymion*, though it is curiously half-hearted. The Hymn to Pan in the first book, drawing on a bewildering range of classical, Elizabethan and modern sources of which the familiar team of 'Ovid and Lemprière' are the most important, expresses a reluctance to abandon Pan and the poetically transformed world of nature:

> Be still the unimaginable lodge
> For solitary thinkings, such as dodge
> Conception to the very bourne of heaven,
> Then leave the naked brain; be still the leaven,
> That spreading in this dull and clodded earth
> Gives it a touch ethereal, a new birth.   (*Endymion* I.293–8)

In his wanderings through lush woodland Endymion thinks he has come upon the Proserpine of Milton and the *Metamorphoses* (perhaps the most widely travelled heroine in Ovid), but she melts into the melancholy figure of Ovid's Echo, still a part of the same coherently imagined world (*Endymion* I.931–59). Ovidian lore shadows Endymion right through the poem. His encounters with the moon-goddess upon earth are followed by adventures below the earth and then, in Book III, beneath the sea, where he finds a calm and peaceful old man.

This Wordsworthian figure turns out to be Glaucus the lover of Scylla, represented both in Salvator Rosa's painting of 'Glaucus and Scylla' which may have influenced Keats and in the 13th and 14th books of the *Metamorphoses* (13.906–68; 14.1–74). But Keats modifies Ovid's story considerably, mingling it with features of an episode in *The Faerie Queene* and introducing a benign magic book on loan from Shakespeare's Prospero in *The Tempest*.[55] This literary enrichment signals a moral departure from the Ovidian world under the (temporary) influence of Christian humanism. Ovid told of a Glaucus who became a sea-god and fell in love with the nymph Scylla. When she fled from his wooing he sought Circe's aid only to find that the enchantress wanted him to love her instead. When he refused she made her rival Scylla into a sea-monster though she refrained from harming Glaucus. Keats's Glaucus, like

Spenser's Fradubio in the first book of *The Faerie Queene*, is less highminded:
both betray their love of another by succumbing to the lures of an enchantress,
for 'Who could resist? Who in this universe?' (*Endymion* III.453). Glaucus
yields not so much to Ovid's Circe as to the moralised Circe of Renaissance
tradition, identified by Natalis Comes and George Sandys in his commentary
on Ovid with *libido* or lust. Glaucus comes to realise that he had degraded
himself in surrendering to lust and Circe when he discovers that the animals
which roam her island were once human, now degraded into beasts. For the
Renaissance moralists sensuality was a dehumanising agency: it had turned
Spenser's Fradubio into a tree. When Keats's Glaucus attempts to escape from
Circe he is prompted not merely by his preference for Scylla as in Ovid but by
repudiation of the lust that had cost Fradubio his humanity. Circe cuts off his
retreat, however, and condemns him to an old age of a thousand years on the
seabed. Soon he encounters Scylla, not turned into a sea-monster as in Ovid but
simply drowned. If Keats's moralising departures from Ovid have given
Glaucus sinful lust and a nightmare punishment they also offer an opportunity
to atone. A book of magic recovered from a shipwreck instructs him to assemble
drowned lovers side by side until he meets a youth 'by heavenly power loved
and led' (III.708) who will help him bring them to life again. The youth is
Endymion. The restless visionary dreamer and the chastened and benevolent
humanitarian, representing the two aspects of Keats's poetic aspiration, can
now work together to restore life and happiness to the drowned lovers. Scylla
too comes back to life, while Glaucus recovers his youth, and there is rapturous
celebration in the Temple of Neptune. In the midst of this Endymion swoons
and has an intimation of eternal bliss with his own beloved, the elusive Cynthia.

Triton blows his horn at the end of the episode as he does in Wordsworth's
sonnet 'The world is too much with us' and this draws attention to the
Wordsworthian character of the whole episode. Endymion's encounter with
Glaucus corresponds to a morally encouraging interview with a Wordsworthian
solitary. The whole attempt to retune Ovidian Pan-pipes to play the still sad
music of humanity is in accordance with Keats's earlier determination to pass
beyond the world of Flora and old Pan. But one is left with the impression that
Ovid gave him more imaginative stimulus than the old leech-gatherer and that
far more than Wordsworth he remained a 'pagan suckled in a creed outworn'.

Keats used Ovid not merely for incidental mythological reference but to
supply the substance of a particular imaginative orientation. The Glaucus story
functions as a self-contained episode or interlude in the adventures of
Endymion. Ovid was always a useful source for such interludes: his stories,
particularly in the *Metamorphoses*, were conveniently detachable but always
lucid and concise, participating in a distinctive and coherently imagined world
of myth which librettists and painters as well as poets loved. Not surprisingly,
from Monteverdi's *Orfeo* (1607) to Offenbach's *Orfée aux Enfers* (1858) the
brilliant artifice of opera, incorporating spectacle and dramatic feeling, found

Ovid indispensable. The formalisation of powerful emotion into a grand rhetorical set-piece is characteristic both of the great arias of opera and of Ovid's *Heroides*, and Ovid's men can feel no less deeply than his women. The disconsolate Orpheus musically bewailed the loss of his Eurydice: *resedit/dis genitus vates et fila sonantia movit* ('the heaven-descended bard sat down and smote his sounding lyre') (*Met.* 10.88ff). Gluck's librettist for *Orfeo ed Euridice* (1762) obligingly wrote the words for him: *Che farò senz' Euridice?* ('What shall I do without Eurydice?'), and Offenbach irreverently imported the air into his *Orfée aux Enfers*, giving it (frequently) to his comic Orpheus to emphasise his robust remoteness from operatic grief. The operatic qualities of Ovid were as well suited to comedy as tragedy, for his narratives proffered a sometimes evasive, even equivocal tone or quality of feeling which could be rendered sympathetically, or comically subverted according to taste. Sorrowing deserted Ariadne, with or without her saviour Bacchus, was a favourite set-piece for Victorian painters such as G. F. Watts and Frederick Leighton, inspired as much by Titian as by Ovid.[56] It was as a set-piece that she had gone on stage, providing a suitably elevated subject for the pretentious M. Jourdain to contemplate in the interlude which was incorporated in a German version of Molière's *Le Bourgeois Gentilhomme*. Hugo von Hofmannsthal improved this into a libretto for Richard Strauss as *Ariadne auf Naxos* (1912). But why stop at opera? John Davidson had gone the whole way and turned the tale into a satirical pantomime, *Scaramouch on Naxos* (1888).

Pantomime and opera, especially comic opera, are fairly remote from the fastidious sensibility of Matthew Arnold, but he too could write an Ovidian interlude, adapting the story of Cadmus and Harmonia to the singing-voice of Callicles in *Empedocles on Etna*. For all his admiration of things Hellenic it was in the Latin poet that Arnold found a narrative of limpid clarity to insert as a serenely lyrical interlude in the stoical musings of Empedocles, a thinly veiled modern consciousness linked with the Romantic melancholy of nineteenth-century French literature. Ovid describes the unhappy Cadmus and Harmonia, transformed into snakes, as mild creatures remembering what once they were, *quidque prius fuerint, placidi meminere dracones* (*Met.* 4.603). Arnold, however, absolves them from the pangs of modern consciousness and grants them peace by allowing them to

> wholly forget their first sad life, and home,
> And all that Theban woe, and stray
> For ever through the glens, placid and dumb.
>
> (*Empedocles on Etna* I ii 458–60)

Pindar as well as Ovid contributes to Callicles' song, pitched to harmonise with Empedocles' strain of undespairing calm amidst life's inevitable reverses. The faint Miltonic echo of 'all that pain' which Ceres endured as she wandered through the world in search of Proserpine enriches the song with another glimmering of (ultimately) Ovidian lore and very gently hints at an anguish at the heart of things articulated in myth for which there may yet be healing or oblivion.

Ovid is useful to Arnold in a small way in *Empedocles*. It is in a similarly modest fashion that he is useful to Burne-Jones, William Morris and Charles Kingsley as a source for their different versions of the story of Perseus and Andromeda.[57] In their hands the tale modulates into a piece of decorative Victorian chivalry. As usual, Ovid almost disappears in the process: in Kingsley's long poem 'Andromeda', it is Sir Walter Scott's *Marmion* rather than the *Metamorphoses* that supplies Perseus with the 'falchion' to slay the sea-monster.[58] For much of the nineteenth century Ovid seems to lurk in odd corners, given generous hospitality by John Keats but by few others. Shelley the champion of Hellas dismissed him along with Horace and Catullus as a mere imitator of the Greeks, though he did not disdain to draw on him for 'Arethusa' and 'Song of Proserpine', lyrical interludes in Mrs Shelley's drama *Proserpine*.[59] Nineteenth-century Hellenism, taking its tone from Shelley, looked askance at Ovid but did not completely annihilate him. Just occasionally stray reflections from the glory that was Greece could place him in a new and warmer light. Walter Pater became aware of the distinctiveness of Ovid's version of the Proserpine story in the *Fasti* as he considered the Greek *Hymn to Demeter* and paid tribute to the delicate sadness and 'pathos caught from humble things' which characterises Ovid's narrative.[60] In a sense this is a Wordsworthian reading of Ovid, but it is a perceptive comment which serves to remind us that Wordsworth himself had found in Ovid a sympathetic imagination.

Ovid was part of the Romantic and Victorian literary consciousness, but a small and conveniently detachable part. Wordsworth and Keats were drawn to him and yet in different ways and with different success tried to establish their distance from his world. For Byron he was an easily disowned *alter ego*, the impudent rogue he sometimes liked to appear himself. Browning and Swinburne identified in him a challenge to conventional pieties which they exploited for their own ends. Poets, painters, librettists all found in Ovid a useful imaginative resource which they seldom troubled to acknowledge. Time which devours all things, as Ovid tells us (*Met.* 15.234), did not destroy Ovid in the nineteenth century. It changed him as his Arethusa was changed into a fountain from which wayfarers could drink without always recognising the source.

15

T. S. ELIOT'S *METAMORPHOSES*: OVID AND *THE WASTE LAND*

Stephen Medcalf

G. K. CHESTERTON remarks in the opening paragraph of his novel *The Ball and the Cross* that 'the world of science and evolution is far more nameless and elusive and like a dream than the world of poetry or religion; since in the latter images and ideas remain themselves eternally, while it is the whole idea of evolution that identities melt into each other as they do in a nightmare'.[1]

He is describing here something about modernity which he detests because it involves a revolt against the recognition that being oneself involves the acceptance of limitations and the following of moral laws. In his essay *A Defence of Rash Vows* he attacks an aspect of this revolt against identity, the 'terror of one's self, of the weakness and mutability of one's self [which] is the real basis of the objection to vows of any kind' whose end is 'that maddening horror of unreality which descends upon the decadents'.[2]

In describing this complex of feelings as something close to the heart of the modern world, Chesterton is no doubt right, and also right in implying that now it claims to find a justification in the theory of evolution in its various forms, biological, sociological, psychological. But it does not seem to be a thing peculiar to the modern world, nor by any causal necessity connected with modern science. For could one not give as a possible reading of Ovid's *Metamorphoses*, both of the repeated theme of change of body, and of the cunning intricate sliding of the book's whole structure, that some such amorality, some such shrinking from commitment lies behind it? As Karl Galinsky has very well said,

One obvious characteristic of metamorphosis is that, by its very nature, it eliminates a true solution to the moral issues raised by the myths. For instance, lust and passion in metamorphosis stories seldom are actually defeated or resisted, seldom faced head-on in a true moral conflict that can only be resolved in moral terms. Instead, the passions are represented as they work upon the personality of the character involved until he or she is changed into the bestial or elemental equivalent of that passion...[3]

To the modern eye, this reading is enhanced by the poem's being given the form of a history of the world: the sense of an evolution which first creates, then endlessly varies forms, is explicit in Ovid's account of the creation, and for us – with our post-Darwinian sense of the unity of all flesh – tends to raise itself out of the subsequent narratives, where perhaps for him it was latent in his sense of history, and even, as in Pythagoras' oration in the 15th book, of biology.

Now this flight from identity is present in one famous modern use of the *Metamorphoses*, T. S. Eliot's note to line 218 of *The Waste Land*:

> Tiresias, although a mere spectator and not indeed a 'character', is yet the most important personage in the poem, uniting all the rest. Just as the one-eyed merchant, seller of currants, melts into the Phoenician Sailor, and the latter is not wholly distinct from Ferdinand Prince of Naples, so all the women are one woman, and the two sexes meet in Tiresias. What Tiresias *sees*, in fact, is the substance of the poem.[4]

As with all the notes to *The Waste Land*, one wonders how seriously to take it, a wonder emphasised by its going on 'The whole passage from Ovid is of great anthropological interest' and then beginning a quotation of 19 lines from the account of Tiresias in Book 3 of the *Metamorphoses* (320–8) two-thirds of the way through a sentence, which as a result becomes quite hard to construe, although in the original it is lucid. Most probably the selection was arbitrary, and dictated by the amount of space which required filling in the printed text. The note is beloved by scholars and critics anxious to demonstrate the unity of *The Waste Land*, for it suggests that to the serious, the sophisticated, the scholarly, in short to the initiated, there is a hidden unity under the mystery which the uninitiated may be rebuked for not perceiving. But this very inclination of the natural initiate is something that Eliot, the ironist and devotee of P. G. Wodehouse, might have wished to prick.

For the natural reading of *The Waste Land* is not characterised by meltings nor by absence of distinctions. Its structure is abrupt, block succeeding block and tone breaking violently in against tone in a manner very like the music of Stravinsky's *The Rite of Spring*, which may have been the poem's catalyst. In both works there are thematic unities, echoes and repetitions: but they are not achieved by sliding and melting. Neither artist goes in, in these works, for the deft turns of Ovid: they stress the breaks.

It would be possible for this to be true of the structure and yet for the personages inhabiting its discrete blocks to melt into one another. And the (apparently mostly male) figures who carry the narration, the series of 'I's which addresses the son of man in the desert, watches the purposeless crowd flow over London Bridge, thinks silent thoughts in the presence of the nervous woman, weeps by Lake Leman, as prince Ferdinand fishes in the canal, is addressed by the Smyrna merchant, as Tiresias tells the encounter of the typist and the clerk, hears the mandoline in Lower Thames Street, comes to Carthage, walks through the desert, struggles with *give*, *sympathise* and *control*, fishes again, and shores up its ruins[5] – this series certainly is uncertain whether it makes up an identity or has sufficient distinctions within it to remain a sequence of phantasmagoric echoes.

Eliot certainly wanted them to become a unity. This can be deduced from three pieces of evidence:

1 The note on Tiresias itself.
2 The suggestion which he made to Pound and from which Pound dissuaded him, that *Gerontion* be prefixed to *The Waste Land*. For the old, prophetic, apparently blind man being read to by a boy, in *Gerontion*, waiting for rain, very clearly fits into the sequence, and *The Waste Land* would have seemed simply what its last line proclaims *Gerontion* to be –

> Thoughts of a dry brain in a dry season.[6]

3 Something curious, which can only be deduced from the *Metamorphoses*. For the passage quoted by Eliot continues with Tiresias' first prophecy, that Narcissus would live to see a long, ripe old age '*si se non noverit*' – if he never knew himself (*Met.* 3.348). This, which sounds like a deliberately impudent inversion on Ovid's part of the Delphic advice to know oneself, must have been known to Eliot. It might very well lie behind his poem *The Death of St Narcissus*, which is more Ovidian than *The Waste Land*, both in its treatment of metamorphosis, as Narcissus remembers being a tree,

> Twisting its branches among each other

a fish

> With slippery white belly held tight in his own fingers

and a girl

> Knowing at the end the taste of his own whiteness –

and in its surreal or mannerist vision, its amorality, and the smoothness with which it recounts rape and murder –

> ...his white skin surrendered itself to the redness of blood and satisfied him.[7]

All its imagery seems to develop from an expression of self-consciousness –

> His eyes were aware of the pointed corners of his eyes –

which although it is Eliotic rather than Ovidian, and indeed seems to express an obsession with introspection peculiarly modern, nevertheless could be a development of *si se non noverit*.

Two versions of *The Death of St Narcissus* are among the manuscripts associated with *The Waste Land*, and its first five lines –

> Come under the shadow of this grey rock
> Come in under the shadow of this grey rock
> And I will show you a shadow different from either
> Your shadow sprawling over the sand at daybreak, or
> Your shadow leaping behind the fire against the red rock[8]

became part of the first speech by a prophetic voice, already perhaps Tiresias, in *The Waste Land*.

But these are only evidences of a wish on Eliot's part to give *The Waste Land* a single observer, Gerontion or Tiresias, who would, had he come into full existence, have transformed the poem, distancing the profoundly disturbing stream of images which now flow from the poet's mind directly into the reader's, by interposing a persona and rendering the whole sequence into a dramatic monologue.

The struggle to make Tiresias the one who sees the substance of the whole poem does indeed enter its structure. He appears at almost its exact centre, and after his entry the successive pictures do begin to compose more continuous stories (a journey down the Thames to the sea, a journey from the city through a desert), stories which suggest a firmer resolve – a not very Ovidian resolve – to look for a moral resolution to the chaotic contrasts of the first two and a half parts of the poem. And the note does indicate at least one thing which is true within the poem, and which explains why this quest for a moral resolution should seem to become possible through Tiresias, although it is ultimately frustrated. For Tiresias is both male and female, and, therefore, 'throbbing between two lives' (218), lives both in the sad typist and in the aggressive clerk whose coition he observes. In this episode, therefore, the fear is momentarily lifted that is confirmed at the end of the poem, that we live isolated in our own prisons –

Thinking of the key, each confirms a prison. (414)

But, it would seem, Tiresias' vision is only one of those rumours at nightfall which revive us, and in the end it confirms the isolation of the typist and clerk.

And in fact this contrast runs through the poem. The narrative 'I' from time to time half forms tentatively distinct figures, but they melt back into its one self: the figures it contemplates are irremediably isolated, irremediably distinct. Most of them, although not quite all, are female: there is no conceivable sense which would be true of the poem that could be given to Eliot's statement that 'all the women are one woman'. The typist and the daughters of the Thames are indeed not very distinguishable from each other: but, in terms of emotion, will, background and language, they are sharply distinguished from Marie the archduke's cousin, the hyacinth girl, Madame Sosostris, Philomela, and the women who seem to be reflections of the two women in Eliot's household, Vivien Eliot and their lady help Ellen Kellond. And all these are in a few lines sharply and abundantly characterised in contrast with each other. And while Mr Eugenides and Phlebas the Phoenician may melt into each other as a perennial Mediterranean merchant (a resemblance more tragically complete if one could regard Eliot as having had a premonition, in bringing Mr Eugenides from Smyrna, of what happened just as *The Waste Land* was in the press, the massacre at Smyrna in September 1922 which might have made even Mr

Eugenides a sacrifice) they do not in the least resemble the male narrators nor do either they or the narrators resemble the young man carbuncular.

These figures indeed, more particularly the female ones, may be said to be trapped in their roles, and indeed not only trapped figuratively but usually also insulted, injured, forced. If we may be said on the one hand to enjoy or inhabit in the poem the consciousness of a fluid series of narrative figures who scarcely establish a fixed identity, whose type from Ovid is Tiresias, what on the other hand we contemplate, on the screen as it were, are sharply defined, compelled, even sacrificial figures, whose type from Ovid is Philomela –

> As though a window gave upon the sylvan scene
> The change of Philomel, by the barbarous king
> So rudely forced...   (98–100)

Philomel and Tiresias are brought close together in *The Fire Sermon*, as Philomel's fate is rehearsed in the middle of her call as a nightingale

> So rudely forc'd
> Tereu   (205–6)

and I take it that 'Tereu', though it primarily calls on Tereus, also introduces twelve lines later the like sound of Tiresias.

Kierkegaard described both types of person in *The Sickness unto Death*,[9] and defined both their conditions as varieties of despair: the Philomel figure lost in despair of finitude, the fear that the human personality is determinate, unfree, wholly expressible in terms of social pressure and mechanical causation – the Tiresias figure lost equally in despair of infinity, the fear that the human personality is undetermined, incapable of definition, aimless, subject as in our opening quotation from Chesterton to 'that maddening horror of unreality which descends upon the decadents'.

The contrast is neither Ovidian nor even classical: it is Christian and, as Kierkegaard is well aware, only resolvable in a dialectic of infinite and finite of which the model is the Incarnation: so, many years later, Eliot presented it in *Murder in the Cathedral* and *Four Quartets*. While he was writing *The Waste Land*, we know that he was seriously considering turning to Buddhism. In his original draft there was a line which suggests an entertainment of belief in transmigration of souls:

> London, your people is bound upon the wheel![10]

He rejected it: but its original existence is one of a number of witnesses to his being torn at the time of writing *The Waste Land* between contrasting beliefs about the soul and personality. This tension is expressed in personal terms in the tension of his essay *Tradition and the Individual Talent*, between a wish to attack 'the metaphysical theory of the substantial unity of the person'[11] altogether, and so strong an awareness of possessing 'personality and emotions' as to 'know what it means to want to escape from these things'.[12] Religiously, it expresses itself in the three possibilities of *The Waste Land* – the Buddhist sense of an illusory soul bound up with our captivity to time and desire, escape from which is Nirvana, the Christian sense of a soul whose choices in time create its destiny in eternity, and a frivolous or despairing sense of beliefless futility. Although it was the Christian that finally triumphed in Eliot, the Buddhist and the beliefless emotions are both severally and together stronger than it in *The Waste Land*, and – one may hazard the guess – bring him close to Ovid, whose metamorphoses find their only moral or metaphysical rationale in the 15th book, in Pythagoras' metempsychosis.

Now, the doubt about the soul, caught between finite and infinite in *The Waste Land*, has further aspects which are relevant to Eliot's relation with Ovid:

1 First, in the nature of Tiresias' vision. In the incident which explicitly he sees, it is noticeable that the actions which he sees are all in the present tense – strives...clears...lights...lays out...arrives...guesses...is ended...is bored and tired...endeavours...are unreproved...assaults...encounter...requires...makes a welcome...bestows...gropes...turns...looks...allows...paces...smoothes...puts...(220–56). His own vision of it is in a medley of tenses – can see...perceived...foretold...awaited...have fore-suffered (219–43). The contrast fits with his own undetermined and in fact timeless nature, which is further confirmed by Eliot's taking him not only from Ovid, but from Sophocles –

> I who have sat by Thebes below the wall (245)

and the *Odyssey*

> And walked among the lowest of the dead. (246)

Superimposed in fact on Ovid's prophet is someone in whom the contrast of finite and infinite takes another form – that of time and the everlasting, which again is unresolved. Tiresias cannot help, but only suffer in clerk and typist.

2 In the *Odyssey*, (10.493–5; 11.90–1), Tiresias' consciousness alone remains firm, while the other ghosts are unrecognising and inarticulate. Perhaps this contrast is in Eliot's putting the song of the nightingale eight lines before his speech:

> Twit twit twit
> Jug jug jug jug jug jug
> So rudely forc'd,
>
> Tereu (203–6)

All through *The Waste Land* there is a feeling that language and consciousness may change, or relapse, or be transmuted into something which may be music, or birdsong, or the sound of the river, or simply broken speech. In the metamorphosis of Philomel into the nightingale it is expressed at its most beautiful:

> yet there the nightingale
> Filled all the desert with inviolable voice
> And still she cried, and still the world pursues,
> 'Jug jug' to dirty ears. (100–3)

238

Ovid makes nothing of this, and leaves the change with the tonguelessness of Philomela, which I think may be echoed in Eliot's despairing next lines:

> And other withered stumps of time
> Were told upon the walls...   (104–5)

For I suppose those stumps may more naturally suggest Philomela's tongue than what they commonly suggest to readers, the arms of Lavinia, similarly abused in *Titus Andronicus*. Romantic rather than classical, Eliot remains uncertain whether to long for, or to leave aside as holding no hope for humanity, the unconscious delight and lamentation of the birds and the song of the river Thames

> Weialala leia   (270, 290)

which is the same as the song of Wagner's Rhine-daughters, and therefore evokes music that seems to convey a similar self-absorbed delight.

Eliot ends these longings with a quotation from the *Pervigilium Veneris*, where his note reasonably directs us to think also of the *Metamorphoses* and of Philomela's sister Procne, the swallow –

> Quando fiam uti chelidon   (*Waste Land* 428)
> When may I become like the swallow...

Human speech condemned to dumbness and transformed into bird song presents a tension between inarticulate and articulate which is a further variation of the poet's being caught between finite and infinite. Nietzsche in *The Birth of Tragedy* speaks of this condition in a passage which I think is behind the quotations from *Tristan and Isolde* in the opening of *The Waste Land*: for he describes the contrast between the music which opens the scene from which Eliot quotes and which accompanies the particular words quoted – *oed' und leer das meer* – as exemplifying the way in which 'Myth shields us from music while at the same time giving music its maximum freedom.' When we see the individual grief of Tristan, 'what before had seemed a hollow sigh echoing from the womb of things now says to us simply "Waste and empty the sea"...Pity saves us from the radical pity of things'.[13]

Now this tension between myth and music reveals a further depth in Eliot's reading of Ovid. He had a nearer model for handling the tension than Wagner's *Tristan*, in Stravinsky's *Rite of Spring*. We have already observed the structural similarity between the two works, the particular kinds of juxtaposition, unity and contrast. This structural similarity is presumably an expression of the aesthetic ideals which Eliot outlined in his review of *The Rite of Spring* in September 1921:

The spirit of the music was modern, and the spirit of the ballet was primitive ceremony. The Vegetation Rite upon which the ballet is founded remained, in spite of the music, a pageant of primitive culture. It was interesting to any one who had read The Golden Bough and similar works, but hardly more than interesting. In art there should be interpenetration and metamorphosis. Even The Golden Bough can be read in two ways: as a collection of entertaining myths, or as a revelation of that vanished mind of which our mind is a continuation. In everything in the Sacre du Printemps, except in the music, one missed the sense of the present. Whether Stravinsky's music be permanent or ephemeral I do not know; but it did seem to transform the rhythm of the steppes into...the barbaric cries of modern life; and to transform these despairing noises into music.[14]

This – *Golden Bough* and Vegetation Rite as revelations of a vanished mind interpenetrating the modern mind which continues it, primitive rhythm transformed into modern rhythm, a metamorphosis of the whole into music which has a sense of the present – is clearly a picture of what Eliot was aiming for in *The Waste Land*, which took shape in the following three months. Among other purposes, then, it is clear that Eliot is in *The Waste Land* doing something oddly parallel to what Ovid was doing in the *Metamorphoses* – providing a version of the cycle of ancient myths in a form which would strike the mind of his own epoch as having a sense of the present. But unlike Ovid he thinks of this in terms of a sort of psychologised anthropology – of a primitive largely unconscious collective mind welling up into our minds; in the welling up there is to be a conscious metamorphosis into music. He sees something of the same process happening in Ovid: at least that would be the implication of the last remark in his note on Tiresias, that the whole of Ovid's description of how Tiresias gained his gift of prophecy 'is of great anthropological interest'. What, I wonder – if we take that remark seriously – did he have in mind? The idea of the physically blind man made a seer? The seer who is both male and female, a notion which Frazer in *The Golden Bough* connects with the transvestite effeminate priests of Attis, whom he regards as a god of fertility and vegetation? Or the fact that it was striking asunder two coupling snakes that changed Tiresias' sex? I have a suspicion that it was the last, because of the letter which Lady Ottoline Morrell wrote to Stephen Spender about Eliot when she had 'showed him photographs of Greek IVth and Vth Century Statues and he said they gave him the Creeps. They were so akin to "Snake Worship".'[15] He would no doubt have been thinking of the snake that was fed monthly on honey cakes in the Erechtheum, and is described in *The Golden Bough*.

Whichever of these it was he primarily had in mind, there is present in his note on Tiresias, and in his passages on Tiresias and Philomel his very physical sense of the 'daemonic, chthonic powers'[16] which drive our minds and bodies: there is present too 'the horror' which Kurtz speaks of when he dies after having had human sacrifices offered to him in the passage from Conrad's *Heart of Darkness* which Eliot originally intended to use as the epigraph to *The Waste Land*.[17]

Ovid lived closer to the rituals and sacrifices which were the horror of Kurtz and of Eliot. Is it because he is so close to them that he seems so much less moved to horror by the story of Philomela, Tereus and Procne? – moved rather to the almost amused elegance of the style with which he describes them. One might almost reverse Nietzsche's terms and say that this elegance of style is the music with which Ovid contrives to shield us from myth while at the same time giving myth its maximum freedom.

It seems likely that Eliot was fascinated by this duality in Ovid. It is certain that at the time of writing *The Waste Land*, he would have dissented from one possible reading of it – the reading which would hold Ovid to his word for the ambiguously moral sentiments which he expresses either in his own person or in character. Thus Tennyson in 1889:

> Video meliora, proboque
> Deteriora sequor.
>
> A quotable snatch of Ovidian song
> And a saying true to the letter.
> Yet – if we follow the worse too long
> We may cease to believe in the Better.[18]

Thus too Geoffrey Hill in 1968:

> Ovid in the Third Reich.
> non peccat, quaecumque potest peccasse negare
> solaque famosam culpa professa facit
>
> I love my work and my children. God
> is distant, difficult. Things happen.
> Too near the ancient troughs of blood
> Innocence is no earthly weapon...[19]

Both poets respect but finally condemn what they present as Ovid's divorce between contemplation or word and act. But Eliot in his essay on *Andrew Marvell*, written in 1921, while *The Waste Land* was struggling to be born, notes Ovid as one of the poets who share Marvell's 'alliance of levity and seriousness (by which the seriousness is intensified)'. Eliot regarded this alliance as a 'quality of a sophisticated literature',[20] and it would seem to be one of the qualities he aimed at in *The Waste Land*, and particularly in the passages where Philomel and Tiresias appear.

Philomel is seen in a passage of deliberately fine rhetoric in which, somewhat after the manner of Eliot's earlier *Portrait of a Lady*, a lady contemplates herself in the mirrors of myth and poetry, as Cleopatra, as Dido, as Imogen and Philomel. Apart from Philomel these figures are not named, and it would require turning up the relevant passages in Shakespeare and Virgil to name them, and in particular to remember that Imogen was reading the story of Philomel in a chamber closely resembled by this lady's before Iachimo in *Cymbeline* (II ii) betrayed her in her sleep. But the bewildering poetry of luxury and mirrors, in which the self is lost in reflections, cannot be mistaken: a world, might one say, of metamorphosis? Paradoxically, however, it is with the naming of the one figure out of Ovid's *Metamorphoses* that a real pity and a sense of the power of poetry enters.

Indeed, in *The Waste Land*, metamorphosis, whatever it meant to Ovid, does seem to be associated with the hope of an escape from the human condition, perhaps with a way of resolving the tension between despair of infinity and despair of finitude. Philomel escapes into poetry: Tiresias' transformations between male and female enable him to enter into the experience of typist and clerk: at the end, the poet cries out for the power to be transformed like Procne into the swallow. But the power in each case is simply the power to make poetry. It would perhaps not be too merely clever to suggest a connection between Eliot's use of the image of metamorphosis and the creative 'inter-penetration and metamorphosis' of which he speaks in the review of *The Rite of Spring*, which presents primitive myth with a sense of the present.

I would suggest that Eliot began in *The Waste Land* by hoping to make this transformation by the 'alliance of levity and seriousness'. But this is not quite what happens: it is not how we read the poetry of *A Game of Chess*. And in the episode of Tiresias, although Eliot originally composed it in quatrains which have something of Ovid's smoothness, when he revised it, he broke up their smooth running – except where, as in the physical moment of seduction, the now unexpected smoothness of style accentuates the shock of what is happening. It is not, I think, a coincidence that when Eliot transferred the Ovidian lines from *The Death of St Narcissus* to *The Waste Land* he transformed them also, omitting the movement of the shadow leaping behind the fire, and replacing the violent horror of the 'bloody cloth and limbs' with the chill horror of 'fear in a handful of dust'.

It is probable that Ovid was in his mind even in this last change. For it is easy to associate the fear of this handful of dust with the Sibyl whose longing to die introduces *The Waste Land* in its final version. In Golding's translation of the *Metamorphoses* (advocated by Pound with Eliot's support in *The Egoist*) the Sibyl tells Aeneas how she made the fatal request for long life to Apollo when he desired her maidenhead:

> I taking full my hand of dust, and shewing it him there
> Desyred like a foole to live as many yeeres as were
> Small graynes of cinder in that heape. I quight forgot to crave
> Immediately, the race of all those yeeres in youth to have.[21]

If indeed the Sibyl was in Eliot's mind in the handful of dust, it would account for his choice of the passage from the *Satyricon* as his epigraph when Pound objected to Kurtz's dying message: again a change from violent horror to chill horror.

In general the levity of Ovid and the associated aesthetic delight in violence are things for which Eliot had the capacity, but which tended to vanish from *The Waste Land* in the act of writing. As they vanish, the anthropology in Ovid tends to rise to the surface, as we can see by looking through *The Waste Land* with him in mind.

Ovid and *The Waste Land*

First, it may be said that Ovid broods over the roots of *The Waste Land*. I was told at school by one of our classics masters, G. H. Webb, that the whole of *The Golden Bough* was an attempt to explain one line in the *Fasti*. I have not been able to verify that this was literally true: it may be a deduction from the immense commentary, alluding to and drawing on *The Golden Bough*, which Frazer gives in his edition of the *Fasti* (3.271–2) on the couplet which he quotes in *The Golden Bough* itself:

> Regna tenent fortesque manu, pedibusque fugaces
> Et perit exemplo postmodo quisque suo

The strong of hand and fleet of foot do there reign kings, and each is slain thereafter even as himself had slain.[22]

The couplet does of course describe the custom which Frazer set out to explain, but for which he offers other classical evidence in addition to Ovid – that in Ovid's time and long after, the priest of Diana's grove at Nemi was always a runaway slave who had gained the office by killing his predecessor in combat, and remained priest until he was killed himself in turn. Frazer explains the custom in terms of the need to have a virile and lively priest or king to ensure the fertility of the land which he governed, and remarks in the manner of Gibbon that 'such a custom savours of a barbarous age, and, surviving into imperial times, stands out in striking isolation from the polished Italian society of the day, like a primeval rock rising from a smooth-shaven lawn'.[23] Did it seem so isolated, in the world of gladiatorial shows and animal sacrifices, to Ovid? To Eliot, it certainly carried primitive horror, and provides, with the similar story of the Fisher-King whose wound in the Grail legend keeps his land waste, something continuous with the allusions he makes to the dead of our culture who do not return, or whose return he makes nightmarish in imagery of sprouting corpses and hallucinatory companions – Christ, the dead of the world war, our very selves – dead kings of a land which will not regain its fertility.

After the Sibyl's endlessly sterile life has joined with Narcissus' obsession with his own shadow to contribute to the fear underlying the Waste Land, there follows the evocation of another figure whom Frazer would identify with the god who must die and rise again with the vegetation – Hyacinth, whom Ovid deals with because when he died through Apollo's love for him, he returned as the flower named after him. Ovid's dealing with the story (if we allow that it affects Eliot's writing, or allow it to affect our reading of the poignant intense glimpse of the girl with her arms full from the Hyacinth garden) adds perhaps a sense of the sadness of a young death, of the death of a beloved, of the death of spring flowers, and helps perhaps to generalise the sense of loss so that it includes from the next, contrastingly satiric block of lines, the drowned Phoenician Sailor. Eliot's note at line 126

> I remember
> Those are pearls that were his eyes

during the altercation of husband and wife reads 'Cf. Part 1, l.37, 48': which makes better sense if it is really 'Cf. Part 1, ll.37–48,' for that would join the hyacinth girl and the drowned sailor, lost objects of love perhaps, together as the 'nothing' that is in the silent husband's head. If so, the note probably records a regret on Eliot's part at having excised the line which made this link explicit in the husband's thoughts in his first draft:

> I remember
> The hyacinth garden. Those are pearls that were his eyes[24]

Perhaps Eliot wanted to commemorate Jean Verdenal, who died at Gallipoli and whom he remembered in Paris carrying lilac, without introducing the irrelevance of homosexuality, which the association of drowned sailor and Apollo's love Hyacinth might have seemed to do.

But these pursuings of Eliot's possible lines of thought, these chasings into possible lines of connection among metamorphoses and ancient myths, lie open to a charge of forsaking the poem. How many commentators have been led into this maze by looking for a meaning behind *The Waste Land*, and find no end in endless error lost! But then it is *The Waste Land* that tempts us to do it: that is what the waste land is. Nietzsche in the *Birth of Tragedy*, two chapters after the dealings with *Tristan and Isolde* from which I have quoted, speaks contemptuously of 'a culture without any fixed and consecrated place of origin, condemned to exhaust all possibilities and feed miserably and parasitically on every culture under the sun': and again 'Man today, stripped of myth, stands famished among all his pasts and must dig frantically for roots, be it among the most remote antiquities.'[25]

These sentences, I am inclined to think, lie behind the lines immediately before those suggesting Narcissus, Tristan and Hyacinth:

> What are the roots that clutch, what branches grow
> Out of this stony rubbish? (19–20)

and

> A heap of broken images, where the sun beats (22)

Even if they do not lie behind those lines, still they illuminate what Eliot means, and what his commentators do, and do almost inevitably, and do futilely.

This is not true of Eliot's next allusion to Ovid, the change of Philomel which we have already thought about. Here the link between Eliot and Ovid is overt: there is no need to posit ritual or primitive processes of the mind: the sharp pain, the horror and the beauty are all present in the story, and only have to be detached from Ovid's distancing of them in aesthetics to make a natural comment on the helpless, though only mental and verbal suffering of the conversation which follows. Horrible as it is, this myth really does fill the waste land with 'inviolable voice'.

The nightingale's song returns, as we have also already seen, just before

Tiresias is named. It is preceded, in fact, by what only Eliot's note makes clear is another reference to ancient myth and a dying victim – the words about Sweeney coming to Mrs Porter, which, Eliot tells us, are parodied from Day's *Parliament of Bees*, where they refer to Actaeon and Diana.[26] The connection is at best jazz age black farce: yet it makes thus a proper contrast with the nightingale's song. Charles Williams's description of the world of *The Waste Land* as 'Hell varied by intense Poetry'[27] is very much to the point.

Tiresias follows: and again what in Ovid seems to be a sophisticated renovation of ancient folly, a joke partly against women, partly at the expense of old myths, in Eliot's hands, while not quite losing its sophisticated irony, becomes also a desperate striving to renew whatever primitive wisdom was present in the myths in Ovid's day. The attempt fails, as we have seen, although the music with which it ends becomes associated with the most hopeful part of the poem – the pleasant whining of the mandoline near St Magnus Martyr's inexplicable splendour, and the song of the Thames.

There is no more of Ovid now until the end: the wisdom after which the poem henceforth reaches without attaining it, is, except for the image of Phlebas, all Christian and Hindu or Buddhist, not at all classical, until the call to be like the swallow, Philomela's sister, among the helpless flurry of quotations at the end. Perhaps it is significant of this abandonment of hope for help from pagan antiquity, that Ovid here is subsumed in a quotation from the *Pervigilium Veneris*, a very late echo of dying paganism. However that may be, it is striking that Eliot does not appear in *The Waste Land* or later to associate the myths *positively* with the divine story which in the end he accepted, the story of Christ. C. S. Lewis was led to do so in the same decade by the chance remark of a colleague: 'Rum thing. All that stuff of Frazer's about the Dying God... Looks as if it had really happened once.'[28] And C. H. Sisson seems to do something similar in his brief rehandling of Ovid, *Metamorphoses*, which culminates in the birth of Christ, 'The metamorphosis of all'.[29]

C. S. Lewis concludes that the myths are echoes of a true myth, the only way in which God can communicate truth to our myth-making minds; Sisson, it seems, uniting metamorphosis with Darwinian evolution, that myth-making is what differentiates humanity from the animals, transforms the rutting stag into an Actaeon capable at least of conscious sexual love and perhaps of beholding Diana – so that if there is a further transformation of humanity, an incarnation, it will be in some way by the same means.

But the positive acceptance of myth was not in the event Eliot's way. His remarks about *The Rite of Spring* and some very similar contemporaneous comments on Joyce's *Ulysses* indicate that *The Waste Land* may have been meant as an experiment in that direction. But it did not produce the desired result. On the contrary, as R. G. Collingwood points out in what I judge to be the most perceptive account of *The Waste Land*, the last pages of his *Principles of Art*, the poem is purgative, an example of what he would regard as art about its proper business. We were, we are, in our ancient civilisation, the victims of false consciousness. Our consciousness being so corrupt, we cannot see what is wrong with us. The myths which we inherit do not help us: Nietzsche's diagnosis was itself part of the disease which he intended to cure, the beliefless culture which (without the faith needed to hand on the images which were its *raison d'être*) either surrendered the Bible and the classics to a rage for individual freedom and force, or surrendered freedom and force in the attempt to preserve the forms even without their life.

Ovid, in a not wholly dissimilar situation, brought off a tremendous paradox. With ironic levity, speed and elegance of form and syntax, he gave a new narrative attraction to the myths which he loved, in the *Metamorphoses* and to some extent in the *Fasti*. But in his love there was an element of antiquarianism: that is of a love too much tempered by scepticism, and of the mere will to restore old forms because they are the only forms to be had. He does not test the myths to find which still have life in them, and what kind of life.

The painful abrupt fragments of *The Waste Land*, like some kinds of memory and remorse at the end of sleep, make it their business to wake us and to keep us awake. 'This poem is not in the least amusing. Nor is it in the least magical',[30] as Collingwood puts it, in his own rather special senses of these words as indicating motives for art other than the purgative and the prophetic. The myths, like other features of modern civilisation, are put to a hard test in the violent music of *The Waste Land*: and it would seem that only their strength as metaphors for human pain or weariness or fear, and their poignant beauty survive, not their power to grant salvation. Even Christ's story takes its place among them negatively as another myth of the dying God. It took another testing, in *The Journey of the Magi* and *Ash Wednesday*, and further meditation on the nature of image and belief, before Eliot distinguished myth from the Incarnation of the Word.

But the myths survive with whatever modification of their function. In our time, classical scholarship is presented with a choice, if it is to survive, between the humanist way, which was also Eliot's way, of seeing European literature as a whole in which the ancient literatures interpenetrate the English and other modern literatures, and the pure scholar's defence of boundaries between each domain. In Ovid's time, it was possible for the revival of tradition to present itself as part of the Roman state's care for civilisation. In our decade, finance and government appear to be supporting the purist in a practice of diminution and limitation, against which the theory of Eliot's essay *Tradition and the Individual Talent* and the vision of *The Waste Land* stand and fight.

APPENDIX

Daedalus and Icarus in Art
Niall Rudd

The following list is confined to items for which, in the time available, I have been able to find published illustrations. As a result, some of the works mentioned by A. Pigler in *Barockthemen* (Budapest 1956) have been omitted. For the same reason several items have been excluded which I know only from photographs in the Warburg Institute. In the case of emblem literature, where numerous published illustrations *are* available, I have cited a few basic works and added a couple of bibliographical references. In spite of its limitations I hope the list will indicate the range and quality of the works inspired by the myth.

ANTIQUITY
Bronzes

1   Statuette of a winged boy (Icarus ?), reputedly 4th cent. BC Etruscan. *Apollo* (June 1981) 3.

2   Statuette of Icarus from Smyrna, 4th cent.

A. Furtwängler, *Sammlung Somzée* (München 1897), section 85, pl. 33. See also *Greek Anthology*, Book 16, no. 107 (Loeb trans.).

Bulla

Gold bulla with two figures Taitle (Daedalus) and Vikare (Icarus) reputedly found near Ferrara. Date between 475 and 450 BC.

G. M. A. Hanfmann, *American Journal of Archaeology* 39 (1935) 189ff.

Frescoes

P. H. von Blankenhagen, 'Daedalus and Icarus on Pompeian Walls', *Mitteilungen des Deutschen Archaeologischen Instituts, Römische Abteilung*, 75 (1968) 106–43.

C. M. Dawson, *Romano-Campanian Mythological Landscape Painting* (Rome 1965).

For coloured reproductions of the picture in pl. 1 see

A. Baumeister, *Denkmäler des Klassischen Altertums* (1885–8) 2, pl. 22.

E. Pfuhl, *Malerei und Zeichnung der Griechen* (München 1923), vol. 3, 335.

Gems

1   G. M. A. Richter, *Engraved Gems of the Greeks and Etruscans* (London 1968) 211; pl. 862 (?), 863 (?).

2   A. Furtwängler, *Die Antiken Gemmen* (repr. Amsterdam 1965) vol. 1, pl. 25, no. 2 (vol. 2, 124); vol. 1, pl. 28, no. 27 (vol. 2, 140); vol. 1, pl. 37, no. 12 (vol. 2, 177); vol. 1, pl. 42, no. 1 (vol. 2, 199); vol. 1, pl. 58, no. 9 (vol. 2, 265); vol. 1, pl. 63, no. 32 (vol. 2, 285). See also vol. 3, 339–40.

3   G. M. A. Richter, *Engraved Gems of the Romans* (London 1971) 70; pls. 330–2.

Appendix

Lamp

Earthenware lamp from Pozzuoli, 1st cent. AD.

Archaeologische Zeitung 10 (1852) 39.2, 423ff.

H. B. Walters, *Catalogue of the Greek and Roman Lamps in the British Museum* (London 1914) no. 656, pl. 22.

Medallion

Bronze medallion, first half of 2nd cent. AD (?).

C. Bérard, 'Une représentation de la chute d'Icare à Lousonna', *Zeitschrift für Schweizerische Archäologie unde Kunstgeschichte* 23 (1963) 1–9.

C. Bérard et M. Hofstetter, 'Dédale et Icare: tradition ou renouveau?' *Bronzes hellénistiques et romains* (Lausanne 1979) 121–6.

Mosaic

J. W. Salomonson, *Le mosaique aux chevaux de l'antiquarium de Carthage* (1965) 66, pl. 46.3.

Reliefs

1 M. Robertson, 'Two Question-Marks on the Parthenon', in *Studies in Classical Art and Archaeology*, ed. G. Kopke and M. B. Moore (New York 1979).

2 Relief from 2nd cent. AD found on the Palatine.

H. Beck and P. C. Bol, *Forschungen zur Villa Albani* (Berlin 1982), pl. 59, Abb. 108.

J. Winkelmann, *Monumenti Antichi Inediti* (Roma 1767) pl. 95.

3 Relief on the Porte Noire, Besançon.

E. Espérandieu, *Recueil général des bas-reliefs de la Gaule romaine* 7 (1918) 11; cf. 5.3804, 4065; 7.5270.

4 Funerary relief from Carnuntum.

E. Diez, 'Mythologisches aus Carnuntum', *Carnuntum Jahrbuch* 1963–4 (1965) 43–7, pl. 1, fig. 2.

Sarcophagi

1 C. Robert, *Die Antiken Sarkophag-Reliefs* (Berlin 1890–1919) vol. 3, part 1, 51, pl. 11, figs. 37 and 38.

2 P. P. Bober and R. O. Rubinstein, *Renaissance Artists and Antique Sculpture* (Oxford 1986) pl. 45. Cf. Robert, *Die Antiken Sarcophag-Reliefs* 3.3. no. 440.

3 M. Lawrence, 'Additional Asiatic Sarcophagi', *Memoirs of the American Academy in Rome* (1951–2) 133–5, pl. 19.

Statues

1 Icarus

D. Mustilli, 'L'Icaro di Via dell'Impero', *Bolletino d'arte* 28 (1934–5) 466–70.

D. Mustilli, *Il Museo Mussolini* (Roma 1939) pl. 53.

Enciclopedia dell'Arte Antica (1961) 81, pl. 104.

2 Daedalus

M. J. H. Iliffe in *Studies Presented to D. M. Robinson*, vol. 1 (1951) pl. 75–80.

Appendix

H. Möbius, 'Ein hellenistischer Daidalos', *Jahrbuch des Deutschen Archäologischen Instituts* 68 (1953) 96–101, pls. 1–3.

See also C. Picard, 'Les "symplegmata" du gymnase d'Éphèse', *Comptes Rendus de l'académie des inscriptions* (1955) 24.

Vases

1 Attic trefoil-mouthed olpe; late 7th cent. BC (Daedalus?) *JHS* 59 (1939) pl. 13b.

2 Black-figure vase from Acropolis, first half of 6th cent. BC. Two legs with winged boots; inscription IKAROS.

J. D. Beazley, 'Icarus', *JHS* 47 (1927) fig. 2.

3 Small red-figure lekythos, *c.* 470 BC; winged boy (Icarus?) sinks sideways into the sea.
Beazely, *JHS* 47 fig. 6.

4 Red-figure Italiote cotyle, *c.* 400 BC; Daedalus adjusts Icarus' wings.
Beazely, *JHS* 47 pl. 21.2.

5 Late 4th cent. volute crater; Daedalus fastens wings on Icarus.
Beazely, *JHS* 47 fig. 5.

6 Earthenware jug, N. African type; mid. 3rd cent. AD; on one side Icarus flies, on the other Daedalus points upwards.

Bronzes hellénistiques et romains (Lausanne 1979) pl. 75.

M. R. Hampe, 'Daedalus und Icarus auf spätrömischer Sigillatakanne', *Mansel'e Armağan* 1 (1974), pls. 17 and 18.

MIDDLE AGES

Alexander

1 R. S. Loomis, 'Alexander the Great's Celestial Journey,' *Burlington Magazine* 32 (1918) 136–40, 177–85.

2 G. Cary, *The Medieval Alexander*, ed. D. J. A. Ross (repr. Cambridge 1967) 134–5, pl. 1.4; pl. 9.

Bladud

Illustration from Percie Enderbie's *Cambria Triumphans* reproduced in P. Haining, *The Compleat Birdman* (London and New York 1976) between pp. 32 and 33.

Daedalus and Icarus

Illustration from *Ovide Moralisé*, French, 14th cent.

Reallexikon zur Deutschen Kunstgeschichte, 3, 978.

Daedalus

Andrea Pisano, bas-relief in the Campanile, Florence. (Pl. 2a)

A. Venturi, *Storia dell'Arte Italiana*, 4 (repr. 1967) 459.

Eilmer

Stained glass window in Malmesbury Abbey (1928), W. end of S. aisle.

Reproduced in the pamphlet on the Abbey, ed. by P. Barton.

Appendix

Simon Magus

See Chapter 2, note 26.

Wayland the Smith

The Franks Casket (c. AD 700)

1 British Museum postcard.

2 *Encyclopaedia Britannica*, ed. 11, vol. 28, 532.

RENAISSANCE AND AFTER

Alciati, A., see below under *Emblems*

Anonymous, French, 18th cent.

D. Finn and F. Licht, *Canova* (New York 1983) 157.

Armstrong, J., *Illustrated London News*, May 11 (1968) 24.

Ayrton, M. (1921–75)

P. Cannon-Brookes, *Michael Ayrton* (Birmingham 1968) pls 128–30, 134, 137–44, 153, 156–7, 165.

Bol, H. (1534–90)

M. D. Henkel, *Illustrierte Ausgaben von Ovids Metamorphosen im XV, XVI und XVII Jahrhundert*, Bibliothek Warburg Vorträge, 1926–7 (Leipzig 1930), 110, Tafel xxvII, Abb. 50.

Bruegel, P. (1525/30–69)

1 Etching (1553)

Jacques Lavalleye, *Pieter Bruegel the Elder and Lucas Van Leyden* (London, 1967) pl. 2.

2 Painting (Musée des Beaux Arts)

Bob Claessens and Jeanne Rousseau, *Our Bruegel* (Antwerp 1969) pl. 43.

3 Painting (Van Buuren Collection)

Claessens and Rousseau, *Our Bruegel pl.* 44.

4 J. Guichard-Meili, ed., *Bruegel: la chute d'Icare* (Fribourg 1974) includes black-and-white illustrations of versions by Bol, de Momper, Verhaecht, and others.

Cambiaso, L. (1527–85)

B. S. Manning and W. Suida, *Luca Cambiaso: la vita e le opere* (Milano 1958) pl. 308.

Canova, A. (1757–1822)

D. Finn and F. Licht, *Canova* (New York 1983) 27, 156, 157.

Carracci, A. (1560–1609)

J. R. Martin, *The Farnese Gallery* (Princeton 1975) 64–5, pl. 92. (This painting was probably done by Domenichino on the basis of Carracci's pen sketch.)

de Cauļléry, L. (16th to 17th centuries)
Sotheby's Catalogue, Feb. 1986.

Cessari, G. (d. 1640)
The ceiling of the Single Cube Room, Wilton House (Wilts.)
Country Life May 16 (1963) 1111.

Appendix

Chagall, M. (1887–1985)

Susan Compton, *Chagall* (London 1985) 139, p. 115.

David, G. (1743–90)

E. W. Bredt, *Der Götter Verwandlungen* (München 1920) 2, 68.

Deineka, A. (1899–1969)

Alexander Deineka (Aurora, Leningrad 1982) pl. 156.

Domenichino, (1581–1641) see under Carracci, A.

[Donatello (c. 1386–1466)]

Marmortondi in court of the Palazzo Ricardi in Florence *c.* 1460 attributed to Donatello by P. Schubring, *Donatello* (Berlin 1922) 156. Attribution rejected by H. W. Janson, *The Sculpture of Donatello* (Princeton 1963) 83.

Draper H. J. (1863 1920)

Tate Gallery postcard.

Duncan, C.

Illustrated London News May 11 (1968) 24.

Emblems

Alciati, A. *Emblemata cum Commentariis* (1531; the Padua edn of 1621 repr. 1976) 432, no. 104.

Horatii Emblemata (Antwerp 1607; 1612 edn repr. 1979) 19.

de Marolles, Michel, *Tableaux du temple des Muses* (Paris 1655, repr. 1976) illustration facing p. 267.

Vaenius, O., *Amorum Emblemata* (Antwerp 1608) with plates by Cornelius Boel, ed. by S. Orgel under the title *The Philosophy of Images* (New York and London 1979) 43.

Van de Passe, Crispin, *Metamorphoseon Ovidianarum* (Cologne 1602, repr. with notes by S. Orgel, New York and London 1979). Daedalus and Icarus are among the illustrations of *Met.* 8. (The pages are not numbered.)

J. Hutton, *The Greek Anthology in Italy to the Year 1800* (Ithaca, New York, London 1935) 195–208.

M. Praz. *Studies in Seventeenth Century Imagery*, 2nd edn (Rome 1964).

P. M. Daly, *Literature in the Light of Emblem* (Toronto 1979).

Ferrat, J. J.-H. Romain (1822–82).

P. Fusco and H. W. Janson, *The Romantics to Rodin* (Los Angeles and New York 1980) pl. 136.

Filarete (c. 1400–c. 1469)

H. Roeder, 'The Borders of Filarete's Bronze Doors to St. Peter's', *JWCI* 10 (1947) 150–3, especially p. 153.

J. Lees-Milne, *St Peter's* (1967) 120 shows a photograph of the doors, but the details are not distinct enough for our purpose.

Gilbert, Sir Alfred (1854–1934)

R. Dorment, *Alfred Gilbert* (New Haven and London 1985) 46–8, and 55.

Appendix

Giulio Romano (1499–1546)

1 *Catalogue of the Ellesmere Collection*, Drawings by Giulio Romano, facing p. 125.

2 F. Hartt, *Giulio Romano* (New Haven 1958) 2, pl. 471.

Gowi, J. P. (17th cent.)

S. Alpers, *Corpus Rubenianum*, part 9 (1971), pl. 128.

Grass, P. (1801–1876)

P. Fusco and H. W. Janson, *The Romantics to Rodin* (Los Angeles and New York 1980) pl. 158.

Leighton, Lord Frederic (1830–96)

G. Jackson-Stops, ed., *The Treasure Houses of Britain* (Washington, New Haven, London, 1985) pl. 554.

Matisse, H. (1869–1954)

J. Guichard-Meili, *Matisse: Paper Cutouts* (London 1984) nos. 10 and 11.

N. Watkins, *Matisse* (Oxford 1984) pl. 189.

Montorsoli, G. A. (*c.* 1507–1563)

E. H. Gombrich, *Symbolic Images* (London 1975) pl. 6.

Perrier, F. (1590–1650)

Apollo (December 1977) 69.

Picasso, P. (1881–1973)

1 UNESCO poster of mural in UNESCO building, Paris.

2 Douglas Cooper, *Picasso Theatre* (London 1967) 415.

3 Douglas Cooper, *Picasso Theatre* 419.

Riederer, Fr., *Spiegel der Waren Rhetorik* (1493) contains woodcut reproduced in P. Haining, *The Compleat Birdman* (London 1976) 28.

Rodin, A. (1840–1917)

1 A. E. Elsen, *In Rodin's Studio* (Oxford and Paris 1980) pl. 43.

2 I. Jianou and C. Goldscheider, *Rodin* (Paris 1967) pl. 33.

Rubens, P. P. (1577–1640)

J. S. Held, *The Oil Sketches of Peter Paul Rubens, a Critical Catalogue*, 1 (Princeton 1980) no. 198, pl. 207

M. Jacobs, *Mythological Painting* (Oxford 1979) 27.

Sacchi, A. (1599–1661)

A. S. Harris, *Andrea Sacchi* (Oxford 1977) pl. 87.

Saraceni, C. (1585–1620)

M. Jacobs, *Mythological Painting* 27.

del Sarto, A. (1486–1530)

S. J. Freedberg, *Andrea del Sarto* (Cambridge, Mass. 1963) 2, pl. 3.

Appendix

(?) Tintoretto, J. (1518–94)

R. Pallucchini and P. Rossi, *Tintoretto* (Milan 1982) 2, p. 304, no. 38.

(The interpretation of the scene is doubtful.)

Van Dyck, A. (1599–1641)

G. Glück, *Van Dyck* (Stuttgart 1931) 268.

Wood, F. Derwent

R. de la Bère (ed.) *Icarus: An Anthology of Flight* (London 1938), Frontispiece.

NOTES

I INTRODUCTION

1 See John Dixon Hunt, *Garden and Grove: The Italian Renaissance Garden in the English Imagination: 1600–1750* (London and Melbourne 1986) especially chap. 4 'Ovid in the garden' (though Hunt attributes specifically to Ovid some features which result from a more generalised classicism).

2 See Niall Rudd, 'Pyramus and Thisbe in Shakespeare and Ovid', in David West and Tony Woodman, eds., *Creative Imitation and Latin Literature* (Cambridge 1979) 239 note 25

3 Illustrated in colour in L. T. Stanley, *Collecting Staffordshire Pottery* (London 1963) opposite 105; as in an earlier Derby group, an arrow replaces the spear of Ovid's version, perhaps to ease the potter's task.

4 *Illinois Classical Studies* IX.2 (1984) ed. J. K. Newman, preface x

5 See the present editor's *Virgil and his Influence: Bimillennial Studies* (Bristol 1984), intr. 1ff

6 Frank Kermode, ed., *Selected Prose of T. S. Eliot* (London 1975) 38–9

7 For the former, W. R. Johnson, 'The Problem of the Counter-classical Sensibility and its Critics', *California Studies in Classical Antiquity* 3 (1970) 123–51 (138ff); for the latter, Douglas Little, 'The Speech of Pythagoras in Metamorphoses 15 and the Structure of the Metamorphoses', *Hermes* 98 (1970) 340–60

8 *Preface to Fables Ancient and Modern*, in George Watson, ed., *John Dryden: Of Dramatic Poesy and other Critical Essays*, 2 vols. (London and New York 1962) II.270 (this preface contains the celebrated comparison of Ovid and Chaucer).

9 See Howard Hibbard, *Bernini* (Harmondsworth 1965) 48–54, 235–6; Rudolf Wittkower, *Gian Lorenzo Bernini: The Sculptor of the Roman Baroque* (London 1966) 183–4 and pl. 14

10 For some speculations see Harold Skulsky, *Metamorphosis: The Mind in Exile* (Cambridge, Mass. and London 1981)

11 Christine Rees, 'The Metamorphosis of Daphne in Sixteenth- and Seventeenth–Century English Poetry', *Modern Language Review* 66 (1971) 251–63 (263)

12 See H. E. Wethey, *The Paintings of Titian: vol. III: The Mythological and Historical Paintings* (London 1975) 91–3 and pls. 170–2

13 So A. G. Lee, 'An Appreciation of *Tristia* III viii', *Greece and Rome* 18 (1949) 113–20 (115)

14 So A. G. Lee, 'Ovid's Lucretia', *G & R* 22 (1953) 107–18 (115–17)

15 From *The Pentameron* (1837); the speaker is Petrarch. Quoted by Wilfried Stroh, *Ovid im Urteil der Nachwelt: Eine Testimoniensammlung* (Darmstadt 1969) 114.

16 From *Aeneidea* vol. 1 (1873) 618. Quoted by A. G. Lee in the introduction to his edition of *Metamorphoses* I (Cambridge 1968) 24.

17 R. G. M. Nisbet, 'Great and Lesser Bear (Ovid, *Tristia* 4.3)', *Journal of Roman Studies* 72 (1982) 49–56 (49)

18 See S. G. Owen, 'Ovid and Romance', in G. S. Gordon, ed., *English Literature and the Classics* (Oxford 1912) 171–3; L. P. Wilkinson, *Ovid Recalled* (Cambridge 1955) 102, 107.

19 C. Martindale, 'Paradise Metamorphosed: Ovid in Milton', *Comparative Literature* 37 (1985) 301–33

20 W. R. Johnson, 'The Problem of the Counter-classical Sensibility', 148

21 R. G. M. Nisbet, 'Great and Lesser Bear', 56

22 So L. P. Wilkinson, *Ovid Recalled*, 102. For children in Latin poetry see also Lucretius 3.894–6, Virgil, *Georgics* 2.523, Juvenal 14.

23 From *The fable of Ovid treating of Narcissus* (1560). Quoted by Frederick S. Boas, 'Ovid and the Elizabethans', in *Queen Elizabeth in Drama and Related Studies* (London 1950) 101–21 (105).

24 Prefixed to *Examen Poeticum*, John Dryden: *Of Dramatic Poesy* 1.167

25 For a discussion of all three works see Winton Dean, *Handel's Dramatic Oratorios and Masques* (London, New York, Toronto 1959) 18–20, chaps. 8 and 16. Dean wrongly sees *Semele* as Greek in spirit.

26 See too Charles Tomlinson, *Poetry and Metamorphosis* (Cambridge 1983)

27 E. M. Forster, *Aspects of the Novel* (reprinted London 1949) 27

28 For the opposition between hunting and love discussed in structuralist terms see Gregson Davis, *The Death of Procris: 'Amor' and the Hunt in Ovid's Metamorphoses* (Rome 1983)

29 So G. K. Galinsky, *Ovid's Metamorphoses: An Introduction to the Basic Aspects* (Oxford 1975) 186–90. Similarly Nicholas Horsfall, 'Epic and Burlesque in Ovid, *Met. VIII.260ff*', *Classical Journal* 74 (1979) 319–32 (329–30) takes the joke in 406–7 as a key to the anti-heroic character of the whole episode of the Calydonian boar hunt. Close to my own position is David West, 'Orpheus and Eurydice,' *JACT Review* 4 (1986) 7–11.

30 So C. P. Segal, *Landscape in Ovid's Metamorphoses: A Study in the Transformations of a Literary Symbol* (Wiesbaden 1969) 23–6. Nevertheless I owe much in this section to his useful discussion.

31 'On Stories', in C. S. Lewis, *Of This and Other Worlds*, ed. Walter Hooper (London 1982) 25–45

32 Illustrated in colour in Michael Jacobs, *Mythological Painting* (Oxford 1979) 22

33 So C. P. Segal, *Landscape in Ovid's Metamorphoses*, 10

34 T. F. Higham, 'Ovid: Some Aspects of his Character and Aims', *Classical Review* 48 (1934) 105–16 (105)

35 *Humanist Essays* (reprinted London 1964) 85–6

36 T. F. Higham, 'Ovid: Some Aspects of his Character and Aims', 114

37 See Stephen Hinds, 'Booking the return trip: Ovid and Tristia I', *Proceedings of the Cambridge Philological Society* 211 (N.S. 31) (1985) 13–22

38 Christine Rees, 'The Metamorphosis of Daphne', 251

39 E. W. Leach, 'Ekphrasis and the Theme of Artistic Failure in Ovid's *Metamorphoses*', *Ramus* 3 (1974) 102–42 (131)

40 E. J. Kenney, Introduction to A. D. Melville's translation (Oxford, New York 1986) xxvii

41 E. W. Leach, 'Ekphrasis and the Theme of Artistic Failure', 106

42 For this painting see José López-Rey, *Velázquez' Work and World* (London 1968) 105–9; Enriqueta Harris, *Velazquez* (Oxford 1982) 158ff and pl. 171

43 R. A. Lanham, *The Motives of Eloquence: Literary Rhetoric in the Renaissance* (New Haven and London 1976) 64 and 56

44 L. P. Wilkinson, *Ovid Recalled*, 197

45 So E. K. Rand, *Ovid and his Influence* (New York 1963) 172: 'I venture to see in Ovid a spirit more mature than this. His mimic world is no toy fancy, a thing apart. He rather has absorbed life into it as into the only verity that remains eternal amid the flux and flow'; cf. E. J. Kenney's review of G. Rosati, *Narciso e Pigmalione: Illusione e spettacolo nelle Metamorfosi di Ovidio* (Florence 1983) in CR N.S. 34 (1984) 186–8.

46 R. G. M. Nisbet, 'Great and Lesser Bear', 51

47 *Preface to Ovid's Epistles* in *John Dryden: Of Dramatic Poesy*, I. 41

48 See Howard Jacobson, *Ovid's Heroides* (Princeton, New Jersey 1974) chap. 18

49 The point derives from Euripides, *Medea* 243ff

50 See E. J. Kenney, 'Ovid' in E. J. Kenney and W. V. Clausen, eds., *The Cambridge History of Classical Literature II Latin Literature* (Cambridge 1982) 423–4; this is now the best brief introduction to Ovid in English.

51 M. C. Bradbrook, *Shakespeare and Elizabethan Poetry: A Study of his Earlier Work in Relation to the Poetry of the Time* (London 1965) 74

I would like to thank my wife Michelle for supplying me with some of my material and assisting me thereafter; an earlier draft was read and improved by A. D. Nuttall, Robert Parker and Niall Rudd. I dedicate this introductory essay to the memory of Tom Stinton, my tutor at Wadham College, an inspiring teacher and scholar of rare integrity.

2 DAEDALUS AND ICARUS (I) FROM ROME TO THE END OF THE MIDDLE AGES

1 For Greek versions of the legend William Smith's *Dictionary of Greek and Roman Biography and Mythology* (London 1844) is still useful. *Dédale* by F. Frontisi-Ducroux (Paris 1975) is an interesting modern study. The specialist, however, will still have to brave the articles in Roscher and Pauly-Wissowa.

2 I say 'probably', because some scholars doubt whether Theseus is part of the design.

3 See, e.g., Horace, *Carm.* 3.3.49 and Ovid, *Met.* 1.138

4 E.g., Apollodorus 3.9; Servius on *Aen.* 6.14

5 See the maps supplied by J. S. Traill, 'The Political Organisation of Attica', *Hesperia*, Suppl. 14, 1975, where the form Ikarion is preferred.

6 *Die Griechische Heldensage* I (1920) 173

7 P. Green, 'The Flight Plan of Daedalus', *Classical News and Views* 23 (1979) 30–5. Green believes that a memory of the truth has survived in the Scholiast's note on Euripides, *Hipp.* 887, which says that Icarus died πρὸς τὸ παράλιον πέλαγος. Green takes this to mean 'the sea by the Paralia', i.e. the coastal waters of Attica. One would like to see parallels, however, for παράλιον ('coastal') used with πέλαγος ('sea'). Schwartz emended to παρ' 'Ασίαν.

8 Cf. *Tr.* 1.1.90; 3.4.21

9 Seneca, *Oed.* 892–910; *Hercules Oetaeus* 687–97

10 Cf. Dio Chrysostom, *Disc.* 21.9 (Loeb vol. 2, 280–1). Where not otherwise indicated translations are my own.

11 Lucian, Loeb vol. 5. 347ff. As a serious concern with astrology is inconsistent with Lucian's normal attitude, the piece has been regarded as early, or ironical, or spurious. See J. Hall, *Lucian's Satire* (New York 1981) 381ff.

12 The Greek says οἳ κατά τινα κῆρα πτερυσσόμενοι ἄνω. This could be translated as 'flying upwards by virtue of some evil design of fate'; cf. Plutarch, *Ant.* 2: ὥσπερ τινα κῆρα.

13 A. Alciati, *Emblemata cum Commentariis* (Padua 1621, repr. 1976), 432, *In Astrologos*, Emblema 104 with a picture of the falling Icarus. Such a picture, we are told, was to be seen in the Amsterdam Town Hall, above the door leading to the bankruptcy court.

14 See F. Gadan and R. Maillard, eds., *A Dictionary of Modern Ballet* (London 1959) 214–15

15 See D. Cooper, *Picasso Theatre* (London 1967) 415–19

16 For this kind of entertainment see Friedländer, *Roman Life and Manners*, vol. 2, 74

17 These summaries, which are found in certain MSS of the *Metamorphoses*, were attributed to Lactantius Placidus by Renaissance scholars. The real author is unknown, as is the date; but the summaries must surely belong to antiquity, as E. Martini says (*Einleitung zu Ovid* (repr. Darmstadt 1970) 40). The text is given by D. A. Slater in *Towards a Text of the Metamorphoses of Ovid* (Oxford 1927).

18 Some directly relevant examples, based on Virgil and Ovid, are cited by Courcelle, e.g. (i) a fourth-century epitaph by the neoplatonist Manlius Theodorus on his sister Manlia Daedalia: like her mythical model 'she cherished immortal thoughts in her mortal breast and always longed for a path to reach heaven' (ii) a passage of St Ambrose in which we are exhorted to avoid the heat of this world 'lest, in the terms of the myth, the wax may melt in the sun's heat, our wings may fall off, and our Icarian flight come to an end' (iii) a passage of St Augustine which urges those who long for their homeland to take the wings of love (one the love of God, the other the love of one's neighbour). See *Revue des études anciennes* 46 (1944) 65–73.

19 Defending Homer against ignorant charges of impiety, Heraclitus says: πάντα γὰρ ἠσέβησεν, εἰ μηδὲν ἠλληγόρησεν. But, as the book proceeds to show, Homer allegorised all the time; hence there was no impiety. For the text see *Héraclite: Allégories d'Homère*, ed. F. Buffière (Paris 1962) opening section.

20 John of Garland, *Integumenta Ovidii*, ed. F. Ghisalberti (Messina–Milan 1933). See F. J. E. Raby, *Christian Latin Poetry*, 2nd edn. (Oxford 1953) 385–9.

21 *Le Roman de la Rose*, ed. E. Langlois (Paris 1920) vol. 2, ll. 5205–33, especially 5226–9

22 *Ovide moralisé*, ed. C. de Boer, M. G. De Boer, J. Van't Sant (Amsterdam 1931), vol. 3, Book 8, 1767–1915

23 Rigaut de Barbesieux, *Le Canzoni*, ed. Mauro Broccini (Florence 1960) 25–6

24 Petrarca, *Rime e Trionfi*, a cura di Raffaello Ramat, 2nd edn. (Milan 1971) *Rime sparse* no. 307

25 For Simon Magus see the article by G. N. L. Hall in Hastings' *Encyclopaedia of Religion and Ethics*. For the text of Hegesippus see the edition by C. F. Weber and J. Caesar (Marburg 1864). Ovid took over Virgil's *remigium* in *Ars* 2.45 and *Met.* 8.228.

26 The Irish crosses at Kells and Monasterboice are tenth-century; see H. Roe, *The High Crosses at Kells* (Meath 1967) 40 and F. Henry, *Irish Art during the Viking Invasions* (London 1967) 104 and 186–7. The capital at Autun is twelfth-century; see the excellent photos in *Gisalbertus, Sculptor of Autun*, D. Grivot and G. Zarnecki (London 1961) pl. 35 and 38. For the mosaics at Palermo and Monreale see Henry, fig. 35c, and O. Demus, *The Mosaics of Norman Sicily* (London 1949) pl. 83. The frescoes are from San Paolo fuori le Mure and the former St Peter's. Stained glass: Bourges, chapel of N. Dame de Lourdes, central window; Chartres, window 32, scene 29; Tours, great choir clerestory, window 6, scene 16. Among other examples are sculptures at Toulouse (south door), and a painting in Siena (*c.* 1265) for which see P. Torriti, *La Pinacoteca Nazionale de Siena* (Genoa 1971) 41, no. 15.

27 For Wayland the Smith see *Corpus Poeticum Boreale*, ed. G. Vigfussen and F. York Powell (Oxford 1883) vol. 1, 168–75. The story is represented in carved whalebone on the Franks Casket (Northumbria, *c.* AD 700); see *Encycl. Brit.* (11th edn.) vol. 28.432. Today Wayland's forge is still to be seen on the Ridgeway just outside Oxford. He is also connected with Berkshire by a tradition which was taken up by Scott in *Kenilworth*. Of the dramatic versions composed in the nineteenth century the most notable is Wagner's,

in which Wieland outwits the rascally King Envy (Neidung) and then flies off to join his beloved swan-maiden, Schwanhilde. See *Richard Wagner's Prose Works*, trans. W. A. Ellis (London 1895) 215–48.

28 The passage of the Thidreksage is taken from F. Niedner, *Thule*, vol. 22, Die Geschichte Thidreks von Bern (Jena 1924) 141–2

29 See B. Schmidt, *Griechische Märchen Sagen und Volkslieder* (Leipzig 1877) 91 – 3. Other parts of the story recall the lock of Nisus, Arion's dolphin, and the young man who regains human shape on marrying a princess.

30 Geoffrey of Monmouth, *Historia Regum Britanniae* (London, New York, Toronto 1929) 2.10, 262. The variant version is edited by J. Hammer (Camb. Mass. 1951); the quotation is on p. 46. The whole matter is very fully presented by H. C. Levis in *The British King Who Tried to Fly* (London 1919). See also J. P. Tatlock, *The Legendary History of Britain* (Berkeley 1950).

31 Percy Enderbie, *Cambria Triumphans* (1661) 23

32 William of Malmesbury, *De Gestis Regum Anglorum Libri Quinque*, ed. W. Stubbs (London 1887 and 1889) vol. 1.276–7. See also Lynn White Jr, *Medieval Religion and Technology* (Univ. of California 1978) chap. 4.

33 The text is in Migne, *PG* 139, 458. The first edition of the history (*LXXXVI Annorum Historia*) was printed in Basel in 1557. For the incident described see p. 60.

34 See K. Clark and D. Finn, *The Florence Baptistery Doors* (New York 1980) 25ff

35 This is illustrated in I. Lavin's article 'Cephalus and Procris', *Journal of the Warburg and Courtauld Institutes* 17 (1954) 260–87; even more relevant is his later piece 'Underground Transformations' (*ibid.* 366–72). See also E. H. Gombrich, 'Così fan tutte' (*ibid.* 372– 4).

3 DAEDALUS AND ICARUS (II) FROM THE RENAISSANCE TO THE PRESENT DAY

1 See P. H. Wicksteed and E. G. Gardner, *Dante and Giovanni del Virgilio* (London 1920) 316–17. Giovanni's text is printed by F. Ghisalberti in 'Giovanni del Virgilio espositore delle Metamorfosi', *Giornale Dantesco* 34, N.S. 4 (Florence 1933) 81.

2 See F. Ghisalberti, 'L'Ovidius Moralizatus di Pierre Bersuire', *Studij Romanzi* 23 (1933) 5–136. This very useful article includes a study of Bersuire's life and work, and explains the rather complicated history of the allegories. It also prints the text.

3 Thomas Walley's edition of Bersuire's *Metamorphosis Ouidiana Moraliter...Explanata* was printed in 1511. There the labyrinth is the world of sin; to escape it one must take the wings of contemplation and fly to the celestial realms. In 1563 a beautiful little book appeared, with elegiacs by Spreng and some excellent woodcuts by Virgil Solis of Nuremberg. The comment on Daedalus and Icarus concludes:

> Gratia sed Christi levibus nos instruit alis,
> Haud quicquam nostra perficiemus ope.

> The grace of Christ provides us wings to mount;
> We can do nothing on our own account.

Robert Holkot's *In Librum Sapientiae Regis Salomonis Praelectiones* was printed in 1586. There the devil encloses a person's monstrous sin within his conscience, and makes it impossible for a confessor to find his way in, except by means of a thread. In 1589 and 1606 came the *Interpretatio Ethica, Physica, et Historica* by Georgius Sabinus: Daedalus' wings are ships' sails; do not try to be too clever (Lucian's remarks on astrology are cited); behave as a father or son should; do not attempt to rise above your allotted level.

4 Albrecht von Halberstadt's paraphrase (1210) was modernised by Jörg Wickram (1544). For a list of these and other works, see R. R. Bolgar, *The Classical Heritage and its Beneficiaries* (Cambridge 1954) 526–41.

5 See J. H. Turner, *The Myth of Icarus in Spanish Renaissance Poetry* (London 1976) chap. 2. This is a valuable collection of material to which I am much indebted.

6 A. Golding, *Ovid's Metamorphoses*, ed. J. F. Nims (New York and London 1965) 410. In 1480 Caxton had published a translation of Bersuire's paraphrase with a few allegories, but none of Daedalus and Icarus.

7 G. Sandys, *Ovid's Metamorphosis*, ed. K. K. Huxley and S. T. Vandersall (Lincoln Nebraska 1970) 384

8 F. Bacon, *De Sapientia Veterum, Icarus Volans* in *Works*, ed. Spedding, Lewis, and Heath (London 1870) vol. 6.677. An intermediate work was the translation of Bacon by Sir Arthur Gorges (1619), but Sandys's phrasing is not close enough to suggest that he used it.

9 See S. H. O'Grady, ed., *Catalogue of Irish Manuscripts in the British Museum* (London 1926) vol. 1.437–8

10 E.g. '*ala vero est potentia sursum ducens, per quam animae quidem divinae dicuntur alatae*' (*In Phaedrum* 7) – 'The wing is the power leading upwards, on account of which divine souls are called winged'; '*solem namque et Deum ita invicem comparat ut quemadmodum se habet sol ad oculos ita ad mentes se Deus habet*' (*In Repub.* 6) – 'He compares the sun and God thus: as the sun is to the eyes so God is to men's minds'; '*Platonis nostri sententia est, ea potissimum ingenia, quae ad amorem propensiora sunt, alas, quibus revolatur in coelum, posse recuperare*' (*Epist.* 7) – 'Our friend Plato believes that those souls which are especially prone to love can acquire wings on which one can fly back to heaven.' For a general study see M. J. B. Allen, *The Platonism of Marsilio Ficino* (Berkeley, Los Angeles, London 1984) chap. 4.

11 Laurentius Valla, *De Libero Arbitrio*, ed. M. Anfossi (Florence 1934) 13, 120–6

12 Pico della Mirandola, *De Hominis Dignitate*, ed. E. Garin (Florence 1942) 122

13 See Nesca Robb, *Neoplatonism of the Italian Renaissance* (London 1935) chap. 4

14 Giordano Bruno, *Opere Italiane*, vol. 2, ed. G. Gentile (Bari 1908) 336

15 *Ibid.* 342. The poem is also printed in *Lirici del Cinquecento*, ed. L. Baldacci (Milan 1975) 461–2. For Giordano Bruno see Allen, *The Platonism of Marsilio Ficino*, chap. 2 and J. C. Nelson, *Renaissance Theory of Love* (New York 1958) chap. 3.

16 Printed in *Icarus, An Anthology of Flight*, ed. R. de la Bère (London 1938). Compare Tansillo's sonnet *Amor m'impenna l'ale* in Baldacci, *Lirici del Cinquecento* 461 and the madrigal *S'un Icaro, un Fetonte* (*ibid.* 475).

17 Sannazaro, ed. A. Mauro (Bari 1961), *Sonetti e Canzoni*, Parte Seconda, 195, no. 79

18 See J. Graciliano Gonzalez Miguel, *Presencia Napolitana en el Siglo de Oro Español* (Salamanca 1979) 50–9

19 See F. Yates, 'The Emblematic Conceit', *Journal of the Warburg and Courtauld Institutes* 6 (1943) 101–21, especially 105–6

20 See Turner, *The Myth of Icarus*, 83–4 and 137–9

21 Ronsard's poem begins 'Ce fol penser pour s'en voler plus hault'; see his *Amours*, ed. H. and C. Weber (Paris 1963) 107. Ariosto's begins '*nel mio pensier che così veggio audace*', see Turner, 51.

22 The sonnet begins 'Dois-je voler emplumé d'esperance' (H. and C. Weber, 373)

23 H. and C. Weber, 407

24 Desportes, *Les Amours d'Hippolyte*, ed. V. Graham (Geneva/Paris 1960) 11

25 Printed in *Icarus*, ed. de la Bère, 152

26 See Turner, *The Myth of Icarus*, 74–5 and his references. For a use of the myth in literary theory see Sidney, *An Apology for Poetry*, ed. G. Shepherd (London 1965) 132–3.

27 In the account of his career given in *Grand Larousse*, vol. 7.193–4, he is described as *élégant et subtil cavalier, très souple et zélé*. He was the subject of countless lampoons.

28 From Robert Jones's *Second Book of Songs and Airs* (1601), printed by N. Ault in *Elizabethan Lyrics* (London 1925) 320

29 M. Drayton, *Works*, ed. J. W. Hebel (Oxford 1931) vol. 1, *Ideas Mirrour, Amour* 22

30 J. Leslie, *De origine, moribus, et rebus gestis Scotorum*, Lib. 8, 345–6. J. Dalrymple's translation (1596) was published by the Scottish Text Society in 1895 as nos. 5, 14, 19, and 34. The story of Simon Magus was popularised in *The Golden Legend*, a collection of legendary lives of saints by Jacobus de Voragine in the thirteenth century. Versions appeared in Scotland in the fourteenth century and in England in the fifteenth.

31 See *The Poems of William Dunbar*, ed. J. Kinsley (Oxford 1979) 159–60 and 161–4

32 A comma is inserted after 'melting' by Fredson Bowers in his 2nd edn. (Cambridge 1981); but this produces awkward syntax and destroys the poetic collocation 'melting heavens'.

33 H. Levin, *Christopher Marlowe: the Overreacher* (repr. London 1967)

34 Lucian was also referred to by Sandys, who says 'Lucian will have Dedalus an excellent Astrologian who instructed his sonne Icarus in that art', *Ovid's Metamorphoses* (n. 7 above) 385

35 The forces of caution and conservatism are studied by J. W. Ashton, 'The Fall of Icarus', *Phil. Quart.* 20 (1941) 345–51

36 See C. H. Gibbs-Smith, *Aviation* (London 1970), Clive Hart, *The Dream of Flight* (London 1972) and *The Prehistory of Flight* (Univ. of California 1985), Peter Haining, *The Compleat Birdman* (London 1976)

37 *Quel privilège peuvent avoir les oiseaux pour nous exclure de leur séjour, tandis que nous sommes admis dans celui des poissons?* The pamphlet is thought to have been published *c.* 1742. It is ascribed to Rousseau in the edition published by the Institute of Aeronautical History Inc. (Pasadena Cal.).

38 Though Goethe may not have known it, the Faust legend at an early stage became conflated with the story of Simon Magus. See H. B. Cotterill, *The Faust Legend and Goethe's Faust* (London 1912) 22–4.

39 A. Gillics, *Goethe's Faust* (Oxford 1957) 170

40 M. Z. Shroder, *Icarus: the Image of the Artist in French Romanticism* (Cambridge, Mass. 1961)

41 See M. Ayrton, *The Testament of Daedalus* (London 1962), *The Maze Maker* (London 1967), and the sculptures illustrated in *Virgil*, ed. D. R. Dudley (London 1969), pls. 7, 10, 11, 12. A full account of his work is contained in P. Cannon-Brookes, *Michael Ayrton* (Birmingham 1978).

42 The page-numbers are those of *The Essential James Joyce*, ed. H. Levin (Penguin 1969). The Daedalus parallel is not explored in the earlier work, *Stephen Hero*.

43 Why did Daedalus/Joyce read in the National Library in Kildare St instead of in University College? The answer is given in *A Page of Irish History: the Story of University College, Dublin, 1883–1909*, compiled by the Fathers of the Society of Jesus (Dublin 1930), a reference kindly provided by Prof. John Richmond: 'In the College there was not any library worth speaking of, whereas the National Library was peculiarly well stocked…Moreover, the Librarian, Mr. Charles Lyster, had nothing more at heart than to make his institution helpful to students, and he had no objection to hear it called jokingly "The Library of University College"' (p. 235; cf. p. 68: 'The Catholic University books had been carted away').

44 *Ulysses* (Vintage Books 1961), 210

45 I had thought of the words of the prodigal son: '*pater, peccavi*'; but they are no closer.

46 In view of the ibis-headed Thoth, it might be suggested that Joyce was thinking of the hawk-head of Ra or Horus. But neither of those deities is mentioned, and the transition to Thoth could have been made quite easily from the hawklike Daedalion without any intermediate step. The word 'weltering' in the final quotation recalls the drowning of another young man, lamented in *Lycidas*: 'He must not...welter to the parching wind' (12–13). It is perhaps worth adding that Daedalion was the son of Lucifer, another proud faller who appears in *A Portrait* (142; cf. 'I will not serve' 247). See Isaiah 14.12–15.

47 Bertholt Brecht, *Plays, Poetry, and Prose*, ed. J. Willett and R. Mannheim, *Poems*, Part 2 (1929–38) 243–4

48 G. D'Annunzio, *Poesie, Teatro, Prose*, ed. M. Praz e F. Gerra (Milan, Naples, n.d.) 323. There is also a passage of almost hysterical excitement about flight at the end of his novel *Forse che si, forse che no*.

49 M. Praz, *The Romantic Agony* (New York 1951) 387–8

50 In *Clinical Studies of Personality*, ed. A. Burton and R. E. Harris (New York 1955), vol. 2, 615–41

51 Such delusions are dateless. In his autobiography Benvenuto Cellini describes how he was held prisoner in the Castel S. Angelo by a jailer who intermittently flapped his arms and emitted faint bat-like squeaks (Everyman edition, 228–9).

4 OVID THE CRUSADER

1 A critical edition of Gilo's work formed the present writer's Ph.D. thesis (Bedford College, University of London, 1982), written under the supervision of Dr J. B. Hall, to whom I am also greatly indebted for many helpful suggestions and comments with regard to this essay. Any errors or omissions which are contained in the present work I accept as being my own. A revision of the Ph.D. edition is currently being prepared for publication in the *Oxford Medieval Latin Texts* series. The numeration given in the essay for quotations from Gilo's work refers to the 'Combined edition' of both Gilo and his anonymous continuator; Gilo's five books form books 4, 5, 7, 8 and 9 of this version.

2 Paris, BN MSS Lat. 12607, 13090; extracts printed in Migne, *PL* CLIX, 909–19

3 Gilo's mission is recorded in William of Tyre's *Historia* 1.73, lib.xiii. 23. His letter to Bernard, patriarch of Antioch, is printed in Migne, *PL* CLXXIII, 1389.

4 Peter the Venerable, *Letters* 2.4, 2.30

5 *Claudian, De Raptu Proserpinae*, ed. J. B. Hall (Cambridge 1969) 69

6 L. D. Reynolds and N. G. Wilson, *Scribes And Scholars: A Guide To The Transmission Of Greek And Latin Literature* (2nd edn Oxford 1974) 98–9

7 Franco Munari, *Ovid im Mittelalter* (Zurich, Stuttgart 1960) 10, my translation

8 E.g. in Munari, *Ovid* 9; E. R. Curtius, *European Literature and the Latin Middle Ages* (London 1953); J. de Ghellinck, *L'Essor de la littérature latine au XIIIᵉ siècle* (Brussels 1946); C. H. Haskins, *The Renaissance Of The Twelfth Century* (Cambridge, Mass. 1928), among many others

9 L. P. Wilkinson, *Ovid Recalled* (Cambridge 1953) 376

10 R. W. Hunt, 'The Deposit Of The Classics In The Twelfth Century', in R. R. Bolgar, ed., *Classical Influences on European Culture AD 500–1500* (Cambridge 1971) 54

11 L. D. Reynolds, ed., *Texts and Transmission: A Survey of the Latin Classics* (Oxford 1982) 258, 259

12 E. P. M. Dronke, *Medieval Latin and the Rise of European Love-Lyric* (2nd edn Oxford 1968), and especially 163ff

13 E. P. M. Dronke, 'Functions Of Classical Borrowing In Medieval Latin Verse', in Bolgar, ed., *Classical Influences on European Culture*, 159

14 B. L. Ullman, 'Tibullus In The Medieval Florilegia', *Classical Philology* 23 (1928) 131

15 Quoted by Munari, *Ovid*, 23
16 B. Bischoff, 'Living With The Satirists', in Bolgar, ed., *Classical Influences on European Culture*, 84
17 Cf. E. R. Curtius, *European Literature and the Latin Middle Ages*, 40
18 *Galteri de Castellione Alexandreis*, ed. M. L. Colker (Padua 1978)
19 Ullman, 'Tibullus in the Medieval Florilegia', 133
20 E. Faral, *Les Arts poétiques du XIIe et XIIIe siècles (Recherches et documents sur la technique littéraire du Moyen Age)* (Paris 1924), 86ff
21 E. R. Curtius, *European Literature and the Latin Middle Ages*, 82ff 'Affected Modesty'
22 E. R. Curtius, *European Literature and the Latin Middle Ages*, 128ff
23 The Image is also found in Statius, *Silvae* 3.3.83–4, and Propertius, 3.3.22. One other source, which Gilo may well have known, is Quintilian, *Inst.* 12.10.37.
24 Bischoff, 'Living With The Satirists'. Cf. also L. P. Wilkinson, *Ovid Recalled*, 376: 'the young poets of the Cathedral schools made Ovid their master'.
25 *Oxford Book Of Medieval Latin Verse*, ed. F. J. E. Raby (Oxford 1959) poem 239
26 R. W. Southern, *Medieval Humanism* (Oxford 1976) 120
27 Cf. L. P. Wilkinson, *Ovid Recalled*, 377
28 On *annominatio*, cf. E. R. Curtius, *European Literature and the Latin Middle Ages*, 278ff
29 Cf. E. R. Curtius, *European Literature and the Latin Middle Ages*, 286ff, for a full discussion of this device

5 CHAUCER AND OVID: A QUESTION OF AUTHORITY

1 Quotations from Chaucer are from *The Works of Geoffrey Chaucer*, ed. F. N. Robinson (2nd edn, London 1957). The standard abbreviations for individual works are used: *BD*, *Book of the Duchess*; *CT*, *Canterbury Tales*; *HF*, *House of Fame*; *LGW*, *Legend of Good Women*.
2 Chaucer's major debts to Ovid are surveyed by E. F. Shannon, *Chaucer and the Roman Poets*, Harvard Studies in Comparative Literature 7 (Cambridge, Mass. 1929) and R. L. Hoffman, *Ovid and the Canterbury Tales* (Philadelphia 1966); John Fyler's *Chaucer and Ovid* (New Haven and London 1979) is a more general study of resemblances.
3 See Carleton Brown, 'The Man of Law's head-link and the Prologue of the Canterbury Tales', *Studies in Philology* 34 (1937) 8–35, and Helen Cooper, *The Structure of the Canterbury Tales* (London 1983) 16
4 The relevant sections of Deschamps and Dryden are reprinted by Derek Brewer, ed., *Chaucer: The Critical Heritage* vol. 1 (London 1978) 39–41, 160–4. Chaucer implicitly adds himself on to the line of poets of 'Virgile, Ovide, Omer, Lucan, and Stace' at the end of *Troilus and Criseyde* (5.1792), and makes a more extensive comparison of himself with Ovid in the Introduction to the Man of Law's Tale, *CT* II.45–93, discussed at the end of this essay.
5 The history of the concept of Fama and the richness of its meanings in the fourteenth century are explored by Piero Boitani, *Chaucer and the Imaginary World of Fame*, Chaucer Studies 10 (Cambridge and Totowa, NJ 1984).
6 Meg Twycross demonstrates that it is 'a very strong probability, to go no further, that Chaucer knew Bersuire's work in a full, and not an abridged or excerpted form' (*The Medieval Anadyomene: A Study in Chaucer's Mythography*, Medium Ævum Monographs N.S. 1 (Oxford 1972) 14). The first redaction of Bersuire's work and the first chapter of the second are edited by J. Engels, *Werkmateriaal* 1, 2 and 3 of the Instituut voor Laat Latijn of Utrecht (1960–6); Chaucer apparently knew the later version, made around 1350. The Ovid commentary forms Book 15 of Bersuire's *Reductium Morale*, and

is still frequently found mis-attributed to Thomas Walleys. Chaucer's use of the work, and his preference for the literal and historical over the spiritual or moral, are also discussed by A. J. Minnis, *Chaucer and Pagan Antiquity*, Chaucer Studies 7 (Cambridge and Totowa, NJ 1982) 11–21, 109–18.

7   J. L. Lowes ('Chaucer and the *Ovide moralisé*', *PMLA* 33 (1918) 302–25) believed there to be distinct traces of the French poem in Chaucer's Legend of Philomela, but the parallels he cites are mostly trivial or incorrect (see also Shannon, *Chaucer and the Roman Poets*, 260–82); the Philomela section of the *Ovide* was in any case originally a separate poem (ascribed to Chretien de Troyes) and could have been known to Chaucer independently. Lowes' more cautious conclusions on Chaucer's versions of the story of Theseus and Ariadne in *HF* and *LGW* were strengthened by Sandford Brown Meech, 'Chaucer and the *Ovide moralisé*: a Further Study', *PMLA* 46 (1931) 182–204, but his main piece of evidence, Chaucer's knowledge of the life of Androgeus, could have its source in a gloss to the *Heroides* (M. C. Edwards, 'A Study of Six Characters in Chaucer's *Legend of Good Women* with Reference to Medieval Scholia on Ovid's *Heroides*', Oxford B.Litt. diss. 1970, 80–1). James Wimsatt's study of the *Ovide* and the *BD* sees the evidence of relationship as inconclusive ('The Sources of Chaucer's "Seys and Alcyone"', *Medium Ævum* 36 (1967) 238–40). The ingenious attempt by A. J. Minnis to demonstrate that the book of fables read by the narrator in *BD* before he falls asleep is the *Ovide* is frustrated by the imprecision of Chaucer's wording, and by the fact that the premise of the identification, that the book is real and not fictional, is unprovable ('A Note on Chaucer and the *Ovide moralisé*', M Æ 48 (1979) 254–7).

8   Chaucer's story of Phoebus and the crow in the Manciple's Tale has been extensively studied in relation to the *Ovide*, and the evidence is again inconclusive: there are more similarities to Machaut's *Voir Dit* than to the *Ovide*, but few enough to either. The texts are edited by J. A. Work in W. F. Bryan and Germaine Dempster, eds., *Sources and Analogues of Chaucer's 'Canterbury Tales'* (1941, repr. NJ 1958) 699–722, and the state of scholarship is summarised by D. C. Baker, ed., *The Manciple's Tale*, Variorum Edition of the Works of Geoffrey Chaucer, vol. 2, part 10 (Norman, Oklahoma 1984) 4–11.

9   *Ovide moralisé* 12.1657–1708, 11.772–968, ed. C. de Boer, Verhandelingen der Koninklijke Akademie van Wettenschappen te Amsterdam: Adfeeling Letterkunde, Nieuwe Reeks 37 (1936). The full text is spread across vols. 15, 21, 30, 37, 43 (1915–38).

10 *CT* III.952–82, 865–81

11 The king who rides back to his castle is also a figure for John of Gaunt, but within the poem must refer to the Emperor Octavian rather than to the knight: see e.g. the discussion by David Lawton, *Chaucer's Narrators*, Chaucer Studies 13 (Cambridge and Dover, NH 1985) 53–7, which includes some thought-provoking comments on the use of the *Metamorphoses* (though he is wrong in saying that the story of Ceyx and Alcyone is told by Orpheus).

12 See D. R. Howard, *The Idea of the Canterbury Tales* (Berkeley and Los Angeles 1976) 305, 331; Cooper, *Structure*, 195–202; *Manciple's Tale*, ed. Baker 31–7

13 The main contenders would be Gower's *Confessio Amantis* (III.783–817), Machaut's *Voir Dit* and the *Ovide* (see note 8 above). The only link between Chaucer and Gower is Chaucer's use of the *Confessio* formula 'My sone –' at the end of the tale. The non-Ovidian detail found in Chaucer that the crow cries before 'tempest and rayn' was a commonplace item of bestiary lore (sometimes supported by *Georgics* 1.388), and the attempts to link it to another moralised Ovid, the *Integumentum Ovidii*, or a more distant analogue in the *Seven Sages of Rome*, can be dismissed.

14 Edwards, 'Study', 113–19; the particular type of commentary known to Chaucer is identified on p. 41

15 *Met.* 5.295–307, 669–78. That this is the correct interpretation of the allusion is confirmed

by the fact that the Muses are not called the Pierides in the *Metamorphoses*. The false Muses are described only as the daughters of Pierus, but the term 'Pierides' for them is used at this point in Bersuire's commentary (Engels, vol. 2, p. 90) and was probably familiar as a marginal finding-note.

16 The 'metamorphoses' image is explored in terms of the categories used by Ovidian commentators by J. B. Allen and T. A. Moritz, *A Distinction of Stories: Chaucer's Fair Chain of Narratives for Canterbury* (Columbus, Ohio 1981).

6 LESSONS FROM THE GREAT CLERK: OVID AND JOHN GOWER

1 Quoted in Beryl Smalley, *English Friars and Antiquity in the Early Fourteenth Century* (Oxford 1960) 319

2 The standard edition of Gower's works in four volumes is by G. C. Macaulay (Oxford 1899–1902).

3 Statistics from E. W. Stockton, *The Major Latin Works of John Gower* (Seattle 1962) 27

4 B. Harbert, ed., *A Thirteenth-century Anthology of Rhetorical Poems* (Toronto 1975) 54–60

5 *ibid.* p. 70

6 C. Mainzer, 'John Gower's Use of the Medieval Ovid in the *Confessio Amantis*', *Medium Ævum* 41 (1972) 215–29

7 Petrus Berchorius, *Ovidius Moralizatus* (Werkmateriaal 1, Utrecht 1962)

8 Harbert, ed., *A Thirteenth-century Anthology*, and Paul Lehmann, *Pseudo-Antike Literatur des Mittelalters* (Leipzig 1927). On the medieval history of the legend see the Introduction to F. Branciforti, ed., *Piramus et Tisbé* (Biblioteca dell'Archivum Romanicum, serie 1, vol. 57 (Florence 1959))

9 4187–222; see Mainzer, 'John Gower's Use of the Medieval Ovid'

10 4243–361; see Mainzer, 'John Gower's Use of the Medieval Ovid'

11 *Mirour* 27337–48; 14090. For Gower's biography see J. H. Fisher, *John Gower* (London 1965).

For a sophisticated defence of Gower's merits as a poet see Christopher Ricks, 'John Gower: Metamorphoses in other words', in *The Force of Poetry* (Oxford 1984) 1–33 (reprinted from A. J. Minnis, ed., *Gower's 'Confessio Amantis': Responses and Reassessments* (Cambridge 1983)).

7 ORIGINAL FICTIONS: METAMORPHOSES IN *The Faerie Queene*

1 See, e.g., Anon. 'The Fable of Ovid treting of Narcissus' (1560)

2 *Fabularum Ovidii Interpretatio, Ethica, Physica, et Historica, tradita in Academia Regiomontana* (Cambridge 1584) 2. '*Ovidii consilium fuit, contexere mundi historiam usque ad sua tempora*' ('Ovid's plan was to put together a history of the world up to his own times') *ibid.* sig.¶ 2b.

3 John Lyly, *Euphues, The Complete Works of John Lyly*, ed. R. W. Bond, 3 vols. (Oxford 1902) 1.240. Cf. Sabinus: '*Titulus inscribitur Metamorphosis, hoc est, transformatio. Fingitur enim hic converti ex hominibus in belluas, qui in hominis figura belluae immanitatem gerunt: quales sunt ebriosi, libidinosi, violenti & similes, quorum appetitus rectae rationi minime obtemperat.*' ('The book is called Metamorphosis, that is transformation. For it is imagined here that men are changed into beasts who in the shape of men had the rough character of beasts: such are drunks, lechers, brawlers and the like, whose appetites are not governed by Right Reason.') sig.¶ 8b.

4 *Poetry and Metamorphosis* (Cambridge 1983) 6

5 *Aen.* 3.22–48; *Orlando Furioso* VI.26–53; XXXIX.26–8

6 See Daniel Javitch, 'Rescuing Ovid from the Allegorizers: The Liberation of Angelica, *Furioso X*', in Aldo Scaglione, ed., *Ariosto 1974 in America* (Ravenna 1976) 85–98

7 *Gerusalemme Liberata* X.68–9; *Discourses on the Heroic Poem* ed. and trans. Mariella Cavalchini and Irene Samuel (Oxford 1972) 16; 36–7

8 *The Faerie Queene* I vii 4–5. All references are to *The Works of Edmund Spenser: A Variorum Edition*, ed. Edwin Greenlaw *et al.* 11 vols. (Baltimore 1932–49). Spenser's use of Ovid for this sinister sort of *locus amoenus* is discussed by Richard J. DuRocher, *Milton and Ovid* (Ithaca and London 1985) 210–16.

9 For a list of examples where this happens, see William S. Anderson, 'Multiple Changes in the *Metamorphoses*', *Transactions and Proceedings of the American Philological Association* 94 (1963) 5

10 e.g. *Fast.* 1.1; *Met.* 4.794; 9.2. See L. P. Wilkinson, *Ovid Recalled* (Cambridge 1955) 154 n.

11 I vii 7. For the association of water and lust, see the note on this passage in *The Faerie Queene* ed. A. C. Hamilton (London 1977). Chapman shows the currency of the idea when he mistranslates a passage of the *Odyssey*: 'This no moist man is (nor watrish thing, / That's ever flitting, ever ravishing...)' *Odysseys* 6.311–12. Text from *Chapman's Homer*, ed. Allardyce Nicholl, 2 vols., 2nd edn (London 1967).

12 'The interlude beside the fountain shows Redcrosse being both idle and voluptuous' S. K. Heninger Jr, 'The Orgoglio Episode in *The Faerie Queene*', *ELH* 26 (1959) 175. A less moralistic interpretation is offered by P. J. Alpers, *The Poetry of 'The Faerie Queene'* (Princeton 1967) 137–51.

13 See R. B. Gottfried, 'Spenser and the Italian Myth of Locality', *Studies in Philology* 34 (1937) 107–25

14 Book II of *E. W. his Tameseidos* (1600) tells the story of Medway's rape by a satyr. She is banished by Diana, and dissolves into a tearful river when her child metamorphoses at birth into catstail. Churchyard's description of the Oshe, *The Worthines of Wales* (London 1587) sig. C4a, is typical.

15 See, for instance, the story of Brecan's daughters (IV 95–106), or the chaste metamorphosis of Sabrina into the Severn, VI 130–78

16 See *Variorum* II.196. Cf. also Cyane's tearful metamorphosis into a stream, *Met.* 5.425–37. Cf. Areta's change into the well of Sanajo in Giangiorgio Trissino, *L'Italia liberata dai Goti*, 3 vols. (London 1779) 1.139–40. This well, however, unlike Spenser's bountiless version of it, cures all ailments.

17 *Ovids Metamorphosis ⟨sic⟩ English'd, Mythologiz'd and Represented in Figures.* G[eorge] S[andys] (Oxford 1632) 485. Cf. Sabinus, *Fabularum Ovidii Interpretatio*, 584: '*Anaxarete in saxum conversa fingitur, propter duriciem animi.*'; Ovid's standard Renaissance humanist editor Regius reproduced a similar comment by Lactantius Firmianus: '*ob nimiam crudelitatem animique duritiam in vestigio sui a Venere saxo durata est*' ('because of the excessive cruelty of her heart she was hardened to stone right where she stood') *Publii Ovidii Nasonis Sulmonensis Metamorphoseos Librorum XV* (Lyons 1528) fol. 125b. For a descriptive account of all these commentaries, see Ann Moss, *Ovid in Renaissance France*, Warburg Institute Studies 8 (London 1982).

18 Northrop Frye notes that Diana's wrathful chastity often suggests the Old Law in *The Faerie Queene*, *Fables of Identity* (New York 1963) 80

19 See *Variorum* II.195; A. C. Hamilton, 'A Theological Reading of *The Faerie Queene*, Book II', *ELH* 25 (1958) 155–62; Alastair Fowler, 'The Image of Mortality: *The Faerie Queene*, II i–ii', *Huntington Library Quarterly* 24 (1961) 91–110; James Nohrnberg, *The Analogy of 'The Faerie Queene'* (Princeton 1976) 288. Fredson Bowers, '*The Faerie Queene*, Bk. II: Mordant, Ruddymane, and the Nymph's Well' in *English Studies in*

Honor of James Southall Wilson, University of Virginia Studies 4, (Charlottesville 1951) 243–53 argues that mortal contact with an absolute purity like that of the Nymph is deadly.

20 Hamilton, 'A Theological Reading' 156. Rather remarkably he makes no reference at all to the etiological fiction.

21 Fowler, 'The Image' 102

22 '*Nimphae sunt numina, quae generationi praesunt. Ideo dicuntur aquas inhabitare, vel sylvas, quoniam generatio, & per humorem expletur, & descendit ad sylvam, id est, materiam primam.*' ('Nymphs are deities which preside over generation. For this reason they are said to inhabit waters or woods, since generation is brought about by moisture and descends into *sylva*, wood or matter.') Marsilio Ficino, *Opera*, 2 vols. (Basle 1576) II.1374. Cf. Natales Comes *Mythologiae, sive explicationum Fabularum, Libri Decem* (Paris 1583) 470: '*universae generationis parentes sunt vocatae*' ('they are called the parents of universal generation').

23 For the idea of a well which dislikes wine – although Acrasia's curse is clearly the main cause of Mordant's death – Spenser may have had Ovid's description of the Clitorian spring at the back of his mind. It induces total abstinence '*odiumque meri permansit in undis*' 15.328 ('and hatred of wine remains in its waters'). Interestingly enough it is described by Pythagoras immediately after the well of Salmacis, the main source for the fountain in Book I.

24 As Gower's moral to the tale of 'Araxarathen' ⟨*sic*⟩ puts it 'He was to neysshe [eager] and sche to hard' *Confessio Amantis* 4.3681; *Works*, ed. G. C. Macaulay, 4 vols. (Oxford 1901).

25 Aquinas, *Summa Theologiae* Sec. Sec. Qu.142 Art.1: '*Utrum insensibilitas sit vitium*'. My translation.

26 *Ibid.* Sec. Sec. Qu.152 Art.3; cf. Prim. Sec. Qu.64 Art.1 (3). For a discussion of the importance of Aquinas in Book II (which may rather overstate the case) see Gerald Morgan, 'The Idea of Temperance in the Second Book of *The Faerie Queene*', *Review of English Studies*, N.S.37 (1986) 11–39.

27 See C. S. Lewis, *The Allegory of Love* (Oxford, 1936). This essay owes a great deal to Lewis.

28 The theologically based articles of Fowler and Hamilton (note 19 above) are replies to A. S. P. Woodhouse, 'Nature and Grace in the *Faerie Queene*', *ELH* 16 (1949) 194–228, who argues that II moves purely in the realm of Nature.

29 *Comus* 823–57. M. S. Gohlke, 'Embattled Allegory: Book II of *The Faerie Queene*', *English Literary Renaissance* 8 (1978) 127 notes the infertility of the Nymph and relates it to Guyon's own.

30 The latter is modelled on Arachne's weaving, *Met.* 6.103–28. For the theme of lying artifice, see Lewis, *The Allegory of Love*, 327–9.

31 See Douglas Bush, *Mythology and the Renaissance Tradition in English Poetry* (Minneapolis 1932) 108; Caroline Jameson, 'Ovid in the Sixteenth Century' in J. W. Binns, ed., *Ovid* (London 1973) 237

32 For Ovid's use of this technique, see C. P. Segal, *Landscape in Ovid's 'Metamorphoses': a Study in the Transformation of a Literary Symbol* (Wiesbaden 1969) 39–70. See also A. E. Friedman, 'The Diana–Acteon Episode in Ovid's *Metamorphoses* and *The Faerie Queene*', *Comparative Literature* 18 (1966) 289–99.

33 Clark Hulse, *Metamorphic Verse: the Elizabethan Minor Epic* (Princeton 1981) 277 calls the link 'the flimsiest of pretexts, the most "ingenious" of Ovidian transitions to so exalted a vision'.

34 See Hugh Parry, 'Ovid's *Metamorphoses*: Violence in a Pastoral Landscape', *TPAPA* 95 (1964) 268–82. He notes the particular peril of the sun, 277. Cf. Segal, *Landscape* 4.

35 See Hamilton's note on this passage and *Hamlet*, ed. Harold Jenkins (London 1982) 534–42

36 Diana's absence from this incarnation story is significant in the light of Frye's identification of her and the old law. See note 18 above. On the hermaphrodite in Spenser, see C. S. Lewis, *Spenser's Images of Life*, ed. Alastair Fowler (Cambridge 1967) 36–44. Spenser used the hermaphrodite as an image of amorous contentment with which to end the three-book *Faerie Queene* of 1590 (III xvii 43–7).

37 Ovid goes on to compare the process with spontaneous generation from Nile slime, 422–5

38 Ernst Cassirer, *The Philosophy of Symbolic Forms*, 3 vols., trans. Ralph Manheim (New Haven 1955) II.105

39 Scholars of Ovid do not attach enough importance to the crescendo of frustration represented in Orpheus' songs. See Brooks Otis, *Ovid as an Epic Poet*, 2nd edn (Cambridge 1970) 185.

40 Spenser may have looked to the Adonis of the Orphic hymns as made available to him by Comes rather than to the Adonis of which Ovid's Orpheus sings: '*Orpheus in hymno in Adonim, illum esse solem, cum illum rebus omnibus praebere nutrimentum, & esse germinandi autorem dixerit*', *Mythologiae* 527. ('Orpheus in his hymn to Adonis said that he is the sun, since that affords nourishment to all things and is the author of generation.') See Henry Gibbons Lotspeich, *Classical Mythology in the Poetry of Edmund Spenser*, Princeton Studies in English 9 (Princeton 1932) 32.

41 *Spenser's Faerie Queene. A New Edition*, ed. John Upton, 2 vols. (London 1758)

42 William Nelson suggested that Malbecco's crooked claws recall Daedalion's at 342, *The Poetry of Edmund Spenser: A Study* (New York and London 1963) 324–5.

43 This connection has also been suggested by Harold Skulsky, *Metamorphosis: The Mind in Exile* (Cambridge, Mass. and London, 1981) 132.

44 *Mercator fuerat gemmis praedives & auro, / Aesacus, historiae ceu monumenta docent, / Cui merces olim rapidis periere procellis, / Hinc avis amissas aequore quaerit opes.* ('Aesacus was a merchant very rich in gems and gold, as the monuments of history tell, whose wealth once perished in a violent hurricane, and hence this bird seeks its lost wealth in the sea.') Johanus Sprengius, *Metamorphoses Ouidii, Argumentis quidem soluta oratione, Enarrationibus autem & Allegoriis Elegiaco versu accuratissime expositae* (Paris 1583) fol. 144b. Sabinus offers the same story, 458.

45 *Works*, ed. J. W. Cunliffe, 2 vols. (Cambridge 1907) 1.423. This source was noted by W. Nelson, 'A Source for Spenser's Malbecco', *Modern Language Notes* 68 (1953) 226–9; W. F. NacNeir, 'Ariosto's Sospetto, Gascoigne's Suspicion, and Spenser's Malbecco', *Festschrift für Walther Fischer* (Heidelberg 1959) 34–48 notes that the Suspicion episode in Gascoigne's *Adventures of Master F.J.* derives from Ariosto's *Cinque Canti* II x–xx. However, he takes such a rigorous view of what constitutes a source that he denies either passage any bearing on the Spenserian episode, despite important similarities.

46 See Hamilton's note on this passage; cf. Alpers, *The Poetry* 220

47 *Works* 1.422

48 Angus Fletcher, *Allegory: The Theory of a Symbolic Mode* (Princeton 1964) 49–50 regards Malbecco as more or less archetypical of the mode.

49 See further Harry Berger Jr, 'The Discarding of Malbecco: Conspicuous Allusion and Cultural Exhaustion in *The Faerie Queene* III ix–x', *Studies in Philology* 66 (1969) 135–54

50 Cf. Hermann Fränkel, *Ovid: A Poet Between Two Worlds* (Berkeley and Los Angeles 1956) 101: 'We know how sorely [Ovid] lacked the nerve for finality.' Perhaps Spenser sensed the affinity.

51 See W. P. Cumming, 'The Influence of Ovid's *Metamorphoses* on Spenser's "Mutabilitie Cantos"', *Studies in Philology* 28 (1931) 241–56. The best account of Ovid in the 'Mutabilitie Cantos' is Michael Holahan, '*Iamque Opus Exegi*; Ovid's Changes and Spenser's Brief Epic of Mutability', *English Literary Renaissance* 6 (1976) 244–70.

52 Cf. *Met*. 2.454–7

53 Cf. *Met*. 2.451–2 where Ovid slyly hints that Diana's Nymphs were rather more experienced than the goddess herself, who failed to notice that Callisto was pregnant: '*et, nisi quod virgo est, poterat sentire Diana / mille notis culpam; nymphae sensisse feruntur.*' ('And if she hadn't been a virgin, Diana could have spotted it by thousands of signs. It's rumoured the Nymphs noticed all right.')

54 *Met*. 3.192–252. Spenser's source for the version of the tale without the metamorphosis is probably Comes. Even in this version, however, Actaeon is mutilated: '*Alii dixerunt Actaeonem cervi pelle a Diana tectum laniatum fuiise a canibus ad eum lacerandum incitatis, ne Semelen uxorem duceret.*' *Mythologiae* 666. ('Others say that Actaeon was covered with a deer skin by Diana and torn apart by dogs goaded on to maul him, lest he should marry Semele.')

55 'The Faunus Episode', *Modern Philology* 63 (1965) 14

8   OVID AND THE ELIZABETHANS

Two valuable collections that reprint most of the epyllia are:
E. S. Donno, ed., *Elizabethan Minor Epics* (London 1963)
Nigel Alexander, ed., *Elizabethan Narrative Verse* (London 1967)
As well as Pearcy, Braden and Lewis cited below (notes 2, 5 and 9), other critics who have dealt with this material include:
Douglas Bush, *Mythology and the Renaissance Tradition in English Poetry* (Minneapolis and London 1932)
Roma Gill, '*Musa Iocosa Mea*: Thoughts on the *Elegies*', in A. J. Smith, ed., *John Donne: Essays in Celebration* (London 1972) 47–72
Clark Hulse, *Metamorphic Verse: The Elizabethan Minor Epic* (Princeton, New Jersey 1981)
William Keach, *Elizabethan Erotic Narratives: Irony and Pathos in the Ovidian Poetry of Shakespeare, Marlowe and their Contemporaries* (Hassocks 1977)
J. F. Kermode, 'The Banquet of Sense', *Bulletin of the John Rylands Library* 44 (1961) 68–99
D. D. Rubin, *Ovid's Metamorphoses Englished: George Sandys as Translator and Mythographer* (New York and London 1986)

1 *Ovid's Metamorphosis, Englished, Mythologized, and Represented in Figures*, ed. K. K. Hulley and S. T. Vandersall (Lincoln 1970), commentary to book 3, p. 151

2 Gordon Braden, *The Classics in English Renaissance Poetry: Three Case Studies* (New Haven 1978) introduction xii

3 *To the Gentleman Students of both Universities* (Preface to Robert Greene's *Menaphon*) 1589, in R. B. McKerrow, ed., *The Works of Thomas Nashe*, 5 vols. (Oxford 1966) III.312

4 Francis Meres, *Palladis Tamia: Wit's Treasury* (London 1598) 281–2

5 L. T. Pearcy, *The Mediated Muse: English Translations of Ovid 1560–1660* (Hamden, Conn. 1984) chaps. 1 and 2 (p. 6)

6 Thomas Baines's 'Note containing the opinion of one Christopher Marly concerning his damnable judgement of Religion and scorn of God's word' is reprinted e.g. in Millar Maclure, ed., *Marlowe: The Critical Heritage 1588–1896* (London, Boston and Henley 1979) 36–8.

7 Thomas Fuller, *History of the Worthies of England: Warwickshire* (1662); reprinted e.g. in C. M. Ingleby *et al.*, eds., *Allusions to Shakespeare* (New Shakespeare Society, London 1879 and 1886), 247

8 Letter to Sotheby, 10 Sept. 1802, in E. L. Griggs, ed., *Collected Letters of Samuel Taylor Coleridge*, 6 vols. (Oxford 1956–71) II.459

9 C. S. Lewis, *English Literature in the Sixteenth Century Excluding Drama* (Oxford 1954) 499

9 OVID'S NARCISSUS AND SHAKESPEARE'S RICHARD II: THE REFLECTED SELF

All references to Shakespeare are to *The Riverside Shakespeare* (Boston and London 1974), though I have retained the traditional spelling of Bolingbroke.

1 'In the Roman Pontifical, of which the order of Coronation is really a part, there is no form for the inverse process, no "rite of degradation"...It is as if Shakespeare had in mind some such inverted rite, like those old ecclesiastical or military ones, by which human hardness, or human justice, adds the last touch of unkindness to the execution of its sentences, in the scene where Richard "Deposes" himself, as in some long, agonizing ceremony, reflectively drawn out, with an extraordinary refinement of intelligence and variety of piteous appeal, but also with a felicity of poetic invention...', Walter Pater, *Appreciations* (London 1910) 198

2 On mirror imagery see Herbert Grabes (trans. Gordon Collier), *The Mutable Glass: Mirror-imagery in titles and texts of the Middle Ages and English Renaissance* (Cambridge 1982)

3 Unless we ascribe *The Two Noble Kinsmen*, II ii 120 and IV ii 32 to Shakespeare (both occur in scenes usually given to Fletcher).

4 *Met.* 3.394; in Arthur Golding's translation (1567), 3.491; in the edition by J. F. Nims (New York 1965) 74

5 R. K. Root, *Classical Mythology in Shakespeare*, Yale Studies in English, ed. A. S. Cook (New York 1903)

6 J. A. K. Thomson, *Shakespeare and the Classics* (London 1952) 154

7 T. W. Baldwin, *William Shakspere's Small Latine and Lesse Greeke*, 2 vols. (Urbana 1944) II.418. V. K. Whitaker takes a similar view; see his *Shakespeare's Use of Learning* (San Marino 1953) 26.

8 On Renaissance editions of Ovid, see D. P. Harding, 'Milton and the Renaissance Ovid', *Illinois Studies in Language and Literature* 30 (1946) 11–105, especially the Bibliography on pp. 100–2. Further information is available in Madeleine Doran, 'Some Renaissance Ovids', in Bernice Slote, ed., *Literature and Society* (Lincoln, Nebraska 1964) 44–62 and D. T. Starnes and E. W. Talbert, *Classical Myth and Legend in Renaissance Dictionaries* (Chapel Hill 1955). There are 330 entries under Ovid in the index to J. W. Velz's *Shakespeare and the Classical Tradition: A Critical Guide to Commentary, 1660–1960* (Minneapolis 1968).

9 See Caroline Jameson, 'Ovid in the Sixteenth Century', in J. W. Binns, ed., *Ovid* (London 1973) 210–42, esp. p. 213. Caxton's translation of the *Metamorphoses* had appeared earlier – in 1480. When D. P. Harding published 'Milton and the Renaissance Ovid' the first nine books of Caxton's translation were missing. These have now been found and reunited with the rest in the Pepys Library at Magdalene College, Cambridge; see N. F. Blake, *Caxton and His World* (London 1969) 239.

10 My attention was drawn to this line by Mr Robert Carver.

11 Louise Vinge has suggested that the curious confusion of pronouns in Thomas Edwards's *Narcissus* (London 1595) is deliberate, miming a confusion of poem and poet. See her *The Narcissus Theme in Western Literature up to the Early Nineteenth Century* (Lund

1967) 175. I find it difficult to believe that Edwards's ramshackle poem is really so subtle. See the Roxburghe Club edition, Thomas Edwards, *Cephalus and Procris. Narcissus*, ed. W. E. Buckley (London 1882) esp. p. 52 where the fact that Edwards's Narcissus takes the image to be that of a woman leads to an inept marring of the reciprocity effect so brilliantly managed by Ovid.

12 The immediately following *inopem*, 'poor' obliges the translator to choose 'wealth' from the various senses of *copia* if the poetic figurative language is to be retained. At the same time however the implication of sexual opportunity or availability (clear in *emoriar, quam sit tibi copia nostri* at 3.391) is surely also present.

13 *Chameleon*, December 1894; in *The Works of Oscar Wilde, 1856* [*sic*, properly 1854] – *1900*, ed. G. F. Maine (London 1948) 1114

14 Ovid, *Metamorphoseon*, ed. Jacobus Pontanus (Antwerp 1618) 144. This is available in a facsimile produced by Garland Publishing (New York and London 1976).

15 By Stephen Orgel in a note prefixed to the Garland Publishing facsimile of Pontanus' edition.

16 *Ovid's Metamorphosis English'd, Mythologiz'd and Represented in Figures by G.S.* (Oxford 1632) 103. Also available in facsimile by Garland Publishing (New York and London 1976).

17 G. K. Galinsky, *Ovid's Metamorphoses: An Introduction to the Basic Aspects* (Oxford 1975) 53, 60. See also C. R. Edwards, 'The Narcissus Myth in Spenser's Poetry', *Studies in Philology* 74 (1977) 63–88, esp. 63–7. Hermann Fränkel's observation that in this passage the Delphic command is 'enigmatically reversed' is very much to the point. See his *Ovid: A Poet Between Two Worlds* (Berkeley 1945) 213. Franz Bömer in his commentary expresses a proper mistrust of the wilder kind of twentieth-century reading but concedes that Fränkel's 'moralisch-allegorisch-metaphysische' reading is persuasive, and then further concedes that although Ovid has given us an ancient tale of Nemesis he has also chosen to give that story a Euripidean (psychologising) colour (P. Ovidius Naso, *Metamorphosen*, edited with a commentary by Franz Bömer, 7 vols. (Heidelberg 1969–86) vol. 1.538).

18 *Tusculan Disputations*, I XXII 52 and I XXVII 67, in the edition with an English translation by J. E. King, Loeb Classical Library (London 1927) 62 and 78

19 Euripides, *Hippolytus*, ed. W. S. Barrett (Oxford 1964) 363. The Greek is cited from Barrett's text.

20 Joseph Glanville, *The Vanity of Dogmatizing* (London 1661) 18; available in facsimile, ed. Stephen Medcalf, from the Harvester Press (Hove 1970)

10 ILLUSTRATING OVID

1 Translated by Peter Green in *Ovid: The Erotic Poems* (Harmondsworth 1982) 89

2 See generally A. Pigler, *Barockthemen* (Budapest 1956) 8–258 and E. Paratore, ed., *Bibliografia Ovidiana* (Sulmona 1958). G. K. Galinsky, *Ovid's 'Metamorphoses': An Introduction to the Basic Aspects* (Oxford 1975) and S. Viarre, *L'Image et la Pensée dans les 'Metamorphoses' d'Ovide* (Paris 1964) are useful on the compositional structure of the poem.

3 The expression appears to be a corruption of the title given to the second edition of Mansion's version of the text *La bible des poets* (Paris 1493).

4 For interior and exterior visualisation see M. Baxandall, *Painting and Experience in Fifteenth-Century Italy* (Oxford 1972) 45, where the notion is applied to representations of religious scenes.

5 However, see the claims of A. Minucci in her 'Quid ex Ovidii operibus in Leonardi Vincii scripta sit derivatum' in N. Barbu *et al.*, eds., *Acta Conventus Omnium Gentium Ovidianis Studiis Ferendis* (Bucharest 1976) 451–8

6 Piranesi studied Latin with his brother Angelo, a Carthusian monk, in Venice in 1740. He wrote the *Parere* in 1765 after 20 years in Rome. See R. Wittkower in *Journal of the Warburg Institute* (now *Journal of the Warburg and Courtauld Institutes*) 2 (1938/9) 147ff, and J. Wilton-Ely, *The Mind and Art of Giovanni Battista Piranesi* (London 1979).

7 For Cardinal de'Medici's letter see R. Lefèvre in *L'Urbe* 32 (1960) 6–7

8 C. Gould, *National Gallery Catalogues: The Sixteenth-Century Italian Schools* (London 1975) 272 note 25

9 M. Schapiro, *Words and Pictures: On the Literal and Symbolic in the Illustration of a Text* (The Hague and Paris 1973) 9

10 There is no general survey of Ovidian illustration. Studies are listed in the notes that follow.

11 For a brilliant exposition of the choosing of moments in a narrative cycle see M. Podro, *Piero della Francesca's 'Legend of The True Cross'* (55th Charlton Lecture) (Newcastle-upon-Tyne 1974)

12 The literature spawned by these few words is vast. For a recent bibliography see various references in the periodical *Word and Image* 1 i (1985).

13 See N. Bryson, *Word and Image* (Cambridge 1981) chap. 1, 'Discourse, figure'

14 M. Schapiro, 'On Some Problems in the Semiotics of Visual Art: Field and Vehicle in Image-Signs' in A. J. Griemas, ed., *Sign, Language, Culture* (Paris 1970)

15 J. Culler, *Saussure* (London 1976) 35–44 and generally R. Brilliant, *Visual Narratives: Storytelling in Etruscan and Roman Art* (Ithaca and London 1984) 'Introduction'

16 Claude Lorrain sometimes did; see Nigel Llewellyn, 'Virgil and the Visual Arts' in Charles Martindale, ed., *Virgil and his Influence: Bimillennial Studies* (Bristol 1984) 130ff

17 Schapiro, *Words and Pictures*, 9

18 For ancient Ovidian art see H. Bartolome, *Ovid und die Antike Kunst* (Leipzig 1935); E. J. Bernbeck, *Beobachtungen zur Darstellungesart in Ovids Metamorphosen* (Munich 1967); P. Schonfeld, *Ovids Metamorphosen in ihrem Verhältnis zur antiken Kunst* (Leipzig 1877); C. Buccino, *Le opere nell'arte nel Metamorfosi di Ovidio* (Naples 1913); W. Wunderer, *Ovids Werke in ihrem Verhältnis zur antiken Kunst* (Erlangen 1889)

19 J. M. C. Toynbee, *Art in Britain under the Romans* (Oxford 1964) 262–5 with references

20 For other ancient depictions of this theme see that from Room 1 of the House of the Dioscuri, Ostia, illustrated in W. Dorigo, *Late Roman Painting* (London 1971) pl. 203 and the Pompeian fresco now mounted on panel in the Museo Nazionale, Naples (pl. 103 of A. Stenico, *Roman and Etruscan Painting* (Contact History of Art) (London 1963)). For comment on this visual tradition see O. Wattel-De Croizant, 'Ovide et l'enlèvement d'Europe, aspects littéraires et mosaïques du 1er siècle' in R. Chevallier, ed., *Colloque Présence d'Ovide* (Paris 1982) 79–100.

21 M. C. Dawson, 'Romano-Campanian Mythological Landscape Painting', *Yale Classical Studies* 9 (1944); P. Grimal, 'Les Métamorphoses d'Ovide et la peinture paysagiste de l'époque d'Auguste', *Revue d'Etudes latines* 16 (fasc.i) (1938) 145ff

22 For Ovid in the Middle Ages see D. M. Robothan's chapter in J. W. Binns, ed., *Ovid* (London 1973); S. Viarre, *La Survie d'Ovide dans la Littérature Scientifique des XIIe et XIIIe siècles* (Poitiers 1966); J. Engels, *Etudes sur l'Ovide moralisé* (Groningen 1943); A. Monteverdi, 'Ovidio nel Medio Evo' in *Studi Ovidiani* (Rome 1959)

23 In certain quarters the suspicion of Ovid never died. Juan Luis Vives (d. 1540) called him dangerous and 'sensual', see O. H. Green, *Spain and the Western Tradition* (Madison and London 1968) III.456 and note 162. For medieval, moralising editions of Ovid, J. Seznec *The Survival of the Pagan Gods* (Princeton (Bolligen Series 38) 1953) 92–3 and a recent study of the illustrative tradition by Carla Lord, 'Three Manuscripts of the *Ovide moralisé*', *Art Bulletin* 57 (1975) 161–75.

24 For this scholastic tradition see P. O. Kristeller, *Renaissance Thought and its Sources* (New York 1979) 231 and 316–17 note 14

25 By the fifteenth century the synthesis was virtually complete, see Antonio Filarete's bronze doors for the papal basilica of St Peter's, Rome of *c*.1440–5 which show Ovidian scenes in their ornamental framework; Carla Lord, 'Solar Imagery in Filarete's Doors to St Peter's', *Gazette des Beaux-Arts* 87 (1976), 143–50

26 M. D. Henkel, *De Houtsneden van Mansions 'Ovide moralisé' Bruges 1484* (Amsterdam 1922) and the remarks by E. Schenk van Schweinsburg in *Der Cicerone* 16 (1924) 321ff. Recent work on Mansion's edition includes the entry on pages 63–4 of the catalogue to *Le Livre illustré en occident du haut Moyen Age à nos jours* (Bruxelles 1977); S. Hindman and J. D. Farquhar, *Pen to Press* (Exhibition Catalogue, University of Maryland and Johns Hopkins University 1977) 25 and 193. For Ovidian prints generally see L. M. Prindle, *Mythology in Prints. Illustrations to the 'Metamorphoses' of Ovid 1497–1824* (Burlington, Vermont 1939).

27 For *De Pictura* and *Della Pittura*, the translation which soon followed it, see M. D. K. Baxandall, *Giotto and the Orators* (Oxford 1971) *passim*

28 Baxandall, *Painting and Experience* 45

29 L. B. Alberti, *On Painting*, ed. J. R. Spencer (New Haven and London 1966) 90–1. See too D. Cast, *The Calumny of Apelles: a Study in the Humanist Tradition* (New Haven 1981) but only in the light of Jean Michel Massing's review in *Art History* 5 (1982) 510–11.

30 On gardens see, for example, G. L. Hersey, 'Ovid, Vico and the Central Gardens at Caserta', *Journal of Garden History* 1 (1985) 3–34

31 These came to light in the relevant file of the Photographic Collection of the Warburg Institute, to whose staff I owe due thanks. A similar range would be unearthed from the files containing illustrations of other popular myths.

32 Raffaelo Borghini, *Il Riposo* (Milan edn. 1967) 1.64–5. On the relationship between the picture and the textual source in *Metamorphoses* 10 and elsewhere see C. Hope, *Titian* (London 1980) 126. Amongst other censures of this sort Francesco Milizia's attack on Bernini in G. C. Bauer, ed., *Bernini in Perspective* (Englewood Cliffs 1976) 55: 'He was the first to introduce license and errors under the pretext of grace...'

33 The apparent looseness is rarely understood by critics who search, in vain, for *the* text. For an explanation of '*Venus and Adonis*' of this sort see W. Keach, *Elizabethan Erotic Narratives* (Hassocks 1977) 52–84. Titian's picture was, probably very briefly, in London in 1554 and some feel Shakespeare may have come under its influence via a woodcut. There is no real evidence for this despite E. Panofsky, *Problems in Titian Mostly Iconographical* (New York 1969) 153ff.

34 See Cecil Gould, *National Gallery Catalogue*, who cites the recent literature in his discussion of *Bacchus and Ariadne* (Pl. 8), a *poesia* done not for Philip II but for the Gonzaga family. On the *poesia* see Charles Hope, 'Poesie and Painted Allegories', in C. Hope and J. Martineau, eds., *The Genius of Venice 1500–1600* (Exhibition Catalogue) (London 1983) and D. Rosand, '"Ut Pictor Poeta": Meaning in Titian's "Poesie"', *New Literary History* 3 (1971/2) 527–46.

35 His first visit to Spain was in 1603; he was ennobled by Philip IV in June, 1624.

36 See Rubens's letter of 1638 commenting on the Florence 'Effects of War' as quoted by K. Downes in *Rubens* (London 1980) 21–2

37 For this cycle see S. Alpers, *The Decoration of the Torre de la Parada* (Brussels, London and New York 1971) *passim* (Corpus Rubeniarum Ludwig Burchard, vol. IX). For other examples of decorative schemes on Ovidian themes see the cycle in the lunettes of the Sala del Frigio, Villa Farnesina, Rome, painted in the second decade of the sixteenth century; the Appartamento delle Metamorfosi, with its ceiling panels of about 1616 in the Palazzo Ducale, Mantua by Antonio Viani (1555/60–1629); the Carracci cycle of 1597–1602 in

the Gallery of the Palazzo Farnese, Rome; the late seventeenth-century decorations now housed in the Jeffry Museum, London with a later, English painted cycle.

38 There is a considerable literature on illustrated editions of Ovid, a topic which cannot adequately be surveyed here. For example, M. D. Henkel, 'Illustrierte Ausgaben von Ovide Metamorphosen in XV, XVI und XVII Jahrhunderten', *Vorträge der Bibliothek Warburg 1926–7* (Leipzig and Berlin 1930); superseding G. Duplessis, *Essai bibliographique sur les différentes éditions des œuvres d'Ovide ornées des planches publiées aux XVe et XVIe siècles* (Paris 1889). Amongst later, specialised studies are two by A. Moss: *Ovid in Renaissance France* (London 1982) and *Poetry and Fable: Studies in Mythological Narrative in Sixteenth-Century France* (Cambridge 1984). See too L. Donati, 'Edizioni quattrocentesche non pervenuteci delle 'Metamorfosi' *Atti Convegno Internazionale Ovidiano. Sulmona 1958* (Rome 1959) I.111ff.

39 The placing of mythological pictures in sequences determined primarily by their form has been identified as a way of organising room decoration in sixteenth-century Italy; see C. Hope, 'The "Camerino d'Alabastro" of Alfonso d'Este' in *The Burlington Magazine* 113 (1971) 641–50 and 712–21.

40 For details on this and the many important Ovidian pictures by this artist see A. F. Blunt, *Nicolas Poussin* (London and New York 1967) Catalogue vol. no. 151 (109–10).

41 We cannot here survey the complete series of sets of illustrations which artists have made of Ovid's text, from well before Poussin up to Picasso's etchings for A. E. Watts's translation published by the University of California Press (Berkeley 1954). The most famous series is by Antonio Tempesta (1551–1630) whose 150 scenes published in *Metamorphosen...Ovidianarum* (Amsterdam 1606) became a standard repertory for mythological pictorial narrative (reprinted New York and London 1976 as vol. XIX in S. Orgel, ed., *The Renaissance and the Gods*).

42 See J. Costello, in *JWCI* 28 (1955) 296ff

43 See Brancusi's reference to Narcissus in his sculpture 'Self-Love' described in M. Popa, 'Ovide et Brancusi – confluences mythiques' in N. Barbu *et al.*, eds., *Acta Conventus Omnium Gentium Ovidiani Studiis Ferendis* 495–502

44 Blunt, *Nicolas Poussin*, Text vol. 125

45 See P. A. Reidl, *Gian Lorenzo Bernini. Apollo und Daphne* (Stuttgart 1960)

46 See R. Wittkower, *Gian Lorenzo Bernini: The Sculptor of the Roman Baroque* (3rd edn, Oxford 1981) 6. Borghini talks of 'anzi in concetto, ed in disegno, che in effetto' (S. Battaglia, *Grande Dizionario della Lingua Italia* (Turin 1961 etc.) III *vid* 'Concetto'.

47 For example, in Antonio Pollaiuolo's (*c.* 1432–98) version on panel (National Gallery, London) of *c.* 1450. See L. D. Ettlinger, *Antonio and Piero Pollaiuolo* (Oxford 1978) 141 and pl. 28

48 Quoted by H. Hibbard, *Bernini* (Harmondsworth 1965) note on p. 235

49 See now, G. M. Ackerman, *The Life and Work of Jean-Léon Gérôme* (London and New York 1986) 134 and 269 (Catalogue no. 385). Ackerman makes no mention of Ovid.

50 For Borghese patronage (Scipione was later to become Pope Urban VIII) see F. Haskell, *Painters and Patrons* (rev. edn, New Haven 1980) chap. 2. On sculpture collections, F. Haskell and N. Penny, *Taste and the Antique* (New Haven and London 1981) especially cap. 2.

51 Domenico Bernini of 1713 quoted in translation by G. C. Bauer, *Bernini in Perspective* 26–7

52 See Hibbard, *Bernini*, 53

53 See the transcription and commentary of J. M. Fletcher, *JWCI* 36 (1973) 383 and n. 21

54 D. H. Solkin, *Richard Wilson. The Landscape of Reaction* (Tate Gallery, London 1982) 186 points out an Ovidian series starting in the mid-1750s, with *Venus & Adonis*

(Victoria and Albert Museum, London) from *Met*. 10; *Destruction of Niobe's Children* (Yale Centre, New Haven) (Book 6); *Ceyx and Alcyone* (National Museum of Wales, Cardiff) (Book 11); *Meleager and Atalanta* (Tate Gallery, London) (Book 8).

55 C. Whitfield and J. Martineau, eds., *Painting in Naples from Caravaggio to Giordano* (Exhibition Catalogue, RA) (London 1982) 176–8

56 See D. Freedberg, *JWCI* 34 (1971) 242

57 Panofsky, *Problems in Titian, passim.*

58 See C. Gould, *The Paintings of Correggio* (London 1976) 131ff and 275ff. The picture was part of a group, possibly presented to Charles V by Federigo Gonzaga.

59 H. Bardon, 'Ovide et le baroque' in N. I. Herescu, ed., *Ovidiana. Recherches sur Ovide* (Paris 1958) 75ff *idem*, 'Sur l'influence d'Ovide en France au 17ème siecle' in *Atti del Convegno Internazionale Ovidiano. Sulmona 1958* (Rome 1959) 2 vols. 1.69–83; *idem* 'Ovide et le Grand Roi' in *Les Etudes Classiques* (1957) 402ff; J-P. Neraudau, 'Ovide au Château de Versailles, sous Louis XIV' in R. Chevallier, ed., *Colloque Présence d'Ovide* 323–44

60 For a recent, full entry on this picture see *Watteau 1684 1721* (Paris 1984 5) 417 19

61 E. De Goncourt, *Catalogue raisonné de l'Œuvre peint, dessiné et gravé d'Antoine Watteau* (Paris 1875)

62 E. and J. De Goncourt, *French Eighteenth-Century Painters*, 'Boucher' (Oxford 1972) 64–5

63 *Lettre sur le cessation du Sallon (sic) de peinture* (Cologne 1749) (See Bibliothèque Nationale, Paris: Deloynes Collection, Cabinet des Estampes, No. 49)

64 Quoted by T. Crow, *Artists and Public Life in Eighteenth-Century Paris* (New Haven and London 1985) 12

65 On the pictorial rendering of this myth: O. Wattel-De Croizant, 'Ovide et l'enlèvement d'Europe'; F. Panofsky, *Problems in Titian*; P. Fehl, 'Iconography or *Ekphrasis*; the Case of the Neglected Cows in Titian's 'Rape of Europa' in *Congrès Internationale de l'Histoire de l'art Granada 1973 Actas* II 1977 (reference courtesy of Dr Marcia Pointon); C. Hope, 'Problems of Interpretation in Titian's Erotic Paintings' and C. Ginsburg 'Tiziano, Ovidio e i codici della figurazione erotica nell'1500' both in *Tiziano e Venezia* (Venice 1980) 111–35, the latter previously published in *Paragone* 29 (1978) 2–24; P. Fehl & P. Watson, 'Ovidian Delight and Problems of Iconography. Two Essays on Titian's 'Rape of Europa', *Storia dell'Arte* 16 (1976) 23–30; C. Buccino, *Le opere nell'arte nel Metamorfosi di Ovidio* II.26–34; P. F. Watson, 'Titian's 'Rape of Europa': A Bride Stripped Bare', *SA* 28 (1976) 249–88; A. Pope, *Titian's Rape of Europa* (Boston, Mass. 1960); M. L. Schapiro, 'Titian's "Rape of Europa"', *Gazette des Beaux-Arts* (Sè sér.) 77 (1971) 109–16; A. Smart in *Apollo* 85 (1967) 420–31. Most of this literature relates Titian's picture to one or more literary text, sometimes Ovid's. I have not been able to consult M. Combaret, *La légende d'Europe à travers la littérature latine et l'art figuré* (Mémoire de maîtrise, Clermont-Ferrand 1970).

66 J. M. C. Toynbee, *Art in Britain under the Romans*, 263

67 See, for example, the Pompeian fresco of this subject where there is eye-engagement in a scene otherwise short of 'actors'. (A. Stenico, *Roman and Etruscan Painting* pl. 103)

68 By Philippe Fehl in *SA* 16 (1976) 27

69 Suggested by R. Cocke, *Veronese* (London 1980) 14–15

70 D. Rosand, *Painting in Cinquecento Venice*; *Titian, Veronese, Tintoretto* (New Haven and London 1982) 'Temporal Structures' (167–77)

71 Nicolo di Agostini's, reprinted many times; for example, 1522, 1533, 1537 and 1538. See D. Stone Jr, 'The source of Titian's "Rape of Europa"', *Art Bulletin* 54 (1972) 47–9

72 Boucher's oil sketch (in the Musée de Picardie, Amiens) shows the head of the bull turned

towards Europa – it was not always part of the composition: see A. Laing *et al.*, *François Boucher 1703–1770* (Exhibition Catalogue, Paris 1986) 157–60.

73 Translation by A. D. Melville (Ovid) *Metamorphoses* (Oxford 1986) 50

74 This lack of dignity is brought in by artists in various ways to suggest the games and gestures between Jupiter and Europa. See, for example, the suggestive way in which she grasps his horn in an influential cycle of six frescoes by Bernardino Luini (d. pre-1532) painted in the early 1520s for the Palazzo of Gerolamo Rabia, Milan, since detached and now hanging in Berlin (See B. Berenson, *Italian Pictures of the Renaissance* (London 1968 edn) vol. III pl. 1486 and Watson's reference in *SA* 16 (1976) 252. Watson wrongly numbers them as six; there are at least ten.) The Mellon Collection, Washington contains a similar set of nine scenes of the legend of Cephalus and Procris, also from the Palazzo Rabia.

75 The composition for this picture is repeated in a lost cartoon for a tapestry, one of a series of the loves of the gods for the Beauvais works (see A. Ananoff and D. Wildenstein, *L'Opera completa di Boucher* (Milan 1980) Catalogue nos. 365–6. The tapestries themselves were woven in 1749–74.

76 A. Laing *et al.*, *François Boucher* 237–40 where no mention is made of the treatment of narrative.

77 Some literary critics have brought out this dark side, see H. Parry, 'Ovid's "Metamorphoses": Violence in a Pastoral Landscape', *Transactions of the American Philosophical Association* 95 (1964) 268–82.

78 An extraordinary academic rendering of *Europa* by Ingres is in the Fogg Art Museum, Cambridge, Mass. Signed and dated 1863 Ingres added inscriptions giving the source of the image, a Greek vase acquired by the British Museum in 1846 and another speculating on a reference to such a work by Pliny the Elder (see E. Camesasca and E. Radius, *L'Opera completa di Ingres* (Milan 1968) 119.

79 See, for example, Fragonard's *The Swing*, Wallace Collection, London

11 DRYDEN AND OVID'S 'WIT OUT OF SEASON'

1 See *Controversiae* 2.2.8–12, in The Elder Seneca, *Declamations*, ed. M. Winterbottom, 2 vols. (Cambridge, Mass. and London 1974) 1.259–65. I am indebted to my colleagues Dr Tom Mason and Professor Niall Rudd for their detailed comments on an earlier draft of this essay.

2 *Declamations* II 324–5

3 Quintilian, *Institutio Oratoria*, ed. H. E. Butler, 4 vols. (Cambridge, Mass. and London 1922) IV.51

4 Ovid is here making deliberate play with Horace, *Ars Poetica* 29–30

5 Seneca, *Naturales Quaestiones*, ed. T. H. Corcoran, 2 vols. (Cambridge, Mass. and London 1971–2) 1.278–81

6 See, for example, the remarks of Johann Christian Jahn quoted and translated by W. S. Anderson in 'Playfulness and Seriousness in Ovid's *Metamorphoses*', *Mosaic* 12. 1–2 (1981) 192–210

7 See G. Williamson, *The Proper Wit of Poetry* (London 1951)

8 John Dryden, *Poems*, ed. J. Kinsley, 4 vols. (Oxford 1958) 1.47. All quotations from Dryden are taken from this edition.

9 *Poems* 1.80

10 *Poems* IV.1451. Joseph Addison closely echoed Dryden's remarks about Ovid's treatment of Narcissus in the notes to his translation of *Metamorphoses* Book 3 in *Poetical Miscellanies: the Fifth Part* (London 1704) 591.

11 Myrrha, the girl in Book 10 of the *Metamorphoses* consumed with an incestuous passion

for her father, includes the following among her complaints: 'Our Kindred-Blood debars a better Tie; / He might be nearer, were he not so nigh.' See *Poems* IV.1575.

12 As did Addison, in the translation referred to in note 10

13 See Brooks Otis, *Ovid as an Epic Poet* (2nd edn Cambridge 1970) 281; H. Fränkel, *Ovid: a Poet Between Two Worlds* (Berkeley and Los Angeles 1956) 232; L. P. Wilkinson, *Ovid Recalled* (Cambridge 1955) 168; Otis 39; G. K. Galinsky, *Ovid's 'Metamorphoses': an Introduction to the Basic Aspects* (Oxford 1975) 137

14 *Poems* IV.1666

15 See particularly Otis, *Ovid as an Epic Poet*, 331–61, 421–3; Galinsky, *Ovid's Metamorphoses* 146–6 sees the main pleasure to be had from the piece as that of a connoisseur for a bravura display of literary parody, though he also comments very appreciatively (146) on Ovid's distinctive blend of lightness and seriousness in his handling of Ceyx and Alcyone's love, calling it (159) 'a humor which does not mean to wound or hurt but keeps just the right equilibrium between detached amusement and sympathy'.

16 See G. Lafaye, ed., *Ovide: les Métamorphoses,* 3 vols. (Paris 1928–30) III.21, 25

17 G. M. Murphy, ed., *Ovid: Metamorphoses, Book XI* (Oxford 1972) 71–2

18 Fränkel, *Ovid* 102; see also Galinsky, *Ovid's Metamorphoses* 126–8 and G. Lafaye, *Les Métamorphoses d'Ovide et leurs modèles grecs* (Paris 1904) 117

19 O. S. Due, *Changing Forms: Studies in the Metamorphoses of Ovid,* Classica et Mediaevalia: Dissertations x (Copenhagen 1974) 148

20 See, for example, the first edition of Otis (Cambridge 1966)

21 See, for example, the second edition of Otis, and R. Coleman, 'Structure and Intention in the *Metamorphoses*', *Classical Quarterly* 21 (1971) 461–77

22 See Galinsky, *Ovid's Metamorphoses*, and D. L. Arnaud, 'Aspects of Wit and Humor in Ovid's *Metamorphoses*', Ph.D dissertation, Stanford 1968

23 Despite an occasional local inclusion of a modern colouring in the rendering for example, allusions to the violence of the Civil War and to Roman Catholic religious practices in 344–5

24 See, for example, Alexander Ross, *Mystagogus Poeticus* (2nd edn London 1648) 55–7; P. Du-Ryer, *Les Métamorphoses d'Ovide...avec de nouvelles explications historiques, morales et politiques sur toutes les fables* (Brussels 1677) 395; N. Renouard, *Les Métamorphoses d'Ovide...avec quinze discours contenant l'explication morale des fables* (Paris 1640) 229; Natalis Comes, *Mythologiae* (Venice 1567) 215; George Sandys, *Ovid's Metamorphosis, English'd, Mythologiz'd and Represented in Figures* (1626; rev. edn 1632; repr. London 1640) 231; *Shakespeare's Ovid: Being Arthur Golding's Translation of the Metamorphoses,* ed. W. H. D. Rouse (London 1904) 6

25 See, for example, Mark Van Doren, *John Dryden: a Study of his Poetry,* rev. edn (Bloomington 1963) 219; William Myers, *Dryden* (London 1973) 185

26 Cf. *Paradise Lost* 7.471

27 All quotations from Ovid are taken from Borchard Cnipping's variorum edition, 3 vols. (Amsterdam 1683), one of the editions used by Dryden (see J. McG. Bottkol, 'Dryden's Latin Scholarship', *Modern Philology* 40 (1932–3) 241–54). Accompanying prose translations are from the Loeb edition, occasionally modified for greater accuracy or to fit the text used by Dryden. In his commentary on *Aeneid* 2 (Oxford 1964), R. G. Austin comments that Ovid 'hideously develops' the idea in Virgil's 277.

28 In 435–6, Dryden reworks and develops Sandys: 'Vnwakened with the tumult of this fray / Dissolv'd in death-like sleep, *Aphidus* lay'.

29 *Poems* IV.1666

30 R. S. Lang, ed., *P. Ovidii Nasonis Metamorphoseon Liber XII* (Oxford 1927) 65; *P. Ovidii Nasonis Opera, e textu Burmanni,* 5 vols. (Oxford 1826) IV.286

31 Cf. *Paradise Lost* 4.720; 5.137, 377

32 *Opera, e textu Burmanni* IV.288; Lang 67
33 *Opera, e textu Burmanni* IV.289
34 Lang, 68; Franz Bömer, in his recent edition of *Metamorphoses 12–13* (Heidelberg 1982) questions (145–7) the lines' authenticity on the grounds that they do not appear in the best MSS, and that 438 contains a metrical irregularity. On the obscurities of the passage (which Bömer considers to have been overstressed), see Lang 68.
35 See Cnipping's note on 433; the 'parallel' passage is in *Fasti* 4.769–70
36 See Michael West, 'Dryden's Ambivalence as a Translator of Heroic Themes', *Huntington Library Quarterly* 36 (1972–3) 17–38
37 With Ovid 245–53 (Celadon's eyeballs extruded), cf. *Iliad* 13.616–17, 16.740–2; with Ovid 254–7 (Amycus spitting out blood and teeth), cf. *Aeneid* 5.470; with Ovid 270–9 (Charaxus' hair set alight), cf. *Aen.* 12.300–1; with Ovid 293–5 (Evagrus speared through the mouth), cf. *Iliad* 16.346–50; with Ovid 335–6 (Helops speared through both ears), cf. *Iliad* 20.472–4; with Ovid 380–92 (Dorylas disembowelled), cf. *Iliad* 21.180–2
38 S. Johnson, *Lives of the Poets*, ed. G. B. Hill, 3 vols. (Oxford 1905) 1.20
39 *Lives* I.21
40 *Lives* I.20
41 *Lives* I.20
42 Otis, *Ovid as an Epic Poet*, 232; E. Fantham, 'Ovid's Ceyx and Alcyone', *Phoenix* 33 (1979) 330–45
43 Professor Rudd has, however, pointed out to me that Ovid's '*non...sustinet*' (584–5) could imply that Juno gives way not out of impatience but because she can no longer bear to do nothing.
44 Cf. *Paradise Lost* 8.182–4; Raphael has taught Adam 'to live, / The easiest way, nor with perplexing thoughts / To interrupt the sweet of Life,...'; Dryden puts the phrase 'the sweets of life' into the mouth of Diomedes in his *Aeneis* 11.417, when the hero is describing all that the cruelty of the gods has denied him.
45 Charles Hopkins, *Epistolary Poems; on Several Occasions* (London 1694) 58; on Dryden's use of this volume, see my 'Two Hitherto Unrecorded Sources for Dryden's Ovid Translations', *Notes and Queries* 21 (1974) 419–21
46 Sandys, 207
47 Dryden took the hint for 33 from Hopkins: 'They sweep o're all the earth, swell all the Main.'
48 Dryden remembered Golding, 547–8: 'The chamber did renew a fresh her smart, / And of her bed did bring to mynd the deere departed part.'
49 Dryden may have been prompted to make the connection by his feeling that Virgil, too, had viewed his heroine in a way that included both sympathy and objective distancing. The obtrusive rhetorical figure (*polyptoton*) in the last line of the quotation – a characteristically 'Ovidian' device – is in direct imitation of the equivalent moment in Virgil's Latin: *illum absens absentem auditque videtque* (*Aen.* 4.83).
50 For a full discussion of this aspect of the episode, see Arnaud, 104–36
51 Dryden took a hint for his depiction of the tenth wave (165–6) from Hopkins: 'With more than common ardour in his breast, / And higher hopes, spurr'd further than the rest.'
52 Dryden was here perhaps recollecting a couplet in Cowley's poem, *On the Queens repairing Somerset-House*: 'For the distrest and the afflicted lye, / Most in their Care, and always in their Eye.' The couplet is (mis)quoted in the Epistle Dedicatory to *Don Sebastian*.
53 *The Tempest* I II 5–9
54 See Murphy, *Ovid: Metamorphoses, Book XI* 73–4
55 *Macbeth* II II 33–6

56 It is no accident that, in composing his version of the scene, Dryden both drew on and contributed to the tradition of mock-heroic poetry. See my 'Dryden's Cave of Sleep and Garth's *Dispensary*', *NQ* 23 (1976) 243–5.

57 Murphy, *Ovid: Metamorphoses, Book XI* 77

58 Ibid. 78

59 Sandys: 'Thither forth-with (ô wonderfull!) she springs; / Beating the passive ayre with new-growne wings'; Hopkins: 'Thither (almost beyond belief) she springs, / Born thro' the yielding air, on new-grown wings.'

60 On the afterlife of the phrase, see P. J. Smallwood, 'Pope's "short excursions" and Dryden: an Unrecorded Borrowing', *NQ* 26 (1979) 540–1

61 Borrowed from Golding, 857: 'They treade, and lay, and bring foorth yoong'.

62 Cf. Sandys: '*Alcyon* sits upon her floating nest'; Hopkins: 'Seven days she sits upon her floating Nest.'

12 THE *HEROIDES* AND THE ENGLISH AUGUSTANS

1 Dryden, *Poetical Works* (Oxford Standard Authors 1910) 518

2 See *New Cambridge Bibliography*, vol. II.329, *de arte Amandi* (translator unidentified)

3 *The Minor Poets, or the Works of the Most Celebrated Authors*, 2 vols. (Dublin 1751) I.271

4 Johnson, *Lives of the Poets*, 2 vols. (World's Classics, Oxford 1906) II.318

5 Reuben Brower, *Pope, the Poetry of Allusion* (London, Oxford, New York 1968) 65

6 *Works of Michael Drayton*, ed. Hebel (Oxford 1932) vol. II.257 ll 133–49

7 Dryden, *Poems*, ed. J. Kinsley (Oxford 1958) vol. II. 903 ll 60–4

8 Dryden, *Poetical Works* 518, 37–40

9 Johnson, *Lives*, II.236–7

10 *The Rape of the Lock and other Poems* (London and New Haven 1954) 284–6

11 *Ibid.* 290

12 *Minor Poets* II.272

13 'The *Heroides*' in J. W. Binns, ed., *Ovid* (London and Boston 1973) 81

14 Richardson, *Clarissa Harlowe*, 18 vols. (The Shakespeare Head edition, London 1930) II.xiv

15 Robert Dodsley, ed., *A Collection of Poems by Several Hands*, 6 vols. (London 1763) IV.86

13 SOME VERSIONS OF PYGMALION

1 Clement of Alexandria, *Protrepticus* 4.51:

So the well-known Pygmalion of Cyprus fell in love with an ivory statue; it was of Aphrodite and was naked. The man of Cyprus is captivated by its shapeliness and embraces the statue. This is related by Philostephanus. There was also an Aphrodite in Cnidus, made of marble and beautiful. Another man fell in love with this and had intercourse with the marble, as Posidippus relates. The account of the first author is in his book on Cyprus; that of the second in his book on Cnidus.

2 Arnobius, *Adversus Gentes* 6.22:

Philostephanus in Cypriacis auctor est, Pygmalionem regem Cypri simulacrum Veneris, quod sanctitatis apud Cyprios et religionis habebatur antiquae, adamasse ut feminam, mente, anima, lumine rationis iudiciique caecatis; solitumque dementem, tamquam si uxoria res esset, sublevato in lectulum numine copularier amplexibus atque ore, resque alias agere libidinis vacuae imaginatione frustrabilis. consimili ratione Posidippus in eo libro, quem scriptum super Cnido indicat, superque rebus eius, adolescentem haud ignobilem memorat, sed vocabulum eius obscurat, correptum amoribus Veneris, propter quam Cnidus in nomine est, amatorias et ipsum miscuisse lascivias, cum eiusdem numinis signo genialibus usum toris, et voluptatum consequentium finibus.

Philostephanus relates in his *Cypriaca* that Pygmalion, King of Cyprus, loved as a woman an image of Venus, which was held by the Cyprians holy and venerable from ancient times, his mind, spirit, the light of his reason and his judgement being darkened; and that he was wont in his madness, just as if he were dealing with his wife, having raised the deity to his couch, to copulate with it by embraces and by mouth, and to do other vain things, carried away by a foolishly lustful imagination. Similarly Posidippus in the book which he mentions to have been written about Cnidus and about its affairs relates that a young man of noble birth – but he conceals his name – carried away with the love of Venus because of whom Cnidus is famous, joined himself also in amorous lewdness to the image of the same deity, stretched out on the genial couch, and enjoying the pleasures which ensue.

3 See C. Müller, *Fr. Hist. Graec.* 3.28–34 (incomplete); Gisinger, *R.E.* 20 (1941) cols. 104–18

4 R. Pfeiffer, *History of Classical Scholarship. From the Beginnings to the End of the Hellenistic Age* (Oxford 1968) 151

5 See P. M. Fraser, *Ptolemaic Alexandria*, 2 vols. (Oxford 1972) 1.523ff

6 'An essential feature of this vegetation cult was the hieros gamos (sacred marriage), the union of the Mother Goddess with a male figure in order to ensure human fertility and the fruitfulness of the fields': B. C. Dietrich, *The Origins of Greek Religion* (Berlin 1974) 11

7 Both Fathers were writing treatises exposing the shortcomings of paganism. To this end they emphasised the discreditable aspect of pagan cults.

8 'The most famous centres of the cult were the Greek islands, Cyprus, Cythera and Crete': L. R. Farnell, *Cults of the Greek States*, vol. II (Oxford 1896) 618

9 H. Dörrie, *Pygmalion Ein Impuls Ovids und seine Wirkungen bis in die Gegenwart* (Oplonden 1974) 13

10 O. S. Due, *Changing Forms. Studies in the Metamorphoses of Ovid* (Copenhagen 1974) 134ff

11 H. Fränkel, *Ovid: A Poet Between Two Worlds* (Berkeley 1945) 93

12 Pygmalion's stance seems itself strange and negative in the context. Ovid emphasises the sterility of this bachelor life and uses words which accentuate the lack of a necessary ingredient for a full life; '*sine coniuge*', '*consorte carebat*'. When one remembers that the story is set on Aphrodite's own island and that as a goddess she represents generation and fertility, Pygmalion's behaviour appears all the more unsatisfactory.

13 In fact she is the product of only male seed (Uranus' testicles) like Pygmalion's statue: the ancients thought that both sexes had seed which was mingled in procreation.

14 Although it is clear that what Pygmalion conceives is a passion the use of '*concepit*' and '*nasci*', combined with the emphatic '*sui*' ('his own'), hints at the notion that the statue is, in a sense, Pygmalion's child.

15 The phrase recalls Ovid's description of the cave of Diana, where Actaeon is about to meet his fate: *simulaverat artem/ingenio natura suo* (*Met.* 3.158–9: 'Nature by her own skill had imitated art').

16 Note that Pygmalion takes one piece of advice in particular given by Ovid in the *Ars Amatoria*:

> nec dominam iubeo pretioso munere dones;
>
> parva, sed e parvis callidus apta dato.   (*Ars* 2.261–2)

nor do I order you to give your mistress expensive gifts: let them be small but choose your small gifts cunningly and well.

The list of small gifts is strongly reminiscent of Propertius 3.13.27ff and there are also echoes of Theocritus' *Idylls*: he mentions flowers, apples, birds and locks of hair as presents given by lovers (5.86ff; 11.10ff; 11.56ff).

17 F. Bömer, *Metamorphosen – Kommentar Buch 1–11* (Heidelberg 1976–80) 102f concludes that the passage 'is not so much an "art historical" memory of the fact that "ancient art did not have naked idols"' (Haupt-Ehwald), as a refined variant of erotic literature'.

18 The phrase '*socia tori*' appears quite often throughout the *Metamorphoses*, in the sense of 'bed-partner' or 'wife' e.g. 1.620–1.

19 Both Clement and Arnobius mention Poseidippos' story about the Aphrodite of Cnidus, and the Agathe Tyche in Athens was also alleged to have been used in this way. Aelian *Var. Hist.* 9.39 relates how an unknown young man, frustrated in his attempt to own the statue, eventually killed himself before it. Bömer also lists other examples; Cleisophus of Selymbria lying with a lithine kore at Samos (Alexis fr. 40 and Philemon fr. 139), Alcetas of Rhodes loving the Eros of Praxiteles (Pliny 36.22).

20 See Horace, *Carm.* 3.26.1; 1.9.22; *Serm.* 1.5.82; *Epist.* 1.18.74. Ovid at *Am.* 2.2.34 observes: '*quod voluit fieri blanda puella, facit.*' Propertius also uses '*puella*' thus at 1.5.19; 1.8.24; 3.3.23 and 3.23.15.

21 '*Simulacrum*' is generally used to mean 'resemblance', 'likeness' or 'representation'. It can, therefore, be used to refer to an image in a mirror or water. Note that '*simulacrum*' would also be used to refer to images of the gods.

22 A. H. F. Griffin, 'Ovid's Metamorphoses', *Greece and Rome* 24 (1977) 57–60

23 Shaw expands this notion in the Epilogue: 'If an imaginative boy has a sufficiently rich mother who has intelligence, personal grace, dignity of character without harshness, and a cultivated sense of the best art of her time to enable her to make her house beautiful, she sets a standard for him against which very few women can struggle, besides effecting for him a disengagement of his affections, his sense of beauty, and his idealism from his specifically sexual impulses.' (This separation does not exist in the ancient versions of the Pygmalion legend.)

24 The name Galatea for the statue is comparatively modern. It seems to have appeared first in 1770 in Rousseau's *Pygmalion* (see M. Reinhold, 'The Naming of Pygmalion's Animated Statue', *Classical Journal* 66 (1971) 316–19).

25 M. Meisel, *Shaw and the Nineteenth-Century Theater* (Oxford 1963) 161

26 In *Original Plays by W. S. Gilbert. First Series* (London 1876)

27 It is obviously impractical for her to be totally innocent: cf. Shaw's treatment both in *Pygmalion* and *Back to Methuselah*. The comedy lies in this selective innocence. For example, she can speak but says things she should not. She is ignorant of the meaning of simple words but capable of complex thought (e.g. she does not know the meaning of 'soldier' yet replies to an explanation of it with the phrase 'paid assassin'). For a discussion of this technique in Gilbert's and Shaw's work, see Meisel 420ff.

28 Introduction to the Signet edition of the play (1963), xxxiv

29 There are indeed many interesting, close parallels between Shakespeare and Ovid. Apart from the question of Nature versus Art and the whole vivification scene, there is also, for example, the sexual theme which contrasts Leontes' insane passion with Perdita's pure sexuality.

30 The Pygmalion Series. There are two versions, one in the Joseph Sutton collection in Paris and the more famous series now owned by the Birmingham City Art Gallery (see M. Harrison and B. Waters, *Burne-Jones* (London 1979)).

31 The painter's technique (use of tone rather than colour, doorways and staircases leading in and out of pictures, artistic symbols, wistful and dreamy facial expressions) lends support to such an interpretation.

32 Penelope Fitzgerald, *Edward Burne-Jones: A Biography* (London 1975) 36

33 Fortunée de Lisle, *Burne-Jones* (London 1904). The pictures are sub-titled as follows:
  1 The Prologue – Pygmalion thinks of the ideal.
  2 The Limitation of Human Power – Pygmalion realises he can do no more.
  3 The Completion of the Human Work by Divine Power.
  4 Human Aspiration attains Divine Realisation.

14 OVID AND THE NINETEENTH CENTURY

1 Hermann Fränkel, *Ovid: a Poet between Two Worlds* (Berkeley and Los Angeles 1945) 2

2 Joseph Warton, *Essay on Pope* (1756) cited in Douglas Bush, *Mythology and the Romantic Tradition in English Poetry* (Cambridge, Mass. 1937) 32; J. W. von Goethe, *Dichtung und Wahrheit*, tr. Minna Steele Smith (as *Poetry and Truth*), 2 vols. (London 1908) 1.369

3 According to the Royal Academy Catalogues West exhibited an Ovid-derived *Arethusa* and an *Orion* in 1802 and a *Phaëton* in 1804; Frederick Leighton's *Perseus and Andromeda* was completed in 1891 and is reproduced as pl. 167 in L. and R. Ormond, *Lord Leighton* (New Haven and London 1975).

4 John Dryden, *Love Triumphant; or, Nature will Prevail*, (1694), II i [28]

5 Discussed in Pearl Hogrefe, *Browning and Italian Art and Artists* (Lawrence, Kansas 1914) (the picture is reproduced as the frontispiece of H. C. Duffin, *Amphibian. A Reconsideration of Browning* (London 1956)); Austin Dobson, *Collected Poems*, 5th edn (London 1902) 167ff (the *Morte di Procri* is reproduced as pl. 22 in Mina Bacci, *Piero di Cosimo* (Milan 1966)).

6 Byron, 'Hints from Horace' 1.663

7 J. S. Blackie, *Selected Poems* (London 1896) 212–18; *Fast.* 3.459f; *Theogony* 947–9

8 *Paradise Lost* 4.268–71; compare Ovid, *Met.* 5.391–571

9 See N. J. Richardson, ed., *The Homeric Hymn to Demeter* (Oxford 1974) 65–7

10 Tennyson's classical sources for the poems are discussed by J. C. Collins, *Illustrations of Tennyson* (London 1891) 173f and W. P. Mustard, *Classical Echoes in Tennyson* (New York and London 1904) 121.

11 J. W. Mackail, *Latin Literature* (London 1895), 1899 edn, 139

12 Both made the allusion in letters: Marx to his wife, 21 June 1856, quoted in S. S. Prawer, *Karl Marx and World Literature* (Oxford 1976) 210; Flaubert to Louise Colet, 23 October 1853, *Correspondance*, 9 vols. (Paris 1926–33) III.372

13 Quoted by Lord David Cecil, *The Young Melbourne* (London 1960 edn) 143

14 *Don Juan* VI xvii 7ff; Horace, *Carm.* 1.10.5 ('*auream...mediocritatem*'); compare *Epist.* 1.18.9 ('*Virtus est medium vitiorum*' ('Virtue is a mean between the vices [of bluntness and flattery]')); Ovid, *Met.* 2.136

15 I lxxxvi 4; compare Ovid, *Met.* 7.10–12

16 Sidonius Apollinaris, 'To Consentius', *Poems*, Loeb edn tr. W. B. Anderson (Cambridge, Mass., and London 1936) 23.158–61

17 T. H. Dyer, 'On the Cause of Ovid's Exile', *The Classical Museum* 4 (1847) 229–47; for biographical speculations see A. J. Church, *Ovid* (London 1876) 44–52 and bibliography of A. L. Wheeler's Loeb edn of *Tristia* and *Ex Ponto* (Cambridge, Mass., and London 1924) xlii.

18 *The Ring and the Book* II.1183; compare *Tr.* 2.135–7; *Ring* II.1222; compare *Pont.* 1.6.33, 56

19 Chaucer, *The House of Fame* 1487–9

20 *Guardian*, 9 July 1851 reviewing *Poems* (London 1851), quoted in Phyllis M. Barrett, ed., *Poems of George Meredith*, 2 vols. (New Haven and London 1979) II.1172

21 *Tr.* 4.10.51; W. M. Thackeray, *The History of Henry Esmond* (London 1852) Book 3, chap. 5
22 Private notes on his reading in Calcutta 1835–7, published in G. O. Trevelyan, *Life and Letters of Lord Macaulay* (London 1876), 1883 edn, 691ff
23 William Preston, *Some Considerations on the History of Ancient Amatory Poets* (London 1805) 14
24 Walter Savage Landor, *Works and Life*, 8 vols. (London 1872) II.414, II.475, IV.124, V.291
25 J. A. Symonds, letter to *The Academy*, 27 September 1885, *Letters*, ed. H. M. Schueller and R. L. Peters, 3 vols. (Detroit 1967–9) III.82; A. C. Swinburne, letter to *The Athenaeum*, 26 May 1875, *Letters*, ed. C. Y. Lang, 6 vols. (New Haven and London 1960) III.30–2
26 Edmund Gosse, *The Life of Algernon Charles Swinburne* (London 1917) 112
27 Euripides [?], *Meleager* (fragment) 14ff; Aeschylus, *Choephoroi* 602–12
28 W. R. Rutland, *Swinburne. A Nineteenth-Century Hellene* (Oxford 1931) 106
29 *Iliad* 9.529–99; Apollodorus, *Library* 1.8.2; *Met.* 8.445–525
30 E. Gosse, *Swinburne* 112
31 See R. M. Dorson, 'The Eclipse of Solar Mythology', *Journal of American Folklore* 68 (1955) 393–416
32 A. C. Swinburne, *Atalanta in Calydon* in *Collected Poetical Works*, 2 vols. (London 1924) II.249; 'Itylus', *Poetical Works* 1.55; compare *Odyssey* 19.518 and *Met.* 6.424–674
33 Tacitus, *Germania* 40, discussed in J. M. Kemble, *The Saxons in England*, 2 vols. (London 1849) I.375, and Jakob Grimm, *Deutsche Mythologie* (1835), 3 vols. (Tübingen 1953) I.212
34 *Poetical Works* 1.72, 740; J. G. Frazer, *The Golden Bough* (London 1890), one-vol. edn, 1922, chap. 44, 'Demeter and Persephone'
35 *Balaustion's Adventure* 2625; for an exhaustive discussion see Robert Spindler, *Robert Browning und die Antike*, 2 vols. (Leipzig 1930) I.82, 301, etc
36 *Tr.* 4.10.25ff; Alexander Pope, 'Epistle to Dr Arbuthnot' 1.127
37 Herbert Paul, 'The Decay of Classical Quotation' (1896) repr. in *Men and Letters* (London 1901) 59
38 Matthew Arnold, 'The Study of Poetry' (1880), *Complete Prose Works*, ed. R. H. Super, 11 vols. (Ann Arbor, Michigan 1960–77) IX.181
39 J. J. Howard, tr., *The Metamorphoses of Ovid* (London 1807) Dedication to the Earl of Lonsdale
40 F. H. Hummel and A. A. Brodribb, *Lays from Latin Lyres* (London 1876) 51 (*Amores* 1.1); 61 (*Met.* 1.539)
41 Pope, 'Essay on Criticism' 298
42 See [G. C. Lewis] 'Mythology and the Religion of Ancient Greece', *Foreign Quarterly Review* 7 (1831) 33–52; [G. Eliot] Review of R. W. Mackay's *The Progress of the Intellect*, *Westminster Review* 54 (Jan. 1851) 353–68
43 George Sandys, *Ovid's Metamorphoses Englished* (Oxford 1632) 31–3; *Paradise Lost* 11.10–14; H. E. Ryle, *The Early Narratives of Genesis* (London 1909) 104; C. E. Ceram, *Gods, Graves and Scholars* (Penguin edn 1979) 290–2
44 *Poetry and Truth* 1.369
45 Ruth Mulhauser, *Sainte-Beuve and Greco-Roman Antiquity* (Cleveland and London 1969) 60, 183; C. A. Sainte-Beuve, *Portraits Littéraires*, 3 vols. (Paris [?1880]) II.2f
46 Wordsworth's note on 'Ode to Lycoris' (1817) quoted in Douglas Bush, *Mythology and the Romantic Tradition* 57
47 F. von Schiller, 'Die götter Griechenlands', st. 2, translated as 'The gods of Greece' in E. Bulwer Lytton, *Poems and Ballads of Schiller* (London 1844) 1897 edn, p. 304

48 'The world is too much with us' (1807) 13ff: *Met.* 1.333, 2.8f, 13.918ff
49 'Laodamia' (1814) 73f, 141f; 158–63 in 1815 and 1820 editions, in 1827 edition, in 1832 and subsequent editions. See note in *Poetical Works*, ed. T. Hutchinson and E. De Selincourt (London 1950) 702f.
50 *Her.* 13; *Aen.* 6.447f
51 *Ars.* 3.536–8; compare *Tr.* 2.445
52 'I stood tip-toe upon a little hill', 153. See the notes, to which I am indebted, in Miriam Allott's edition of the *Poems* (London 1970).
53 *Sleep and Poetry* 334–6; *Endymion* 4.240ff; 'Ode to a Nightingale' 32
54 *Sleep and Poetry* 102–5; *Hyperion* 1.2; *The Fall of Hyperion* 1.295
55 *The Faerie Queene* I ii 30–45; discussed in C. L. Finney, *The Evolution of Keats's Poetry*, 2 vols (New York 1963) I.257ff, 310–14
56 G. F. Watts, *Ariadne on Naxos* (1860s) is pl. 115 of L. and R. Ormond, *Lord Leighton*; Leighton's *Ariadne abandoned by Theseus* (c. 1868) is pl. 114; Titian's *Bacchus and Ariadne* (National Gallery) is pl. 9 in Charles Hope, *Titian* (London 1980)
57 Burne-Jones's Perseus series of paintings was commissioned in 1875: some are reproduced in *Burne-Jones* (London 1975) (Arts Council of Great Britain) 58–62. William Morris retells the story in the 'The Doom of Acrisius', *The Earthly Paradise*, 1868–70; Kingsley's narrative poem 'Andromeda' (1858) was reprinted in his *Poems* (1871).
58 'Andromeda' 227; Sir Walter Scott, *Marmion* 6.xxvi
59 K. N. Cameron, *Shelley, the Golden Years* (Cambridge, Mass. 1974) 201; Douglas Bush, *Mythology and the Romantic Tradition* 135ff
60 Walter Pater, 'Demeter and Persephone' (1876) in *Greek Studies* (London 1928 edn) 119

15 T. S. ELIOT'S *METAMORPHOSES*: OVID AND *THE WASTE LAND*

The number of books on T. S. Eliot is so great that it is impossible to know what one's debts are. I am most aware of having used B. C. Southam's *A Student's Guide to the Selected Poems of T. S. Eliot* (London 1968), Grover Smith's *Eliot's Poetry and Plays* (Chicago 1956) and Derek Traversi's *T. S. Eliot: the Longer Poems* (London 1976). Laura Marcus pointed out the condition of the women of *The Waste Land* to me.

1 G. K. Chesterton, *The Ball and the Cross* (London 1910) chap. 1
2 G. K. Chesterton, *The Defendant* (London 1901) 'A Defence of Rash Vows'
3 G. K. Galinsky, *Ovid's Metamorphoses* (Oxford 1973) 13
4 T. S. Eliot, *The Waste Land* (New York 1922) 218n
5 *The Waste Land* 19ff, 60ff, 115ff, 182ff, 187ff, 206ff, 215ff, 258ff, 307, 359ff, 400ff, 423ff, 430
6 T. S. Eliot, *Gerontion* (in *Ara vos prec* – the first book printed, coincidentally, by The Ovid Press, London 1920), final line
7 T. S. Eliot, *Poems Written in Early Youth* (London 1967): also in *The Complete Poems and Plays of T. S. Eliot* (London 1969)
8 T. S. Eliot, *The Waste Land: A Facsimile and Transcript of the Original Drafts Including the Annotations of Ezra Pound*, ed. Valerie Eliot (London 1971) 95
9 S. Kierkegaard, *The Sickness unto Death* (in the original Danish, Copenhagen 1849; tr. W. Lowrie, in *Fear and Trembling and The Sickness unto Death*, Princeton 1941)
10 *Waste Land: A Facsimile* 30–1
11 T. S. Eliot, *Selected Essays* (Third enlarged edition, London 1951) 'Tradition and the Individual Talent', 19
12 *Selected Essays*, 21
13 F. Nietzsche, *The Birth of Tragedy*, tr. F. Gollffung (New York 1956) chap. 21

14 *Dial*, New York, LXXI 4 (October 1921) 452–5
15 S. Spender, *Eliot* (London 1975) 20
16 T. S. Eliot, *The Dry Salvages* v
17 *Waste Land: A Facsimile* 2–3
18 *The Poems of Tennyson*, ed. C. Ricks (London 1969) 1425: cf. Ovid, *Met.* 7.20–1
19 Geoffrey Hill, *Collected Poems* (Harmondsworth 1985) 61: cf. Ovid, *Am.* 3.14.5–6
20 *Selected Essays* 296–7
21 Arthur Golding, *The XV Bookes of P. Ovidius Naso, entytuled Metamorphosis* (London 1567) 14.161–4
22 Ovid, *Fast.* 3.271–2: ed. and trans. Sir J. G. Frazer, 5 vols. (London 1929) vol. 1.132–3
23 Sir J. G. Frazer, *The Golden Bough* (London 1913) Part 1, vol. 1.10
24 *Waste Land: a Facsimile* 12–13
25 *Birth of Tragedy* chap. 23
26 *Waste Land* note to 197
27 Charles Williams, *Poetry at Present* (Oxford 1930) 166
28 C. S. Lewis, *Surprised by Joy* (London 1955) chap. 14
29 C. H. Sisson, *Metamorphosis* (London 1968) Title–poem
30 R. G. Collingwood, *The Principles of Art* (Oxford 1938) 335

BIBLIOGRAPHY

Short Bibliography with suggestions for further reading (including other writings by contributors)

Four useful bibliographies are:

Carlsen, Hanne, *A Bibliography to the Classical Tradition in English Literature*, Anglica et Americana 21 (Copenhagen 1985)

Kallendorf, Craig, *Latin Influences on English Literature from the Middle Ages to the Eighteenth Century: An Annotated Bibliography of Scholarship, 1945–1979* (New York and London 1982)

Stroh, Wilfried, *Ovid im Urteil der Nachwelt: Eine Testimoniensammlung* (Darmstadt 1969)

Aufstieg und Niedergang der Römischen Welt, II.31.4 (Berlin 1981) 2214–45, 2254–63

Baldwin, T. W., *William Shakspere's Small Latine and Lesse Greeke*, 2 vols. (Urbana 1944), II chap. 42 on Ovid

Barkan, Leonard, *The Gods Made Flesh: Metamorphosis and the Pursuit of Paganism* (New Haven and London 1986)

Beller, Manfred, *Philemon und Baucis in der europäischen Literatur: Stoffgeschichte und Analyse*, Studien zum Fortwirken der Antike 3 (Heidelberg 1967)

Binns, J. W., *Ovid* (London and Boston 1973): includes essays on Ovid's influence by Caroline Jameson and Dorothy Robathan

Bush, Douglas, *Mythology and the Renaissance Tradition in English Poetry* (Minneapolis and London 1932)

   Mythology and the Romantic Tradition in English Poetry (Cambridge, Mass. 1937)

Donaldson, Ian *The Rapes of Lucretia: A Myth and its Transformations* (Oxford 1982)

Dörrie, Heinrich, *Der heroische Brief: Bestandsaufnahme, Geschichte, Kritik einer humanistische-barocken Literaturgattung* (Berlin 1968)

   Pygmalion Ein Impuls Ovids und seine Wirkungen bis in die Gegenwart (Oplonden 1974)

Ghisalberti, Fausto, 'Mediaeval Biographies of Ovid', *Journal of the Warburg and Courtauld Institutes* 9 (1946) 10–59

Goldin, F., *The Mirror of Narcissus in the Courtly Love Lyric* (Ithaca 1967)

Harbert, Bruce, 'The Myth of Tereus in Ovid and Gower', *Medium Aevum* 41 (1972) 208–14

   'Chaucer and the Latin Classics' in Derek Brewer, ed., *Geoffrey Chaucer* (*Writers and their Background*) (London 1974) 137–53

Harding, Davis P., 'Milton and the Renaissance Ovid', *Illinois Studies in Language and Literature* 30 (1946)

Bibliography

Hoffman, Richard L., *Ovid and the Canterbury Tales* (USA, London etc. 1966)

Holahan, Michael N., '*Iamque opus exegi*: Ovid's Changes and Spenser's Brief Epic of Mutability', *English Literary Renaissance* 6 (1976) 244–70

Hopkins, David, 'Dryden's "Baucis and Philemon",' *Comparative Literature* 28 (1976) 135–43

'Nature's Laws and Man's: The Story of Cinyras and Myrrha in Ovid and Dryden', *Modern Language Review* 80 (1985) 786–801

Hulse, Clark, *Metamorphic Verse: The Elizabethan Minor Epic* (Princeton 1981)

Jacobsen, Eric, *Translation, a traditional craft: an introductory sketch with a study of Marlowe's Elegies*, Classica et Mediaevalia, Dissertationes, VI (Copenhagen 1958)

Keach, William, *Elizabethan Erotic Narratives: Irony and Pathos in the Ovidian Poetry of Shakespeare, Marlowe and their Contemporaries* (Hassocks 1977)

Martindale, Charles, ed., *Virgil and his Influence: Bimillennial Studies* (Bristol 1984)

John Milton and the Transformation of Ancient Epic (London and Sydney 1986), chap. 4 on Ovid (a revised version of *Comp. Lit.* 37 (1985) 301–33)

Moss, Ann, *Ovid in Renaissance France: A Survey of the Latin Editions of Ovid and Commentaries printed in France before 1600*, Warburg Institute Surveys VIII (London 1982)

Poetry and Fable: Studies in Mythological Narrative in Sixteenth-Century France (Cambridge 1984)

Munari, Franco, *Ovid im Mittelalter* (Zurich, Stuttgart 1960)

Nuttall, A. D., 'Ovid Immoralized: The Method of Wit in Marvell's "The Garden"', in Peter Bilton *et al.*, eds., *Essays in Honour of Kristian Smidt* (Oslo 1986) 79–89

Ogilvie, R. M., *Latin and Greek: A History of the Influence of the Classics on English Life from 1600 to 1918* (London 1964), chapter on 'Ovid and the Seventeenth Century'.

Rudd, Niall, 'Pyramus and Thisbe in Shakespeare and Ovid: *A Midsummer Night's Dream* and *Metamorphoses* 4.1–166', in West, David and Woodman, Tony, eds., *Creative Imitation and Latin Literature* (Cambridge 1979) 173–93; also contains an essay by K. W. Gransden on Ovid, *Amores* 1.13, Chaucer and Donne.

Schmitt-von Mühlenfels, Franz, *Pyramus und Thisbe: Rezeptionstypen eines Ovidischen Stoffes im Literatur, Kunst und Musik* (Heidelberg 1972)

Shannon, Edgar Finley, *Chaucer and the Roman Poets*, Harvard Studies in Comparative Literature 7 (Cambridge, Mass. 1929)

Stechow, Wolfgang, *Apollo und Daphne* (repr. Darmstadt 1965)

Tomlinson, Charles, *Poetry and Metamorphosis* (Cambridge 1983)

Turner, J. H., *The Myth of Icarus in Spanish Renaissance Poetry* (London 1976)

Vinge, Louise, *The Narcissus Theme in Western European Literature up to the Early Nineteenth Century* (Lund 1967)

Wilkinson, L. P., *Ovid Recalled* (Cambridge 1955) esp. chaps. 11, 12 and epilogue.

1 Fresco from Pompeii, Daedalus finds Icarus

2b Van Dyck, *Daedalus and Icarus*

2a Andrea Pisano, Daedalus

3b Chagall, *The Fall of Icarus*

3a Deineka, *Nikitka, the Russian Icarus*

4 Titian, *Venus and Adonis*

5 Rubens, *Venus and Adonis*

6   Poussin, *Echo and Narcissus*

7b *Mars from* Ovide moralisé *(Bruges, 1484)*

7a *Mercury and Argus, MS from Lyons*

8 Titian, *Bacchus and Ariadne*

9   Giordano, *Perseus and the companions of Phineus*

10b Bernini, *Apollo and Daphne*

10a Gérôme, *Pygmalion and Galatea*

11b Watteau, *Judgement of Paris*

11a Correggio, *Jupiter and Io* (detail)

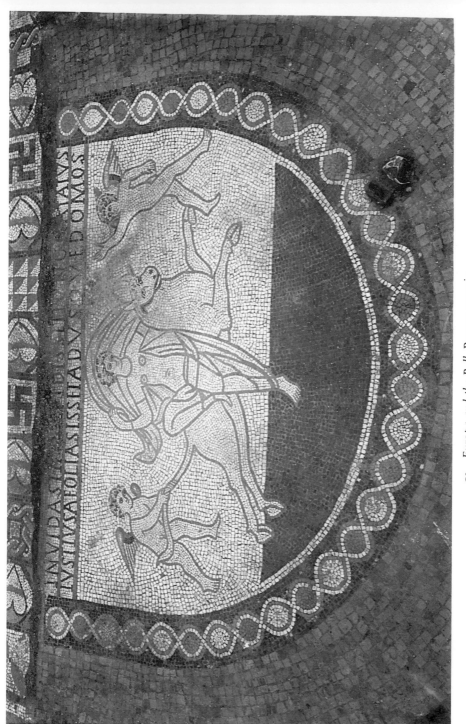

12 *Europa and the Bull*, Roman mosaic

13   Titian, *Rape of Europa*

14   Boucher, *Jupiter and Europa* (1734)

15   Boucher, *Jupiter and Europa* (1747)

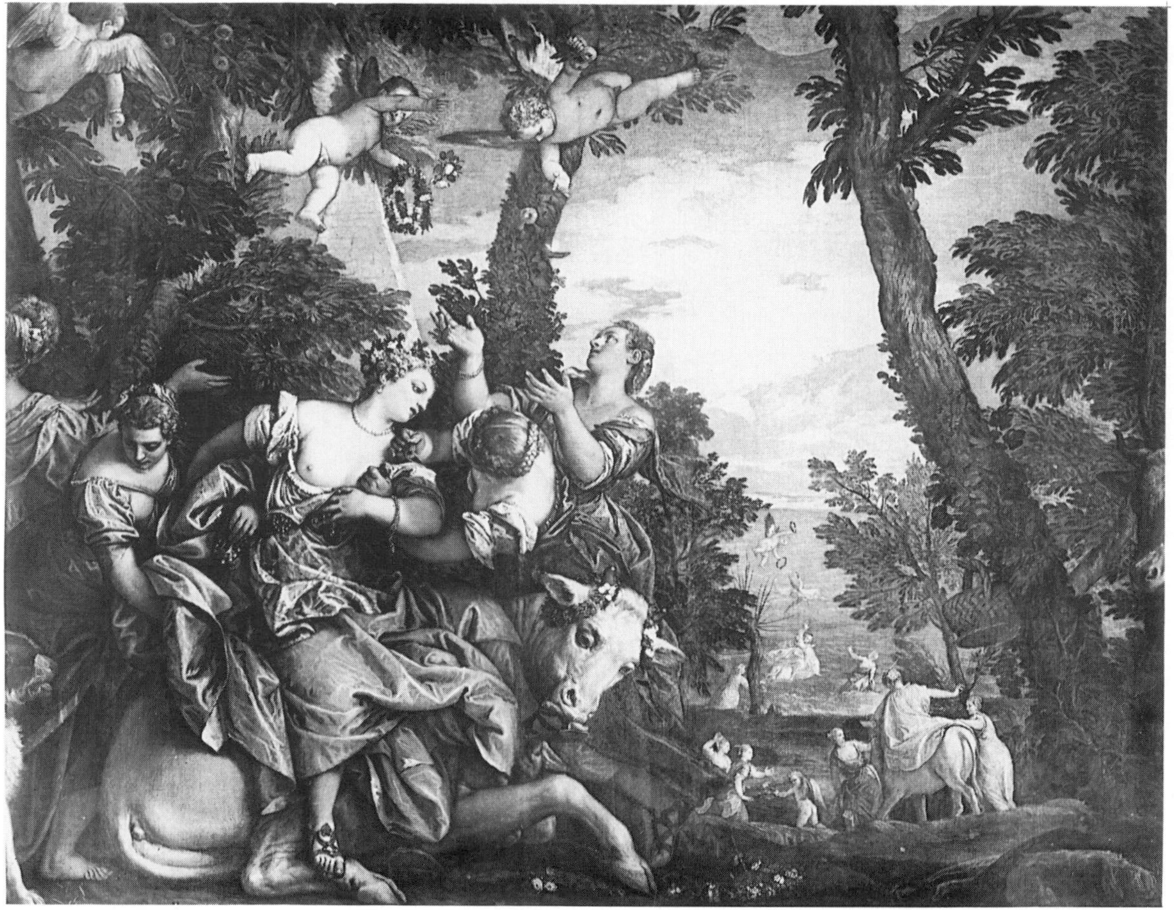

16 Veronese, *Jupiter and Europa*

INDEX OF OVIDIAN PASSAGES

289

GENERAL INDEX